New Directions in Print Culture Studies

New Directions in Print Culture Studies

Archives, Materiality, and Modern American Culture

Edited by
Jesse W. Schwartz and Daniel Worden

BLOOMSBURY ACADEMIC
NEW YORK • LONDON • OXFORD • NEW DELHI • SYDNEY

BLOOMSBURY ACADEMIC
Bloomsbury Publishing Inc
1385 Broadway, New York, NY 10018, USA
50 Bedford Square, London, WC1B 3DP, UK
29 Earlsfort Terrace, Dublin 2, Ireland

BLOOMSBURY, BLOOMSBURY ACADEMIC and the Diana logo are trademarks of Bloomsbury Publishing Plc

First published in the United States of America 2022
Paperback edition first published 2024

Copyright © Jesse W. Schwartz and Daniel Worden, 2022

Each chapter copyright © by the contributor, 2022

For legal purposes the Acknowledgments on p. x constitute an extension of this copyright page.

Cover design by Eleanor Rose |
Cover image: Gudrun Zapf von Hesse, "Alphabet," 1995. Courtesy of the RIT Cary Graphic Arts Collection

All rights reserved. No part of this publication may be reproduced or transmitted in any form or by any means, electronic or mechanical, including photocopying, recording, or any information storage or retrieval system, without prior permission in writing from the publishers.

Bloomsbury Publishing Inc does not have any control over, or responsibility for, any third-party websites referred to or in this book. All internet addresses given in this book were correct at the time of going to press. The author and publisher regret any inconvenience caused if addresses have changed or sites have ceased to exist, but can accept no responsibility for any such changes.

A catalog record for this book is available from the Library of Congress

Library of Congress Cataloging-in-Publication Data
Names: Schwartz, Jesse W., editor. | Worden, Daniel, 1978- editor.
Title: New directions in print culture studies : archives, materiality, and modern American culture / edited by Jesse W. Schwartz and Daniel Worden.
Description: New York : Bloomsbury Academic, 2022. | Includes bibliographical references and index. |
Summary: "New Directions in Print Culture Studies examines new methods and approaches to the literary and historical study of print and media culture in the Americas"– Provided by publisher.
Identifiers: LCCN 2021060067 (print) | LCCN 2021060068 (ebook) | ISBN 9781501359736 (hardback) | ISBN 9781501393020 (paperback) | ISBN 9781501359743 (epub) | ISBN 9781501359750 (pdf) | ISBN 9781501359767
Subjects: LCSH: Printing–United States–History. | Printing–Social aspects–United States–History. | Periodicals–Publishing–United States–History. | LCGFT: Essays.
Classification: LCC Z208 .N49 2022 (print) | LCC Z208 (ebook) | DDC 686.209–dc23/eng/20220223
LC record available at https://lccn.loc.gov/2021060067
LC ebook record available at https://lccn.loc.gov/2021060068

ISBN:	HB:	978-1-5013-5973-6
	PB:	978-1-5013-9302-0
	ePDF:	978-1-5013-5975-0
	eBook:	978-1-5013-5974-3

Typeset by Integra Software Services Pvt. Ltd.

To find out more about our authors and books visit www.bloomsbury.com and sign up for our newsletters.

Contents

List of Figures — vii

Acknowledgments — x

Introduction: Archives, Materiality, and Modern American Culture, *Jesse W. Schwartz and Daniel Worden* — 1

Part One Print Culture's Pasts and Presents

1. Story-Paper Origins in the United States: The Unknown Public and *The New York Ledger*, *Ayendy Bonifacio* — 23

2. "And They Think A Strike Is War": John Reed, *Metropolitan Magazine*, and Print-Socialism Beyond Borders, *Jesse W. Schwartz* — 41

3. Laying the Type of Revolution: Historicizing US Feminism in and through Print Culture, *Agatha Beins* — 63

4. The Instant Classic in the Age of Digital Print Culture: Claude McKay's *Romance in Marseille*, *Gary Edward Holcomb* — 81

5. The Real Productivity: Creative Refusal and Cultish Tendencies in Online Print Journal Communities, *Michelle Chihara* — 97

Part Two Archives, Exhibits, Images, and Sounds of Print Culture

6. Hold Still: Coming Undone Reading Print Culture Like a Work of Art, *Monica Huerta* — 115

7. Engraving Class: Gender, Race, and the Pictorial Politics of the 1877 General Strike, *Justin Rogers-Cooper* — 139

8. Sounding: Black Print Culture at the Edges of the Black Atlantic, *Kristin Moriah* — 167

9. "A Traveling Exhibition": Magazines and the Display and Circulation of Art in the Americas, *Lori Cole* — 173

| 10 | Comics in the Archive: Approaches to the April 1956 Newsstand, *Rebekah Walker and Daniel Worden* | 203 |

| 11 | Icons and Archives: James Baldwin and the Practice of Celebrity, *Robert F. Reid-Pharr* | 225 |

Part Three Print Culture Studies in Practice

| 12 | Reimagining Literary History, and Why It Matters Now, *Kelley Kreitz* | 239 |

| 13 | Anthologizing Alternatives: June Jordan and Toni Cade Bambara's Publishing Pedagogies, *Danica Savonick* | 257 |

| 14 | Hybrid Scholarly Publishing Models in a Digital Age, *Krystyna Michael, Jojo Karlin, and Matthew K. Gold* | 277 |

| Notes on Contributors | 292 |
| Index | 296 |

Figures

0.1 Unidentified actor (the "Little Man"), Claudia McNeil, and John Bouie in the stage production *Simply Heavenly*, 1957. Photo by Friedman-Abeles © The New York Public Library for the Performing Arts — 11

0.2 Scene from the stage production *Simply Heavenly*, 1957. Photo by Friedman-Abeles © The New York Public Library for the Performing Arts — 13

0.3 Afua Richardson's Orynthia Blue comic book in the series *Lovecraft Country*, 2020. © Home Box Office, Inc. All rights reserved — 16

0.4 Afua Richardson's illustrated atlas in the series *Lovecraft Country*, 2020. © Home Box Office, Inc. All rights reserved — 17

1.1 *New York Daily Tribune* (December 6, 1856) — 37

1.2 *New York Daily Times* (December 6, 1856) — 39

2.1 P. Thompson, "Ruins of the Ludlow Tent Colony." *Metropolitan Magazine* (July 1914) — 53

2.2 Corona Folding Typewriter advertisement. *Metropolitan Magazine* (July 1914) — 54

2.3 B. Robinson, "Hospital at Nish." *Metropolitan Magazine* (August 1915) — 59

2.4 B. Robinson "But for the smoke, it might be part of a Galician town." *Metropolitan Magazine* (January 1917) — 61

5.1 Images from Panda Planner (pandaplanner.com) and Bullet Journal (bulletjournal.com) websites, December 2020 — 98

5.2 Google Image search results for "Bullet Journal December Spreads," December 2020 — 99

5.3 Rachel Stephen, "what i was doing wrong in my bullet journal," *YouTube* (June 12, 2019). https://www.youtube.com/watch?v=mIy5RnDuIGk — 110

6.1 *Redeemed in Virginia by Catherine S. Lawrence. Baptized in Brooklyn.... by Henry Ward Beecher, May 1863. Fannie Virginia Casseopia Lawrence, a Redeemed Slave Child, 5 years of age*, created by Renowden (1863). Courtesy of Schomburg Center for Research in Black Culture, Photographs and Prints Division, *Cartes-de-Visite* Collection — 122

6.2 *Fannie Virginia Casseopia Lawrence – a redeemed slave child, 5 years of age – redeemed in Virginia.* c. 1863. Library of Congress Prints and Photographs Division Washington, DC — 127

6.3　*Rebecca, An Emancipated Slave from New Orleans* (1863), created by Kimball. Courtesy of Schomburg Center for Research in Black Culture, Photographs and Prints Division, *Cartes-de-Visite* Collection　127

6.4　Rebecca, Charley, and Rosa. c. 1863. Photographed by M. H. Kimball. Library of Congress Prints and Photographs Division, Washington DC　128

6.5　Rebecca, Augusta, and Rosa. c. 1863. Photographed by M. H. Kimball. Library of Congress Prints and Photographs Division, Washington DC　128

6.6　"Oh! How I Love the Old Flag," Rebecca, a Slave Girl from New Orleans. c. 1864. Created by Charles Paxon. Library of Congress Prints and Photographs Division, Washington DC　135

7.1　D. Bendann, "The Great Strike—The Sixth Maryland Regiment Fighting Its Way Through Baltimore." *Harper's Weekly* (New York) vol. 21, no. 1076 (August 11, 1877)　148

7.2　E.A. Abbey, "The Frenzy, and What Came Of It," *Harper's Weekly* (New York), vol. 30, no. 1077 (August 18, 1877)　150

7.3　"Pennsylvania—An Armed Mob Marching to the Scene of Action in Pittsburgh," *Frank Leslie's Illustrated Newspaper* (August 4, 1877)　155

7.4　"Rioters Soaping the Track," reprinted in J.A. Dacus, *Annals of the Great Strikes in the United States* (Burt Franklin: New York, 1969), 290　161

7.5　"Women Leading a Mob in Baltimore" in Allan Pinkerton, *Strikers, Communists, Tramps, and Detectives* (London: G.W. Carleton & Co., 1882), 194　162

7.6　"Pennsylvania.—The Railroad Riot at Pittsburgh—The Philadelphia Militia Firing on the Mob," *Frank Leslie's Illustrated Newspaper* (August 4, 1877)　164

9.1　"El museo de arte moderno americano," *Forma: Revista de artes plásticas* (Mexico City) vol. 1, no. 3 (1927): 21, featuring Gabriel Fernández Ledesma, *Primera Comunión* (First Communion), 1925. Printed with the permission of Mauricio Bidault Fernández Ledesma　175

9.2　"Arte Nacional: Expocisión de 'La Casa del Arte,'" "Salón de 'La Giralda,'" and "Exposición Pesce Castro," *La Pluma* (Montevideo), vol. 2, no. 6 (May 1928): 35. Courtesy of The Library of the University of California, Berkeley　181

9.3　Delia Demicheli, "Bajorrelieve," and Guillermo Rodríguez, "Escenas Camperas," *La Pluma* (Montevideo), vol. 2, no. 6 (May 1928): 50. Courtesy of The Library of the University of California, Berkeley　181

9.4　The "Theatre Number" of *The Little Review* (New York), vol. 11, no. 2

	(Winter 1926). Photo: Beinecke Rare Book and Manuscript Library, Yale University	190
9.5	Fernand Léger, *Machine Age Exposition* Cover (New York: *Little Review*, 1927). © 2021 Artists Rights Society (ARS), New York/ADAGP, Paris. Photo: Beinecke Rare Book and Manuscript Library, Yale University	194
9.6	*The Bla!*, no. 1 (1916). © 2021 Estate of Stuart Davis/Licensed by VAGA at Artists Rights Society (ARS), NY	197
9.7	*Spawn*, vol. 1, no. 3 (March 1917). © 2021 Estate of Stuart Davis/Licensed by VAGA at Artists Rights Society (ARS), NY	199
10.1	Cover of *Detective Comics* #230. National Comics Publications, April 1956. Stephen Neil Cooper Synchronic Comic Book Collection. Cary Graphic Arts Collection, Rochester Institute of Technology Libraries	207
10.2	Cover of *Comic Book Marketplace* (April 1999). Stephen Neil Cooper Synchronic Comic Book Collection. Cary Graphic Arts Collection, Rochester Institute of Technology Libraries. Courtesy of Stephen Neil Cooper	215
10.3	Comic book genres in April 1956, by percentage. Count of primary and secondary genres combined for overall percentages. Rebekah Walker. Rochester Institute of Technology, Spring 2019	218
10.4	Female protagonist costume prototype. Sally Boniecki. Rochester Institute of Technology, Spring 2019. Used with permission. sallyjaysparrow.com	221
10.5	Screenshot of color comparison slider between original and digital reprint. Andrew Lefurge. Rochester Institute of Technology, Spring 2019. Used with permission	222
10.6	Flesch Kincaid Reading Level of books in the Cooper collection. Green bars represent the spread of the data, and the red line indicates the grade level of individual stories Jake Sikorski. Rochester Institute of Technology, Spring 2019. Used with permission	223

Acknowledgments

This project started with a seminar at the American Comparative Literature Association (ACLA) in 2016, and five years later, we continue to be inspired by the work of the contributors to this book, the participants in that initial ACLA seminar, and the many other colleagues and friends who have been a part of this project along the way. We wish to give particular thanks to Mark Noonan and the other faculty and participants in the 2016 and 2020 NEH Institutes on "New York and the Periodical Press." This book wouldn't exist without those gatherings. Many thanks to Haaris Naqvi and Amy Martin at Bloomsbury for their editorial guidance and support.

Jesse W. Schwartz would like to thank the many friends and colleagues he's spoken with about print culture (and everything else) over the years as well as all the teachers, mentors, and guides he's been fortunate to have along the way. He would also like to thank his parents, who raised him in a house full of the many cultures of print well before he ever heard the phrase. Thanks most of all to Jones the basenji, who curled up stoically behind me nearly the entire time I worked on this project, and to Yvette Grant, who deserves extra gratitude for bringing home a bacon, egg, and cheese the morning this manuscript was due (and for a million other things besides). Thank you for always making sure I get across the finish line.

Daniel Worden would like to thank the Cary Graphic Arts Collection at the Rochester Institute of Technology for providing a place for print culture studies exhibits, research, and teaching; Sean Latham and the participants in the 2010 NEH Seminar on "Magazine Modernism"; and the many colleagues and friends who have helped me to think about print culture. Special thanks to Cat and Clementine, and to Jordan Alexander Stein, who helped me to read books outside of the walls we sometimes put them in.

Introduction: Archives, Materiality, and Modern American Culture

Jesse W. Schwartz and Daniel Worden

The phrase "print culture" names both a methodology and an object. On the one hand, print culture is a prominent historicist method across cultural and literary studies. In this methodology, a scholar considers the production, reception, circulation, or other material conditions of a text, alongside its content features, such as plot or character. On the other hand, print culture names the messy, unquantifiable amount of printed material that any given culture generates. It is intentionally a medium-specific, and not genre-specific, term, as a print culture scholar should be able to analyze any print artifact, whether it's an issue of *Poetry* magazine or the *New England Journal of Medicine* (at least in theory, though less often in practice due to disciplinary constraints). Anchored in the history of the book, inflected by materialist approaches to culture honed by feminist, Marxist, and New Historicist methodologies, and already widely influential in early American and nineteenth-century literary studies, this method has expanded the fields of modernist studies and contemporary literary studies, too. As the number of twentieth-century works in the public domain increases every year, alongside the growth of special collections in research libraries devoted to modernist and contemporary arts cultures, scholars have turned to newspapers, magazines, pamphlets, chapbooks, zines, liner notes, comics, artist's books, and other print media formats for more complex histories of modernity, modernism, and postwar cultures than our undergraduate *Norton* anthologies provided us with in the 1990s and 2000s. A number of critical impulses have made print culture artifacts deeply appealing to humanities scholars today, and indeed to our culture writ large.

The twinned intellectual and material commitments of print culture studies offer something to us today that we usually lack—a clear connection between our minds and reality. A first edition of an old novel and a thoughtfully preserved magazine from decades ago often feel more "original" to us than contemporary printings of the same material, and indeed we've written grants, secured funding, rented housing, temporarily relocated our families, and schlepped across the country just to be in the presence of an "original" text of that nature, when we could have read a reprint without doing anything but picking up our smartphone. It's pretty absurd when we put it like that, but it's also not absurd at all when we think about what those original texts offer us. Of course, it's easy to get caught up in the romance of books as commodities—we love them, we love local bookstores, and we love ourselves and others through them[1]—and forget that the love of a print object is intertwined with a love for the experience of reading, a love for a kind of absorption that many of us have found in print. This experience of reading cannot be bought, sold, and traded itself—instead, we buy print objects as stays against time, as bricks that we can use in a dam against temporal erosion. The print artifact draws us into the kind of reading experience that is necessary to critical thought and that is increasingly only available to us in our working lives if we stake it out.

This book brings together scholars who grapple with the innate messiness of print culture in ways that connect the material print artifact to the larger contours of cultural and literary history. Not so much a new methodology as an accelerated focus and increasing historical purview, print culture studies offers us ways to ground our cultural work in material conditions. And more importantly, it allows us to be honest about what we are studying when we study modern American culture. There is no way around the fact that we study commodities. Everything that we have ever written about has been a commodity in some form, either in its original publication or in its afterlife as an appraised, insured special-collections manuscript. Capitalism is the condition of the cultural histories that we study and the condition that we inhabit as well. Overcoming this system requires analyzing and revealing its fundamental structuring of our culture, in both the commodity objects we study and the ideologies that give those objects value. It also requires the elaboration and imagining of other life-affirming cultural systems, systems in which cultural experiences do not compete with clothes, food, or shelter for our wages.[2]

Our emphasis on wages above is intentional. Indeed, while scholars of the history of the book, early American literature, and periodical studies have long studied printing history, the field of print culture has grown in recent years to include wide-ranging work in American studies, art history, comics studies, communication, environmental

---

[1] In the first chapter of his foundational study of American magazines, Richard Ohmann pauses for a moment and reflects on the pile of old magazines on his desk. They represent a radical shift from an agrarian society to an industrial economy, one in which even basic necessities were increasingly advertised and branded in the pages of magazines. Ohmann notes that "Today, nothing in this room is *not* a commodity, except for the dust, cats, and the cordwood; and of course I used commodities to cut, haul, and split the wood." Richard Ohmann, *Selling Culture: Magazines, Markets, and Class at the Turn of the Century* (New York: Verso, 1996), 9.

[2] For an account of ideology critique today that we have been inspired by, see Caren Irr, "Ideology Critique 2.0," *South Atlantic Quarterly* 119, no. 4 (2020), 715–24. Recent print culture projects have equally inspired our commitments here. These include Ronald Wimberly's broadsheet-sized *LAAB Magazine* (2018–present); the artisanal publishing projects of worker-owned printer and publisher Radix Media (radixmedia.org); postal-based print projects like Caitlin Cass's Great Moments in Western Civilization Postal Constituency (caitlincass.com) and John Porcellino's *King-Cat Comics* (king-cat.net); and a number of venues for popular criticism, in both print and digital forms, such as *The Believer, Jacobin, Los Angeles Review of Books, n+1, Public Books, Teen Vogue*, and many more. And, for an account of labor in our contemporary moment that is particularly relevant to higher education, see Sarah Jaffe, *Work Won't Love You Back: How Devotion to Our Jobs Keeps Us Exploited, Exhausted, and Alone* (New York: Bold Type, 2021).

humanities, history, modernist studies, visual culture, and more.[3] Interdisciplinary work on print culture has contributed, for example, to the popularization of revisionist histories of the book that consider China and Japan's early technologies alongside those in Europe, and thus complicate the traditional "Gutenberg as Inventor of Print" narrative's Eurocentrism.[4] Recovery projects have also radically expanded the

---

[3] There is more work in these fields than we can cite here. Some recent examples of work in American print culture studies that give a sense of the breadth of the field include Agatha Beins, *Liberation in Print: Feminist Periodicals and Social Movement Identity* (Athens: University of Georgia Press, 2017); Janet Borgerson and Jonathan Schroeder, *Designed for Hi-Fi Living: The Vinyl LP in Midcentury America* (Cambridge: MIT Press, 2017); Amanda Borsuk, *The Book* (Cambridge: MIT Press, 2018); Daphne A. Brooks, *Liner Notes for the Revolution: The Intellectual Life of Black Feminist Sound* (Cambridge: Harvard University Press, 2021); Eric Bulsom, *Little Magazine, World Form* (New York: Columbia University Press, 2017); Jim Casey and Sarah Salter, eds., "Forum: Locating the Practices of Editors in Multiethnic Periodicals," *American Periodicals* 30, no. 2 (September 2020), 101–25; Amy Hildreth Chen, *Placing Papers: The American Literary Archives Market* (Amherst: University of Massachusetts Press, 2020); Hillary Chute, *Why Comics?: From Underground to Everywhere* (New York: Harper, 2017); Jean Lee Cole, *How the Other Half Laughs: The Comic Sensibility in American Culture, 1895–1920* (Jackson: University Press of Mississippi, 2020); Lori Cole, *Surveying the Avant-Garde: Questions on Modernism, Art, and the Americas in Transatlantic Modernism* (University Park: Penn State University Press, 2018); Eurie Dahn, *Jim Crow Networks: African American Periodical Cultures* (Amherst: University of Massachusetts Press, 2021); Louis Dietrich, *Writing Across the Color Line: U.S. Print Culture and the Rise of Ethnic Literature, 1877–1920* (Amherst: University of Massachusetts Press, 2020); Vincent DiGirolamo, *Crying the News: A History of America's Newsboys* (New York: Oxford University Press, 2019); Marcy J. Dinius and Sonia Hazard, eds., *Keywords in Early American Literature* and Material Texts, special issue of *Early American Studies* 16, no. 4 (Fall 2018); Sherrin Frances, *Libraries Amid Protest: Books, Organizing, and Global Activism* (Amherst: University of Massachusetts Press, 2020); Cathryn Halverson, *Faraway Women and the* Atlantic Monthly (Amherst: University of Massachusetts Press, 2019); Donna Harrington-Lueker, *Books for Idle Hours: Nineteenth-Century Publishing and the Rise of Summer Reading* (Amherst: University of Massachusetts Press, 2018); Charles Hatfield and Bart Beaty, eds., *Comics Studies: A Guidebook* (New Brunswick: Rutgers University Press, 2020); N. Katherine Hayles, *Postprint: Books and Becoming Computational* (New York: Columbia University Press, 2021); Melissa J. Homestead, *The Only Wonderful Thing: The Creative Partnership of Willa Cather & Edith Lewis* (New York: Oxford University Press, 2021); Daniel Kane, *"Do You Have a Band?": Poetry and Punk Rock in New York City* (New York: Columbia University Press, 2017); Aaron Kashtan, *Between Pen and Pixel: Comics, Materiality, and the Book of the Future* (Columbus: Ohio State University Press, 2018); Catherine Keyser, *Artificial Color: Modern Food and Racial Fictions* (New York: Oxford University Press, 2019); Lee Konstantinou and Dan Sinykin, *Publishing American Literature, 1945–2020*, special issue of *American Literary History* 33, no. 2 (Summer 2021); Rodrigo Lazo and Jesse Alemán, eds., *The Latino Nineteenth Century* (New York: NYU Press, 2016); Aaron Lecklider, *Love's Next Meeting: The Forgotten History of Homosexuality and the Left in American Culture* (Berkeley: University of California Press, 2021); Kirsten MacLeod, *American Little Magazines of the Fin de Siècle: Art, Protest, and Cultural Transformation* (Toronto: University of Toronto Press, 2018); Jessica Pressman, *Bookishness: Loving Books in a Digital Age* (New York: Columbia University Press, 2020); Leah Price, *What We Talk About When We Talk About Books* (New York: Basic, 2019); Anne M. Royston, *Material Noise: Reading Theory as Artist's Book* (Cambridge: MIT Press, 2019); Sophie Seita, *Provisional Avant-Gardes: Little Magazine Communities from Dada to Digital* (Stanford: Stanford University Press, 2019); Jonathan Senchyne, *The Intimacy of Paper in Early and Nineteenth-Century American Literature* (Amherst: University of Massachusetts Press, 2020); Jordan Alexander Stein, *When Novels Were Books* (Cambridge: Harvard University Press, 2020); Rebecca Wanzo, *The Content of Our Caricature: African American Comic Art and Political Belonging* (New York: New York University Press, 2020); Qiana Whitted, *EC Comics: Race, Shock, and Social Protest* (New Brunswick: Rutgers University Press, 2019). This list is not exhaustive by any means, but we believe it does convey the wide range of exciting new work in print culture studies during this time.

[4] For example, see James Raven, ed., *The Oxford Illustrated History of the Book* (New York: Oxford University Press, 2020).

archives and corpus available in print, in research collections, and in digital archives, a transformation that has happened rapidly during our two decades in higher education. Though we were trained to write about and teach novels, poetry, and plays, and to assign those works as textbooks in our classes, we are now just as likely to assign a comic book; magazine; newspaper article; old television show; or selection of visual, textual, and mixed media, curated as a series of files and links on our university's web-based learning management system. In other words, we research and teach print culture more so than we do canonical literary texts. Indeed, we're cusp academics—neither Gen X nor millennials—so we read spools of microfilm while dissertating and then had to figure out what the "digital humanities" were as junior faculty—and all of this well before we could afford a cell phone with a touchscreen. As with so many internet-era explosions of activity, this rise in print culture studies has not been accompanied by a concordant rise in systemic support for our work in the humanities in US higher education (except maybe for the digital humanities, though that bubble may have inevitably burst already). Yet even the shrinking economic realities of the humanities have perversely contributed to print culture studies today. Personally, our careers have been inflected by the increasing pressure from our academic environments and institutions to apply for research grants, which has often meant grounding our research projects in a well-funded archive, and to work more quickly with more texts, in deeply contextual historicist projects or data-driven inquiries. The pressure to meet institutional expectations about grant funding has pulled us into the archives, even if we had not already been there in the first place. (And it is not at all difficult to imagine future scholars writing about this "grant-writing turn" in the humanities.)

While our immediate economic reality and our intellectual interests pulled us toward print culture research, other intellectual movements have also made print culture a site of new possibility. In recent years, the field of literary studies has been exploring methodologies like affect theory, surface reading, and postcritique that seek to foreground the passions and pleasures of aesthetic experiences.[5] These methods have provided us with new tools for both reading and teaching with print culture, and we have found in our work that the processes of aesthetic experience and ideology critique are not necessarily at odds with one another. Indeed, the Marxist cultural project at least in part seeks to synthesize both historical realities (the structures that are uncovered and diagnosed in "paranoid" reading) and utopian visions (the pleasures and experiences we gather when we encounter works of art) into an account of our cultural world. We need to be both paranoid and surface-oriented as readers, and fortunately, print culture demands that we engage both habits at the same time.

[5] There are a wide range of approaches and methodologies that fall under the broad headings of affect theory, surface reading, and postcritique. Influential definitions, articulations, and critiques of these ideas can be found in Elizabeth Anker and Rita Felski, eds., *Critique and Postcritique* (Durham: Duke University Press, 2017); Lauren Berlant, *Cruel Optimism* (Durham: Duke University Press, 2011); Stephen Best and Sharon Marcus, eds., *The Way We Read Now*, spec. iss. of *Representations* 108, no. 1 (Fall 2009); Andrew Cole, ed., *The Ideology Issue*, spec. iss. of *South Atlantic Quarterly* 119, no. 4 (October 2020); Rita Felski, *The Limits of Critique* (Chicago: University of Chicago Press, 2015); Sianne Ngai, *Our Aesthetic Categories: Zany, Cute, Interesting* (Cambridge: Harvard University Press, 2012); Jason Potts, ed., *Dossier: Surface Reading*, spec. iss. of *Mediations* 28, no. 2 (Spring 2015).

We don't think we're alone in this conviction, and with the skepticism of middle-aged scholars, and the optimism of Marxist intellectuals, we think that print culture studies is one viable future for the humanities today.

As we understand it, print culture studies' hybrid methodology and field of analysis draws upon periodical studies, histories of the book, literary studies, American studies, art history, science and technology studies, design studies, history, economics, sociology, education, material culture, visual culture, and more. Radically interdisciplinary, newly globalized and decolonized in historical accounts that have pushed beyond the Eurocentric framework of the Gutenberg-centered history of the book, and expanded by newly available digital archives, print culture is one way of naming the reorganization of professional practice that has been taking place in literary studies and other aesthetically minded fields in the humanities and social sciences. Since at least the gradual articulation of the "New Historicism" as a method in the 1990s and 2000s, and increasingly in our moment of "surface reading" and intensive historicist revision of our cultural history, scholars working in print culture have expanded the range of ideas we can talk about when we talk about texts.

The Past, Present, and Future of Print Culture Studies

In order to explain what print culture studies does for us as scholars today, we will turn to a few clusters of texts that demonstrate both the varied modes of culture that we can talk about as "print culture" and the aesthetic/political ideologies that inflect print culture in our contemporary moment. We begin with the print culture format of the newspaper column, and particularly Langston Hughes's folksy interlocutor character, Jesse B. Simple. Hughes often featured Jesse B. Simple in his syndicated weekly column in *The Chicago Defender* newspaper. Hughes's column ran in the *Defender* from 1943 to 1962, and later in the *New York Post* until 1965.[6] In the "Simple Stories," as they are commonly named, the Harlem native Jesse B. Simple pontificates about contemporary life, offering a humorous take on political reality.[7] First printed in African American newspapers across the country, and then in the *New York Post*, these "Simple Stories"

---

[6] For a thorough history and interpretation of Hughes's Simple stories, see Donna Akiba Sullivan Harper, *Not So Simple: The "Simple" Stories by Langston Hughes* (Columbia: University of Missouri Press, 1995), and for a bibliographic survey of the Simple stories, see Don Bertschman, "Jesse B. Simple and the Racial Mountain: A Bibliographic Essay," *The Langston Hughes Review* 13, no. 2 (Winter/Summer 1995), 29–44. For more recent readings of Hughes's Simple stories, see Ali Brox, "Simple on Satire: Langston Hughes, Gender, and Satiric Double-Consciousness," *Studies in American Humor* 21 (2010), 15–28; David Chinitz, *Which Sin to Bear?: Authenticity and Compromise in Langston Hughes* (New York: Oxford University Press, 2013), 106–9; Brian Dolinar, *The Black Cultural Front: Black Writers and Artists of the Depression Generation* (Jackson: University Press of Mississippi, 2012), 71–124; Cedric R. Tolliver, *Of Vagabonds and Fellow Travelers: African Diaspora Literary Culture and the Cultural Cold War* (Ann Arbor: University of Michigan Press, 2019), 97–125.

[7] For a reading of Jesse B. Simple's character and the poetic principle of simplicity in Hughes's work, see Karen Jackson Ford, "Do Right to Write Right: Langston Hughes's Aesthetics of Simplicity," *Twentieth Century Literature* 38, no. 4 (Winter 1992), 436–56.

were collected by Hughes in five books during his lifetime, and he also adapted them into a play titled *Simply Heavenly*.[8] In a 1976 article comparing Jesse B. Simple to James Thurber's "everyman" character Walter Mitty, the literary critic Melvin G. Williams argued that Jesse B. Simple's literal approach to newspapers is a striking alternative to the escapist daydreaming in Thurber's short story "The Secret Life of Walter Mitty," first published in the March 18, 1939, issue of the *New Yorker*. In Hughes's Simple stories, Williams argues, daydreaming and fantasy are critical and imaginative tools. While Thurber's daydreamer is a perpetual loser, Hughes's dreamer is a charmingly naive yet politically brilliant critic. Williams's closing paragraph begins with a quotation from James Thurber:

> "In a triumphant daydream, it seems to me, there is felicity and not defeat. You can't just take a humiliation and dismiss it from your mind... The thing to do is to visualize a triumph over the humiliator, so vividly and so insistently that it becomes, in effect, an actuality." James Thurber wrote these words about his own dreamers, yet they also apply every bit as well to Langston Hughes's best known dreamer. For he too is a kind of Walter Mitty—a Black Walter Mitty.[9]

Writing through a different methodological lens—this is immediately apparent when reading Williams's essay, as most of it is made up of direct quotations from Hughes's prose—Williams encounters through close reading the difference between Mitty's individualistic daydreaming and Simple's political fantasies. While Thurber's Mitty "generally needs someone else—especially his wife—to bring him back to reality," Hughes's Simple is left to dream. As Williams notes, Langston Hughes places himself in these newspaper columns through Boyd, a writer character who narrates most of Simple's stories. In most Simple stories, Boyd narrates Simple's various antics, and per Williams, "Even though [Boyd] tells Simple, 'You seem to dwell in a world of fantasy,' he does not wish to change him. 'Dream on' is his sound advice."[10] In Williams' analysis, Mitty's fantasies merely equip him to bear life's burdens while Hughes's Simple stories imagine alternative realities.

While Williams does not comment on the print and adaptation histories of either the Simple stories or "The Secret Life of Walter Mitty," there is nonetheless a remarkable parallel as both of these figures—Jesse B. Simple and Walter Mitty—emerge in the periodical press and then move outward into other print and media incarnations. Moreover, they are both representational vehicles for the relationship between print culture and readers. In the Simple stories, Jesse Simple often responds to newspaper articles that he has just read, or invokes them in conversation. For example,

---

[8] For an account of Hughes's *Simply Heavenly*, see Beth Turner, "'Simplifyin': Langston Hughes and Alice Childress Re/Member Jesse B. Semple," *The Langston Hughes Review* 15, no. 1 (Spring 1997), 37–48.

[9] Melvin G. Williams, "Langston Hughes's Jesse B. Semple: A Black Walter Mitty," *Negro American Literature Forum* 10, no. 2 (Summer 1976), 69.

[10] Ibid.

in the first collection of Simple stories, *Simple Speaks His Mind*, Simple is reading a newspaper as Boyd approaches him: "When he saw me, he threw the paper down."[11] In another Simple story, Simple bases his ruminations on print culture, "Look at these here headlines, man."[12] Throughout the Simple stories, Simple invokes newspapers, magazines, and comic books as the basis for his reflections on society, and also as a site for imaginative possibility. Not merely escaping into the popular press, Simple imagines new social relations.

In a Simple story titled "Puerto Ricans," Simple accidentally buys a Spanish-language comic book at a Harlem newsstand. Simple realizes his mistake, strikes up a conversation with a Puerto Rican man next to him on the subway, and gives him the comic book. Simple then reflects on "what a difference a foreign language makes. Just speak something else and you don't have to be colored in this here U.S.A."[13] Noting that Puerto Ricans face fewer housing restrictions than African Americans in cities like "New York, Chicago, anywhere, where an ordinary American-speaking Negro can't get a foothold, much less a room or an apartment," Simple imagines an anti-racist humor publication that would print funny stories about white people.[14] His imagined comic book would bring together the English-speaking Simple and the Spanish-speaking Puerto Rican next to him on the subway:

> I wonder why somebody don't make comic books out of the funny way white folks in America behave—talking democracy out of one side of their mouth and, "Negro, stay in your place," out of the other. I wish I could draw, I would make me such a book. I would start a whole series of comics which I bet would sell a million copies—Jess Simple's *Jim Crow Jive*, would be the title. I would make my books in both English and Spanish so the Puerto Ricans could laugh, too. Because it must tickle them to see what a little foreignness will do. Just be foreign—then you don't have to be colored.[15]

Langston Hughes would return to this idea in the foreword to his 1957 collection *Simple Stakes a Claim*, which included "Puerto Ricans." In the book's foreword, Hughes places his Simple stories in the context of African American print culture:

> My favorite reading is the Negro press. I know it should be the *Iliad*, the *Odyssey*, Shakespeare, or Tolstoy, but it isn't. It is the Negro press. Every week the Lord sends, if possible, in Harlem, I buy the *Courier*, the *Afro*, *Jet*, the *Amsterdam News*, and, of course, the *Defender* for which I write—so I can read myself. Also I buy

---

[11] Langston Hughes, "Simple Prays a Prayer," in *The Collected Works of Langston Hughes*, Vol. 7: *The Early Simple Stories*, ed. Donna A. Harper (Columbia: University of Missouri Press, 2002), 27.
[12] Langston Hughes, "There Ought to Be a Law," in *The Collected Works of Langston Hughes*, Vol. 7: *The Early Simple Stories*, ed. Donna A. Harper (Columbia: University of Missouri Press, 2002), 95.
[13] Langston Hughes, "Puerto Ricans," in *The Collected Works of Langston Hughes*, Vol. 8: *Later Simple Stories*, ed. Donna A. Harper (Columbia: University of Missouri Press, 2002), 63.
[14] Ibid.
[15] Ibid., 65.

whatever local colored papers there are in whatever city I may be when traveling. Whenever I find myself in a town where the colored papers are not available—like Carmel, California—I feel on weekends as though I were completely out of this world and have lost contact with my people. Abroad, the two things that I miss most are American ice cream and Negro newspapers.[16]

Yet Hughes tempers his love for African American print culture by noting that despite their occasional wordplay, "Negro newspapers do not intend to be funny—and usually they are not. For a race with so great a sense of humor, however, as that of the Negro people, it is strange that we have no primarily humorous publications."[17] Just like Simple in "Puerto Ricans," Hughes imagines an African American humor publication: "Since we have in our race a number of excellent cartoonists—some unsurpassed in America—and since we have several good writers capable of creating fun on paper, a humorous Negro monthly magazine should be a welcome addition to American cultural life and a happy success from the beginning."[18] Hughes then lists talented African American cartoonists, writers, and performers who could contribute to such a publication. A kind of African American *Mad* magazine, Hughes's imaginary periodical would have an intentionally critical and political edge, which Hughes compares to magazines "in the Latin countries":

> The humorous magazines there are often more dangerous to a crooked but ambitious politician than the most serious articles in the intellectual press. Think what colored people in the United States could do with a magazine devoted to satire and fun at the expense of the Dixiecrats. Since we have not been able to moralize them out of existence with indignant editorials, maybe we could laugh them to death with well-aimed ridicule.[19]

Hughes's own endorsement of the "Jess Simple's *Jim Crow Jive*" comic book imagined by Jesse B. Simple shows us that Hughes's commitment to print culture encompassed the varied popular periodical formats circulating through American newsstands at the time. Like Walter Mitty, Jesse B. Simple is engaged by American newsstands. He reads newspapers, comic books, and magazines; compares the white press to the African American press; charts the changing demographics of New York City through his encounters with a Spanish-language periodical at his local newsstand; and imagines a new periodical that would unite diverse readers with a shared, anti-racist identity.

The Simple stories imagine print culture as both our everyday reality and a vehicle for activism and change. Simple connects his print culture-inspired fantasies directly to reality, in a way that is at once humorous and profound. For example, in another

---

[16] Langston Hughes, "Foreword: Let's Laugh a Little," in *The Collected Works of Langston Hughes*, Vol. 8: *Later Simple Stories*, ed. Donna A. Harper (Columbia: University of Missouri Press, 2002), 19.
[17] Ibid., 20.
[18] Ibid.
[19] Ibid., 20–1.

Simple story collected in *Simple Stakes a Claim*, "News in Print," Simple remarks that the New York *Daily News* only ever features white people on its front page, unless "a race riot or a lynching or a boycott and a whole lot of us have been butchered up or arrested. Then they announce it."[20] Simple then goes on to describe American print culture and his vision for it in a characteristically humorous way. His objection to the New York *Daily News* is not that white American print culture ignores all but the most easily stereotyped stories about African American communities; Simple notes that the African American press covers what the white press neglects. Instead, Simple argues that African Americans do not get to have the same kinds of experiences in the real world as white people due to the cultural and imaginative limits enforced by white print culture. A lack of representation in mainstream print culture results in a reduction of cultural and social possibility, and even of experience. Simple uses the widely reported 1950s surge in UFO sightings to make his case:

> Take anything else on the front pages. Take flying saucers in the sky. Everybody but a Negro has seen one. If a Negro did see a flying saucer, I bet the papers wouldn't report it. They probably don't even let flying saucers fly over Harlem, just to keep Negroes from seeing them. This morning in the subway I read where Carl Krubelewski had seen a flying saucer, also Ralph Curio saw one. And way up in Massachusetts a while back, Henry Armpriester seen one. Have you ever read about Roosevelt Johnson or Ralph Butler or Carl Jenkins or anybody that sounded like a Negro seeing one? I did not. Has a flying saucer ever passed over Lenox Avenue? Nary one! Not even Daddy Grace has glimpsed one, neither Mother Horne, nor Adam Powell. Negroes can't get on the front page no kind of way. We can't even see a flying saucer.[21]

Simple's imagination of a world where flying saucers cruise over Lenox Avenue posits print culture as both the cause and effect of social change, with the mainstream media both a barometer of white supremacy and crass consumerism, and a site of political and representational struggle. Moreover, as Hughes makes clear when he imagines a new humor magazine in *Simple Stakes a Claim*, print culture is also a cultural system that Hughes can use to form community and imagine political consensus, even if that vision of consensus is already saturated with nostalgia by 1957. Through Simple, Langston Hughes thinks of print culture's forms as creating our social fabric, and he imagines participation in print culture as not just a reader but also producer and participant. Print culture's genre tropes; its representational formats; its blending of aesthetic, economic, and industrial labor—all of these complex clusters of systems, structures, activities, and material objects make up our shared cultural reality.

---

[20] Langston Hughes, "Name in Print," in *The Collected Works of Langston Hughes*, Vol. 8: *Later Simple Stories*, ed. Donna A. Harper (Columbia: University of Missouri Press, 2002), 107.
[21] Ibid., 108. A version of this appears in the play *Simply Heavenly*, as well. See Langston Hughes and David Martin, *Simply Heavenly* (New York: Dramatists Play Service, 1987), 30–1.

In Hughes's 1957 theatrical production of *Simply Heavenly*, print culture is consistently visible on set. The "Prop List" for the play includes the following print culture artifacts:

> Stage money–bills and coins... Bible/Fashion magazine/Travel folders and timetables/Newspaper/Newspaper with puzzle/Copy of *Daily News*/3 copies of *Amsterdam News*/3 copies of *Herald Tribune*/Paper portfolio... Deck of cards/2-3 comic books/Wrapping paper... Paper bag (to hold 3 liquor bottles)... 3 letters (handwritten)... Divorce paper (blue roll with gold seal)/Legal form (apartment application)... Note Pad/Pencils[22]

Indeed, *Simply Heavenly* requires something like a library cart for its print culture artifacts, ranging from specific newspaper titles to generic writing tools. In the play, Simple uses his family Bible as a bank—he tucks money into its pages, saving in order to marry his new love Joyce—and a repository for family wisdom. The comic books and playing cards, though, connote commercial print culture; both are sold at newsstands alongside the "Pack of Cigarettes" also listed on the play's "Prop List."

The "Prop List" specifies the *Amsterdam News* and *Herald Tribune* to provide a clear sense of setting. By including both newspapers, the play presents Harlem as both a unique African American community with its own newspaper, the *Amsterdam News*, and a part of New York City, whose white-dominated perspective is offered through the *Herald Tribune*. Unlike the newspapers, the comic books aren't described in detail in the "Prop List." Yet in the play, they are. In the play, when Simple receives the comic books, he responds by saying two titles out loud: "Oh! *Horror in Hackensack. Terror in Trenton...* This makes me feel better already." Meant to connote unwholesome reading, these horror comics titles would not have been available as new publications on American newsstands in 1957, when this play was first produced. The Code of the Comics Magazine Authority of America effectively removed horror comics titles from American newsstands between 1954 and 1955. The first rule of its "General Standards—Part B": "No comic magazine shall use the word horror or terror in its title." Famously driving the horror comics publisher EC Comics out of the medium altogether by 1956, the Comics Code ended what is now considered to be the "Golden Age" of comic books, and the Code ushered in the medium's "Silver Age," wherein it is generally thought that comics entered into a period of aesthetic and economic decline.[23] *Simply Heavenly*'s invocation of banned horror comics recalls a then-recent moment in print culture history, as does the play's earlier invocation of highbrow print culture.[24]

---

[22] Hughes and Martin, *Simply Heavenly*, 78.
[23] See Shawna Kidman, *Comic Books Incorporated*; Amy Kyste Nyberg, *Seal of Approval*; and Rebekah Walker and Daniel Worden's chapter in this volume.
[24] As Ken Quattro points out in his history of Black comics artists, Langston Hughes wrote a positive review of the National Urban League's *Negro Heroes* comic book in a May 3, 1947, *Chicago Defender* column. For a history of Black comics publishing in 1947, including *Negro Heroes* and the more genre-oriented *All-Negro Comics*, see Ken Quattro, *Invisible Men: The Trailblazing Black Artists of Comic Books* (San Diego: IDW, 2020), especially 204–30.

In *Simply Heavenly*, Paddy's Bar is the play's central setting. In the original production, the bar room occupies center stage, flanked on either side by smaller sets for Simple's and Joyce's rooms. In the public setting of Paddy's Bar, print materials circulate freely alongside other newsstand items like playing cards and cigarettes. Characters sit on barstools and tables, reading newspapers, doing crossword puzzles, playing cards, and writing notes for prospective book projects about Harlem. In the play's first scene, print culture is presented as a major theme itself, as an unnamed character enters Paddy's bar. Described in the play's notes as "A Little Man in nose glasses, carrying an umbrella ... with an armful of highbrow papers and magazines,"[25] this unnamed character is immediately put up for ridicule by Paddy's regular, Mamie, "There comes that character trying to make people think he's educated"[26] (Figure 0.1). The "Little Man" accuses the patrons of Paddy's Bar of being "just stereotypes, that's all," and soon after leaves the bar "clicking his tongue in disgust."[27] Representing the

Figure 0.1 Unidentified actor (the "Little Man"), Claudia McNeil, and John Bouie in the stage production *Simply Heavenly*, 1957. Photo by Friedman-Abeles © The New York Public Library for the Performing Arts.

[25] Hughes and Martin, *Simply Heavenly*, 14.
[26] Ibid.
[27] Ibid., 16–17.

elitist perspective of the "highbrow papers and magazines" that he carries with him, Hughes's "Little Man" is allergic to the folk types and genre conventions that structure the popular press, as represented in the play by Paddy's Bar and its clientele. After all, Paddy's bar is a site for the circulation of both the Black press and the white mainstream press as well as other media forms like the blues and recreational games commodified through print artifacts like sheet music and playing cards. *Simply Heavenly* presents the character Boyd, Hughes's mouthpiece in the Simple stories, as an alternative to the elitist "Little Man." As Mamie points out: "One thing I like about Boyd here, even if he is a writer, he ain't alway trying to impress folks. Also he speaks when he comes in a public place."[28] Boyd's role as a writer places him as a mediator figure, between the vernacular and popular print culture "stereotypes" that populate Paddy's bar, and the play's own audience, who may find in the character of Simple a stereotype. Boyd then serves as a point of identification and authentication for the play's own audience. Indeed, via the play's banishment of the elitist "Little Man"—he leaves Paddy's Bar never to return again—Boyd in turn authorizes the play's characters as authentic, despite their clear references to popular genre types. In fact, the playwright Alice Childress would write a critical letter to Hughes after seeing a performance of *Simply Heavenly*, questioning whether Hughes had achieved "a truthful portrayal of Negroes, honest, unsentimentalized, respectful, etc."[29]

Just as it may balance the stereotypes of high and low culture, the play balances its use of popular periodicals with Simple's family Bible and the various legal documents that Simple puts underneath his Christmas tree at the play's happy conclusion (Figure 0.2). The play's closing scene enacts Simple's symbolic emancipation, as he presents his signed divorce papers to Joyce. She exclaims, "Jess, you're free! Just like in Uncle Tom's Cabin!"[30] And then Simple proposes to Joyce through three gifts: a letter from Joyce's father approving their coupledom, a ring, and an application for an apartment in a new urban housing development. They both sign the application in a symbolic marriage and enter into respectable middle-class life. Just as Boyd enters into print culture through his writings about Simple's Harlem, so does Simple enter into American society by participating in print culture through legal documents.

This print-cultural complexity, revisionist practice, and production of political imaginaries is perhaps best captured today—in an admittedly bleaker register—by the current revival and manifold reworkings of another writer, Howard Philip Lovecraft, better known today, of course, as H.P, the chronically broke writer was convinced by late 1919, perhaps rightly, that no one understood his stories and even fewer wanted to pay for them—sentiments which he bitterly related in dozens of letters to many recipients. Worst of all, though, his beloved little corner of New England was changing rapidly in appearance, tone, and demographics, and he was having *none* of it. To be fair, change was in the air—and not just in New England: 1919 in the United States had seen Congress pass the Nineteenth Amendment to the Constitution,

---

[28] Ibid., 14.
[29] Alice Childress quoted in Leslie Catherin Sanders, "'Also Own the Theatre': Representation in the Comedies of Langston Hughes," *The Langston Hughes Review* 11, no. 1 (1992), 6.
[30] Ibid., 75.

Figure 0.2 Scene from the stage production *Simply Heavenly*, 1957. Photo by Friedman-Abeles © The New York Public Library for the Performing Arts.

which would give women the right to vote the following August. It was also another banner year for migrants from Europe heading toward American shores, particularly Italians, Austro-Hungarians, and Russian Jews. And the inaccurately named "Spanish Flu" was still in the process of killing over 675,000 Americans (depending on who's counting). This early twentieth-century pandemic was partially blamed, of course, on the aforementioned immigrants.[31] As if that weren't enough, a Great Migration of

---

[31] See Alan M. Kraut, "Immigration, Ethnicity, and the Pandemic," *Public Health Reports* 125, no. 3 (2010): 123–33 and Laura Murphy, "The Mexican Germ Invasion Is Just the Right's Latest Anti-Immigration Myth," *Guardian* (July 2, 2014), https://www.theguardian.com/.

African Americans from the South continued its steady pace to the cities of the North, where they were welcomed by dozens of race riots that erupted from the center of Chicago to the cotton fields of Elaine, Arkansas, destroying thousands of Black homes and businesses, and taking hundreds of Black lives. Meanwhile, Attorney General A. Mitchell Palmer (eagerly abetted by an ambitious young man named J. Edgar Hoover, who would cite his job at the Library of Congress as excellent practice for collating and capturing crooks) launched the first formal Red Scare, arresting thousands of putative radicals from Seattle to Boston on charges that had far more to do with the suspects' ethnicities than their politics. Further afield, Lenin and his party faithful had the nerve to consolidate their revolutionary movement in Russia beneath the mantle of the Third International. And right in Lovecraft's comparative backyard, the Boston police went on strike, leaving an already gloomy H.P. certain that *all* of the above were somehow connected. When the Massachusetts State Guard filled in for the striking cops, he wrote to his friend Frank Belknap Long that these were all, of course, mere "symbols of the strife that lies ahead in civilization's struggle with the monster of unrest and bolshevism."[32]

In response to these concerns, Lovecraft dashed off a short story titled "The Street," written in the style of the "weird fiction" he did so much to bring into being.[33] Indisputably weird, the tale was also a wildly racist bit of historical revisionism set against the various immigrant groups, smoke-belching factories, and novel political forms Lovecraft believed were "invading" his beloved New England, particularly the cities of Boston, Providence, and nearby factory towns. Rhetorically organized in the language of myth, "The Street" begins, as it were, at the beginning of Anglo-Saxon settlement in New England with the Puritans landing upon a wild but idyllic and unspoiled land where "Men of strength and honour fashioned that Street; good, valiant men of our blood who had come from the Blessed Isles across the sea."[34] The meaning of the "our" here is obvious when placed in conjunction with the "Blessed Isles," as Lovecraft continues to relate to an imagined audience of in-crowders a world of "bonneted wives and sober children" wherein indigenous populations can be dealt with in a single sentence: "There was a war, and thereafter no more Indians troubled." In fact, all early conflict is just as bloodlessly retold in "The Street." For example, the War for Independence is essentially just a vexillological handoff, "when they furled the Old Flag and put up a new Banner of Stripes and Stars."

Of course, into this white Eden "of many trees; elms and oaks of great dignity" "came days of evil," thanks to industrialization in the form of "strange puffings and shrieks from the river a mile away" which left the "air not quite so pure as before." But

---

[32] H. P. Lovecraft, letter to Frank Belknap Long, November 11, 1920; cited in S. T. Joshi and David E. Schultz, *An H. P. Lovecraft Encyclopedia* (Westport, CT: Greenwood Press, 2001), 254.

[33] The street, while written in late 1919, was first published in the December 1920 issue of the amateur journal *Wolverine*. For recent accounts of "weird fiction," see Julius Greve and Florian Zappe, eds., *The American Weird: Concept and Medium* (New York: Bloomsbury Academic, 2021), and Roger Lockhurst, James Machin, and Timothy Jarvis, eds., *Weird Fiction*, special issue of *Textual Practice* 31, no. 6 (2017), 1041–163.

[34] All quotations are from H.P. Lovecraft, "The Street," *The H.P. Lovecraft Archive*. Available online: https://www.hplovecraft.com/writings/texts/fiction/s.aspx

things really start to go downhill when, before they knew it, the "town was now a city," marked by the arrival of "new kinds of faces... swarthy sinister faces with furtive eyes and odd features." Thanks to them, the "trees were all gone now," the "rose-gardens were displaced by the back of cheap, ugly new buildings," "Push-carts crowded the gutters," and a "sordid, undefinable stench settled over the place."

So far, so subtle—but when Lovecraft hits his present day, that's when the situation really takes a dive. The First World War may be troubling, but the far more important issue is a "revolution... raging across the seas; a dynasty had collapsed, and its degenerate subjects were flocking with dubious intent to the Western Land." Readers at this point may not be surprised to find out that these "alien makers of discord" also settled on "the street" in order "to strike the Western Land its death-blow" just like the "assassins had mounted in that unhappy, frozen land from whence they had come." The planning for this American Revolution takes place in lairs with names like "Petrovitch's Bakery" or "the squalid Rifkin School of Modern Economics," and this great revolutionary moment is to occur, of course, on "the fourth day of July," their "appointed day of blood, flame, and crime." Spoiler: it never happens, thanks to what we might call, in true Lovecraftian spirit, a "Cthulhu ex machina." After a strange and "tremendous climax," the titular street apparently destroys itself rather than suffer further mongrel indignities, and we know this because a "poet" who arrived on the scene sees reflected in the arc-lights "there loomed above the wreckage another picture wherein he could descry moonlight and fair houses and elms and oaks and maples of dignity."

We sojourn with Lovecraft, his abysmal politics, and his even more abyssal fictions not to exculpate them in any way but because they surface an enduring truth about print culture writ large: Like the destruction of "the street" and the poet who witnessed the palimpsestic spirit of an imagined past floating above it, the vagaries cohered to print objects and the cultures they engage also pile wreckage atop wreckage. But unlike Benjamin's famous "Angel of History" blown helplessly backward in its tragic idealism, these objects—in their writing, witnessing, and revision—can also be recycled, reused, reworked, and remade (nearly) anew.[35] Lovecraft's blinkered and brutal literary response to the events of 1919 centers not only the persistent resonance of these enduring tensions in our own time—as inescapable as a tentacular creature from his own dark fictions—but also, in this moment of an astonishing Lovecraftian recrudescence, the ways in which so many contemporary writers of "weird fiction," many of whom might have seen *themselves* in the later arrivals to "the street," are now rewriting Lovecraft the way Lovecraft rewrote US history. And these very processes of seriality, recursion, and iterativity—so central to the magazines Lovecraft published in—are also in large part the mechanics of print culture itself. Victor LaValle, for example, a mixed-race horror writer raised in New York City (a place Lovecraft also despised for the racially diverse throngs he found there), refers to his 2016 novel,

---

[35] For Benjamin's influential figuration of the "Angel of History," see section IX of Walter Benjamin, "On the Concept of History," trans. Dennis Redmond, *Marxists Internet Archive*, 2005. https://www.marxists.org/reference/archive/benjamin/1940/history.htm

The Ballad of Black Tom, as "a literary mash-up of H.P. Lovecraft with a Black Lives Matter undercurrent."[36] But most importantly here, despite LaValle's understandable revulsion at and disavowal of Lovecraft's abhorrent views, he is also a *fan*, and one whose rewritings of Lovecraftian themes are foremost an attempt to salvage these mutable creations from their obdurate creator. In other words, LaValle's writing is a deep and serious practice of care. Or, as he puts it, "You have to love the work to a certain level to engage with it that deeply."[37]

LaValle isn't remotely alone. The popular interest in Lovecraft received prestige television treatment in HBO's 2020 series *Lovecraft Country*, an adaptation of Matt Ruff's 2016 novel of the same name. *Lovecraft Country* is not only deft reworkings of original materials, but also a showcase for the wending traditions of print culture production. And the particular genius of both these versions of Lovecraft countries is that the very horror Lovecraft himself experienced at the non-white bodies in the cities and towns of the Northeast has now been reworked into the horror of *being* a non-white body in a country populated by Lovecrafts, a notion made memorably visible in the 2017 film *Get Out*. Foregrounding the ways that popular genres and their concomitant racist stereotypes travel through print culture objects, the HBO television series *Lovecraft Country* prominently features books and magazines as *actors* in the narrative, particularly a hand-drawn comic book and an illuminated atlas (Figures 0.3 and 0.4). These handmade artifacts help imagine and even attempt to help *bring into being* an anti-racist print culture, a print culture that has never been mainstream but is still emergent today.

Figure 0.3 Afua Richardson's Orynthia Blue comic book in the series *Lovecraft Country*, 2020. © Home Box Office, Inc. All rights reserved.

---

[36] Lincoln Michel, "Victor LaValle's New Novel Is H.P. Lovecraft, Without the Horrific Racism," *Vice* (March 2, 2016), https://www.vice.com/
[37] Ibid.

Figure 0.4 Afua Richardson's illustrated atlas in the series *Lovecraft Country*, 2020. © Home Box Office, Inc. All rights reserved.

This contemporary return to Lovecraft, which is also a return to print culture and the popular press, also resounds for less celebratory reasons. About a century after Lovecraft finished "The Street," over half a million Americans have died from Covid-19, around ten million are unemployed, and the summer of 2020 saw the largest protest movement in the history of the country emerge after a Minnesota cop murdered George Floyd by kneeling on the restrained man's neck for nine minutes and twenty-nine seconds. Meanwhile, a decidedly non-Bolshevik Russia has nevertheless returned three decades after the dissolution of the Soviet Union—this time as online troll farm and one of the standard bearers (alongside a disturbing number of Americans) for a white Christian nationalism as grim as it is cruel. The specter of socialism, however, has made its own comeback in both the swelling ranks of the Democratic Socialists of America and in the mouths of right-wing politicians who lob that charge at anyone radical enough to think fewer children should starve in the richest nation on Earth. And of course, on January 6, 2021, the MAGA crowd obeyed their master's whistles and convoyed into DC, storming the Capitol Building and looking for a vice president or a few House members to hang. Sometimes history rhymes. Sometimes it clangs. A century on, Lovecraft was right about the plotting, but the faces in the actual insurrection probably looked a little different than the people he imagined at the "Rifkin School."

Indeed, what could possibly be more Lovecraftian, more "weird fiction," more wedded to print culture than QAnon—which was also born serially, recursively, and iteratively; shared and expanded endlessly through digital communities; turned into print objects; and carried as slogans into a violent coup attempt. A global cabal of Satanic cannibalistic child molesters who run the world when they're not too busy indulging in bloody rituals and rites, only to be eventually exposed and undone by the

Storm of a Great Awakening? Even "The Street" would be impressed. It seems to be entirely Lovecraft's country now, and we're all just reading, writing, and weirding in it.

Plan of the Book

In *New Directions in Print Culture Studies*, we have brought together scholars who share an interest in the world-making projects associated with print culture. The contributors to this book imagine and then enact a model of print culture studies that is materialist in both critical and utopian modes. On the one hand, as we've mentioned earlier, print culture is a historical and cultural record, one that has become newly available to us as scholars. Our role is to approach print culture as a material phenomenon, bounded not by the imaginary limits of creative expression but by the necessary conditions of capitalist production and exploitation, under which every print culture format in America today must negotiate. On the other hand, particular print culture formations can imagine new communities and new worlds. Imaginatively untethered from material constraints and notoriously indifferent to economic realities, many print culture endeavors are utopian projects. Like so many failed Mom & Pop restaurants in small town America, archives of now-defunct periodicals, remaindered books, and yellowing pamphlets resonate to us today as artifacts of possible worlds, historical documents of paths not taken, visions not fully implemented, ideas that were unheard, communities that thrived momentarily before foundering, institutions that emerged only to recede, and many more instances when people allowed themselves to imagine otherwise. Tending to these possibilities and locating our contemporary struggles in these artifacts from the past frames our history through the tensions not just of abstract ideas and aesthetic history, but also of the material conditions that make those ideas and histories palpable and, therefore, cultural. By understanding these struggles "from the ground up," we hope to be able to teach our students how to enter the world with some degree of preparation for the struggles that await them.

The chapters in this book each present archivally based readings and approaches to texts as well as reflections on the methodological work of print culture studies. We have divided the chapters into four thematic clusters, though these in no way exhaust the connections among this book's chapters (or, of course, any number of other ways we might have organized them). In Part One, "Print Culture's Pasts and Presents," Ayendy Bonifacio reexamines nineteenth-century story papers in order to answer the long-running scholarly debate of who actually read these print objects and why. With the popular *New York Ledger* as his case study, Bonifacio argues that because this periodical resembled the broadsheets of newspapers while also publishing poets and serialists featured in literary monthlies, the *Ledger* occupied an interstitial place in the print market world between popular culture and genteel culture. This allowed the *Ledger* to successfully cater to a capacious "unknown public." Next, Jesse W. Schwartz engages with John Reed's numerous articles in *Metropolitan* magazine during his rise to reportorial stardom. Mutually beneficial at first, Schwartz investigates how their differing definitions of "socialism" fractured this relationship over the magazine's support for the First World War, and therefore forced Reed to obviate potential censorship by using literary techniques and devices to suture his disparate articles into a larger story resembling, in many ways, a serial novel. Then, Agatha Beins returns to the vibrant feminist print culture of the late 1960s and 1970s, such as the *L.A. Free Press*, *RAT* (New York City), *Berkeley Barb*, *Great Speckled Bird* (Atlanta), and *Kaleidoscope* (Chicago). New technologies like the mimeograph machine were a precondition for the explosion of feminist media in this period, and it was these neglected precursors, she argues, that literally materialize the political commitments of US feminism. Next, Gary Edward Holcomb discusses the surprising surfeit of attention around Claude McKay's newly published (if never quite lost) novel, *Romance In Marseille*. Navigating the circuitous life and reception history of McKay and his novels alongside the broader field transformations around African American literary studies as a whole, Holcomb asks what it might mean to become an "instant classic" in the age of digital media. And finally, Michelle Chihara surveys the strange and thoroughly contemporary world of online print journal communities. Heavily enmeshed within the neoliberal discourses of self-actualization and entrepreneurship, these practices and communities can be remade, Chihara argues, to offer strength and solidarity against the cult of productivity.

In Part Two, "Archives, Exhibits, Images, and Sounds of Print Culture," Monica Huerta focuses on *cartes de visite* of children taken from slavery and into the north during the Civil War. By engaging with the celebrity that surrounded some of these children and their *cartes*, Huerta explains how these images reverberated against the active and tumultuous signifying in a public sphere fractured by the Civil War and its unfixed geographies. Then, Justin Rogers-Cooper surveys a number of engraved images of the 1877 general strike that appeared in nineteenth-century periodicals. By examining the vast print culture around the 1877 labor struggles, Rogers-Coopers demonstrates how race and gender inform and complicate our contemporary understanding of the strike's class conflicts and its multiform layers of class consciousness. Next, Kristin Moriah engages with the many tangled intersections between race, gender, performativity, and sound in the late nineteenth century. Considering sound in the absence of recordings, Moriah turns toward press coverage of Black performers who travelled during the high point of racist violence in the United States. With these print objects, she stitches together the impact of these performances and obviates in part the lack of a sonic record. Lori Cole revisits the life and times of art magazine *Spawn*, which its creator, Stuart Davis, dubbed a "travelling exhibition." Devoid of text and simply offering art for sale, *Spawn* radically reimagined the expectations for both a magazine and a gallery. Yet, as Cole argues, *Spawn* was one of many, and she offers several case studies to explore the ways in which magazines functioned as or supplemented exhibition spaces, allowing editors to circulate art on their own terms and, in so doing, to reimagine the magazine as a medium. This is followed by Rebekah Walker and Daniel Worden's analysis of comic books available on US newsstands in the month of April 1956. They explore how primary source research is transforming our understanding of comics history, and how comic book archives can be used in the classroom to pose questions about print culture. And finally, Robert Reid-Pharr uses

James Baldwin as an entry point to reexamine the archives of African America. Long (and understandably) organized around a sense of absence and "lack" 400 years after slavery began in the United States, Reid-Pharr nonetheless argues that celebrity and celebration are also central to contemporary African American and African Diasporic intellectual and cultural life through what he names "the practice of celebrity."

In the third and final section, "Print Culture Studies in Practice," Kelley Kreitz considers the place of the Spanish-language press in the late nineteenth-century United States to reimagine literary history with an emphasis on empowering students. A recent archival turn in teaching in Latinx Studies and adjacent fields, she argues, makes classrooms sites of investigating print culture to connect the past's lost voices to today's ongoing struggles for racial justice. Next, Danica Savonick analyzes the publishing histories of four literary anthologies edited by Black feminist authors June Jordan and Toni Cade Bambara in the late 1960s and early 1970s. By showing how these anthologies emerged, in part, from Jordan and Bambara's collaborative publishing efforts with their students, Savonick argues for the centrality of the classroom, as a space not only for the reading and reception of American literature but also for its active production. Then, Krystyna Michael, Jojo Karlin, and Matthew K. Gold explore the tension between books as printed objects and books as digital experiences. By illustrating how these pressures animate ongoing discussions of the present state and future possibilities of digital publishing, and in place of a model that considers print and digital publishing as inherently separate processes, they advocate for a "hybrid publishing" that involves concurrent print and digital editorial and publication processes.

Taken together, these chapters showcase how print culture mediates and facilitates our imaginations of the world. In our excursions through Hughes's "simple" and Lovecraft's "weird," we have detailed some of the ways that print culture can figure into texts, both as an immediate historical context and as a framework for questioning our assumptions about cultural history. In print culture studies, we find both the methods and the objects that allow us to understand how history unfolds in the present and how others have imagined future worlds yet to come. The contributions to this volume demonstrate the range and promise of print culture studies today.

Part One

Print Culture's Pasts and Presents

1

Story-Paper Origins in the United States: The Unknown Public and *The New York Ledger*

Ayendy Bonifacio

Published from the 1830s until the early 1900s, story papers were hebdomadals, or weekly periodicals, that were closely related to newspapers and literary magazines. Varying in size from tabloid sheets (8.5 × 11.5 inches) and broadsheets (14 × 18 inches) to mammoth sheets (22 × 32 inches), story papers featured illustrations, serials, poems, and advice columns with little to no news. They were, as Richard Brodhead says, "the large-paged, newspaper-like bearer of column upon column of closely printed fiction (usually with lurid illustrations) often published in tandem with the pamphlet-like dime novel."[1] Many publishers called their papers "family papers" to target a broader audience of the whole family. The print culture of story papers is an important part of the formation of nineteenth-century reading publics, reading practices, and cultural production. Yet they are understudied in such analyses. Not a newspaper or a literary magazine, the story paper is often pushed aside by its more culturally legible periodical counterparts. As the following pages will show, centralizing the reprint culture of story papers reveals how nineteenth-century print audiences were asked to imagine a complex industrial culture through the formats and advertisements of the popular press.

Critics of nineteenth-century story papers have long debated the question of readership and audience: who read story papers and for what reasons?[2] This chapter provides context for these queries via an analysis of the "unknown public" and the "family," ambiguous designations for mid-century story paper audiences. I comb through digital databases like the Chronicling America and Readex: America's Historical Newspapers for ads and columns that specifically address story-paper

---

[1] Richard Brodhead, *Cultures of Letters: Scene of Reading and Writing in Nineteenth-Century America* (Chicago: The University of Chicago Press, 1993), 78.

[2] See, Lori Merish, "The Emergence of Story Papers," in *The Oxford History of Popular Print Culture: Volume Six: US Popular Print Culture 1860–1920* (Oxford: Oxford University Press, 2012); Michael Denning, *Mechanic Accents: Dime Novels and Working-Class Culture in America* (London: Verso, 1998); Daniel A. Cohen, "Winnie Woodfern Comes Out in Print: Story-Paper Authorship and Protolesbian Self-Representation in Antebellum America," *Journal of the History of Sexuality* 21, no. 3 (2012), 367–408. Sara Lindey, "Boys Write Back: Self-Education and Periodical Authorship in Late-Nineteenth-Century Story Papers," American Periodicals 21, no. 1 (2011), 72–88.

readers. These ads and columns are important links between newspapers and story papers that reveal a complex network of readers with similar interests and reading practices. These ads are foundational for understanding how editors conceptualized their readers, that is, how they understood their public's interests, demands, neglects, and incuriosities. I argue that the story paper's material and cultural proximity to newspapers and literary monthlies facilitated a network of social relations of readers from diverse socioeconomic backgrounds.

Among nineteenth-century story papers, Robert Edwin Bonner's *The New York Ledger* is the most significant. Resembling the broadsheets of newspapers, yet publishing poets and serialists often featured in literary monthlies, the *Ledger* occupied an interstitial place in the print market world between popular culture and high culture. While literary magazines like *Munsey's*, *Ladies' Home Journal* and *Cosmopolitan* assumed that their readers were educated and part of the middle class, the *Ledger* catered to a vast and classless "unknown public," which Bonner simply called "the family".[3] The *Ledger* was more like the serious newspapers of the time, casting a wide net which, as opposed to the selective scope of intellectual monthlies, catered to readers regionally and nationally. Because socioeconomic factors did not categorically define "the family," the *Ledger*'s emphasis on the family as reader was an important strategy for reaching an audience of diverse classes and societies. The nomenclature of "family" also implies that the *Ledger* was designed as suitable for children as well as for adults. In other words, as a category for the *Ledger*'s audience, "the family" was an ambiguous designation that did not estrange readers based on their class or interests. The purpose of this chapter is to demonstrate how this seemingly neutral nomenclature effectively garnered the interest of readers of news, serials, poetry, and advice columns helping the *Ledger* achieve tremendous success for a weekly paper. Analyzing the *Ledger*'s intended audience as promoted by its editor and contributors will help us to better understand the enigmatic makeup of story-paper readers.

Origins of the Story Paper

The development and popularity of the story paper would not have been possible without the mass production of literary monthlies and newspapers of the late 1820s. Although many literary monthlies were short-lived, the number of magazines produced between 1820 and 1860 rose from less than one hundred to over six hundred, creating new reading markets for future publishers and editors to explore.[4] Many literary periodicals were based in New York City and Boston, including George Pope Morris

---

[3] Matthew Schneirov, *The Dream of a New Social Order: Popular Magazines in America 1893–1914* (New York: Columbia University Press, 1994), 97.

[4] Frank Luther Mott, *A History of American Magazines 1741–1850* (Cambridge: Harvard University Press, 1966), 120.

and Samuel Woodworth's *New York Mirror*, established in 1823, an early weekly devoted to entertainment; and Nathaniel Parker Willis' *American Monthly Magazine* (Boston), founded in 1829, which helped launch Park Benjamin Sr.'s career in the world of print. Benjamin Sr. would go on to print one of the first successful story papers in the United States, *The New World* featuring American and British reprints.[5]

The technological and social conditions that facilitated the success of newspapers played a significant part in the development of story papers as well. The rapid growth of the penny press—*New York Sun* (founded 1833), *Philadelphia Public Ledger* (1836), and *New York Herald* (founded 1835)—signified a new print economy and an age of non-partisan papers.[6] This new print economy also meant selling cheaply, employing third-party distributors like newsboys, and selling column space for mass advertisements. The emergence of the steam-driven cylinder press and transcontinental rail networks improved technological advancements in methods of production and distribution, which were conducive to the growth of the story paper. These technological developments eventually led to, as Michael Denning argues, "social changes in the emergence of a new reading public, the artisans and mechanics of the eastern cities."[7]

Along with advancements in steam press technologies and an increase in population and literacy in the 1830s came an unprecedented growth in periodical production. With a population of thirteen million, the United States had more periodicals and more readers than any other industrialized nation. England, for example, had a significant periodical industry in the early nineteenth century and imposed a hard stamp tax on newspapers in the 1830s. The United States Post, however, did not obstruct the circulation of papers with a postal tax.[8] In fact, special rates were permitted for mailing anything that resembled a newspaper, turning the postman into the United States' foremost literary salesperson. Some publishers of cheap fiction were subject to postal protocols which made it difficult to sell by subscription. To avoid high postal rates for shipping books in the early 1840s, cheap book publications appeared in the form of newspapers and newspaper supplements which had lower postal rates than books and pamphlets.[9]

---

[5] Sacvan Bercovitch, *The Cambridge History of American Literature: Volume Two Prose Writing 1820-1865* (Boston: Cambridge University Press, 1995), 54.

[6] These non-partisan papers were different from the partisan papers of the previous century—Democratic-Republican Party's *National Gazette* (1791-3), Federalist Party's *Gazette of the United States* (1789-93), and *The New York Evening Post* (1801). The new print revolution consisted of papers that claimed no party affiliation and substantively focused on news, "a genre it invented" (Denning, *Mechanic Accents*, 10).

[7] Denning, *Mechanic Accents*, 10.

[8] David. M. Henkin notes in *The Postal Age: The Emergence of Modern Communications in Nineteenth-Century America*, "As with the proliferation of so many artifacts of the expanding antebellum print culture (including newspapers, novels, political pamphlets, urban signage, and fashion magazines), the increasing availability and affordability of the post encouraged the acquisition, cultivation, and maintenance of literacy" (24).

[9] Vicki Anderson, *The Dime Novel in Children's Literature* (Jefferson: McFarlan & Company, Inc., 2005), 124.

The ethos of industrialism pushed the business of writing with unparalleled force, obfuscating the lines between fact and fiction.[10] In the early 1830s, story papers devoted a substantial amount of space to the news, a custom that Denning claims emerged "out of a gradual but incomplete separation of the news and story functions of the newspaper."[11] In doing so, none of these periodicals were strictly story papers.[12] The increase in cheap daily newspapers in 1833 in Boston, Philadelphia, and New York brought firsthand news to a growing reading public precluding story papers from serving this purpose. Thus, by the mid-1830s, story papers significantly cut their news items from their pages to play up their fiction, poetry, illustrations, and advice columns.

In the 1830s and 1840s, story papers occupied a particularly unique space in this market of popular culture. They were affordable; diverse in content; and, in many cases, claimed to publish "original matter," that is, material exclusively written for the pages of their papers and not reprinted from other sources.[13] Many story papers allotted their content in forty columns, resembling the format of newspaper tabloids and their layouts.[14] In the late 1830s, the story papers competed with the cheaply printed pamphlet novels that newsboys and newsstands sold at a dime or half-dime. Operating the same typesetting used for story paper columns, a great number of story-paper serials were reprinted in paper-covered booklets.[15]

Lori Merish argues that the emergence of story papers can only be understood through what Richard Brodhead calls the "social relations of literary forms," or by comprehending the social implications of new print technologies and a developing capitalist market that included printed materials.[16] Merish argues that "story papers are marked by material conditions of production and the network of social relations

---

[10] The industrialization of periodicals brought about changes to literary production, authorship, and the news. Michael Schudson calls the 1830s development of steam press technology and the consequent pouring out of periodicals the "revolution of the penny press." The editor's ability to express himself in his newspapers did not flourish until this epoch (Schudson 16). According to Mott, this penny press revolution changed "the attitude of the early penny papers toward news itself" (243). As a fundamental journalistic concept, the news is "the report of any new thing; but from the newspaperman's point of view, news is limited to those reports which he thinks his public wishes" (Mott 243). In other words, the news is information considered relevant by the paper's respectable public. Such relevant matters included, "the president's message to congress, and larger questions of trade and commerce" (Mott 243). However, as periodical production increased and readership became more stratified, or as Mott says "no longer 'respectable,'" the very concept of news changed. The newspaperman's definition of news and its reliance on readers' demands inevitably led to a reconceptualization and reprioritization of the news.

[11] Denning, *Mechanic Accents*, 10.

[12] Michael Schudson, *Discovering the News: A Social History of American Newspapers* (New York: Basic Books, 1978), 3.

[13] The story paper's focus on original material was unlike the cheap libraries, for instance, which, according to an 1895 *Publishers' Weekly* contributor, were made up of foreign reprints. In the 1830s and 1840s, the closest iteration of the story paper was the cheaply printed pamphlet novels that newsboys and newsstands sold at a dime or half-dime.

[14] This is the case for the *Ledger* and the *New York Mercury* (1839–96), a popular Sunday paper edited by William Cauldwell, Sylvester Southworth, and Horace P. Whitney.

[15] Anderson, *The Dime Novel*, 137.

[16] Merish, "The Emergence of Story Papers," 46.

in which they emerge."[17] The great story paper flood of the late 1830s and early 1840s began with the publications of Benjamin Henry Day's New York City–based *Brother Jonathan* in 1839 and Park Benjamin Sr. and Rufus Wilmot Griswold's *The New World*. Historian James Barnes claims that "both journals far exceeded the circulation of other American periodicals, with the exception of *Graham's Magazine* and a few of the leading daily newspapers."[18] Benjamin Day's *Brother Jonathan* was a mammoth-sized news and story paper measuring 22 × 32 inches, with a reported circulation of 60–70,000 readers[19] and priced at a dollar for a year's subscription.[20] Story papers like *Brother Jonathan* are mirrors to the ethos of their time of publication, reflecting the cultural and social conditions of their moment. In the 1840s and early 1850s, for instance, when manifest destiny was in full effect as the expansionist doctrine of the land, story papers boasted about their material bigness (particularly in the case of the mammoth sheets of *Brother Jonathan* and *Universal Yankee Nation*). Large in public scope and material size, mammoth papers reflect a new destiny of a great untouched reading public that western expansion made available. Like the history of western expansion, this manifest destiny of print began in eastern metropoles.

New York City was the center of the newspaper industry in the 1840s, but it was behind in the world of story papers.[21] Boston- and Philadelphia-based story papers sold widely in New York City, drowning the sales of even the most popular publishers, brothers Erastus and Irwin Beadle's dime novels. Frederick Gleason's Boston-based story paper, *The Flag of Our Union*, reported the largest circulation for the time, reaching 75,000 in 1852 and "blazoned itself as 'A Paper for the million'" by the 1860s.[22] With celebrity contributors like Sylvanus Cobb, Jr., Joseph Holt Ingraham; and Henry Ames Blood, the *Flag* generated a sizable readership from New York City. However, by the late 1850s, many of the popular Boston- and Philadelphia-based weeklies were facing real competition from New York City–based periodicals publishing original matter—like Bonner's *Ledger*—full of piquancy, suspense, and written by well-paid hacks.[23]

---

[17] Ibid.
[18] James J. Barnes, *Authors, Publishers, and Politicians: The Quest for an Anglo-American Copyright Agreement 1825–1854* (Columbus: Ohio State University Press, 1974), 11.
[19] Paul Erickson, "Readers and Writers," in *Industrial Revolution: People and Perspectives*, eds. Jennifer L. Goloboy and Peter C. Mancall (Santa Barbara: ABC CLIO, 2008), 95.
[20] "A Pioneer in the Journalism; The Busy Life of Benjamin Henry Day. Death of the Founder of The New-York "Sun" at His Home in this City Yesterday," *The New York Times*, December 22, 2010.
[21] Mott, *A History*, 377.
[22] Brodhead, *Cultures of Letters*, 78.
[23] Soon after the New York City–based story papers appeared on the scene, Boston printers commenced publishing the *Nation*, and the *Universal Yankee Nation*, and *The Flag of Our Union*. These papers were competitive and short-lived; and although many employed a nationalist rhetoric, they mainly depended on European reprints of novels (Denning 11). Due to the lack of copyright law, editors were free to lift stories from other publications and republish them in their own papers. Gleason's *Flag*, for instance, following the custom of many editors of the time, reprinted stories and poems from English magazines and newspapers.

Family as Reader

The story-paper reader, and the reading public more generally, were much more stratified than scholars initially surmised. Some historical records narrow the broadness of the story-paper reading public by focusing too assiduously on consumer culture. For example, in W. H. Bishop's 1879 *Atlantic Monthly* essay, "Story-Paper," Bishop describes the story-paper reading public as a mostly homogenous group of readers. Bishop's essay is a retrospective look at the significance and prevalence of New York City–based story papers and their ties to mid-century consumers. The essay takes *Atlantic* readers on a panoramic tour of the story-paper world of nineteenth-century New York City, elucidating where papers were sold and what made them so trendy. Story papers, Bishop argues, garnered a lower-class readership consisting of readers from around the city.[24] He claims that the most ardent patrons of the story paper were boys. Their interest in story papers was consolidated in the publication of a significant number of "boy's journals," "*Boys of New York, Boys of America, Boys of the World, Young Man of New York, Young Men of America.*"[25] The heroes celebrated in these papers were boys often depicted as "competent boy detectives, spies, trappers, buccaneers, guides, captains" or more literarily as the "Boy Robinson Crusoe, the Boy Claude Duval, and the Boy phoenix."[26] Although girls were similarly engaged in reading story papers, Bishop maintains that editors and publishers placed less reliance on their sponsorship. In other words, because girls had less pocket money, more house duties, and were under closer supervision, they had less resources (e.g., time and money) for reading story papers.[27]

Denning claims that the mid-century story-paper public was mainly composed of "craft workers, factory operatives, domestic servants, and domestic workers" absorbed in sensational fiction.[28] However, this working-class readership did not determine the entirety of every story-paper audience or definitively conclude that the story paper was "confined to a working-class public."[29] Denning rather argues that since the working class made up a significant portion of the reading public, their "concerns and accents" are inscribed in cheap periodicals.[30] Denning's important emphasis on the "accents" of the story paper's working-class reader challenges Bishop's male-centered reader stereotype and the larger mid-century romanticizations of the reading public. To this end, Denning posits that "any attention to the story papers shows the importance of girls and women's reading in a picture of cheap sensational fiction of the nineteenth century."[31] Focusing on women and girls and not only on men and boys begins to expand the social network of story-paper readers. But to have a clearer picture of these readers, we must also account for the impact of industrialization on reading practices and spaces.

---

[24] W. H. Bishop, "Story-Paper Literature," *The Atlantic Monthly*, September 1879, 389.
[25] Bishop, "Story-Paper Literature," 385.
[26] Ibid., 385.
[27] Ibid., 385.
[28] Denning, *Mechanic Accents*, 16.
[29] Ibid., 4.
[30] Ibid., 4.
[31] Ibid., 16.

Sensational Reading Practices

The fast-moving and industrializing nineteenth century created social conditions for new reading practices that often distinguished reading newspapers from reading story papers. As residential neighborhoods and factory districts developed and grew far apart from one another, readers travelled longer distances, spending more time commuting to and from work. Reading was a favorite pastime for commuters. Railroads and train stations were crowded with readers of periodicals. For many commuters traveling to and from work, these spaces provided a unique, and perhaps their only, opportunity for leisure and entertaining light reading. One editor, describing the busy lives of fathers, claims, "Every streetcar you enter is filled with fathers of little ones. Each of these fathers, to save an hour's time, is reading the morning's newspaper."[32]

Newspaper articles about reading suggest epistemic shifts that shaped how readers evaluated knowledge and information. Some newspapers championed the specific knowledge and information gained from reading newspapers while at the same disparaged the sensationalism of story-paper fiction. These papers often likened the social value of newspaper reading to that of academic books. For example, the *New York Herald* prints in 1849, "All these, without knowledge of the world; without daily interchange of mind, thought, and sentiment with his fellows, will not make him an intelligent man. This he can acquire by no means but by reading the newspapers of the day."[33]

Although newspapers and story papers are, formally speaking, nearly identical, nineteenth-century readers did not see the consumption of newspapers and story papers as equivalent reading practices. Story-paper reading was often portrayed as deleterious to the intellectual growth of readers, provoking some readers to seek ill-advised adventures and a life of crime influenced by the sensational stories they read. One reader of *The Sun* blamed her misfortunes on story papers: "'Troubles come and go,' Mrs. Graven said last night, 'Last week I buried one child, and now two have run away. My husband is going to Holland tomorrow, and I don't know what to do. All this trouble comes from reading the story papers and books.'"[34] Many newspaper reports implied that story-paper reading had a social correlation with criminality, danger, and could even lead to death. *The Willington Enterprise* reports in 1882, "Don't begin reading story papers or lives of notorious criminals unless you wish to train yourself for a nobody or for an outlaw."[35] Less than a year later, *The Sun* states, "While boys in the East are longing to become bandits and Indian slayers on the Western plains, two ten-year old Nebraska urchins, after reading some story paper descriptions of New York life, bought two pistols with stolen money, and set out for this city to become Broadway ruffians."[36] Another news item titled "What Sensational Literature Can Do" details an attempted suicide by a fourteen-year-old boy from "Corwin, Ohio who had

---

[32] *The Chicago Current*, May 18, 1885.
[33] *New York Herald*, September 16, 1849.
[34] *The Sun*, June 11, 1887.
[35] *Wellington Enterprise*, November 1, 1882.
[36] *The Olean Democrat*, April 10, 1883.

been plentifully supplied with such literature as *Boys of New York*."[37] After describing in detail how the boy pointed an old musket to his chest, the article concludes by emphasizing that "He has spent the greater portion of his time reading sensational story papers."[38] Another paper reported that a woman named Miss Mollie Burdett burned to death after reading a story paper in bed:

> It appears that Miss Mollie Burdett, who was burned to death at Haysville… was in the habit of reading story papers after retiring to bed. On the night in question she retired earlier than usual for the purpose of finishing a serial romance in which she had become interested. There being no gas in the room, she placed an oil lamp on a stand near the head of the bed. It is supposed she read until she fell asleep, leaving the lamp burning, subsequently upsetting it and setting fire to the bed-clothes.[39]

As much as newspapers attempted to distinguish themselves from story-paper fiction, ironically, the genre of newspaper reportage and story-paper serials would evolve into a similar genre in the late nineteenth century. The above plot-driven reports seem to come out of the very sensational story-paper serials the articles caution readers from reading. These reports project, in a sense, the sensationalism of story-paper fiction onto real lives and newsworthy events. In her study of the development of "New Journalism," Karen Roggenkamp argues that "Facing growing rivalries with one another and within a burgeoning print marketplace more generally, urban newspaper felt pressure to create prose that entertained, and the urge to spin attractive and popular tales sometime came at the expense of factual information."[40] For many editors, entertainment was more important than delivering the facts simply because entertainment sold papers, and the mass circulation of story papers like *Ledger* was proven. The reading marketplace craved, albeit secretly, the adventure, travel, and intrigue commonly featured in story-paper serials. Many newspapers had to somehow keep up with these proscribed demands.

City Reading and City Spaces

Story papers moved geographically across the city, from neighborhood to neighborhood, and from the hands of distributors to the hands of readers. Readers picked up story papers from virtually any part of the city. Take Bishop's description of shops where story papers were sold: "shall we choose this dingy one at the Five Points, where the grocery and wood and coal business is combined with the other; or this pretentious store under a lofty new tenement house in the German quarter,

---

[37] *The Eaton Democrat*, February 9, 1882.
[38] *The Advocate*, February 10, 1882.
[39] *Buffalo Weekly Courier*, March 12, 1879. This article was reprinted in over 50 newspapers in 1879.
[40] Karen Roggenkamp, *Narrating the News: New Journalism and Literary Genre in Late Nineteenth-Century American Newspapers and Fiction* (Kent: The Kent State University Press, 2005), xii.

with the joints already warping apart, the paint blistered, and a plate-glass window cracked by uneven settling?"[41] The image of the "dingy" and disorderly Five Points and the "pretentious store" in the decrepit German neighborhood represent a lower-class demographic of readers and the newsstands where these readers purchased their papers. Bishop's voyeuristic sketch continues and moves uptown where readers of story papers are presented with more options for purchasing the latest sensational fictions. He describes "one of the stuffy little, but more prosperous [shops] of the up-town avenues [where] the interior is festooned with school satchels and jumping-ropes... The Egyptian, the Hindoo, and the Golden Wheel of Fortune dream books... in gaudy covers, ornament the window, among the tops and marbles."[42] Bishop's portrayal of the amount of stuff sold in this "stuffy little" uptown shop exemplifies the world of goods which in part made up nineteenth-century material culture and aided the growth of literacy during the period.

The story-paper world of shops and newsstands in Bishop's tour is only part of what David M. Henkin calls the "remarkable network of public words" where readers encountered language.[43] For Henkin, most reading of penny papers was done in public, in park squares, and in sidewalks facing shops and other businesses. Access to public reading increasingly drew into question the partition between private and public spaces. New York City was a place of shop signs and trade bills, which meant that commerce and consumption were a part of the "very process of public communication."[44] By way of selling print, these businesses commodified stories, poems, and advertisements. Literate residents, as targeted consumers, could read the sign for "newsstand" and "bookshop" and find their favorite periodicals, serials, stories, and poems without saying a word to the shopkeeper. The in-store sale of entertainment merchandise in the Five Points, in the German quarter, or uptown makes up a fraction of the sale of story papers. Early and mid-century story papers were largely sold by subscription and distributed by the American News Company.[45]

The Early Years of *The New York Ledger*

The mechanical and economical infrastructure for long-term story papers appeared in the 1850s with the founding of Robert Edwin Bonner's *New York Ledger* (1855–1898).[46] The *Ledger* introduced a format that would be mimicked by competitors for the next forty years.[47] When on the night of May 2, 1839, two Northern-Irish immigrants sailed on a vessel to America leaving behind their family, the world of

---

[41] Bishop, "Story-Paper Literature," 384.
[42] Ibid.
[43] David M. Henkin, *City Reading: Written Words and Public Spaces in Antebellum New York* (New York: Columbia University Press, 1998), 2.
[44] Henkin, *City Reading*, 11.
[45] Anderson, *The Dime*, 124; Henkin, *City Reading*, 15.
[46] Ibid., 11.
[47] Bishop, "Story Paper," 384.

story papers was destined to change. Robert and his older brother, William, arrived in New York twenty-one days after their departure from Londonderry. Upon arrival, William worked on his uncle's farm in Hartford, Connecticut, while Robert found employment in the office of the *Hartford Courant* as an apprentice at $25 a year, with room, board, and washing.[48] Bonner worked diligently and learned the print trade. After a five-year apprenticeship, he was promoted to a fully trained printer. Bonner's awareness of the literary marketplace may have developed during his early years as a printer for the *Hartford Courant*.

Robert left Hartford soon after and reunited with his family in New York City, recently arrived from Ireland. In New York City, Robert found employment in the office of George Pope Morris and Nathaniel Parker Willis' *The Evening Mirror* as a proofreader and advertisement setter. From New York City, he worked as a correspondent for the *Hartford Courant* and for newspapers in Boston, Albany, and Washington DC. Soon after, he opened a small printing shop where he printed newspapers including D. Anson Pratt's *The Merchant's Ledger and Statistical Record*, which at that time had a circulation of about 3,000. According to Frank Luther Mott, the paper was not successful and "after four years of effort, [Pratt] was about to discontinue it at the end of 1850, when Bonner, loath to lose the print of it, offered to take it off his hands for $900—the amount of his savings."[49]

In 1851, the *Ledger* was the antithesis of the popular story paper it would become. In these early years, advertisements consumed the *Merchant's Ledger*. To multiply the failing *Merchant Ledger*'s audience, made up of the dry-goods business owners who advertised in the paper, Bonner expanded the paper's literary contributions. Thus, while continuing to print mercantile advertisement, the shrewd businessman promised literary offerings in the *Ledger*'s future issues.

Changes to the *Merchant's Ledger* were gradual. The goal was to successfully transition from a failing paper with a specialized audience to a literary paper appealing to a general audience. In 1855, Bonner changed the name of his paper, entering in the Library of Congress the new title "The New York Ledger: Devoted to Choice Literature, Romance, the News, and Commerce." Visibly influenced by the popular New York City newspapers of the day, Bonner's story paper was meant to be taken as seriously as *The New York Tribune*, *The New York Herald*, *The New York Sun*, and *The New-York Daily Times*. These newspapers commanded local and national scopes.[50] Bonner's vision for his story paper was to garner a similarly broad readership across the nation. It was the drive to promote his paper in this new light that led Bonner to unprecedented

---

[48] Mary Noel, *Villains Galore: The Heyday of the Popular Story Weekly* (New York: Macmillan, 1954), 60.
[49] Frank Luther Mott, *American Journalism: A History of Newspapers in the United States Through 250 Years 1690 to 1940* (New York: The Macmillan Company, 1941), 356.
[50] Lunde, Erik S., "The Ambiguity of the National Idea: the Presidential Campaign of 1872," *Canadian Review of Studies in Nationalism* 5, no. 1 (1978), 1–23. As an editor, part of Greeley's goal was to reach a national and not merely local audience, which he achieved with the publication of the *Weekly Tribune* in December 1841. According to his biographer, Erik S. Lundes, Greeley introduced to the newspaper world the innovation of having correspondents in Washington. After Greeley, other newspapers followed suit and began sending their own correspondents to the nation's capital.

advertisement strategies. He promoted the *Ledger* in the pages of widely circulating periodicals like the Horace Greeley's *Weekly Tribune*. In 1856, Bonner put out the following boastful little ad:

> Time was when people thought that the Saturday Courier, True Flag, Flag of Our Union, Waverly, &C., were the best family papers in the Union; that time has passed away with 1855 and is buried in oblivion. Now at the birth of 1856, it is known by ALL THE PEOPLE that no paper is equal to the New York Ledger.[51]

Bonner's ad posits that with the publication of the *Ledger* dawns a new age for American family papers. From 1855 through 1856, the *Ledger* doubled in size; the price raised from one dollar "per annum in advance" to two dollars in 1856. According to Bonner, "An elegant family weekly, like the *Ledger*, (containing no advertisements) cannot be afforded at less than these terms."[52] The *Ledger* claimed to have "No traveling Agents" and was sold in "periodical and newspaper stores throughout the United States and Canada."[53]

In the first years after entering the name *The New York Ledger* in the Library of Congress, Bonner began making decisions that would establish his paper as a leading journal of sensational and genteel literatures. He published a number of works deemed "original matter," a feat for any paper during a time when publishing original material was not yet normalized in periodicals. In 1853, for example, he commissioned Lydia H. Sigourney, at the time one of the most widely published poets in the United States, to contribute poems to the *Ledger*. Sigourney wrote for the *Ledger* until her death in 1865. In 1855, Bonner contracted Fanny Fern, then in the height of her fame. He paid her $100 per column, the most paid to any woman columnist at the time. Fern wrote exclusively for the paper during the remainder of her life. Bonner sought and published the biggest names in literature on both sides of the Atlantic. He paid Edward Everett $10,000 for a series of short articles called the "Mt. Vernon Papers", Henry Ward Beecher was paid $25,000 for his *Norwood*, and Horace Greeley obtained a similar sum for his *Recollections of a Busy Life*. Charles Dickens, William Cullen Bryant, George Bancroft, Sarah Piatt, Fitz-Green Halleck, James Gordon Bennet, Henry J. Raymond, Harriet Beecher Stowe, Julia Ward Howe, and many other celebrity writers and editors were published in Bonner's *Ledger*. Bonner broadly advertised the publications of his luminaries as ideal for the "family," a label that would effectively target all members of society. These editorial and marketing decisions successfully transitioned the *Ledger* from a specialized merchants' journal for traders and wholesalers to a literary story paper for the family and the unknown public. Bonner would eventually become one of the wealthiest newspaper editors in the United States, earning the respect of presidents, railroad magnates, and educators.

---

[51] *The Tribune*, January 1, 1856.
[52] *The New York Ledger*, December 27, 1856.
[53] Ibid.

Story Paper as Family Paper

For Bonner, and many other story-paper publishers, the story paper was synonymous with the "family paper," a moniker that emphasized the reader and "family," rather than the paper's content, "story." Some story papers emphasized this in their papers' mastheads featuring titles associated with the family, such as Norman L. Munro's *The New York Family Story Paper*. Bonner advertised his story paper as an "instructive family paper," "good family paper," "the best family paper," and as the "leading high-class illustrated family weekly paper in America."[54] Although the *Ledger* published celebrity writers, the paper was not on par with the serious magazines of the time like *Godey's*, *Harper's*, *Graham's*, and the *Atlantic*. The *Ledger* was, after all, labeled a sensational story paper, a branding that often came with cultural stigmas. In her study of the dime novel, Vicki Anderson argues, "No one wanted to be associated with 'low classness', and sensationalism was low class. The authors of these story paper serials had to add something representing 'class' to their crime stories."[55] Bonner published serials by Sylvanus Cobb Jr. and E. D. E. N. Southworth that catered to readers of tabloids and sensationalism. At the same time, Bonner also published notable writers like Edward Everett who appealed to a genteel readership. In doing so, the *Ledger* straddled the cultural landscape of genteel and sensational culture. In Denning's words, "[the *Ledger*] was the most respectable story paper, [and] the least respectable magazine."[56]

Between 1858 and 1859, Everett signed a contract to write fifty-two weekly columns for the *Ledger* in exchange for a $10,000 donation made to the Mount Vernon Ladies Association for the preservation of George Washington's estate. In Everett's final contribution in 1859, he writes:

> [The *Ledger*] has simply aimed to be an entertaining and instructive Family newspaper, designed, in the first instance, to meet the wants of what is called in a very sensible and striking paper in Dickens' Household Words,... the "Unknown Public." The New York "Ledger" is the first attempt in this country, on a large scale, to address *that* public; and the brilliant success, which has attended it thus far, is a strong confirmation of the truth... that the time is coming when "the readers, who rank by the million, will be the readers, and who will therefore command the services of the best writers of the time.[57]

The reader's ability to determine taste shaped Bonner's growing awareness of a popular-culture audience. The *Ledger* catered to this "Unknown Public," "who rank by the million," and it was the unknown public's taste that commanded who and what the *Ledger* published.

---

[54] *N.W. Ayer & Son American Newspaper Annual* (Philadelphia: N. W. Ayer & Son, 1892), 1403.
[55] Anderson, *The Dime*, 137.
[56] Denning, *Mechanic Accents*, 218.
[57] Edward Everett, *The Mount Vernon Papers* (New York: D. Appleton and Company, 1860), 488.

The *Ledger*'s unknown public was an interstitial audience made up of readers occupying an unidentified gray area between popular culture and genteel culture, which was best described as the family. Garnering a cross-cultural readership as the *Ledger* did meant reaching readers across socioeconomic backgrounds of nineteenth-century society. It meant reaching a popular, genteel, as well as an "Unknown Public" through effective advertisement schemes that focused on the paper's multifaceted offerings.

Changes in the economy concerning major trends like industrialization, urbanization, immigration, the diversification of the market economy, the settlement of the West, and increased social stratification brought about changes to the traditional family structure and the domestic space of the home. Historians claim that the blend of "traditional folkways with the reform vision of many Americans caused social influence, political authority, and the traditional concepts of family to become uncertain, unstable, and somewhat ambiguous."[58] For Bonner, the emphasis on the family as reader was crucial for reaching this unknown audience because the traditional American concept of the family did not depend on one's socioeconomic background. Anyone could, essentially, be part of a family, or at least most readers valued the idea of the family in the nineteenth century. In this sense, the family was a type of euphemism for the "Unknown Public" and an open invitation that flattened political, racial, ethnic, gendered distinctions among readers.

Bonner demonstrated a profound understanding of his family audience. He describes them as complex and at times contradictory. Bonner explains that "Human nature is active, analytic, investigating, and it must have something vital to feed upon."[59] Here, Bonner implies that a good story paper can, in effect, satiate the vitality of human nature. Readers' cravings for story papers manifested from being stuck in between the same worlds that the *Ledger* occupied, the genteel and the sensational. Thus, when Bonner defended the content of his paper, he was also defending the desires of his readers or rather the cravings of human nature.

On the one hand, Bonner's insistence on calling the *Ledger* a family paper was one way to assure his readers that he would not print anything inappropriate for children, who, according to Bishop and Denning, made up a significant part of his readership in the early years of the paper. On the other hand, his label of family paper extended to the outer reaches of an Unknown Public, which included members across political party lines and racial groups. For example, Bonner emphasized his family audience in ads that frequently appeared in abolitionist newspapers, appearing next to article titles like "The 'Rise of Negroes at the South' in *The Anti-Slavery Bugle* (Lisbon, Ohio) and 'What the Democracy of the North Has Done for Slavery' in *The National Era* (District of Columbia)." At the same time, *Ledger* ads appeared in Whig party

---

[58] James M. Volo and Dorothy Dennen Volo, *Family Life in Nineteenth Century America* (Westport: Greenwood Press, 2007), 5.
[59] *The New York Ledger*, January 12, 1856.

papers like *The Daily Whige* (Vicksburg, Mississippi), Democratic weeklies like the *Monmouth Democrat* (Freehold, New Jersey), and Republican papers like *The Missouri Republican* (St. Louis, Missouri).[60] In a sense, there were few papers where Bonner did not advertise.

"The Maecenas of Poets and Romancers": Editorial Practice in the *New York Ledger* Tradition

Story-paper scholars rarely fail to mention Bonner's business-savvy ability to break away from traditional approaches to publishing and marketing.[61] As Bonner deviated from traditions of the publishing world, he introduced innovative and successful methods for publishing: paying contributors large sums of money, publishing mostly women, and introducing new ways of advertising original material. Although critics address the many ways in which Bonner broke away from traditional publishing, fewer address the aspects of the *Ledger* and Bonner's editorial style that are quintessentially traditional. Bonner's paper might have diverged from long-standing values of publishing, but he did not completely do away with printing works that promoted traditional systems of values important to the nineteenth-century family.

As the "story-paper hero" of the nineteenth century, Bonner developed unique ways to reach members of the family as the Unknown Public. On December 6, 1856, Bonner put out an advertisement on page eight of Horace Greeley's *New-York Tribune*. The six-column advertisement covers the entire page of the *Tribune* and makes up a series of iterative copies, repeating four paragraphs about the *Ledger*'s readership, content, and "secret of the *Ledger*" (Figure 1.1).

In iterative copies that repeat throughout the entire first column, Bonner introduces another editor's remark about the *Ledger*:

> The New-York Ledger has been very generally and highly complimented by the country press. We are especially pleased with a remark that one editor makes. He says: "The LEDGER is a particular favorite of our family; and we take particular pleasure in carrying it home, knowing that its influence will be good—and only

---

[60] See, *The National Era*, May 21, 1857; Anti-Slavery Bugle, January 3, 1857.
[61] Mary Noel claims that "The New York Herald, little given to praise in its 'spicy' column, referred to Bonner as the 'Maecenas of poets and romancers—the autocrat, in most respects, of American periodical literature, and certainly its most successful publisher'" (56). See Joyce Warren's *Fanny Fern: an Independent Woman* (1992); Michael Denning *Mechanical Accents: Dime Novels and Working Class Culture in America* (1987); Kathryn Conner Bennett's *The Economics of Loyalty: Robert Bonner, the "New York Ledger," and Sentimental Capitalism*; Ray B. Browne and Lawrence A. Kreiser, Jr's *The Civil War and Reconstruction* (2003); David Dowling's *The Business of Literary Circle in Nineteenth-Century America* (2011); Kenneth Salzer's "Call Her Ishmael: E. D. E. N. Southworth, Robert Bonner, and the 'Experiment' of Self-Made," *Popular Nineteenth-Century American Women Writers and the Literary Marketplace* (2007).

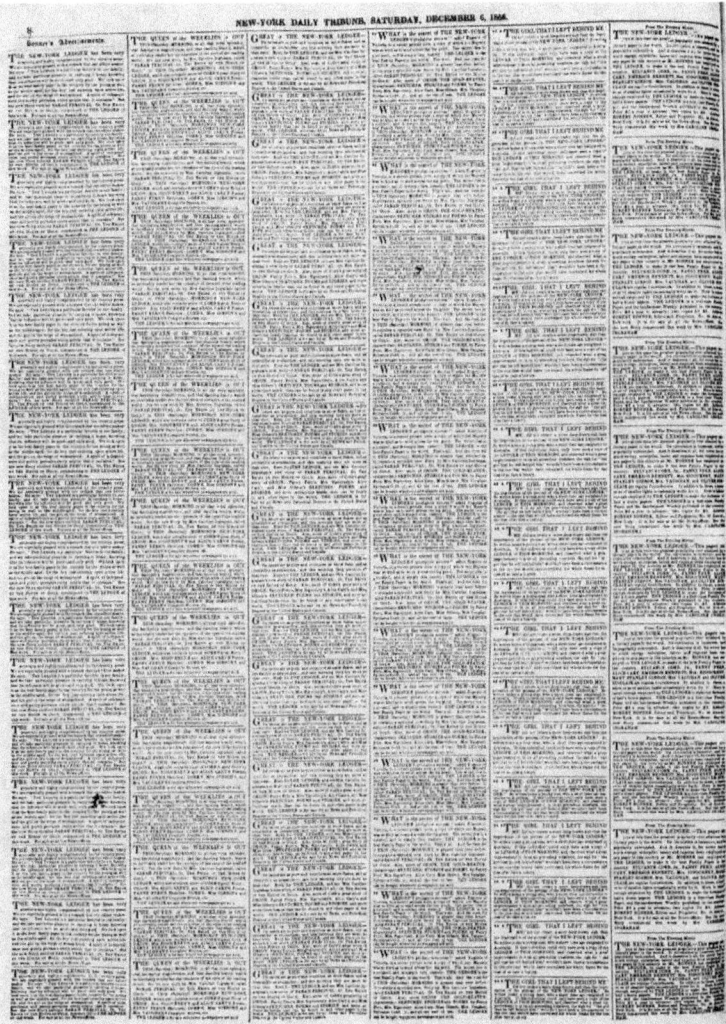

Figure 1.1 *New York Daily Tribune* (December 6, 1856).

good. We look upon it as the best family paper in the country for the young as well and the middle-aged; for the boys just entering upon active life, and the girl on the verge of womanhood. A spirit of independence and purity pervades every article that it contains." See the new Story entitled Sarah Percival; or, The Bride of the House of Gold, commence in The Ledger of this week, for sale at all News-office.[62]

---

[62] *The New York Tribune*, December 6, 1856.

Bonner's family-friendly ad reached the *Tribune*'s record-breaking figure of 200,000 readers.[63] In the confessional voice of "one editor" (possibly referring to Greeley), the reader learns about the *Ledger*'s "spirit of independence and purity," which determines the paper's "good—and only good" influence on the entire family. After the editor's remark, Bonner's voice follows and promotes the publication of a new story. The ad insinuates that the "spirit of independence and purity" is contained in "Sarah Percival," an intricately plotted story of love affairs, death, and the steady social decline of the Percival family. The somewhat disconnected parts of this ad (the editor's remark and the promotion of a story) make for a course transition. But the purpose of the ad is not to make smooth logical transitions between its parts. The ad's blatant promotion of "Sarah Percival" shows that Bonner was more interested in aligning his stories with the idea family-appropriate content and a pervading "spirit of independence and purity."

Bonner's advertisement strategy prompted rebukes from newspaper editors who claimed that the *Ledger*'s ads were ruining the newspaper industry. In perhaps one of the most ironic ads taken out by Bonner, he appropriately, commodifies public disapprovals of his marketing strategy and turns them into ads. For example, in Figure 1.2, Bonner takes out three full columns in the *New York Times*. Like most of the *Ledger*'s ads, these are iteration copies promoting the paper's latest serials. Two of the columns are simply conventional ads of the *Ledger*'s stories. The one in the middle, however, is a meta-ad that self-reflexively converts critiques about Bonner's advertisement technique into a marketing ploy. This ad states:

> "BONNER HAS RUINED THE NEWSPAPER BUSINESS," said a disconsolate publisher the other day. "He puts in such enormous advertisements of that everlasting LEDGER, that it is no use for any other publisher to advertise in a small way any more." There may be a good deal of truth in that remark. See the LEDGER for THIS (Friday) MORNING, WHICH CONTAINS THE GREAT NEW STORY OF "SARAH PERCIVAL.; on; THE BRIDE OF THE HOUSE OF GOLD."[64]

For Bonner, bad publicity is good business. He does not defend his paper for "ruin[ing] the newspaper business." Bonner simply confirms the validity of that statement, interpreting the accusation leveled against him as a type of achievement instead of a crime. If there was ever a competition between newspapers and story papers, the above ad suggests that Bonner's *Ledger*, regardless of its generic form, comes out victorious.

The rapid development of the penny press, the newspaper, and the literary monthly magazine provided the conditions for the emergence of story papers. These periodical developments share a rhizomatic network of print technologies and audiences which made possible unprecedented production of print in the early to mid-nineteenth century and beyond. Story-paper readers were diverse in terms of class, age, gender,

---

[63] Mott, *American*, 269.
[64] *The New York Times*, December 6, 1856.

Figure 1.2 *New York Daily Times* (December 6, 1856).

and race. They encompassed a broad Unknown Public of the family. Bonner's *Ledger* was a leader in the story-paper world, maneuvering between high and low cultures, genteel and sensationalist tastes, and reaching readers of diverse backgrounds. Like many story papers, the *Ledger* provided an escape from the monotony of nineteenth-century life, shaping itself for the public and in turn reshaping the periodical's form and meaning in the popular press.

2

"And They Think A Strike Is War": John Reed, *Metropolitan Magazine*, and Print-Socialism Beyond Borders

Jesse W. Schwartz

John Reed was a radical writer in possession of as much contradiction as he lacked in compromise. Born into one of Portland's most prominent families, literal Harvard cheerleader, would-be-poet-cum-journalist, champion of restive labor and the poor from Mexico to New Jersey to Serbia, and one of the most famous chroniclers of the Russian Revolution, Reed's mercurial positions and positioning might begin to explain why his works have at various times been suppressed, seized by authorities, and often just banned outright by antagonists as politically distant as Woodrow Wilson's United States and the Stalinist Soviet Union. Even the phrase "radical writer" enjoins challenges when examining this slippery historical subject's life and work. For someone who wrote so extensively about the most momentous events of his time, Reed's works are largely ignored *as writing*, even though he considered himself a writer above all and made a living this way for pretty much his entire—if admittedly brief—adult life. Often dismissed (when he's discussed at all) as a man who "never matured into a poet or thinker of power" despite legions of admirers then *and* now, Reed apparently committed several unpardonable literary offenses. First, he was promiscuous in mode, style, and genre—and repeatedly indulged the sin of publishing journalism rather than fiction.[1] So even though he was one of the most popular reporters of his day; wrote a number of plays, short stories, and poetry; and co-founded the Provincetown Players (which helped jumpstart the careers of Eugene O'Neill, Djuna Barnes, and Susan Glaspell, among others), Walter Rideout offers perhaps the best example of this disjunction between Reed's life and work with the arch appraisal that "As far as his influence on the literature of the Left goes, Reed's death was his greatest achievement."[2]

Not only Reed the "writer" comes under scrutiny, though. The "radical" bit often gets demeaned as well—even though he was a respected friend of such far-left American

---

[1] Daniel Aaron, *Writers on the Left: Episodes in Literary Communism* (New York: Columbia University Press, 1992), 38.
[2] Walter Rideout, *The Radical Novel in the United States: Some Interrelations of Literature and Society* (New York: Columbia University Press, 1992), 127.

royalty as "Big" Bill Haywood, Elizabeth Gurley Flynn, Eugene Debs, Mike Gold, and Max Eastman; married to pioneering feminist writer Louise Bryant; admired by Trotsky and many other Bolshevik elites; and had his most famous book, *Ten Days That Shook the World,* blurbed by Lenin himself. Yet, even though he wrote the most renowned on-the-ground English-language chronicle of Red October; famously rented out Madison Square Garden to put on a pageant in support of the striking Patterson silk workers, which featured a cast of hundreds of laborers reenacting their strife before an audience of 15,000; was co-founder of the Communist Labor Party of America; essentially lost his job over his refusal to support the war effort; and is one of only three Americans buried in the Kremlin Wall Necropolis, Reed's radical bonafides are often represented as dilettantish and undertheorized at best, and incoherent and disingenuous at worst.[3] His friend and Harvard classmate Walter Lippmann summarized these biographical challenges: Reed "is many men at once, and those who have tried to bank on some phase of him, to regard him as a writer, a correspondent, a poet, a revolutionist, or a lover, lose him."[4] While I intend to focus not at all on the "lover" he may have been (though most accounts from friends and former paramours report a passionate and engaged partner), I am very much interested in Reed the writer, the correspondent, the poet, and the revolutionist, and particularly the ways in which these deeply imbricated characteristics of his artistic and political life informed, contradicted, and mutually constituted each other—while perhaps also contributing to his perpetually liminal reputation.

The challenges outlined above are evinced both by a general lack of critical work on Reed and within extant scholarship. Daniel W. Lehman, his most extensive contemporary interlocutor (and the only writer, as far as I can find, of a book-length literary-critical analysis of Reed's work) attributes this overall neglect to two main factors: (1) "holdover genre politics within the literary criticism establishment. Even after several decades of canon reformulation, the chief manner by which a nonfiction writer is read seriously today is if he or she had published some measure of acclaimed fiction." And (2) "his personal and political notoriety."[5] While this accords with both terms of the "radical writer" formulation above, and though this essay is deeply indebted to Lehman's book, I am indifferent (contra his own study) in proving Reed's "artistry," arguing for "canonicity," or defending his journalism's sometime loose relationship with "truth." Attempting to locate one "real" Reed, as Lippmann warned, is as impossible as adjudicating the veracity of various scenes or exchanges in his longform journalistic narratives. His archival notes most often capture broadly sketched scenes and snippets of dialogue, a "journalistic code of half sentences, a word, a name."[6] So there's simply

---

[3] For more on Reed's involvement in the pageant, see Robert A. Rosenstone, *Romantic Revolutionary: A Biography of John Reed* (Cambridge, MA: Harvard University Press, 1975), 124–5. The other two Americans buried in the Kremlin are Charles Ruthenberg and William "Big Bill" Haywood.
[4] Walter Lippmann, *Public Persons* (London: Routledge, 2017), 43.
[5] Daniel W. Lehman, *John Reed & the Writing of Revolution* (Athens, OH: Ohio University Press, 2002), 24.
[6] Tamara Hovey, *John Reed: Witness to Revolution* (New York: Crown Publishers, 1975), 174.

no way to prove whether a Mexican doctor really told Reed that General Urbina tried "to shoot his mother" due to drinking too much "*aguardiente*" or that a British lieutenant in Serbia angrily threw his sword into the corner after nearly tripping over it in front of his troops.[7] As for the effects of Reed's critical neglect, when he is read at all it is mostly through three book-length works that correspond to the locations of his best and best-known reporting: *Insurgent Mexico* (traveling around with Pancho Villa during the Mexican Revolution), *The War in Eastern Europe* (where he unsuccessfully chased the First World War around the titular region), and, of course, the book that survived well beyond his own brief thirty-two years, *Ten Days That Shook the World* (Reed's firsthand account of the Bolshevik ascent to power).

Where his work is largely *not* read, however, is where it was nearly all published in the first place: various newspapers and magazines as well-known as the *New York Times* and as "little" as the *Liberator*. Therefore, and contrary to Lehman's injunction to make a case for canonicity so Reed might be "anthologized in composition readers" like other journalists-cum-fiction writers such as Ernest Hemingway, George Orwell, and Stephen Crane, I would make the inverse plea: A century after his death, to read Reed exactly where he was, still is, and probably should mostly remain—in the archives of the magazines he helped fashion, and the ones that helped fashion him in return.[8] By examining these objects *in situ*, as a whole, and within the constellation of other texts that surrounded Reed's work in said magazines, we can far more easily discern Reed as both a radical *and* canny writer traversing the pressures and promotions of the business of journalism itself. From West Coast scion to Greenwich Village radical playboy to sober Bolshevik champion dying from typhus in a Moscow hospital, viewing Reed's works in their original publications iteratively and over time offers a schematic of one writer's attempt to navigate the politics of his increasingly war-mad editorial board (and homeland) while also trying to remain both engaged with his convictions and engaging for readers. And examining Reed's installments for *Metropolitan Magazine* in particular offers us greater purchase on his novel political uses of the serial format itself. In his travels from Portland mansion to Kremlin Necropolis, Reed would, in Gramsci's phrasing, renovate and make critical the already existing activity of seriality to link such seemingly disparate locales and events as the Mexican Revolution, US labor wars, and the battlefields of the First World War into archipelagic examples of the same global struggle against imperial capital. In the spirit, then, of Reed's promiscuous and undoctrinaire Marxism, this chapter seeks to engage the phrase "literary journalism" dialectically, as a linkage of generative tensions inherent in the phrase itself and on several aspects of its production, distribution, and consumption. Reed for his own part seemed pretty unconcerned by this coupling, deploying some of the very techniques of imaginative literature (character construction, repetition, symbol, scene) in his journalism to aid in his politics and also avoid the collaborationist incrementalism of

---

[7] John Reed, "With La Tropa," *Metropolitan* (April 1914), 12; and "Serbia between Battles," *Metropolitan* (August 1915), 4. For more on Reed's note-taking style such as can be discerned from the archives, see Lehman, *John Reed*, 35, 53–6.

[8] Lehman, *John Reed*, 24.

what was increasingly his socialist-lite main magazine. Under the rubric of the word "war" Reed will skillfully repurpose repeated words, phrases, images, and analyses from one struggle to the next to make these linked locations resonate for readers, especially when the connections might at first seem incongruous. So even something as titanic as the First World War, thanks to Reed's careful construction and reworking of the serial form, becomes just another series of battles between belligerents in a worldwide anti-imperialist class struggle. From the aimless filthy crowds of a New Jersey jail to the needless deaths of soldiers and civilians alike during the Mexican Revolution to the industrialized charnel house of the First World War, for Reed the modern world is one of endless natural and human beauty shoved aside by the comprehensively unnecessary but necessarily manmade horrors subtended by imperial capital.

The study of seriality often resembles the old parable about the elephant in a dark room, wherein numerous scholars seem content to describe the phenomenon based on partial aspects important for their own disciplines, fields, and research. Serial form has also become so pervasive in both concept and manifestation when it comes to consuming contemporary culture that its very ubiquity can often stand in for a definition of what it is and does. Therefore, in the words of Sabine Sielke, much work remains "to develop a theoretical and methodological framework out of a proliferating practice and aesthetics of serial forms—serial in the sense of a string, chain, or succession that works recursively, not linearly."[9] And when it comes to the field of periodical studies, there are perhaps few areas of higher importance. As Matthew Levay argues, "we might consider seriality the defining feature of all periodicals; signaling in its name a temporal pattern of production and consumption, the periodical is a material object born from the logic of seriality."[10] But if seriality birthed the periodical, its offspring are a messily complex cacophony of conflicting discourses belying the supposedly neat "logic" that spawned them. Indeed, as Sean Latham reminds us, periodicals might be more productively read as "a collage: a vibrant, often chaotic collection of fragmented pieces that generate meanings far in excess of authorial control or editorial design."[11] One feature that links these chaotic and fragmented collages across both time and space, however, is precisely that of seriality, and therefore the study of periodicals is not only inseparable from the regularized temporality of their iterative form but—because they are *the* material manifestation of seriality, existentially linked with the (usually) standardized instantiations of their appearance—periodicals might also offer us some purchase on seriality itself.

The most famous argument around the political and cultural work of seriality—at least when it comes to the periodical construction of what Benedict Anderson calls

---

[9] Sabine Sielke, "Network and Seriality: Conceptualizing (Their) Connection," *Amerikastudien/American Studies* 60, no. 1 (2015), 83.

[10] Matthew Levay, "On the Uses of Seriality for Modern Periodical Studies: An Introduction," *Journal of Modern Periodical Studies* 9, no. 1 (2018), vi.

[11] Sean Latham, "Serial Modernism," in *A History of the Modernist Novel*, ed. Gregory Castle (New York: Cambridge University Press, 2015), 255.

"the origins of national consciousness"—is his gloss on the generative effect "print-capitalism" has on fashioning (and regularly re-fashioning) the imagined communities of and within a state.[12] Contrasting the "bound seriality" of government instruments such as the census, map, and museum, Anderson explains how the "unbound seriality" of print periodicals are central building blocks to the modern nation-state, offering nothing less fundamental than allowing "rapidly growing numbers of people to think about themselves, and to relate themselves to others, in profoundly new ways" as well as "a new fixity to language" with which to do so, thereby providing the bedrock for "national consciousness."[13] The mutually generative relationship between the development of print-capitalism and the nation allows us to see "from within this logic of the series that a new grammar of representation came into being, which was also a precondition for imagining the nation."[14] Or, as Peter Hitchcock pithily reminds us, "serialization is indeed time's writing system for nation."[15]

However, in the wake of this discursive reproduction and iterative distribution of the nation-state by way of print-capitalism, Reed seemed to understand that this formation might also dialectically contain the seeds of its own contradictions, and that the serial distribution of his works might just as well suture a socialist consciousness *against* national borders—as well as against the world wars that nationalist thinking inevitably gave rise to. If, as Elizabeth Sheehan succinctly notes (following Anderson), seriality is, among other things, "a technique of repetition that helps to produce and reproduce subjects and groups"[16] and, in a self-described "grand statement," Frank Kelleter boils seriality down to its essentials by declaring "what we call culture is fundamentally dependent on the repetition and variation of narratives," then perhaps this endlessly iterative manufacturing of national consciousness might also be short-circuited by seriality as well.[17] Anderson clearly outlined how print-capitalism offered a sense of group belonging to such varied populations as metropolitan businessmen and Southeast Asian freedom fighters. Indeed, many of the radical "little magazines" in New York that Reed wrote for tried to produce similar cohesion across fragmented milieus, so why couldn't the serial production of such groups theoretically extend to those who shared political affiliations rather than a "nation?" The logic of seriality demands a bit of dedicated practice and engagement from readers due to the fact that "repeated temporal overlap between publication and consumption allows serial audiences to become involved in the progress of the narrative. In more general terms,

---

[12] Benedict Anderson, *Imagined Communities: Reflections on the Origins and Spread of Nationalism* (New York: Verso, 2006), 37.
[13] Ibid., 36, 37, 44.
[14] Benedict Anderson, *The Spectre of Comparisons: Nationalism, Southeast Asia, and the World* (New York: Verso, 1998), 34.
[15] Peter Hitchcock, *The Long Space: Transnationalism and Postcolonial Form* (Palo Alto, CA: Stanford University Press, 2009), 23.
[16] Elizabeth M. Sheehan, "To Exist Serially: Black Radical Magazines and Beauty Culture, 1917–1919," *Journal of Modern Periodical Studies* 9, no. 1 (2019), 31.
[17] Frank Kelleter, "From Recursive Progression to Systemic Self-observation: Elements of a Theory of Seriality," *Velvet Light Trap* 79, no. 1 (2017), 99.

seriality can extend—and normally does extend—the sphere of storytelling into the sphere of story consumption."[18] If so, Reed's "print-socialism" might allow him to use the seriality of the magazine form *against* nation by stitching together and reinforcing the transnational linkages between seemingly disparate battles into a single struggle against global capital.

Reed's primary vehicle of serial travel was the sizable portion of his early work published in the pages of *Metropolitan Magazine* between 1913 and 1917. Ranging from longform investigative series to standalone reportage to short stories and even a letter (not to mention several advertisements that used his image and growing fame to sell some typewriters), Reed's time at *Metropolitan* would see him span the distance between reportorial ingenue and literary celebrity—in short, the years and the work that made him "John Reed." *Metropolitan* itself, which ran from 1895 to 1925, is a generative example of the tensions Richard Ohmann outlines during this "inaugural moment" of a truly "mass" culture in the United States: a turn-of-the-century mass-market magazine trying to tread the choppy marketplace waters with arms around the fashionably socialist politics of the time and legs paddling furiously through the exigencies of financial pressures.[19] By focusing primarily on this publication and time period, the magazine becomes emblematic of a number of putatively left-aligned ever-slicker glossies that, in one way or another, eventually twisted their putatively socialist politics into support for the First World War. We can also apprehend the manner in which Reed deployed some of the tropes and techniques of imaginative writing to obviate increasing—if also often tacit—censorship from his editorial paymasters while simultaneously coaxing readers toward a more systemic understanding of seemingly unrelated events.

At the turn of the century, *Metropolitan* was a relative minnow in terms of circulation when compared to its better-known contemporaries, such as *Cosmopolitan* and *McClure's*. Beginning its life as a bawdy rag that "depended on photographs of stage actresses, art models, and bloomered and bathing-suited beauties," *Metropolitan* would become a real player during its heyday in the 1910s, with its new British president, Henry James Whigham (known by both friends and *Metropolitan's* readers as "H.J."), presiding from 1911 on.[20] With his managing editor, Carl Hovey—the man most responsible for recognizing, supporting, and profiting off of Reed's talents—the pair helped steer the magazine into serious relevance right around 1913, which also happens to mark the year John Reed first appeared in its pages. It was Whigham that determined the magazine's new tone would be less scandalous photos and more social conscience, transforming a "naughty picture" monthly into an exemplar of what David Reed calls "mixed function" magazines, which collected news (foreign and domestic),

---

[18] Ibid., 100.
[19] Richard Ohmann, *Selling Culture: Magazines, Markets, and Class at the Turn of the Century* (London: Verso, 1996), 285.
[20] Laura Davis, "Not So Much Art as a Financial Operation: Conrad and Metropolitan Magazine," *Conradiana* 41, no. 2–3 (Summer/Fall 2009), 246.

editorials, general-interest topics, images, and imaginative writing all helpfully within the same issue.[21] By November 1913 Whigham had also increased the size of *Metropolitan* to 11 × 14 so that it could better compete with the popular behemoth (both literally in terms of physical heft and figuratively in terms of circulation number) of the *Saturday Evening Post*. However, *Metropolitan's* politics seem to have been defined in some ways precisely in striking *contrast* to George Horace Lorimer's editorial hand at the *Post*, which he led from 1899 to 1936, during which Lorimer tirelessly defended a sort of yeoman American capitalism from the twin degradations of predatory financial speculation and the leftwing alternatives supposedly "imported" from Europe.[22] In fact, the same month Whigham matched the *Post* in size, he also seemed to commit himself to a gentlemanly war with their editorial position, declaring "In politics and in our philosophy of life we represent the progressive movement which is just beginning to stir the world to real purpose. The object of that movement is to render to the workers of the world the fruits of their labor, and to abolish the tyranny of capital."[23]

But what did this "Progressive or pro-socialist" line mean in both practice and tone?[24] At first, and luckily for both the magazine and the young writer, Reed's early politics were certainly more traditionally progressive than socialist, raised in the ethical bosom of his father, Charles Jerome Reed, who had been appointed by Teddy Roosevelt and abetted by Lincoln Steffens to break the Oregon Land Trust ring, a group of Pacific Northwestern businessmen and politicians defrauding the state with a real-estate scheme.[25] Raised with this sense of righteousness and rectitude from his dad, Reed's politics also at first aligned with a sort of masculinist Rooseveltian conception of duty wherein the strong are obligated to aid the weak, but filtered through an ahistorical rather than critical lens that avoided any systematic critique as to why so many strong and weak existed in the first place. In the beginning, then, Reed and T.R. didn't seem like unlikely magazine-mates, which is good for Reed because *Metropolitan* fawned over the elder politician, filling its pages with extensive coverage of his deeds as well as Roosevelt's own brow-beating editorials in line with the paper's newly stated political stance. Or, as Whigham put it frankly, "Theodore Roosevelt is the only candidate for the Presidency who has any knowledge of or sympathy with the working man."[26] However, as Reed continued to be sent on assignment in more far-flung locales, he seemed to uncover consistently comparable forms of class relations that resulted in similar exploitation and abuse—and a more robust totalizing analysis began to take shape in his work, which would inevitably diverge from Roosevelt and *Metropolitan*.

[21] David Reed, *The Popular Magazine in Britain and the United States 1880–1960* (Toronto: University of Toronto Press, 1997).
[22] See Jan Cohn, *Creating America: George Horace Lorimer and "The Saturday Evening Post"* (Pittsburgh, PA: University of Pittsburgh Press, 1990).
[23] H.J. Whigham, "By the Editor," *Metropolitan* (October 1912), 6.
[24] Davis, "Not So Much," 247.
[25] For more on Reed's early life, see Rosenstone, *Romantic*.
[26] Whigham, "By the Editor," 6.

Both the man and the magazine had a mutually constitutive professional relationship, wherein *Metropolitan* offered the young writer the opportunity to craft the "John Reed" he would become while also having a direct hand in his creation. Alternatively, Reed's reporting—beginning with his career-making coverage of the Mexican Revolution—facilitated the catapulting of *Metropolitan* into national prominence. Indeed, from 1913 to 1917, there were few months when the magazine didn't feature at least *something* by the young reporter. His time in Mexico also inaugurates the repetition of the word, trope, and leitmotif of "war" that Reed would use to suture his disparate dispatches into a scathing global critique of imperial capital (even if an actual "war" would eventually fracture this mutually beneficial relationship).

But we're not there yet: Reed's name may have been made in Mexico, but his first piece of agitational journalism for *Metropolitan* was the September 1913 "Sheriff Radcliff's Hotel," a brutal indictment of the treatment of striking silk workers across the Hudson from Reed's beloved Greenwich Village.[27] The article's entry point is a playful folk ballad about the aforementioned hotel, which immediately by dint of its refrain makes clear that Reed's accounting are part of a robust carceral tradition rather than a singular experience. The song frames readers' expectations of the "hotel" as a trap for the indigent, a cop-led bait-and-switch wherein they might be lured by the "free bed and food" "but they wished they had died/ When they saw it inside." Most importantly, we also see the beginnings of a more capacious institutional critique in his analysis: Reed's report argues from the outset that it is not necessarily bad *individuals* that have produced this human warehouse, but a vast network of powerful organizations interested first and foremost in upholding property rights—and therefore also the unsafe low-wage factory system that helps produce so much protectable property in the first place. Framed like this, and while still terrible on its own terms, the Passaic County Jail in Patterson is "not an usually bad example.... Just ordinary, like dozens of others scattered all over this country."[28] Nearly all incarceration, Reed argues—and certainly the unaccountable and largely unregulated local jails—aren't concerned with rehabilitation, paying a debt to society, or even the righting of wrongs but a disciplining measure meant to undermine workers' rights and also corral superfluous (or restive) labor. While the bestial imagery so common in coverage of immigrant laborers during this period still appears here, Reed also seems to critically invert this trope to show that it is not "savage" men that *enter* the jail, but the dehumanizing prison system that *produces* such "animals"—especially when, with all painful irony, these workers refuse to be beasts of burden down the road at the factory. Or, as he puts it, "A county jail is a place that takes in weak men and turns them out weaker.... It simply saps their strength and their intelligence. It dilutes whatever little manliness they have left."[29]

The jail itself is Dantean in its horrors: the (literally) rotten food, the vermin, the heat, the cold, the filthy cots, and it houses a bestiary of Marx's lumpenproletariat.

---

[27] John Reed, "Sheriff Radcliff's Hotel," *Metropolitan* (September 1913), 14.
[28] Ibid.
[29] Ibid., 60.

Chronicling the triviality of the crimes and the severity of their sentences—the seventeen-year-old convicted of stealing bicycles but "*held as a witness for nine months*" or the twin brothers "kept in jail *because nobody knew what to do with them!*"—alongside the casualness with which the law was unevenly applied to ensure a packed house, Reed showcases an institution within which the pettiest criminals are turned professional and the most vulnerable lose their grasp on reality altogether.[30] Eerily echoing contemporary discussions that directly link the legacies of slavery with our current moment of mass incarceration, Reed announces that "the county jail is a peculiar institution," using such loaded language to hammer home the point that prison is a trap set at the intersections of both race *and* class, a warehouse and warning for white and Black alike.[31] Unsatisfied with any "eye in the sky" survey of the scene, Reed refuses to give his readers an undifferentiated mass of lawbreakers but instead offers a coerced cabal of imaginative individuals trapped between nightmarish working conditions at the factory or attenuated carceral lives where even still: "There was art, and humor, and business, and gambling, and selfishness, and generosity, and every human passion."[32] Or, as his last line implores us to remember, "the guests of Sheriff Radcliff's hotel are very humble and very human."[33] This first piece of "real" reporting for a mainstream magazine also provides a firmer outline of the ways in which Reed would offer radical ideals within a reformist paper: human interest rather than proselytizing, "a satirical style palatable to a broad reading public," vivid first-person description that make the events (if not the conclusions) difficult to debate, and a critique of institutions rather than individuals.[34] Even before Reed ever landed in Europe to cover the battles on its Eastern Front, he began to see "war" all around him, local and global—and this particular word would soon be linking his headlines more than any other.

It was easier for our hero—for that is certainly how *Metropolitan* would soon be advertising him—to find, define, and relate what for him were imbricated scenes of war during his first major series. From February to July of 1914, the "nominally liberal-socialist" magazine published a sequence of six articles on the Mexican Revolution wherein Reed rode near, around, and sometimes straight through battles with Pancho Villa and his men, and the editorial staff back home wasted no time marketing the astonishing access its newest star had wrangled. In fact, the magazine introduced his first dispatch as from the "brilliant fiction writer and poet" even though Reed had received little acclaim and even less remuneration for his previously published creative works. But the editor, Carl Hovey, saw an energetic, ambitious, and talented young man, and was eager to bet on what seemed like a winning horse. Indeed, before Reed ever sent an article from Mexico to New York, Hovey and Co. published together (with the author's consent) two letters

---

[30] Ibid., 16, 59. Italics in original.
[31] Ibid., 14.
[32] Ibid., 16.
[33] Ibid., 60.
[34] Hovey, *John Reed*, 76.

from Juarez, dated December 21 and 26 of 1913, respectively, to inaugurate Reed's coverage. This conceit of unvarnished and putatively unedited text fresh from the maw of revolutionary Mexico advances a ripped-from-the-headlines truth-effect from the commencement of Reed's marquee coverage. And the editorial headnote only increases the sense of import and insider knowledge surrounding the letter, explaining to readers that "Although not intended for publication, these pen pictures are too vivid to be lost."[35] In this appraisal, even Reed's private ephemera are vital enough to be shared, as he relates being part of an irregular army comprised of "Two thousand nondescript, tattered men on dirty little tough horses" all dedicated to a leader represented as more of an infrastructure than a person: "Villa runs the electric light plant, the telephone, the street-cars, the brewery, and almost every public utility"—already the leader of his territories in all but recognition. But perhaps most important is the access Reed promises Hovey, and that Hovey offers *Metropolitan* readers in return: "I had a long talk with Villa today and he promised me that I was to go with him wherever he went, day or night."[36] Simultaneously sidekick and familiar, Hovey establishes Reed establishing his own credentials to be Villa's right-hand chronicler in clear contrast to the other papers whose reporters sat around hotel bars near the border waiting for second-hand news.

When Reed first arrived, the Mexican Revolution at this time had not yet fully cohered around either a stable US policy or a rigid division between "good" and "bad" actors in the press, so many observers peered from palaces and parliaments around the world, waiting to see the fallout and victors before taking firm sides. As the official US position was still being hashed out by President Wilson and his advisors, Reed was one of the central mouthpieces through which American citizens and politicians alike read and apprehended not just the events in Mexico, but also their broader narrative context. In this way, Reed helped Villa be seen as a freedom fighter rather than brigand, and contrary to a number of other early reports of Villa's bloodshed, Reed assures readers that the city of Chihuahua, far from a contagiously anarchic open wound, is instead a tranquil redoubt in the mold of the equitable peace to come. Or, in his own plain words, "There is no danger here."[37]

In "With La Tropa," his first full-length article from the conflict, Reed plays a slick sleight of hand with Villa's General Urbina, who at first appears as an uncomplicated hero to be revered—and then is quickly undermined by Reed, who uses the trusting general to spotlight the mechanics of journalistic character-production itself. After presenting us with a Mexico primarily feudal in its class relations and building up Urbina as a brave soldier and loyal lieutenant, Reed then reports that Urbina would "like me to have me take some pictures of him." Suddenly, this stoic and stern military man can't help but preen like a florid bird for the Yanqui press while Reed offers readers

---

[35] John Reed, "With Villa in Mexico," *Metropolitan* (February 1914), 72.
[36] Ibid.
[37] Ibid.

any number of ways these "characters" might be constructed for an audience in their writerly, imagistic, and editorial choices. As he relates:

> the next hour, I took photographs of General Urbina and his family: General Urbina on foot, with and without sword; General Urbina on three different horses; General Urbina, with and without his family; General Urbina's three children, on horseback and off; General Urbina's mother, and his mistress; the entire family, armed with swords and revolvers; also the phonograph, provided for the purpose, and one of the children holding a placard upon which was inked 'General Tomas Urbina R.'[38]

On offer here—in addition to the cheeky irreverence toward custom and convention that characterizes Reed's multiplicity of possible Urbinas—is in large part the very "fiction" of the news itself, or at least Reed's heavy debt to literary-visual forms and formulae that preceded his go at reportage. Even the landscape intrudes upon any sense of impartial legitimacy because, as Reed reports, "It is almost impossible to get objective about the desert; you sink into it—become a part of it."[39] With some irony, then, the general's final statement as he lies in bed wracked by "rheumatism" is the simple request that Reed "Write the truth."[40] The potential for this "truth," of course, has already been willfully undone by Reed's interruptions that constantly refer back to the necessary mediation between representations of reality, its constructedness, and its chroniclers.

Emerging "as one of the highest-paid" and well-known journalists in the country, Reed left the Mexican Revolution only to be sent straightaway to another battleground—but his July 1914 dispatch from this new "war" might not be the one today's readers imagine.[41] Writing from Ludlow rather than Lille, "The Colorado War" lands Reed squarely in the aftermath of the massacre of miners and their families by various police forces, proxies, and legal representatives of Colorado Fuel & Iron (CF&I), owned wholly at this time by John D. Rockefeller. Or, to simplify the antagonists in the manner of the Bolsheviks that Reed would so famously cover just a few years later, for the first time in the mainstream press he was writing in stark terms about the war between labor and capital. Whereas "Sheriff Radcliff's Hotel" was ostensibly about a labor strike, its content was almost entirely focused on the world inside the prison. In the nearby company town of Trinidad, Colorado, however, there is no institutional intermediary to gather up the angry, underfed, and unemployed. Hovey and the rest of the editorial board make this link explicit in their marketing materials, connecting the Rockies with the Sierra Madres for readers even before Reed himself: "When there is war, John Reed is the writer to describe it. That is why the METROPOLITAN sent him straight from Mexico to Colorado."[42]

---

[38] Reed, "With La Tropa," 12.
[39] Ibid., 13.
[40] Ibid.
[41] Lehman, *John Reed*, 129.
[42] Lehman, *John Reed*, 129; and John Reed, "The Colorado War," (July 1914), 11.

Beginning with the court testimony of the president of CF&I—Dickensianly named "Mr. Welborn"—Reed begins the article proleptically by way of a report delivered to a congressional investigation in the wake of the violence, and he soon further textually intertwines Colorado and Mexico for those who had already read his previous coverage (which, considering it was the very same magazine, was rather likely). Even the very issue links the two between its covers: Reed's last dispatch from Mexico is only twelve pages away from his first report on Colorado. In Mexico, Reed had repeatedly portrayed social relations there as medieval vassalage, essentially a feudal state just south of the border that Villa and Zapata were hoping to liberate. But though Reed has rightly been taken to task for Mexican scenes that can read as a collapse between naturalized and racialized "truths" about Latinx peoples seemingly out of time, these critiques might also take into account that the mountain West in his Colorado coverage comes in for similar treatment.[43] So we might more generously read Reed as renovating and making critical these racialized preconceptions of subjectivity *into* the language of class exploitation. Indeed, from the very first pages of Ludlow, readers could be forgiven thinking they were still in *Metropolitan*'s Mexico, though whereas Villa was a one-man civic works who ruled to keep the peace, Colorado's "feudal coal towns" are Mexico's inversion, wherein "the houses of the workmen, the stores, saloons, mine-buildings, schools, post-offices—all on private property, all fortified and patrolled as if in a state of war" and where "they consider the boss almost a God."[44] But in Colorado, rather than fighting with Federales, we find villages "occupied by armed detectives with machine guns and searchlights" and lives even more precarious than those in Chihuahua.

Canvasing the vast heterogeneity of the immigrant laborers from Mexico to Greece, Reed offers a United Nations of misery and details scenes of "ghastly ruins" (see Figure 2.1) that further yoke Colorado to Mexico (and will eventually recall Serbia during the First World War and even, later on, New Jersey), placing such supposed "precapitalist" forms of labor relations smack in the center of the United States. Reed even explains away the motley ethnic mix in the mines as the result of an old slaver's trick, with owners "deliberately importing ignorant foreigners to fill the mines, carefully massing in each mine men of many different languages, who would not be able to organize."[45] And yet, despite the ferocity of death and exploitation, the mines also contain the potential of the factory floor, serving the useful function of stitching the workers together *across* lines of race and ethnicity. As Reed argues, "There were more than twelve hundred people there, divided into twenty-one nationalities, undergoing the marvelous experience of learning that all men are alike. When they had been living together for two weeks, the petty race prejudices and misunderstandings that had been fostered between them by the coal companies for so many years began to break down."[46]

---

[43] For a representative example, see Christopher P. Wilson, "Plotting the Border: John Reed, Pancho Villa, and *Insurgent Mexico*," in Cultures of United States Imperialism, eds. Amy Kaplan and Donald E. Pease (Durham, NC: Duke University Press, 1993), 340–64.
[44] Reed, "Colorado," 11, 12, 11.
[45] Ibid., 12.
[46] Ibid., 13.

Figure 2.1 P. Thompson, "Ruins of the Ludlow Tent Colony." *Metropolitan Magazine* (July 1914), 11.

Or, as Reed directly connects his two most recent scenes, "As one Mexican said to me: 'We go out despairing and there comes a river of friendship from our brothers that we never knew!'"[47] These kumbayas, though, are quickly qualified by Reed's other main observation: The workers themselves exist within an airless universe of institutional capture, wherein "District attorneys, sheriffs, county commissioners, and judges were practically appointed in the offices of the Colorado Fuel and Oil Company."[48] Even worse, the forces arrayed against miners and their families seem happy to respond to demands for improvements with the bullhorns and bullets of full-scale war.

If *Metropolitan*'s urbane Northern readers had been able to differentiate themselves from the reports out of Mexico with the smug certitude of racial and national distance, they might have been uncomfortably shocked by the rapine violence against civilians—primarily US citizens at that—in Colorado, especially against women and children. Reed offers a litany of quotidian horrors against the innocent: "Every time the wounded boy tried to drag himself in the direction of the tents, the machine gun was turned on him. He was shot no less than nine times. ... A little girl, the daughter of a neighboring farmer, was coming home from school. She was shot in the face."[49] Reed himself also

[47] Ibid., 12.
[48] Ibid.
[49] Ibid., 15.

becomes part of the story in particular fashion, and one that oddly accords with the attention he tried to direct toward the hidden mechanics of journalistic world-building itself: One of *Metropolitan*'s many advertisers, the Corona Typewriter Company, used his likeness as well as a letter Reed ostensibly wrote to Hovey to promote their new folding model (see Figure 2.2). Also referring back to his time in Mexico, the ad not

Figure 2.2 Corona Folding Typewriter advertisement. *Metropolitan Magazine Metropolitan Magazine* (July 1914), 67.

only announces Reed's preference for a particular typing machine but also once again draws attention to the mediation of the news by those writing it. Even the arrow pointing toward the letter almost breaks into the dividing line of the next column of actual news, nearly collapsing the division between naked marketing and supposedly objective "facts."

Governments, industrialists, class exploitation, and, most especially, war would spectacularly combine for Reed and his reporting when *Metropolitan* rerouted him in 1914 from a planned tour of revolutionary China to cover the increasing hostilities in Europe. But if "our hero" was essentially created by the editors at *Metropolitan*, increased exponentially through his reports from Mexico, and his star only risen further in Colorado as the man who speaks truth to power in the mainstream press, Reed was undone—or, perhaps more accurately, willfully undid himself—while trying to cover the First World War. And I use the word "trying" because Reed's European coverage during the war seemed most adept at *missing* the war itself, arriving either too early or too late to witness actual fighting through a series of reports that critic Harry Henderson calls "a dismal failure."[50]

With friend and illustrator Boardman Robinson providing dark and moody charcoal sketches to accompany Reed's "word pictures," the pair travelled around Southern and Eastern Europe looking for battle but finding instead either the tense regimented boredom of soldiers waiting for the enemy or, worse, the deracinating wake of battle, with vast fields and villages nearly abandoned to scavengers and their human carrion. Undeterred, Reed was determined to carry the "truth" of this struggle between empires back to the audiences back home. Granville Hicks, in his biography of Reed, relates an anecdote about the writer and the distinctions he made between fact and truth: When Robinson criticized a detail in one of Reed's stories, saying:

> "But it didn't happen that way; it happened this way." Reed would explode. Crying, "What the hell difference does it make?" he would seize one of Robinson's sketches. "She didn't have a bundle as big as that," he would say; or, "He didn't have a full beard." Robinson would explain that he wasn't interested in photographic accuracy; he was trying to give the right impression. "Exactly," Reed would shout in triumph; "that is just what I am trying to do."[51]

But this somewhat tenuous—or we might more generously call "creative"—relationship to truth was not the only bond to fray: the First World War would prove an entirely different level of mediation with and by *Metropolitan*, and Reed did not yet know that the contradictions between his own political convictions and those of the magazine's editorial staff would no longer paper themselves over through

---

[50] Lehman, *John Reed*, 163.
[51] Granville Hicks, *John Reed: The Making of a Revolutionary* (New York: Macmillan, 1936), 197–8.

mutual renown and financial remuneration. While the seeds of this schism can be seen retrospectively from the start, Reed and Whigham had often seemed in near lockstep as far as their respective voices in the paper were concerned. For example, in the July 1914 issue wherein Reed explained that Rockefeller not only knew but at least tacitly demanded the violent suppression of labor at his Colorado mines, Whigham's editorial followed Reed's work a few stories later, calling the industrialist out by name, and demanding justice for Mother Jones who had been imprisoned essentially at Rockefeller's request. But a localized labor battle is not the same as a global conflict between nation-states, at least as far as a magazine's bottom line is concerned.

From the outset, Reed's first dispatch, "The Approach to War," is anything but: Begun on a Naples-bound steamer in New York Harbor, the "approach" of the title is not about any international cabal of "sleepwalkers" lumbering toward conflict but only Reed's slow crawl toward the Continent by steamship. Less interested in where he's headed than with the ruthless class distinctions already aboard, Reed writes extensively about how these maritime relations seem to distill in miniature the divisions he had already written about firsthand across North America between the well-fed and the fodder. Indeed, Reed doesn't even need to reach Europe to find conflict, for "once on board the Italian steamer that was to carry me to Naples, I came face to face with war."[52] He means this literally: For Reed, the faces he sees *are* the war in both its causes and human cost. Comparing the 150 or so first- and second-class passengers above decks, he peers over the rail to find "three thousand miserable beings thronged the steerage, many without an adequate place to lie at night."[53] Even worse, the largely European crowd below was making this immigrant journey in reverse because they "had been called home to the army... and in a flush of feeling for their country had left behind their business, their home, and even their families to get themselves butchered because their wiser superiors had called it Patriotism."[54] Richard Harding Davis reporting from San Juan Hill this most certainly is *not*. In other words, as with Colorado, Mexico, and New Jersey, the First World War for Reed is just one more class struggle by yet another name. Or, as he titled it succinctly in the actually socialist pages of the *Masses* two months prior, welcome to "The Trader's War."

Reed wastes little time making this point, beginning with a sendup of the self-interested would-be war-profiteering on his home turf, where "the newspapers talked blandly of the advantages which would accrue to the United States because of the European War" such as "how we would grab the South American trade, float the liabilities of Europe at exorbitant rates of interest, and sell our foodstuffs at an outrageous profit to the starving nations of the world."[55] Indeed, the first-class folks around him don't seem to have been infected with any nationalist feeling beyond shared profits. Among "several German barons, an Austrian count, and military officers of

---

[52] John Reed, "The Approach to War," *Metropolitan* (November 1914), 15.
[53] Ibid.
[54] Ibid.
[55] Ibid.

all nationalities" Reed finds, in his most unvarnished callback to earlier stories yet, "an Italian capitalist who *owned a silk mill in Paterson and had helped break the great strike.*"[56] Signaling to his cannier readers a clear reference to the piece that inaugurated his political reporting in *Metropolitan*, Reed links the Great War to the "great strikes"—with the same cast of characters he'd been writing about ever since his prison stint in New Jersey. What's more, the casual cruelty he documents aboard is just as unrelenting and reminiscent of Radcliff's "hotel" or the treatment of company-town residents in Ludlow and Trinidad. The well-placed passengers around him refer constantly to those belowdecks as "Animals!" and "Vermin!" soon to be "exterminated" in battle. In fact, the Patterson capitalist is far crueler—or at least less restrained—than the nobility around him, a fine candidate for an executive position at the Colorado Mine: Reed explains how the silk manufacturer was beside himself with rage when one of the men in steerage had the temerity to disobey an order to disperse that he didn't hear because he was sleeping. "Why didn't they throw the old fool overboard! The beasts!" screams the mill owner. "They ought to be shot or starved to death!"[57] This is followed quickly by another Easter egg that links Reed's prior work with his coverage of Europe: "It was rather extraordinary to see him—a mere lad about thirteen years old—taking actual part in the serious business of war. *It reminded one of Mexico.*"[58]

So while *Metropolitan*, led by star editorializer Teddy Roosevelt, beat a steady rhythm toward war undergirded by a supposedly "reformist" socialism that could stomach aligning itself with industrialized carnage, Reed waged his own contrary struggle in their very own pages, showcasing instead the monotony, cruelty, and largely civilian-borne costs during and after battles. His dispatches from wartime Serbia are probably the pinnacle of his wartime "style" and Boardman's charcoal sketches become their own atrocity exhibition of desperation and casual harm. Heading out from Salonika (Thessaloniki) near the large Allied Expeditionary Force base, Reed also refers back to some "types" we've met before: As in the hotels of Mexico City and the mines of Colorado, Europe is crawling with representatives of US business interests, particularly Rockefeller's Standard Oil, whose repeated appearances in Reed's stories suture together a far more economic underbelly in contrast to the public rallying around the rectitude of war. The agents in Europe kindly offer a bit of gallows humor when the writer and artist share their plans to head toward the fray: "Too bad… So young, too. Do you want the remains shipped home, or shall we have you buried up there?"[59] But their macabre asides aren't at all misplaced: Serbia when they arrive is in the grip of a typhus epidemic brought about and also exacerbated by the war, a "devastated land; where battle-fields, villages and roads stank with the lightly buried dead, and the streams were polluted with the bodies of men and horses."[60] Reed places human war back into the natural world, reminding readers that its casualties are far

---

[56] Ibid. Italics mine.
[57] Ibid.
[58] Ibid., 66. Italics mine.
[59] Reed, "Serbia between Battles," 3.
[60] Ibid., 4.

more innocent and extensive than anything sustained on the battlefield, and he also returns us to his time with Villa, linked by a line of Serbian soldiers that are "ragged, dirty fellows in every variety of half-uniform, with rifle-belts crisscrossed over their breasts like Mexican revolutionists."[61]

The subsequent scenes are a relentless catalog of Boschian detail: splayed out on the grass, they encounter "hundreds of soldiers, sleeping, scratching themselves, stripping and searching their bodies for lice, tossing and twisting in fever… Wherever there was a spot of worn grass, the miserable people clustered, picking vermin from each other."[62] Far from a decontextualized jingoistic conflict, Reed offers instead an image of soldiers at war with pestilence and disease rather than the Central Powers. But it's in the hospitals where we encounter true hopelessness (see Figure 2.3). Even before they arrive, the "wind set our way, carrying the stench of bodies sweating with fever, of sick men eating, of the rotting of flesh" and inside they find cots crammed side to side, with "patients writhing in their dirty blankets, five and six crowded into two beds. Some sat up, apathetically eating; others lay like the dead; still others gave short, grunting moans, or shouted suddenly in the grip of delirium."[63] Robinson's drawings channel Goya's "Disasters of War" series and offer little glamour to match Reed's words. The writer and illustrator would ultimately send back little more than this to the *Metro* offices in New York: Endless descriptions of unmitigated and unnecessary suffering punctuated by moments of bleak humor and references that link the European cannon fodder to the oppressed elsewhere. And though Reed locates a likeness in "the rude wooden crosses, as in Mexico, to mark the spots where men had been assassinated" and found plenty more graves, he never found his war, though he did continue to push against it through reporting that contained little to no fighting, even less heroics, and loads of human pain.

The nightmare of all good New Yorkers, Reed's mainstream career ended where it began: In New Jersey. And apparently not a moment too soon: His final article for *Metropolitan* carried a tone decidedly more impatient and certainly less subtle, while his editors no longer introduced Reed as special correspondent—or, frankly, as anything special at all. After the debacle of his war coverage, however, Reed offers a parting shot that not only stitches together his previous preoccupations but also declares his own small war against *Metropolitan* and "objective" journalism itself. Bringing Mexico, Ludlow, and Serbia to Bayonne, NJ, Reed and Robinson cross the Hudson to chronicle yet another Rockefeller-abetted hellscape, but this time the company isn't pulling strings in feudal towns out West or sending representatives to hunt for opportunities on the edges of world wars. Another strike, another collective of exploited immigrant laborers, another merry-go-round of institutional capture by the local police, press, and courts, more violence, more jail, in other words more of the endless iterations of the same struggle—but this time so close to Reed's beloved Village apartment that it

---

[61] Ibid.
[62] Ibid., 9.
[63] Ibid., 53.

Figure 2.3 B. Robinson, "Hospital at Nish." *Metropolitan Magazine* (August 1915), 6.

can be seen on a clear day from the Battery downtown. Who needs Mexico or Serbia or Trinidad when right across the Hudson is:

> a waste of red New Jersey earth where nothing grows, spotted with garbage and tin-cans, with great red oil-tanks scattered like strange fungi amid mountains of coal… you can look straight out to the flat blue waters of the harbor, and all downtown New York piled up from the sea in a glittering mountain like some

legendary St. Michel. You can see Twenty-six Broadway [the Standard Oil Building], where sits the power that has created all this—and the copper green Statue of Liberty, seeming, by a curious foreshortening, to stand right at its door.[64]

Reed, not yet thirty years old, reads like a worn-out old radical resigned to howling into the storm. There is no longer any coy negotiation of the point or his position. Indeed, his very first line speaks to the normalization of the scenes he spent his short life trying to call attention to: "The growing frequency of violent labor disputes in this country, accompanied by riots, murder and armed battles, has become so familiar to people who live in industrial communities that it is almost taken for granted."[65] In short, he might as well be speaking of the weather.

But this time, going after more than just Rockefeller, Reed takes aim at his readership, his entire "scene," all the other self-proclaimed socialists from the editorial board to the folks aping bohemian chic downtown, and even the platforms he uses to mock them:

> New Yorkers have a hazy idea that these things happen in distant, half civilized countries—the Michigan peninsula, the mountains of Colorado and Minnesota; and the metropolitan press is indignant at capitalistic injustice. But the same injustice goes on in Bayonne, a city visible from the Battery and almost within the city limits of Greater New York, and most of the newspapers will not, or cannot, tell the truth about it.[66]

Primed by and for war, Reed's time in Europe has helped him articulate the resonant inhumanity that also characterizes everyday labor at the plant as if he were still on the battlefield in Nish, while Robinson's charcoal drawings bridge this link directly (see Figure 2.4). Like the Serbian hospital, Reed explains the plight of the "pressmen" who enter the vast stills in the refinery to scrub out the petroleum byproducts left behind. If Nish represented the nadir of literal war, Reed's descriptions of this Rockefeller plant and its army of laborers are even more disturbing precisely because of their quotidian ubiquity and implied repetition at refineries across the country. The effects on the human body, the suffering of which is even more biblically hellish than the carnage of Eastern Europe, are recounted in hideous detail, explaining that the pressmen experience "a temperature of over two hundred degrees" while "wearing iron shoes and wearing layers of layers of sacking" so "almost every day someone collapses" and "has to be rescued."[67] Even then, a local doctor reports that their bodies have become so permeated by fumes that he has "seen *flames coming out of their mouths* after drinking."[68] The lucky ones have a "working-life of ten years" and reportedly look like

---

[64] John Reed, "Industrial Frightfulness in Bayonne," *Metropolitan* (January 1917), 12.
[65] Ibid.
[66] Ibid.
[67] Ibid., 63.
[68] Ibid. Italics in original.

"boiled meat."⁶⁹ War may be hell, but in Reed's words and Robinson's pencil, it's no worse than the millions of daily injuries, deaths, and humiliations that can happen to anyone selling themselves for wage-work the world over. In Bayonne, Reed "saw the same thing in the German-conquered towns in Belgium, before the sniping began." Besides, with the cops and strikers both ready to pounce, the whole town is filled with the "look of war."⁷⁰

But for the smoke, it might be part of a Galician town

Figure 2.4 B. Robinson "But for the smoke, it might be part of a Galician town." *Metropolitan Magazine* (January 1917), 13.

---

⁶⁹ Ibid.
⁷⁰ Ibid., 66.

Not all was *complete* failure and collapse, however: Rockefeller's unofficial motto toward labor organizing had for years been simply "Whenever it shows its head, hit it."[71] But, with some irony considering Reed's stance, the war in Europe had only strengthened labor's hand at home. The Bayonne Strike in particular is often seen as one of the causes behind public—and eventually political—opinion finally turning against Rockefeller and his tentacular organization, with Reed's stories most likely adding a few logs to the pyre of Standard Oil's unapologetic control. With these new pressures on the supply of labor in addition to public anger toward scenes like the one in New Jersey, Rockefeller finally "initiated pension programs and other extensive employee benefits."[72] But we might also hear Reed asking what kind of benefits could possibly be provided for "boiled meat?" or the point of a pension if the laboring lifespan is a mere decade? Bayonne seems to be the moment Reed finally concedes that, after all his travels, there's no place to run in a global war.

Reed never wrote for *Metropolitan* again after Bayonne. His implacable anti-war position "had become an embarrassment" and was impossible to coalesce with T.R.'s drumbeating editorials.[73] In the words of editor Carl Hovey, "It was fine for Reed to hate the war and say so. But the magazine could no longer be his platform."[74] In fact, he never wrote regularly for any mainstream magazine again, saving his "word-pictures" for more politically amenable outlets like the *Liberator, The New York Call,* and the *Masses*. And though he did not of course transform social relations into a socialist paradise or stop the madness of international conflict, he did leave behind a record of one writer deploying literary techniques and tropes in the journalistic service of tying together the Mexican Revolution, labor strikes, prisons, state violence across the United States, and even the First World War into interlinked instances of a single global class war. In fact, by Bayonne, he didn't have much time left, dying from typhus a few days shy of his thirty-third birthday three years later in a Moscow hospital because American authorities wouldn't authorize a return home. Like so many radicals of his time, he sought personal and political apotheosis in the glow of Bolshevik Russia, whose revolution he would chronicle so famously and so well. Obviously, we know how *that* story goes too, but at least Reed was able to die with the conviction that his very last beat might really be the one to change the world.

---

[71] Jill Quadagno, *The Transformation of Old Age Security: Class and Politics in the American Welfare State* (Chicago: University of Chicago Press, 1988).
[72] Ibid.
[73] Hovey, *John Reed,* 153.
[74] Ibid., 154.

3

Laying the Type of Revolution: Historicizing US Feminism in and through Print Culture

Agatha Beins

I often start with statistics when introducing my work about US feminist newsletters and newspapers published during what is commonly termed the "second wave": in 1968 a self-identified feminist periodical appeared in the United States—*The Voice of the Women's Liberation Movement* (Chicago).[1] By 1970, there were around 85 feminist publications, growing to at least 228 the following year, and then to over 550 in 1974.[2] These numbers tell a striking story about the vibrant activism during this era, which included and extended far beyond feminist print culture. For Sara Evans, the late 1960s through mid-1970s are "the golden years" of feminism, and Rosalyn Baxandall and Linda Gordon describe the mid-1960s through 1977 as "the period of the most yeasty ferment, creativity, and mass participation."[3] Writing in the late 1970s, Charlotte Bunch explains that "the existence and visibility today of feminist and especially of lesbian-feminist writing is largely a result of the establishment of feminist presses and periodicals over the past ten years... New ways of exploring subjects has been possible because of the atmosphere created by women's publishing."[4] Therefore, in this moment feminists, in many ways, were "paper feminists," whether they were directly involved in editing and publishing, or if they read mailings, newspapers, or paperbacks from one of the many feminist presses.[5] Periodicals, books, and other print ephemera provided

---

[1] Alice Echols, *Daring to Be Bad: Radical Feminism in America 1967–1975* (Minneapolis: University of Minnesota Press, 1989), 53.
[2] The 1970 number is from Martha Allen, "The Development of Communication Networks among Women, 1963–1983—A History of Women's Media in the U.S.," PhD dissertation (Howard U, 1988); the 1971 number is from Lisa Cobbs, "State of the Press—1976," *Feminist Bulletin* (July–August 1976), 15; the 1974 number is from Anne Mather, "History of Feminist Periodicals, Part 1," *Journalism History* 1, no. 3 (1974), 82.
[3] Sara Evans, *Tidal Wave: How Women Changed America at Century's End* (New York: Simon and Schuster, 2003); Rosalyn Baxandall and Linda Gordon, "Introduction," in their *Dear Sisters: Dispatches from the Women's Liberation Movement* (New York: Basic Books, 2000), 1.
[4] Charlotte Bunch, "Reading and Writing for a Feminist Future," in her *Passionate Politics: Feminist Theory in Action; Essays, 1968–1986* (New York: St. Martin's P, 1987), 219.
[5] Here I borrow from Kate Adams's characterization that "the paper lesbian was a paper feminist" ("Built Out of Books: Lesbian Energy and Feminist Ideology in Alternative Publishing," *Journal of Homosexuality* 34, no. 3/4 [1998], 116).

materials and ideas that invigorated feminism, and a vital part of feminist activism involved the women in print movement.[6]

Although I introduced this chapter with a specific point of origin in 1968, and although that year has been narrated into feminism as such through the Miss America Protest and the widespread media coverage it received, this so-called second wave did not appear spontaneously, like a "big bang" in which women suddenly awoke to gender oppression and took to the streets and the printing presses. Rather, it emerged in relation to the social and political climate in the 1960s, both in the United States and around the world: the Black Panthers and Brown Berets, the civil rights movement, homophile activism, and the New and Old Left carved a national landscape of resistance; uprisings in countries like Cuba, Vietnam, Angola, Mozambique, and Chile offered models for challenging colonialism and imperialism; and figures like Ché Guevara, Mao Tse-tung, and the freedom fighters in Africa, South America, and Southeast Asia also contributed to the visions and practices women took into their organizing. Activist publishing and the US underground press, however, rarely surface as part of this context, even within histories of the 1970s women in print movement. When mentioned, it tends to be folded into the dominant narrative that inaugurates feminism with women "arriving directly from male-dominated, grassroots social justice movements" who "longed for a space where they could talk freely with other women."[7] Print culture in the 1960s, therefore, becomes just another component of the sexist, patriarchal spaces that women rejected in favor of feminist ones. Such a view not only prevents us from seeing aspects of feminist publishing that extended and borrowed from other activist groups but also automatically excludes these groups as sites where feminist activism occurred in and through print.

Complicating this dialectical narrative, I analyze the 1960s as a political-material formation that lay foundations for the type of revolution that feminism became, and is still becoming.[8] After briefly summarizing some key dimensions of 1960s politics in relation to US feminism, I turn to the material, discursive, and ideological facets of periodical publishing within the alternative press through a "history of the book" framework.[9] On the one hand, misogyny in New Left and US third world groups did push women away, causing them to create and become engaged in autonomous feminist formations. On the other hand, print culture illustrates how these movements held space for feminist practices and shaped aspects of women's liberation activism.

---

[6] Trysh Travis, "The Women in Print Movement: History and Implications," *Book History* 11 (2008), 275–300; Kristen Hogan, *The Feminist Bookstore Movement: Lesbian Antiracism and Feminist Accountability* (Durham, NC: Duke University Press, 2016). Although 1970s feminist print culture was part of a transnational conversation of resistance, because this movement was largely situated in the United States, my analysis focuses primarily on this country (on feminist periodicals outside the United States, see Agatha Beins, "A Publishing Assemblage: Building Book History Methodology through Feminist Periodicals," *American Periodicals* 28, no. 2 [2018], 119 note 9).

[7] Baxandall and Gordon, "Introduction," 12.

[8] See Erica Townsend-Bell, who shows how women of color publishing in the 1980s is rooted in their writings during the prior decade ("Writing the Way to Feminism," *Signs* 38, no. 1 [2012], 127–52).

[9] For a brief overview of history of the book scholarship, see Beins, "A Publishing Assemblage."

I thus make an argument that reconfigures the chronological and spatial landscapes of what is commonly referred to as "second wave feminism," expanding and complicating its scope through print culture.[10]

This chapter offers methodological provocations as well. Writing it has involved building an archive through endnotes, one that is both perhaps too extensive and certainly too incomplete, but that at least alludes to the heterogeneity of feminism. Juxtaposing primary and secondary sources and texts from a range of different movement groups offers a new catalog of feminist activism and provides multiple starting points for building an even more expansive view of feminist print culture. History of the book foregrounds the stakes in this process by centering questions about the entirety of a text's lifespan, from the mere idea of its existence through its post-publication survival (or non-survival), for texts are unevenly extant. Whether a newspaper issue is in a box in someone's closet, in an institutional archive but uncataloged, or in digitized open access form affects how it writes and is written into our history. Access is shaped by the positions of a periodical's creators, as well: not all groups saved or archived their work, and the more prominent feminist collectives are more likely to be visible in these archives. Methods of cataloging print culture also matter. When metadata categorizes a newspaper as part of women's liberation or as feminist—or as neither—it can impact historiography. Finally, the politics of citation contribute to feedback loops that amplify the feminist weight of some artifacts and the invisibility of others. For example, in her national history of US feminism, Alice Echols overwhelmingly cites periodicals from the coasts (Washington, DC, New York, and California) and large urban hubs (Chicago, Boston/Cambridge).[11] My point is not to indict Echols for her selection and citation of sources but to emphasize the value of an analysis that centers print culture because it makes available the political, epistemological, *and* material dimensions of these decisions and the forces that give texts life, inviting a more general reconsideration of the archives we use and create to read and write histories.

Publishing Context

Because 1960s print culture reflected the broader landscape of radical politics, I introduce this section with a sketch of activism during that decade. Resistance to the status quo saturated the atmosphere: the civil rights movement, antiwar activism, the New Left, and US third world revolutionary movements (Black, Brown, Yellow, and Red Power) ignited the national imagination with their strident demands and visual spectacles. Within these movements, women became politicized, developing their activist repertoire and building alliances with others working to eradicate inequity,

---

[10] Maylei Blackwell does this for Chicana feminism in *¡Chicana Power! Contested Histories of Feminism in the Chicano Movement* (Austin: University of Texas Press, 2011), 141.
[11] Echols, *Daring to Be Bad*.

injustice, and sexism.¹² However, these so-called "free spaces" manifested a gap between ideology and practice when discourses of equality, participatory democracy, and liberation did not translate into a critical understanding of sexism.¹³ Male domination was reproduced in political praxes and ideals, idealizing masculinity in revolutionary figures and diminishing issues that prioritized women's liberation.¹⁴ Consolidating this political moment through a few paragraphs and endnotes, though, requires some caveats because different activist spaces configured power and privilege differently: women occupied leadership roles within these groups; not all women of color shared the same position in relation to race and gender in their activism; not all women *within* a racial group had the same kind of experience; and not all men were chauvinist pigs. Women in privileged positions (regarding race, class, sexuality, ability, etc.) also bear responsibility for reproducing inequities and reconsolidating their own positions of power. Nevertheless, even with the diversity of activists and activist groups, patterns are apparent: women were involved in a wide range of political movements in the 1960s and 1970s; women of color have a long history of challenging sexism; and in these movements, concerns about gender were often marginalized and trivialized—all of which factored into varied challenges to patriarchal hegemonies at that time and beyond. As foregrounded

---

[12] Sara Evans, *Personal Politics: The Roots of Women's Liberation in the Civil Rights Movement and the New Left* (New York: Vintage Books, 1980); Tiyi M. Morris, *Womanpower Unlimited and the Black Freedom Struggle in Mississippi* (Athens: University of Georgia Press, 2015); Blackwell, *¡Chicana Power!*, chapter 2; Belinda Robnett, "African-American Women in the Civil Rights Movement, 1954–1965: Gender, Leadership, and Micromobilization," *American Journal of Sociology* 101, no. 6 (1996), 1661–93; Echols, *Daring to Be Bad*, chapter 1; Benita Roth, *Separate Roads to Feminism: Black, Chicana, and White Feminist Movements in America's Second Wave* (Cambridge: Cambridge University Press, 2004); Sara Evans, "Women's Liberation: Seeing the Revolution Clearly," *Feminist Studies* 41, no. 1 (2015), 138–49.

[13] See Carol Hanisch and Elizabeth Sutherland, "Women of the World Unite—We Have Nothing to Lose But Our Men!" in *Notes from the First Year* (New York: New York Radical Women, 1968), 12–16; Roth, *Separate Roads to Feminism*, 62–70, 136–9; Kimberly Springer, *Living for the Revolution: Black Feminist Organizations, 1968–1980* (Durham, NC: Duke University Press, 2005); Judy Wu, *Radicals on the Road: Internationalism, Orientalism, and Feminism during the Vietnam Era* (Ithaca, NY: Cornell UP, 2013), 154–9; Ryan Masaaki Yokota, "Interview with Pat Sumi," in *Asian Americans: The Movement and the Moment*, eds. Steve Louie and Glenn Omatsu (Los Angeles: UCLA Asian American Studies Center Press, 2006), 24, (https://www.academia.edu/10127875/_Interview_with_Pat_Sumi); Third World Women's Alliance, "Our History, Our Ideology, Our Goals," April [1971], [4]. Folder 9, box 1, Third World Women's Alliance Papers, Sophia Smith Collection, Smith College, Northampton, MA. (also quoted in Springer, *Living for the Revolution*, 48); Winifred Breines, *The Trouble between Us: An Uneasy History of White and Black Women in the Feminist Movement* (Oxford: Oxford University Press, 2006), 84; see also Lee Bebout, *Mythohistorical Interventions: The Chicano Movement and Its Legacies* (Minneapolis: University of Minnesota Press, 2011), Chapter 3; "Political Education Workshop," Hijas de Cuauhtémoc publication [early 1970s], Oral History Collection: Los Angeles Women's Movement, California State University, Long Beach Special Collections and University Archives.

[14] Jane Rhodes, *Framing the Black Panthers: The Spectacular Rise of a Black Power Icon* (New York: Norton, 2007), 156; on the similarities between *Black Panther* and *Gidra*, see Rychetta Watkins, *Black Power, Yellow Power, and the Making of Revolutionary Identities* (Jackson: University Press of Mississippi, 2012), Chapter 2; Blackwell, *¡Chicana Power!*, 109–19; Agatha Beins, "Radical Others: Women of Color and Revolutionary Feminism," *Feminist Studies* 41, no. 1 (2015), 150–83; E. James West, "Black Power Print," *Radical Americas* 3, no. 1 (2018), https://www.scienceopen.com/document?vid=fa0c8946-050c-49df-a4d1-9b8221da0266.

at the start of this chapter, writing and publishing were an important part of radical politics in the 1960s and 1970s, so I turn to the activist and underground printscape, focusing specifically on periodicals, which constituted a significant output within social movements.[15]

This burgeoning alternative ephemeral print movement—New Left, third world, feminist and otherwise—occurred because activists needed to communicate with each other and because print provided an accessible and adaptable medium for addressing injustice and envisioning new worlds. In the mid-twentieth century, shifts in publishing technologies not only reconfigured the means of production so that people with little prior knowledge and few resources could create their own newsletters and newspapers, but also enabled transformations in the modes of production. Here, "means" refers to the tools and technologies used in periodical publishing, which includes everything from typewriters and typists, mimeograph machines, printing presses, paste used in laying out pages, and bulk mailing labels that made distribution less expensive. "Modes" refer to the practices and the politics that intersect with the means, such as how groups went about putting an issue together, the organizational structures they employed, and the ideals and values that informed their decisions about publishing.

Regarding means, prior to the mid-twentieth century, most periodical publishers used Linotype machines, which revolutionized the newspaper industry after they became common in the 1880s.[16] Although more economical and efficient than previous methods, it still required individuals to manually set lines of type ("line-o-type") to create molds that were then inked for printing. The 1960s, however, brought offset printing, so anyone with relatively cheap and accessible tools like pens, pencils, paper, scissors, rubber cement, and perhaps a ruler if they wanted straight lines could produce a newspaper.[17] One simply designed the pages—with content drawn, typed, pasted on—and sent them to the printer who would photograph the sheet to produce a metal plate that then was inked and "pressed" to make copies. It took only a few hundred dollars to create a few thousand copies of a 16-page tabloid in the 1960s.[18] Even cheaper than offset printing, and allowing groups to bypass a potentially hostile, censor-prone printer, was the mimeograph machine, which could be purchased for

---

[15] The term "printscape" is inspired by Arjun Appadurai's use of "scapes" to describe different aspects of production and circulation within globalization. Arjun Appadurai, "Disjuncture and Difference in the Global Cultural Economy," *Theory, Culture & Society* 7, no. 2–3 (1990), 295–310. On 1960s print culture, see John McMillian, *Smoking Typewriters: The Sixties Underground Press and the Rise of Alternative Media in America* (New York: Oxford University Press, 2014), introduction.

[16] John Hendel, "Celebrating Linotype, 125 Years since Its Debut," *Atlantic*, May 20, 2011, https://www.theatlantic.com/technology/archive/2011/05/celebrating-linotype-125-years-since-its-debut/238968/; see also Rudolph J. Bodmer, *The Book of Wonders* (New York: Presbrey Syndicate, 1915), 569–74, https://archive.org/details/bookofwondersgiv00bodmiala/page/n10/mode/2up.

[17] Matthew T. Pifer, *Dissent and the Dynamics of Cultural Change: Lessons from the Underground* (New York: Routledge, 2020), 6.

[18] McMillan, *Smoking Typewriters*, 7; see also Junko Onosaka, *Feminist Revolution in Literacy: Women's Bookstores in the United States* (New York: Routledge, 2006), 15.

around $550 in the early 1970s ($3700 in 2022 dollars).[19] These changes didn't just enable more groups to publish. Publishing also became less expensive, which facilitated practices like selling copies on a sliding scale and providing issues at no cost to people who were incarcerated or unable to pay.[20]

Means and modes of production inevitably intertwined as technology democratized access to the tools. The mimeo machine enabled self-publishing, and the lower cost of offset printing led to an increase in printers and presses, including many explicitly progressive ones created to serve social movements.[21] As writers, editors, and activists gained more control over the means, they could cultivate modes of reporting and writing that embodied their politics. For example, the Black Panthers saw their publishing as "a process of community building," structuring the editorial work as collaborative and designing it to empower "people with little or no journalism background" (e.g., students and incarcerated people) to contribute to their newspaper.[22] Alternative and underground media thus provided a way for people to speak back to and question the status quo—in the media industry and in politics—through the content of their publications and in their publishing practices.[23]

Although just a snapshot of the alternative printscape in the 1960s, I offer a few examples to illustrate the range of periodicals that appeared during this decade. Dense urban cities and large university campuses shouted disproportionately loudly amid the cacophony, but underground periodicals popped up throughout the country. *The Village Voice*, the *Realist*, and *Mad* magazine appeared in New York City in the 1950s, and the 1960s turned up the volume with rags like the *L.A. Free Press* (Los Angeles), *Berkeley Barb* (Berkeley), *Kaleidoscope* (Milwaukee), the *Great Speckled Bird* (Atlanta), *Capital East*

---

[19] The *Valley Women's Center* Newsletter (Northampton, MA) published an announcement in May 1972 that reads, "The VWC has received a grant from the University Christian Movement for half the price of a new mimeo machine (obviously and desperately needed). We need contributions to raise matching funds (up to $136)" (page 4). If $136 is half of the grant, which covers half the cost of a mimeo machine, the machine would cost about $550.

[20] *Female Liberation* Newsletter from Cambridge, MA, did not charge for their newsletter until April 1972, which was about 18 months after they began publishing (editorial announcement, page 1); *Sister* from Los Angeles offered "free issues on request to women in prison, and... single copies to women who can't afford to buy it" ("The State of Sister," *Sister*, December-January 1987, 15); and the Third World Women's Alliance offered free subscriptions to "brothers and sisters that are incarcerated behind prison walls" ("Note to Readers... " *Triple Jeopardy*, September-October 1972, 2).

[21] Lincoln Cushing, "Red in Black and White: The New Left Printing Renaissance of the 1960s—and Beyond," in *Peace Press Graphics 1967-1987: Art in the Pursuit of Social Change*, eds. Ilee Kaplan and Carol A. Wells (Long Beach: University Art Museum, California State University, 2011); Julie R. Enszer, *The Whole Naked Truth of Our Lives: Lesbian-Feminist Print Culture from 1969 through 1980*, PhD dissertation (University of Maryland, 2013).

[22] Rhodes, *Framing the Black Panthers*, 105. On alternative media as a practice of participatory democracy and prefigurative politics, see McMillan, *Smoking Typewriters*, Chapter 6; Chris Atton, *Alternative Media* (Thousand Oaks, CA: SAGE, 2002); Tony Harcup, "Alternative Journalism as Active Citizenship," in his *Alternative Journalism, Alternative Voices* (New York: Routledge, 2013), 128-43.

[23] The connection between disruption of mainstream printing conventions, freedom of/for the press, and the mimeograph machine extended to literary culture, as well (Chelsea Jennings, "Pirating Pound: Drafts & Fragments in 1960s Mimeograph Culture," *Journal of Modern Literature* 40, no. 1 [2016], 88-108).

Gazette (Washington, DC), and *Rat* (New York City), to name a few.[24] Social-movement groups offered a more explicitly politicized approach to publishing, using newsletters and newspapers as part of their activist repertoire. From Oakland, California, the Black Panthers put out their newspaper of the same name as well as their newsletter *Black Power!*, and the NAACP's *The Crisis* first appeared in 1909 and continues as an online platform today.[25] Chicano activist groups published, as well: the Brown Berets in Los Angeles, the Black Berets in Albuquerque, and the Young Lords put out, respectively, *La Causa*, *Venceremos*, and *Palante*;[26] the Mexican-American Liberation Committee in Tucson published *¡Coraje!*; and *El Grito del Norte*—based in Española, a small city in northern New Mexico—served as a more general movement newspaper.[27] Further expanding the scope of activism in print, *Akwesasne Notes* was first published in 1968 in upstate New York by a group of Mohawk people to advocate for indigenous rights, with the Los Angeles-based *Gidra* appearing the following year as a platform for issues and politics relevant to Asian Americans.

These newspapers and tabloids were created for a broad activist public while others were designed specifically for the group's own members. John McMillian recounts this anecdote from someone visiting the national SDS (Students for a Democratic Society) office in Chicago: the space was "something between a newsroom and a flophouse, drawing attention to 'an unmade cot, several laundry bags, a jar of instant coffee, and a half-eaten chocolate bar.' But one artifact, above all, caught his attention. Taped to one of the walls was a model drawing of a mimeograph machine; just beneath it, someone had written the words, 'Our Founder.'"[28] I'm not sure this label is an overstatement. The mimeograph machine supported project-specific serials for SDS like the *Peace and Research Action Project Newsletter* and the *Vietnam Summer Newsletter*, as well as more general publications such as *Albatross* (published by the Swarthmore, PA, chapter) and the *Membership Bulletin* and *Discussion Bulletin* (put out by the National Council) that coalesced into *SDS Bulletin*. The centrality of these more informal movement periodicals is evident in a 1972 editorial note in *Female Liberation Newsletter* (Cambridge, MA), about a year and a half after they started publishing it: "Our mimeograph has run off more than 1,000,000 sheets of paper. We hit a million on Friday, Feb. 11. No small part of this million comes from the Newsletter. In fact, the Newsletter accounts for about 5,000 sheets a week."[29] This statistic translates into over 12,800 mimeographed sheets

---

[24] "Underground/Alternative Newspapers History and Geography" offers an exciting catalog of these publications across space and time (https://depts.washington.edu/moves/altnews_intro.shtml). See also Lauren Kessler, *The Dissident Press: Alternative Journalism in American History* (Thousand Oaks, CA: SAGE, 1984); Laurence Leamer, *The Paper Revolutionaries: The Rise of the Underground Press* (New York: Simon & Schuster, 1972). For a digital archive of the *Realist*, see http://www.ep.tc/realist/.

[25] On the Black Power press, see West, "Black Power Print."

[26] "Remembering Rito Canales and Antonio Cordova of the Black Berets of Albuquerque," *Siglo de Lucha*, March 3, 2017, https://siglodelucha.wordpress.com/2017/03/03/remembering-rito-canales-and-antonio-cordova-of-the-black-berets-of-albuquerque/; issues of *Palante* are available online: https://www.marxists.org/history/erol/periodicals/palante/index.htm.

[27] For a list of Chicano student periodicals in the 1960s and 1970s, see Harry L. Simón Salazar, "An Overview of Chicana/o Student Newspapers," 2017, http://www.qvole.org/wp/la-causa/chicanaostudentnews/.

[28] Quoted in McMillian, *Smoking Typewriters*, 213.

[29] Announcement, *FLN*, February 21, 1972, 4.

per week and includes usage by other local feminist and activist groups, indicating the extent to which mimeographing catalyzed and fed movement activities.

Alternative and underground publishing provided women with models to emulate and avoid. Setting a tone and style that many feminists periodicals would adopt in some form, this dissident press exemplified characteristics of new journalism, challenging norms in the popular press about what counted as newsworthy and how these topics could or should be covered. The Michigan State University *Paper* and the University of Iowa's *Iowa Defender*, for example, formed to illuminate and critique local and national politics that the official campus papers, *State News* and *Daily Iowan* respectively, shied away from. In their journalistic agendas, these dissidents blended conventional reporting with an eclectic mix of unconventional and often raunchy breaches of decorum, filling their pages with "demonstration scorecards, exposés of the insidious tentacles of foreign and domestic imperialism, caricatures of official buffoonery both local and national, denunciations of drug laws, true tales of military insubordination, and long tomes of righteous doctrine."[30] In other words, contributions rarely strove for neutrality or objectivity, treating professional journalistic norms and civility as optional. Supporting these publishing practices, the Liberation News Service (LNS) and Underground Press Syndicate (UPS) served as news clearinghouses and regularly mailed packets of articles to subscribers. Although leaders of the LNS claimed independence from any particular political stance or party, it would not be mistaken for the more conventional journalism from news resources like the Associated Press or Reuters. As LNS co-founder Ray Mungo stated, "We'd print any kind of crazy shit that anybody sent us."[31]

Hands-on experience with the modes and means of periodical production became part of women's feminist and activist training. When working with the Southern Christian Leadership Conference, Jo Freeman was heavily involved in its information infrastructure. "Until you've written out 300 mass-meeting leaflets by hand," she explains, "you don't know how valuable [the mimeo machine] was to any project director."[32] Black Power activists Kathleen Cleaver, JoNina Abron, and Elaine Brown were involved in publishing *Black Panther*, with Abron eventually serving as an editor from 1978 to 1980.[33] And Elizabeth "Betita" Martinez, who co-founded *El Grito del Norte*, ensured that women regularly had opportunities to contribute as writers, artists, photographers, and editors.[34] The proliferation of student activist groups on university campuses also created opportunities for women to gain publishing experience, which

---

[30] Harvey Wasserman, "The Joy of *Liberation News Service*," *Serials Review* 16, no. 1 (1990), 51.
[31] Quoted in McMillan, *Smoking Typewriters*, 146.
[32] Jo Freeman, "On the Origins of the Women's Liberation Movement from a Strictly Personal Perspective," in *The Feminist Memoir Project: Voices from Women's Liberation*, eds. Rachel Blau DuPlessis and Ann Snitow (New Brunswick, NJ: Rutgers University Press), 174.
[33] Rhodes, *Framing the Black Panthers*, 104–5.
[34] Dennis López, "*El Grito del Norte*, Chicana/o Print Culture, and the Politics of Anti-Imperialism," *Science & Society* 79, no. 4 (2015), 538; see also Juan Gómez-Quiñones and Irene Vásquez, *Making Aztlán: Ideology and Culture of the Chicana and Chicano Movement, 1966–1977* (Albuquerque: University of New Mexico Press, 2004), 85.

Lori Mejia Briscoe and Alexandrina Esparza did as editors, respectively, for *Adelante* (University of California, Riverside) and *El Machete* (San Jose State).[35]

Along with the empowerment women experienced as activists and media makers, they grappled with sexism and misogyny in content and modes of production. Mainstream media did little—if anything—to address gender inequities within their industry: articles and advertising reinforced a hierarchical gender binary through practices such as sex-segregated want ads and hiring practices that left women on the sidelines.[36] *Distaff*, a New Orleans–based feminist newspaper regularly noted these journalistic failures in print, radio, and television. Referring to the now-defunct daily paper the *States-Item*, a 1973 editorial told readers that "in reply to DISTAFF's charge that he does not take women athletes seriously, [sports reporter Nat Belloni] admitted in a July 27 column that he is a 'male chauvinist' and called the women's liberation cause 'stupidity.'"[37] And even putatively supportive coverage fell short. A *New York Times* article on the 1968 Miss America Protest was placed in the Style section, suggesting it was not real news; contextualizing the newspaper's message about where the women's liberation movement belonged, Dow notes that "the protesters' analysis of the political ills that the pageant symbolized received much less attention than the spectacle of the protest itself... The *Times*'s coverage did little to give the protest and its participants political credibility."[38] Women took action to challenge these conventions, including lawsuits and sit-ins that targeted sexism in the *Ladies Home Journal*, *Newsweek*, the *Washington Post*, and the *San Francisco Chronicle*.[39]

Although often more sympathetic to the dynamics of sexism and women's liberation, the underground and alternative press nonetheless replicated patterns in mainstream media by objectifying women; marginalizing, ridiculing, and erasing gender as a site of oppression; and centralizing publishing power in the hands of men. Judy Stewart, who was staff for the San Francisco *Oracle*, recounts, "Two times out of three a cartoon of a naked woman appeared on the [Berkeley] *Barb*'s front cover, in accordance with [editor] Max's mantra, 'Tits Above the Fold. It's how ya sell papers.'"[40] The *Oracle* was anything but unique, likely an effect of the overwhelming dominance of white men in

---

[35] Michael Soldatenko, *Chicano Studies: The Genesis of a Discipline* (Tucson: University of Arizona Press, 2009), 132.

[36] See letter from Ellen Lynch to *Female Liberation Newsletter*, December 16, 1971, 1–2; "A New Year: LWL Reorganizes," *Lancaster Women's Liberation*, September 1973, 3; Daphne Spain, "Women's Rights and Gendered Spaces in 1970s Boston," *Frontiers* 32, no. 1 (2011): 154, 158; "Highlights," *National Organization for Women*, https://now.org/about/history/highlights/.

[37] "Over the Pork Barrell," *Distaff*, August 1973, 8. The Tulane University Library has digitized the full run of *Distaff*, which can be accessed here: https://digitallibrary.tulane.edu/islandora/object/tulane:distaff.

[38] Bonnie J. Dow, *Watching Women's Liberation, 1970: Feminism's Pivotal Year on the Network News* (Urbana: University of Illinois Press, 2017), 33; Dow's analysis continues through page 37.

[39] Dow, *Watching Women's Liberation*.

[40] "Above the fold" refers to the portion of the front page that was visible when an issue was placed in a newspaper vending machine or rack, or simply folded on a counter in a newsstand. Judy Gumbo Albert, "Tits above the Fold," paper presented at "A Revolutionary Moment: Women's Liberation in the Late 1960s and early 1970s," Boston University, March 27–29, 2014, https://www.bu.edu/wgs/files/2013/10/Albert-Tits-Above-the-Fold.pdf.

editorial and staff positions.⁴¹ Also indicating contradictions between revolutionary ideals and revolutionary practices, the dissident press gave feminism little credence. Marilyn Webb (who worked on the long-running Washington, DC, feminist newspaper *off our backs*), describes her time at the *Guardian*, a self-described "organ of the New Left." She explains, "As radical as it supposedly was, the newspaper had an unconscious blackout on feminist news. While demonstrations might be newsworthy, the editors did not consider issues about women—like news on abortion counseling or issues of consciousness-raising—important enough to write about."⁴² And an open letter to the New Left magazine *Ramparts* in response to their "Woman Power" article offers a litany of concerns: it was "condescending" and "patronizing," presented women's activism as "a fashion report," and depicted women as "psycho-physiologically different from, and inferior to men."⁴³ Rhodes, moreover, notes that in *Black Panther*, although women were represented as part of the movement, its content "tended to argue for an assertion of masculine authority and a sexual division of labor," which constructed men as the real revolutionaries.⁴⁴

Responding to chauvinism and male dominance in 1960s activist print culture, women not only formed separate feminist periodicals but also attempted change from within. They voiced their demands on a national scale, proposing a resolution at the July 1969 Underground Press Syndicate conference:

> It is the sense of this conference that the underground press must undergo revolutionary changes in its relationship to and projection of women. Therefore we propose the following:
> 1. That male supremacy and chauvinism be eliminated from the contents of the underground papers. For example, papers should stop accepting commercial advertising that uses women's bodies to sell records and other products, and advertisements for sex, since the use of sex as a commodity specifically oppresses women in this country. Also, women's bodies should not be exploited in the papers for the purpose of increasing circulation.
> 2. That papers make a particular effort to publish material on women's oppression and liberation with the entire contents of the paper.
> 3. That women have a full role in all the functions of the staffs of underground papers.⁴⁵

---

⁴¹ Sinead McEneaney, "Sex and the Radical Imagination in the *Berkeley Barb* and the San Francisco *Oracle*," *Radical Americas* 3, no. 1 (2018), https://www.scienceopen.com/document?vid=bb3dcdc4-981b-4231-af9e-9ffe6aff80f2; McMillan, *Smoking Typewriters*, 148.

⁴² Marilyn S. Webb, "*oob* and the Feminist Dream," *In Insider Histories of the Vietnam Era Underground Press, Part 1*, ed. Ken Wachsberger (East Lansing: Michigan State University Press, 2011), 189.

⁴³ Lynn Piartney, "A Letter to the Editor of Ramparts Magazine," in *Notes from the First Year* (New York: Redstockings, 1968), 22–3.

⁴⁴ Jane Rhodes, "*The Black Panther* Newspaper: Standard-Bearer for Modern Black Nationalism," *Media History* 7, no. 2 (2001), 156.

⁴⁵ Quoted in Teresa Youngblood, "Not Our Newspapers: Women and the Underground Press, 1967–1970," MA Thesis (Florida State University, 2004), 8; see also McMillian, *Smoking Typewriters*, 122.

This statement focuses on the culture and structures of publishing, but women's activism also involved attempts to transform the *modes* of production by controlling the *means* of production. In October 1970 feminists took over the *Great Speckled Bird* for one issue; in it Becky Hamilton wrote an editorial explaining why:

> The men were editors and business people (i.e., circulation, keeping the books, understanding the finances). That left typing for women. Women fought for control of layout, which was the one creative outlet allowed to women ... Out of those first women's [caucus] meetings (not at all confined to *Bird* women) came an idea for a 'women's issue' of the *Bird*. We would prove ourselves to the men. We would write, type, layout—everything.[46]

This occurred with the *L.A. Free Press*, as well, when women gained editorial control for an August 1970 issue. Such actions offered a brief reprieve from gendered hierarchies, but there was at least one longer-term feminist occupation: the takeover of *Rat*, a New York City underground newspaper. In January 1970 a coalition of women ousted its editors and writers and published it as a feminist newspaper for a little more than a year. They put out their first issue in February with triumphant celebrations of women power and scathing indictments of the "counterfeit Left" and their print culture.[47]

Although feminists did not stop pushing back against inequities in the press, they built their own print culture, which carried the influences of radical publishing while also attempting to move beyond its hierarchical, biased practices in modes of production and representation. Feminist presses, periodicals, writing collectives, bookstores, poetry readings, books and anthologies, and distributors all emerged with pointed and passionate energy during the 1970s, and all were shaped by the political, media, and technological context of the radical press.[48] This comes through clearly in the fact that one of the first large purchases by DC Women's Liberation in 1969 was a mimeograph machine, which Kate Adams describes as a "symbol of what would be called the 'Women in Print' movement."[49] And, in many ways, in their modes of production feminists continued the prefigurative political legacies of other radical

---

[46] "Even a Woman Can Do It: Bird Women's Caucus," *Great Speckled Bird* October 11, 1970, 3.

[47] Robin Morgan, "Goodbye to All That," *Rat* February 9-23, 1970, 7. See also Morgan's recollections in *The Word of a Woman: Feminist Dispatches, 1968-1992* (New York: W.W. Norton & Company, 1992), 49-57.

[48] Hogan, *Feminist Bookstore Movement*; Cecilia Konchar Farr and Jaime Harker, eds., *Outrageous, Dangerous and Unassimilable: Experimentation and Second Wave Feminist Literature* (Urbana: University of Illinois Press, 2018); Julie R. Enszer, "Lavender Press, Womanpress, and Metis Press: Lesbian-Feminist Writers and Publishers in Chicago During the 1970s," *Bibliologia* 10 (2015), 71-83; Barb and Joan, "The Invisible Lesbian Feminist Printer," *off our backs* (September 30, 1982), 26; Jaime Harker, *The Lesbian South: Southern Feminists, the Women in Print Movement, and the Queer Literary Canon* (Chapel Hill: University of North Carolina Press, 2018); Travis, "Women in Print Movement"; Amy Farrell, *Yours in Sisterhood: Ms. Magazine and the Promise of Popular Feminism* (Chapel Hill: University of North Carolina Press, 1998).

[49] Adams, "Built Out of Books," 116.

print cultures. Feminists published their activism and published *as* activism, working collectively, challenging the reader/writer, expert/amateur, public/private binaries, and blurring the lines between political, cultural, professional, and personal.[50] Mother Jones Press, based in Northampton, MA, explained,

> We wanted to provide printing to women's groups and community groups at a cost they could afford. We wanted to teach women (starting with ourselves) printing skills which they usually don't have an opportunity to learn. And we wanted to do this by working in a collective, non-hierarchical way. With each of us learning all the various processes involved in printing.[51]

These groups thus attempted to realize the liberated world they envisioned in their periodicals (and other writing), part of which involved pushing back against the status quo not just in mainstream media and politics but, as I elaborated above, also in radical media and politics. At the same time, constructing US feminism as only or primarily a rejection of chauvinistic male political spheres reduces and oversimplifies the scope of the women's liberation movement, as I elaborate below.

Feminist Historiography Redux

In *Feminist Literacies, 1968–75*, Kathryn Thoms Flannery's chapter about 1970s feminist periodicals situates their growth as a response to "male dominance" in the mainstream and alternative media industries, pointing to feminist excoriations of the underground press and movement publications for both their blatant and unstated chauvinism.[52] Affirming this view, *Ain't I a Woman?*, an Iowa City newspaper, calls out the "pig press" in an editorial in their second issue:

> Ain't I A Woman and many other publications by sisters around the country began as we felt a need for alternative media. We have to communicate without the constraints of the pig press where we've always had our page for recipes, fashions and advice on how to please a man.
>
> Working conditions in the pig media demand that any woman who works there must accept a male definition of what women are and should be. Women

---

[50] Springer, *Living for the Revolution*, 90–3; Agatha Beins, *Liberation in Print: Feminist Periodicals and Social Movement Identity* (Athens: University of Georgia Press, 2017), chapter 4; Jennifer Gilley, "Feminist Publishing/Publishing Feminism: Experimentation in Second Wave Book Publishing," in *This Book Is an Action: Feminist Print Culture and Activist Aesthetics*, eds. Jaime Harker and Cecilia Konchar Farr (Urbana: University of Illinois Press, 2016), 23–45; Michal Brody, ed., *Are We There Yet? A Continuing History of Lavender Woman, a Chicago Lesbian Newspaper, 1971–1976* (Iowa City: Aunt Lute, 1985); Stacey Young, *Changing the Wor(l)d: Discourse, Politics, and the Feminist Movement* (New York: Routledge, 1997), Chapter 2.
[51] "Mother Jones Press," *Valley Women's Center Newsletter*, May 1974, 3.
[52] Kathryn T. Flannery, *Feminist Literacies, 1968–1975* (Urbana: University of Illinois Press, 2005), 26–9.

who work as reporters work for the Man. Usually the man with the most contempt for women sits as their editor. Little wonder that the women survive by seeing themselves as exceptions.[53]

Primary and secondary sources like these point to the powerful feminist energy at that time and emphasize the significance of an autonomous print culture for women's liberation activists. It also binds mid-twentieth-century feminist publishing to a certain metanarrative of rejection and separatism, one that parallels historiography of the women's liberation movement more generally: in the United States sexism and misogyny pervaded public institutions and spaces, private spheres, and mainstream and progressive media, leading women to repudiate male dominance and form their own groups.

On the one hand, the creation of feminist publications, presses, distribution houses, conferences, bookstores, and other media services certainly resulted from the misogyny women experienced throughout publishing industries. Jaime Harker and Cecila Konchar Farr attribute the "explosion of women's presses across the country" to mainstream presses' refusal to print women's writing, which echoes the idea that publishing has historically been "a gentleman's profession."[54] Kristen Hogan shows that feminist bookstores and their networks aimed to serve "counter-capitalist revolutionary purposes" by making spaces for minoritized voices and bodies, in contrast to the publishing norms that accommodated literature only if it could be turned into profit.[55] And many within women's liberation refused interviews with male reporters, recognizing the barriers women encountered in the field of journalism and doubtful that men would be able to understand and fairly represent their concerns.[56] Ultimately, no part of the communications circuit—from the author to distributor to subscriber—was untouched by this revolution in print.[57]

On the other hand, this narrative tends to reinforce a linear history and a wave-based chronology, re-center certain urban spaces as activist hubs, reify white women and the New Left as the primary protagonists and antagonists, and locate feminism in its autonomous formations. Such a reject-and-separate framework oversimplifies feminism's heterogeneity, breadth, and depth, by narrowing who, what, and where

---

[53] Editorial, *Ain't I a Woman?* July 10, 1970, 8.

[54] Jaime Harker and Cecilia Konchar Farr, "Introduction: Outrageous, Dangerous, and Unassimilable: Writing the Women's Movement," in their *This Book Is an Action: Feminist Print Culture and Activist Aesthetics* (Urbana: University of Illinois Press, 2016), 5; Eileen Cadman, Gail Chester, and Agnes Pivot, *Rolling Our Own: Women as Printers, Distributors, and Publishers* (London: Minority Press Group, 1981), Chapter 2.

[55] Hogan, *Feminist Bookstore Movement*, 44.

[56] Jo Freeman, *The Politics of Women's Liberation* (New York: Longman, 1975), 113– 14; KNOW, Inc., a feminist news clearinghouse and distribution service launched in Pittsburgh in 1969, developed a list of reputable reporters in 1972 ("Reporters You Can Trust," March 13, 1972, folder 4, box 16, Women's Liberation Collection, 1959–2006, Sophia Smith Collection, Smith College, Northampton, MA).

[57] On the communications circuit, see Robert Darnton, "What Is the History of Books?" *Daedalus* 11, no. 3 (1982), 65–83.

"count" as feminism and as feminist.[58] In the spirit of loosening this framework, I pull some print culture threads: a closer look at feminism through publishing in the 1960s allows me to unsettle the movement's origin stories and ask historiographical questions about the archives in which we research and that we construct to tell these stories. It also creates the opportunity to question what falls within "feminist print culture," as well as how we construct relationships between primary sources and historiography.

Because historiography is so dependent on print, telling richer histories involves not only expanding our primary-source collections but also attending to the layers of an archive—both institutional collections and the body of sources we curate for a research project.[59] Documents reveal much in their explicit content, but many scholars (especially those studying subjugated peoples) have shown that other histories emerge through subtext and silence. Marisa Fuentes, for instance, lays bare the implications of using slaveholders' records to write histories of enslaved people, urging accountability and meta-analysis regarding our methodologies.[60] Her project, similar to many that interrogate the archive, focuses more on practices of reading and of constructing histories that extant sources fragment, misrepresent, and erase. Building on this literature, I integrate a book history methodology to examine how a text's path along a communications circuit—its creation, publication, distribution, preservation—is part of building an archive.

What does this mean for US feminism? As I discussed in the "Publishing Context" section above, women were putting their politics into print throughout the 1960s. Publications from New Left and third world revolutionary movements hold traces of what we might consider feminist energy in their content and labors of publishing. A focus on ephemera also indicates that many tracts circulated informally as mimeographed copies or were printed by a movement press as individual publications; some of these freestanding pieces also appeared in feminist periodicals or anthologies, but others remain accessible only in an archive or in periodicals that aren't categorized as feminist.[61] For example, Betty Christine Eng recalls that an important part of her political education involved reading position papers by Japanese American activist Pat Sumi that—to her knowledge—did not appear in more formally published texts.[62]

---

[58] Premilla Nadasen's work on welfare rights activism is one example of a study that positions feminist praxis in relation to a space not explicitly claiming this identity; see, for example, *Rethinking the Welfare Rights Movement* (New York: Routledge, 2012).

[59] Cait McKinney, *Information Activism: A Queer History of Lesbian Media Technologies* (Durham, NC: Duke University Press, 2020).

[60] Marisa J. Fuentes, *Dispossessed Lives: Enslaved Women, Violence, and the Archive* (Philadelphia: University of Pennsylvania Press, 2016).

[61] Some of the pieces in Robin Morgan's *Sisterhood Is Powerful: An Anthology of Writings from the Women's Liberation Movement* (New York: Vintage Books, 1970) and Toni Cade Bambara's *The Black Woman: An Anthology* (New York: New American Library, 1970) are reprints of this type, and a rich breadth of feminist ephemera is collected in Rosalyn Baxandall and Linda Gordon, eds., *Dear Sisters: Dispatches from the Women's Liberation Movement* (New York: Basic Books, 2000) more recently collected a rich breadth of feminist ephemera.

[62] Betty Christine Eng, "Becoming an Agent of Social Change: Stories of Sweatshops, Sweetshops, and Women's Social Activism," in *Personal—Passionate—Participatory Inquiry into Social Justice in Education*, eds. Ming Fang He and JoAnn Phillips (Charlotte, NC: Information Age Publishing, 2008), 251–52.

A closer look at the history surrounding the 1965 "Sex and Caste" memo by Casey Hayden and Mary King, two white women active in SNCC (Student Nonviolent Coordinating Committee), raises additional questions about social movement forms and formations. While reading Robin Morgan's introduction to *Sisterhood Is Powerful*, I noticed her cite Ruby Doris Smith Robinson as the author of a 1964 memorandum protesting women's treatment by SNCC men that shaped what Hayden and King circulated.[63] But there doesn't appear to be an extant copy of this memo, and secondary sources don't conclusively verify its existence. Carol Giardina, who was active in the Gainesville, FL, women's liberation movement and currently is a professor of history, mentions the 1964 strike and sit-in organized by SNCC women that supposedly occurred in conjunction with Robinson's memo but doesn't discuss the memo (she cites only "Sex and Caste").[64] Stanley Wise, a SNCC activist interviewed for a biography about Robinson, recounts the strikers' concerns about the way men objectified and sexualized them, which he says they expressed in "a memorandum of agreements that these were the kinds of activities that women would no longer tolerate in the organization—from anybody."[65] This statement, if it did exist, could be the one Morgan has in mind, but its link to "Sex and Caste" remains unclear. It is possible, as Winifred Breines elaborates, that different drafts of "Sex and Caste" circulated with an early version misattributed to Robinson.[66] Or perhaps another group of SNCC women led by Robinson *did* coauthor another memo. Regardless, Breines proposes that Morgan's representation of the memo reflects white women's desire to view this moment as one of "cross-racial sisterhood," suggesting that—for each of these accounts—memory's idiosyncrasies and an individual's own desires and investments reveal as much about the person offering it as it does about the story being told.[67]

My point here is not to determine a definitive truth about the memo or memos (if "truth" can ever be definitive), nor simply to argue that we need richer, more expansive archives (which we do), but to highlight the political and epistemological implications of the primary sources we consider and are able to consider when (re)constructing the past.[68] "Sex and Caste" has become canonical in most stories about US feminism because activists and historians have traced its path from SNCC mimeographs to its 1966 publication in the journal *Liberation* and through its widespread circulation. But

---

[63] Robin Morgan, "Introduction," in her *Sisterhood Is Powerful: An Anthology of Writings from the Women's Liberation Movement* (New York: Vintage Books, 1970), xxi.

[64] Carol Giardina, "The Making of a Modern Feminist Vanguard, 1964–1973: Southern Women Whose Leadership Shaped the Movement and the Nation—A Synthetic Analysis," *Journal of Southern History* 85, no. 3 (2019), 611–52; see also Margaret Ripley Wolfe, *Daughters of Canaan: A Saga of Southern Women* (Lexington: University Press of Kentucky, 1995), 195.

[65] Quoted in Cynthia Griggs Fleming, *Soon We Will Not Cry: The Liberation of Ruby Doris Smith Robinson* (Lanham, MD: Rowman & Littlefield, 1998), 151–52.

[66] Breines, *Trouble between Us*, 29.

[67] Ibid.

[68] Many have written about the politics of archiving; on the intersections of feminism and archiving see Kate Eichhorn, *The Archival Turn in Feminism: Outrage in Order* (Philadelphia: Temple University Press, 2013) and Kelly Wooten and Liz Bly, eds., *Make Your Own History: Documenting Feminist and Queer Activism in the 21st Century* (Sacramento, CA: Litwin Books, 2012).

what about other ephemera that haven't registered at the same scale? If Robinson had authored or coauthored a separate memo how and why did its communications circuit become so different from "Sex and Caste"? Questions such as these are useful not only because of the research paths that open but also because they invite us to rethink how a text's material and discursive history is intertwined with the broader history being told. Specifically, the uncertain history of "Sex and Caste" points to a broader constellation of feminist origins than the two white women whose connection to this text has been cemented, thus disrupting the standard periodization of US feminism and the process by which history concentrates around a few agents, moments, locations, and texts.

The "Sex and Caste" example additionally illustrates the imbrication of feminism's racial politics in the archives we construct. Here I join the vibrant field of critiques and renarrations that name and trouble the conflation of "white" and "feminism."[69] Many also show that by shifting the chronology—regarding origins and primary source selections—we might see feminism as an intersectional movement throughout its history.[70] The inextricability of gender, race, sexuality, and class shaped women's activism in civil rights, New Left, and third world liberation movements—as well as prior to the mid-twentieth century.[71] Women of color performed their politics in publications like *El Grito del Norte*, *The Black Panther*, and *Gidra*, so it becomes possible to read these periodicals—and their modes of production—as sites where a feminist praxis or ethic existed. And when women did organize separately, race and class did not disappear, as indicated by the Third World Women's Alliance's newspaper: its name *Triple Jeopardy* refers to the intersections of oppressive forces, which is made explicit in the tag line, "racism, imperialism, sexism," appearing on the cover of each

---

[69] I offer just a small slice of the literature here: Nancy Hewitt, ed., *No Permanent Waves: Recasting Histories of U.S. Feminism* (New Brunswick, NJ: Rutgers University Press, 2010); Stephanie Gilmore, ed., *Groundswell: Historical Perspectives on Second-Wave Feminism in the United States* (Urbana: University of Illinois Press, 2008); Kathleen A. Laughlin, Julie Gallagher, Dorothy Sue Cobble, Eileen Boris, Premilla Nadasen, Stephanie Gilmore, and Leandra Zarnow, "Is It Time to Jump Ship? Historians Rethink the Waves Metaphor," *Feminist Formations* 22, no. 1 (2010), 76–135; Andrea Smith, "Indigenous Feminism without Apology," in *Unsettling Ourselves: Reflections and Resources for Deconstructing Colonial Mentality*, ed. the Unsettling Minnesota Collective (Minneapolis: University of Minnesota, 2009), 158–60, https://unsettlingminnesota.files.wordpress.com/2009/11/um_sourcebook_jan10_revision.pdf; Victoria Browne, *Feminism, Time, and Nonlinear History* (New York: Palgrave Macmillan, 2014).

[70] Intersectionality refers to the social, economic, and political ways in which identity-based systems of oppression and privilege connect, overlap, and influence one another and has been central to much feminist theorizing and praxis. See, for example, Kimberlé Crenshaw, "Mapping the Margins Intersectionality, Identity Politics, and Violence against Women of Color," *Stanford Law Review* 43, no. 6 (1991), 1241–99; Leslie McCall, "The Complexity of Intersectionality," *Signs* 30, no. 3 (2005), 1771–1800; Vivian May, *Pursuing Intersectionality, Unsettling Dominant Imaginaries* (New York: Routledge, 2015).

[71] See, for example, Angela Davis, *Women, Race, and Class* (New York: Vintage, 1983); Dorceta E. Taylor, "American Environmentalism: The Role of Race, Class and Gender in Shaping Activism 1820–1995," *Race, Gender & Class* 5, no. 1 (1997), 16–62; Cheryl Suzack, Shari M. Hundorf, Jeanne Perreault, and Jean Bartman, eds., *Indigenous Women and Feminism: Politics, Activism, Culture* (Vancouver: University of British Columbia Press, 2010).

issue. Integrating these sources into US feminist historiography thus demands that we contend with the movement through a framework that presumes intersectionality, rather than first situating the origins of our research and the movement with white women and their writings—and then adding women of color, lesbians, poor women, and others afterward.

Refracting feminism through book history as I've done also requires caution. My citation practice in this essay imparts a feminist presence to texts not usually perceived as sites of feminism or feminist print culture. Diversifying and complicating US feminism in this way must be accountable to the fact that many women involved in activist movements in the 1960s and beyond did not identify with feminism, whether or not they explicitly worked to challenge patriarchal hegemonies. I resist simply adding adjectives—black feminist, Chicana feminist, lesbian feminist, socialist feminist—to address this concern. Although it allows activists to identify with, yet also differentiate themselves from, "feminism" as a generic term, it can reaffirm the presumption that "feminism" means "white feminism."[72] As a result, I use "feminist" with a commitment to be mindful about those who might reject the label, to continually unsettle the terrain of writing, editing, and publishing that has enacted feminism, and to create space in the archive for "feminist" to be performed without fixing it to someone as an identity.[73]

Investigating social movements through book history, as I argue, highlights the acts and materials of writing, editing, and publishing as integral to social movement formation. The San Diego–based *Feminist Bulletin*'s "State of the Press—1976" explains, "Feminist publishing is our own tool, to use and develop, or let grow rusty from neglect… It is one of our few guarantees of free expression, for a virtually uncooptable medium."[74] And in an open letter, KNOW, Inc. described itself as a group of "feminists who believed that you can't have a revolution without a press and went out and bought one."[75] In other words, means and modes of publishing are not separate from the political visions that are published, so a text and its communications circuit become the evidence of activism, contributing to the definition of who and what belong within a social movement. I therefore offer this method as one with relevance beyond feminism, encouraging us to account for and be accountable to the entanglement of materials and ideas construing any historical record along with interpretations and re-presentations of the stories it contains.

---

[72] See, for example, Alma M. García, ed., *Chicana Feminist Thought: Basic Writings* (New York: Routledge, 1997); Julie R. Enszer and Agatha Beins, "Inter- and Trans-national Feminist Theory and Practice in *Triple Jeopardy* and *Conditions*," *Women's Studies: An Inter-disciplinary Journal* 41, no. 1 (2018), 29.

[73] For a beautiful exploration of this tension in feminism, see Jessica Nydia Pabón-Colón, *Graffiti Grrlz: Performing Feminism in the Hip Hop Diaspora* (New York: New York University Press, 2018), Chapter 2.

[74] Lisa Cobbs, "State of the Press—1976," 18.

[75] KNOW, Inc., "To Those Who Wonder," July 1971, Feminist Resources Collection, Department of Archives and Special Collections, University Library, California State University, Dominguez Hills (uncataloged as of 2008).

4

The Instant Classic in the Age of Digital Print Culture: Claude McKay's *Romance in Marseille*

Gary Edward Holcomb

The first four chapters of Claude McKay's *c.* 1929–33 Harlem Renaissance novel *Romance in Marseille*, published by Penguin Classics in 2020, depict a kind of modern middle passage volte-face and its simultaneously surprising and understandable consequences. Self-described "dancing fool" Lafala has become the laughingstock of quayside Marseille after Aslima, a Moroccan prostitute he'd lavished his affection on, boosts all his francs.[1] Down and out and seeking escape, Lafala contrives the curious solution to his troubles of stowing away on a steamer bound for New York. Set in the "time of universal excitement" (4) over the Back to Africa movement, the image of an African modern concealing himself in the bowels of a ship to hitch a ride across the Atlantic into the heart of Whiteness sets in reverse the history of the transatlantic slave trade.

The freedom dream of modern Black movement, however, is exposed as an illusion. Lafala is discovered and, enduring torture evocative of the slave ship, locked in a freezing water closet for the rest of the voyage. The narrative isn't finished with its mordant commentary on being Black in the modern world, however, as on reaching landfall the French shipping line's doctors ascertain that the undocumented immigrant has incurred frostbite in both legs. Lafala is then compelled to rehearse the narrative of institutionalized captivity and trauma—he is rushed to the Ellis Island surgical hospital where, without his consent, his limbs are amputated below the knees.

When the stowaway surprisingly wins a large settlement from the negligent shipping company, *Romance in Marseille* charts the media "blast," depicting how Black Manhattan yellow journalists vie to exploit the story: "*The Bellows of the Belt* shouted: AFRICAN DAMAGED FIFTY THOUSAND DOLLARS" and, not to be outdone, the "*United Negro*... ran: AFRICAN LEGS BRING ONE HUNDRED THOUSAND DOLLARS" (18–19). Throwing weight on the modifier *literary*, the narrative voice

---

[1] Claude McKay, *Romance in Marseille*, eds. Gary Edward Holcomb and William J. Maxwell (New York: Penguin, 2020), 13. Citations of page numbers from *Romance in Marseille* will appear parenthetically throughout.

witheringly remarks: "The African had conquered Aframerica with a whoop. Very literary were the days that ensued for Lafala" (19).

Upon its February 11, 2020 publication, the very institution that *Romance in Marseille* mocks in its opening chapters, the national press, waged a welcome that McKay could have only dreamt of in his own time. "A Book So Far Ahead of Its Time, It Took 87 Years to Find a Publisher" introduced a notion that in a New York minute would go viral.[2] Critics near universally would agree that *Romance in Marseille* is, as the *New York Times* headline states, "ahead of its time." Subsequent print and digital press sustained the prophetic trope, typified by the online version of the headline of *The Washington Post* review: "Claude McKay abandoned 'Romance in Marseille' because it was too daring. He was just ahead of his time."[3] The Pulitzer-Prize winning critic Michael Dirda's declaration that *Romance* is a work that reflects present-day social and political awakening propels the Great Depression-period novel instantly into contemporary discourses: "Today *Romance in Marseille* seems less shocking than strikingly woke, given that its themes include disability, the full spectrum of sexual preference, radical politics and the subtleties of racial identity."[4]

New York magazine writer Molly Young's review, titled "The Best New Novel Was Written 90 Years Ago," also articulates the idea of the text finally finding its moment. The *New York* magazine Vulture.com website article expresses a kind of millennial's hipster irony in response to so queer, Black, differently abled, and obscure a novel appearing so well into the twenty-first century. "If you skipped the introduction and surrendered access to Google, you could easily mistake it for a novel written last year," says Young, unquestionably if understandably overstating its presentness.[5] "It's about bodies, disability, sex, Islam, slavery, and capital. There are lesbians. There is gender-bending. There is socialism."[6] Nearly ninety years after its failure to reach a readership of its own time, *Romance in Marseille* has become the model (Black) modernist text, as the novel exists in two epochs: the period when McKay labored on it and it left the publishing industry cold; and the present, wherein it speaks warmly to contemporary readers.

The reviews articulate among the most revolutionary features of the text: that McKay portrays sexually divergent life on the Marseille Quayside as utterly commonplace. While the queer cast includes the much-liked longshoreman Big Blonde, the male hustler Petit Frère, and Aslima's rival among the Vieux Port sex workers, La Fleur Noire, among the most thought-provoking aspects of the text's queerness is that the narrative doesn't treat the existence of same-sex folk as anomalous. Just as groundbreaking, while in the presence of the gay characters such recognizably straight characters as the Black

---

[2] Talya Zax, "A Book So Far Ahead of Its Time, It Took 87 Years to Find a Publisher," *New York Times* (February 5, 2020). Online.

[3] Michael Dirda, "Claude McKay abandoned 'Romance in Marseille' because it was too daring. He was just ahead of his time," *Washington Post* (February 5, 2020). Online.

[4] Ibid.

[5] Molly Young, "The Best New Novel Was Written 90 Years Ago," *New York* (February 6, 2020). Online.

[6] Ibid.

sailor Babel veer queer, the text suggesting uncommonly contemporary ideas about sexual fluidity—thereby parading, as the Lambda Literary site would note, *Romance*'s "pansexual" content.[7]

Romance in Marseille's popular reception exemplifies the sundry surprising and often riotous demands that we place on those objects circulating the compound cultures of print today. The text exists simultaneously both there and here—acknowledging that *there* is an imaginary if sketchy notion of the past, and *here* is an idea of a present that shifts so swiftly that the meaning changes almost hourly. The capitalist enterprise of contemporary print culture plunges the literary artifact into a dehistoricized place where the signposts leading from past to present are distorted, where the past becomes a kind of version of the present, and the present a kind of repaired past, in incessant need of regular updating.[8]

Romance in fact had lost its archival virtue well in advance of its successful media moment. Transcribing the typescript, correcting errors, and speculating on McKay's occasional puzzling phrasings were all important but familiar components in preparing this unpublished text for current readers. But what truly fashioned the book for twenty-first-century reading was supplementing the primary text with critical materials. In other words, it isn't that William J. Maxwell and I published an altered version of the original text. In fact, our corrections were minimal. By contextualizing the manuscript's historical and cultural significance with our supplementary materials, however, my collaborator and I necessarily translated the raw artifact for contemporary readers. No pure interwar-period *Romance in Marseille* now exists.

Not that a chaste original ever did, given the extratextual correspondence between McKay and publishers, editors, literary agents, critics, and kibitzers that orbited and by turns inflected the original drafting. Because it is more the consequence of mixology—I intentionally mean to use the cocktail trope—than the dissemination of archeological purity, the *Romance in Marseille* that is now in print (by which we should understand to mean both materially and digitally[9]) may be understood to be, to exercise two much-used expressions, a *contemporary classic*, even an *instant classic*, if a unique one. *Romance* is an exceptional specimen of a classic because it redefines the term, thereby stimulating a new way of thinking about print culture. One might say that our job was helping this sleeping, debilitated beauty take to its feet, our duty being to provide the literary scholarly prostheses to a critically impaired body. Doing so inevitably ensured that *Romance in Marseille*'s pastness transformed into a kind of presentness.

---

[7] Michael Kaler, "Claude McKay's *Romance in Marseille* Charts the Misadventures of an Eclectic Bunch of Social Outcasts," *Lambda Literary* (March 25, 2020). Online.

[8] Thanks to Kimberly Holcomb, William Maxwell, Jesse Schwartz, Agnieszka Tuszynska, and Daniel Worden for reading drafts of this essay.

[9] See new digital projects in periodicals studies, such as *Circulating American Magazines*, https://sites.lib.jmu.edu/circulating/; *The Digital Colored American Magazine*, http://coloredamerican.org/; *The Modernist Journals Project*, www.modjourn.org; *Just Teach One*, http://jto.common-place.org/; *The Pulp Magazine Project*, https://www.pulpmags.org/; *The Colored Conventions Project*, https://coloredconventions.org; *City of Print: New York and the Periodical Press*, http://cityofprint.net/.

The Instant Classic, the Press, and Print Culture in the Age of Digital Media

Given that the early 1930s New York publishing industry had roundly snubbed the Great Depression novel, McKay's reaction to seeing the "very literary" text in print nearly ninety years later no doubt would be a mingling of vindication and bitterness. Nothing else apropos the introduction of *Romance in Marseille* to the world, however, was a given. While Penguin hoped that the novel would appeal to a certain demographic, nobody was prepared for the reaction. By the day of the book's release, *Romance*'s discursive identity had been determined. *Romance in Marseille* would wind up trending due to its capacity for being "relatable."

Of all the media, the *New York Times* truly fell for *Romance*, as, all told, the text racked up six notices, the most curious if revealing being an interview with Joseph Stiglitz on his reading habits. The Nobel Prize-winning Georgist economist mentions that, following a conversation about *Things Fall Apart*, his newly formed reading group will be discussing *Romance in Marseille*.[10] The noteworthy implication is that Achebe's ultimate postcolonial classic is, as though the two texts were a couple of bottles of *vin du pays*, being paired with McKay's instant classic for comparative sampling.

Just as germane for the present discussion of the newspaper's *Romance* references was an article tackling the topic of redefining the classic in multicultural terms. Another irony that the satirist McKay would have appreciated, *Romance in Marseille* doesn't qualify as a *classic* simply because prior to winter 2020 it had never been in print.[11] "Penguin Classics and Others Work to Diversify Offerings from the Canon" calls on both Bill Maxwell and the imprint's publisher Elda Rotor. As the *New York Times* piece suggests, a classic in the sense that Penguin traditionally has used the term is virtually synonymous with *canonical*, and over the past few years, under Rotor, Penguin has been redefining the classics category by issuing texts by African American, Latinx, Asian, Asian American, and other writers that, due to their nationality, color, and sex, have been denied a place in the Western or American canon. The very act of identifying these works as perennials challenges the notion of a stable canon, and adding *Romance in Marseille* to the catalog pushes the classics cachet to its limits. *Romance* simultaneously challenges the Western canon while challenging the idea of what the Harlem Renaissance is by appearing as if out of nowhere with the purpose of demanding that the literary study be redefined—and on top of all that, it is a classic that was never a classic.[12] *Romance* insists that it may only be a classic if it is an instant one.

---

[10] See Jillian Tamaki, "The Nobel-Winning Economist Who Wants You to Read More Fiction," *New York Times* (April 9, 2020). Online. See also Brent Hayes Edwards, "A Legless Black Man Comes into a Windfall in This Biting Satire," *New York Times Book Review* (February 11, 2020). Online.; and Concepción de León, "Penguin Classics and Others Work to Diversify Offerings from the Canon," *New York Times* (March 30, 2020). Online.

[11] In the 1990s, the University of Exeter Press planned to publish the novel but the project fell through. See "A Note on the Text" in McKay, *Romance in Marseille*, xlvii.

[12] The attention wasn't confined to popular news media. *The Los Angeles Review of Books* excerpted two chapters. Nearly all the books excerpted in *LARB* are contemporary texts, so to see two chapters from *Romance* was an indication of the exceptional character of the Penguin Classic.

It's fitting that McKay met (and mocked) H. G. Wells because when word of *Romance*'s wokeness spread to public radio,[13] both NPR and the CBC picked up the time-tripper metaphor. As a handful of other formerly unknown or out of print Harlem Renaissance texts recently had appeared, most notably, Zora Neale Hurston's *Barracoon* (2018), the NPR show *1A* invited Bill to join a panel discussion, aired a day after *Romance*'s publication, on "lost secrets of the Harlem Renaissance." Bill did an impressive job of tracing the highlighted texts to their deep historical context. Still, the show's theme—salvaging "lost secrets"—had already established that forlorn novels like *Romance* plainly need an extraordinarily long vintaging period before being cracked open.

Similarly, while the CBC arts program *Q*'s perceptive compere Tom Power understandably was enamored of the idea that *Romance* may be best appreciated many decades after it was written, I, already becoming ambivalent about the presentist response to the novel, stated as a literary historian that I was hesitant about the notion of any archival artifact being understood *primarily* as prescient. I'm not sure that I was entirely successful in offering to Canadian listeners the alternative that "repressed texts may tell us more about that past—and [therefore] the present—than ones that were embraced by mainstream readers," to cite the Q website's near verbatim paraphrasing of my remarks. At the risk of exceeding my tolerated soupçon of self-indulgence, I will complete the advertisement for myself: "[R]eading texts that were lost in the shuffle, and some like *Romance in Marseille* that were effectively repressed, helps us better understand who we are now."[14]

Following years of research and writing about the Harlem Renaissance author, the media celebration made it a little difficult to reconcile the McKay of the archive with the McKay of the Penguin Classic *Romance*. Two McKays suspended before me: the McKay of then, and the McKay of now. But even the past and present character of these two time-bound traces of the writer and the print culture aura surrounding him are indistinct. Thanks to Jean-Christophe Cloutier's discovery and, with his Columbia University advisor Brent Hayes Edwards, coediting of McKay's formerly lost 1941 novel, *Amiable with Big Teeth*, united with the attention paid *Romance*, the McKay of the past has transformed and the world has received him—or is still in the process of receiving him—like never before.[15] Therefore, the McKay of the recent past no longer exists, except in the print culture about him and his own texts that precede the arrival of *Amiable* and *Romance*. And the McKay of the present is no longer the relatively minor queer Black radical artist, to be appreciated (despite his peccadillos) by aficionados. He is instead now a *celebrity*.

---

[13] See Claude McKay, *A Long Way from Home*. 1937, ed. Gene Andrew Jarrett (New Brunswick: Rutgers University Press, 2007), 98–103.
[14] Gary Edward Holcomb, "After 90 years, novel by radical Harlem Renaissance author finally published." Interview by Tom Power. Producer Matt Amha. *Q*. Canadian Broadcasting Company. March 10, 2020. Online.
[15] Claude McKay, *Amiable with Big Teeth: A Novel of the Love Affair Between the Communists and the Poor Black Sheep of Harlem*, eds. Jean-Christophe Cloutier and Brent Hayes Edwards (New York: Penguin, 2017).

Everyone who lives under global capitalism knows that the potential for sales plays as significant a role as the news media in what counts as potentially press worthy and what makes up the print culture. On that measure of all things textual and consumed, that multinational e-commerce Cloud colossus, Amazon.com, the paperback, Kindle, and audiobook led several lists, each characterized by being instructively misleading: "African American Historical Fiction"; Political Fiction"; and, most pertinent, "Classic American Fiction." It also scored high on Prime's "wished-for" lists, which is probably why the gargantuan online emporium ran out of paperbacks on *Romance*'s release date. Penguin quickly issued a second, substantial printing, but Jeff Bezos's octopedal network of fulfillment centers was unable to ship the book on time, and the backed-up preorders delayed the paperback's availability. I take some pride in saying that *Romance in Marseille*, a text that the system once thwarted, broke the system. As if returning to the time of the novel's struggle and failure to appear during its original literary moment, the paperback was eloquently if a little enigmatically only available in bookstores, suggesting among the most interesting features of *Romance*'s public sphere advent. The trace text seemed to insist on returning consumer-readers to the culture of print that most resembles the moment of its hobbling.

I understand why so many are attracted to the concept that a text in its own time was premature and therefore could not find, to use a key McKay metaphor, a *home*. Given that it has no vintage, however, it is downright contradictory that *Romance in Marseille* may be categorized as a classic. The classic *transcends* history; it is unfreighted by the material conditions of its moment. *Romance* was effectively censored and thereby lost in the historical shuffle *because* it was an artifact very much—unfortunately for McKay, too much—of its time. Another classic text, if in literary-critical theory, offers a stimulating analytical approach to this question. Roland Barthes's *S/Z* (1970) advances an influential view on the classic novel, as it distinguishes between "writerly" and "readerly" literary texts. The French structuralist's study disparages perennial favorites, the classics it deems readerly texts, as "reactive" and "products," insisting that they lack a "plurality" of meaning.[16] In contrast, the writerly text (not a classic) exists in "a perpetual present, on which no *consequent* language (which would inevitably make it past) can be superimposed" [italics in original translation].[17] *Romance in Marseille* complicates Barthes's now classic theory, however, as the media response reveals the potential for this singular novel to remain in a continuous state of adapting and growing. *Romance* is both a classic and not a classic. Though it is historical in the way that Barthes means to use the term, it is not static and therefore not *readerly*. It qualifies as being fundamentally writerly, as it has taken on a plurality of meaning. This situation can't be solely because *Romance* was unread, because it never underwent the process of becoming a classic, of being known and therefore becoming potentially static. It must be mostly due to its singular instantness.

---

[16] Roland Barthes, *S/Z*, trans. Richard Miller (New York: Farrar, Straus and Giroux, 1974), 4–5.
[17] Ibid., 5.

So *Romance* is deemed an instant classic, a delightfully self-contradictory term that has the potential to stifle insight into the exceptional situation of *Romance in Marseille* appearing as a Penguin Classic. Everyone who has read the free verse of that timeless New Yorker Walt Whitman or peeped the burgeoning punk sound of the New York Dolls knows what is meant by the idea that an artistic act may prefigure later social and cultural transformation, and McKay's novel, reflecting the very definition of obscure, with its disabled protagonist, radical socialists, and assemblage of queer characters, uncannily both resonates with and is indifferent to present concerns. As it resonates with the present, I would like folks simultaneously to keep in mind that the novel first must be appreciated as a document of its own time for it to be prized now as *relatable*, a text that is or was ahead of its time. *Romance in Marseille* must be understood to resonate with contemporary culture only through understanding it as a historical document which trails the imprint of immobility, one that reflects the social thresholds and (differently) inhibited print culture of its own time. Readers may genuinely appreciate its contemporaneity only when its *pastness* is fully appreciated.

The recovery, editing—paradoxically, our (to use an apt Harlem Renaissance trope) co-midwifing of an *unknown* classic—and publication of and then, not the least, the critical response to the Penguin edition of *Romance in Marseille*, offers a model for rethinking how print culture writ large regulates the very rhetorics of literary history and theory. Awakening, if the reader will, this once effectively disabled text has put on trial the guileless notion that a stable canon of undisputed major literary works forms our literary tastes, cultural consciousness, and, as Toni Morrison discussed in the 1990s,[18] even national identity. Dropping in like a time trekker, the Great Depression-period novel's resonance in the age of post-Black art has revealed how the systems, tensions, and, most important, intertextual conversations that define print cultures in different moments genuinely inform our sense of literary distinction.

The curious case of *Romance in Marseille* therefore poses a series of valuable inquiries for twenty-first-century literary-historical criticism. Its sudden presence asks how we may make material, archival objects aesthetically meaningful. It queries how such objects contest received notions of historical and literary periods. It probes how we may present archival, generally obscure, and often abstruse materials in ways that make them accessible to others. And it interrogates how therefore we may articulate or at least recognize a new set of theoretical commitments that concentrate not exclusively on the *classic* text but, rather, on the material objects that orbit such works, especially those that confront unchallenged ideas of what identifying a work of art as a classic means. In a time when the *print* culture looks to be fading as a culture of print, *Romance in Marseille* appears as a portent, indicating that the classic in today's print and digital culture may not be a perennial in any of the once virtually unchallenged assumptions about what a classic (benchmark, standard, model, masterpiece, and canonical text) is.

---

[18] See Toni Morrison, *Playing in the Dark: Whiteness and the Literary Imagination* (Cambridge: Harvard University Press, 1992).

(Pub) Crawling toward Becoming an Instant Classic (with the Pestilent Hellhound on Our Trail)

Romance's surprising Black History Month 2020 success led to a scramble to hold a New York City book release celebration, which in turn led to a sequence of events that expanded the book's imprint on the contemporary print, digital, and telecommunications culture. As we had relied on the typescript that is housed at Harlem's Schomburg Center for Research in Black Culture, Bill Maxwell and I suggested to Penguin that we hold the publication party at the Center. Unquestionably the Schomburg should be recognized for its role in the book's appearance.[19] The Penguin publicist did her best to arrange an event, but a Harlem happening wasn't to be.

McKay had lived in Harlem before setting off on his twelve-year cruise to Russia, Germany, France, Spain, and Morocco, and then when he returned to New York took up residence again in Harlem. Even though McKay would not return to Harlem until after he was, in both senses of the expression, done with *Romance*, the New Negro movement is obliquely present in the novel, a kind of hangover from all-night cruising. The undocumented Lafala experiences Harlem in Chapter 3 when the lawyer's "runner," Black Angel, runs the double amputee uptown for a private party stimulated by bootlegged liquor (16–17). A true self-reflexively New Negro work of art, the novel repeatedly discourses on complex questions relating to the viability of a genuine Harlem Renaissance.

One year after Alain Locke published the literary florilegium that would define the Harlem Renaissance, *The New Negro* (1925), and two years before McKay published his first novel, the bestselling queer Black Marxist *Home to Harlem*, the literary world witnessed the arrival of the scandalous "Younger Negro Artists."[20] Conducted and ultimately fiscally borne by the cocksure Wallace Thurman with abetting and contributions from jazz and vernacular poet Langston Hughes, anthropologist-fiction writer Zora Neale Hurston, queer gadabout Richard Bruce Nugent, and several other freshly modernized Black *enfants terribles*, the breakaway collective shocked the Black establishment with the one-off *Fire!!* (1926), the most scandalous addition being Nugent's gender-bending and literary genre-breaking "Smoke, Lilies and Jade." Reviving the ghost of gay patron saint Oscar Wilde, cataloging the name of every creative spirit he could think of, and chain-smoking in an epic manner, Nugent's elliptical text is dedicated to the vision that, in the age of modern, urban alienation, cruising for queer love is the ultimate literary and artistic act. The imparting of the idea that living a queer if underground life is just as important as writing a poem or drawing a sketch made the genre-disobedient piece play the central role in the purposefully incited outrage.

---

[19] Specifically, retired Schomburg librarian and new McKay Estate representative Diana Lachatanere should be recognized for making the issuing of *Romance in Marseille* possible.

[20] The cover of the only issue of *Fire!!* states that the magazine is a "Quarterly Devoted to the Younger Negro Artists." See *Fire!! A Quarterly Devoted to the Younger Negro Artists*. 1.1 (1926).

The elder New Negro generation's reaction to McKay's *Home to Harlem*, characterized by Du Bois's declaration that reading the novel made him feel so befouled that he needed to take a thorough soak in the tub, resulted from the still smoldering antipathy for Carl Van Vechten's cluelessly titled *Nigger Heaven*, also published in 1926, and Thurman and Nugent's profane, combustible insolence.[21] Assuming he received the news, no doubt Du Bois didn't mind hearing that, in what must be the most histrionic example of Empyrean irony in the history of print culture, nearly every copy of the *Fire!!* issue was incinerated in a warehouse fire, leaving Thurman with the 1920s' equivalent of an interest-laden student loan: in a state of perpetual debt.[22]

But the fledgling *Fire!!* generation, forming an arty commune at 267 136th Street, the Harlem address they called "Niggerati Manor," wasn't done with playing with its matches. Two years before McKay returned to Harlem, Nugent's comrade in arsonist aesthetics, Thurman, throwing fuel on Nugent's smoking embers, published his droll satire targeting the New Negro movement, *Infants of the Spring* (1932). Thurman's roman à clef rounded up the established generation, including Du Bois and Locke, and burned their (ostensibly) respectable, (allegedly) exhausted renaissance to the ground.

Ironically, even such an impudent gesture was by 1932 already becoming remarkable for its obsolescence. With the entrance of Richard Wright, who would later author the damning if way-off assault on the "so-called Harlem school of expression," "Blueprint for Negro Writing," Great Depression-period US print culture was moving away from any romantic nonsense about a florid renaissance and on to an ascetic vision exemplified by a severe Black Marxist writing.[23] (Wright's screed helped set in motion the still-lingering canard that the Harlem Renaissance was a failure.) It is instructive that when publishers spurned McKay's first attempt at writing a novel in the early 1920s, "Color Scheme," the often-frustrated expat author, in a pique of vexation, cremated his only copy. As justification for the novel's apparently colorful content, in 1925 McKay had written to bibliophile Arturo Schomburg, "I make my Negro characters yarn and backbite and fuck like people the world over,"[24] a comment that equally applies to *Romance in Marseille*. Though he didn't torch *Romance*, McKay must have realized that pitching his fiction of Black-white queer Seventh Heaven into the stark new world of social realism would be futile.

Although a Harlem event wasn't to be, luckily New York University's Glucksman Ireland House was kind enough to arrange an eleventh-hour celebration.[25] A week after the book's release, the lively, standing-room-only panel discussion and Q&A was followed by appropriately high-spirited Greenwich and West Village socializing.[26]

---

[21] See W. E. B. Du Bois, "*Home to Harlem* and *Quicksand*," *Crisis* 35 (June 1928): 202.

[22] See Thurman's letter to Hughes, c. 1928, in *The Collected Writings of Wallace Thurman*, 112.

[23] Richard Wright, "Blueprint for Negro Writing," in *Double-Take: A Revisionist Harlem Renaissance Anthology*, eds. Venetria K. Patton and Maureen Honey (New Brunswick: Rutgers University Press, 2008), 59.

[24] McKay, letter to Arturo Schomburg, June 1925. Langston Hughes Papers, Beinecke Library, Yale University.

[25] Thanks to both Glucksman Ireland House faculty member John Waters and NYU McKay scholar David Hobbs for organizing the event.

[26] Jesse McCarthy, Ernest J. Mitchell, Bill Maxwell, and I formed the panel.

The post-book release party pub scuttle made plain the then/now divide between what a book was and what a book does, as our jaunty band traversed the same turf that McKay, Nugent, Hughes, and other restless New Negroes had covered in their nocturnal cruisings a century earlier.

In fact, Ireland House, smack in the heart of Greenwich Village, was in its way an ideal setting for festivizing *Romance*'s release, not only because McKay was an ardent advocate of Irish-Black insurgent unity,[27] but also because the Village figures as important as Harlem in McKay's queer leftist aesthetic. In fact, Manhattan's radical hub could be considered a second or at least a complementary (if underside) location for the "Harlem" Renaissance. During the early 1920s, before the Black cosmopolitan author departed for England and sojourned abroad, McKay was nearly as much present in the Village as he was in New Negro Harlem.[28] McKay wasn't the only Black artist to hang out in the bohemian enclave, as other queer New Negroes like Bruce Nugent also found the countercultural community friendly to their ways.[29] So, across the street from the archetypal symbol of Greenwich Village's political and cultural progressivism, the Washington Square Park Arch, Ireland House, at the corner of 5th Avenue and Washington Mews, was the perfect site to celebrate McKay's passion for queer Black leftist boundary crossings, the very theme of *Romance in Marseille*.[30] During the period when he was struggling to find a home for himself in the American literary culture, the Jamaican immigrant claimed both the Village and Harlem, Manhattan quarters that were and are if cultural worlds apart only a couple of miles away from each other. As the print culture story of *Romance in Marseille* demonstrates, the present-day outlines and plotlines of Harlem and Greenwich Village are unmistakably demarcated by the inhabitants and events of their pasts.

The day after the Ireland House event, enjoying our *flâneurie* in the great city, Bill and I strolled into the storied Strand Bookstore on Broadway and 12th and discovered that *Romance* was the centerpiece of the Black History Month display.[31] My memento, a photo of myself next to the spectacle, captures the tidy column of *Romance* texts, the effect being a Manhattan tableau of ahistorical literary transcendence. The small *Romance* paperbacks rise like a scale model skyscraper amid popular classics closely stacked up around it—*Zami, Devil in a Blue Dress*, and so on—confirming the novel's suspension in time.[32] In contemporary print culture, it isn't that the classic is abstracted from its historical context. Rather, its historical context exists in a refined circle of

---

[27] See McKay, "Under the Iron Heel," *The Workers' Dreadnought* (August 4, 1920): 2.
[28] For work on Mike Gold and McKay's contentious collaboration on *The Liberator*, see William J. Maxwell, *New Negro, Old Left: African-American Writing and the Communism Between the Wars* (New York: Columbia University Press, 1999), 95–124.
[29] See Thomas H. Wirth, "Introduction," in *Gay Rebel of the Harlem Renaissance: Selections from the Work of Richard Bruce Nugent* (Durham: Duke University Press, 2002), 10.
[30] Penguin arranged with the NYU bookstore to vend copies of the paperback, and I'm told that all the books sold out.
[31] McKay scholar Agnieszka Tuszynska's informing of a Strand employee that *Romance* was accruing critical attention probably inspired its pride of place on the table.
[32] Bill Maxwell took the photo.

other print classics, perennials that exist not in an archive but in another kind of time capsule, even and especially those that embody a past moment. The classic's unaging pod is an exclusive salon—or a members-only speakeasy.

On that same weekend, my spouse, Kim, and I enjoyed the even more surreal and equally enjoyable experience (if the surreal can be enjoyable) of sitting in our Soho hotel room watching the novel being praised on "Bill's Books," a segment of WNBC-TV's Sunday morning talk show, *Weekend Today in New York*. As its repute was becoming discursively fixed, reviewer Bill Goldstein repeats the substance of the already familiar online and print notices: the unexpectedly contemporary character of the book's content. Goldstein goes on to query our introduction's discussion of how *Romance* riffs on *The Sun Also Rises* (1926), Hemingway's modernist-primitivist roman à clef (and a novel that both Thurman and McKay admired immensely[33]).

Eschewing our suggestion of Hemingway's Lost Generation image of sexual unmanning as a kind of negative capability model for former "dancing fool" Lafala's being cut down, Goldstein suggests instead *Porgy and Bess* (1935) and *Tender Is the Night* (1934) as creative stimuli. The Gershwin opera, book by DuBose Heyward, concentrates on a disabled Black vagrant, Porgy, who attempts to rescue his Bess from a couple of toxic male characters. As for the connection to Fitzgerald's novel, presumably what Goldstein had in mind is that it's set on the Côte d'Azur, not far down the coast from Marseille. Bill Maxwell and I appreciated the TV review, but noted that, curiously, Goldstein seemed to have missed the detail that our introduction suggests as an inspiration Heyward's *Porgy*, the 1925 novel on which the jazz opera is based (along with the theatrical version of the same year, script by DuBose and Dorothy Heyward).[34] The TV critic's idea that a jazz opera and another Lost Generation novel—both appearing *after* McKay ceased working on *Romance*—must be influences reinforces how *Romance in Marseille* floats in the historical firmament, out of time but not out of touch. The contemporary classic makes opaque the details of the past, or the details of the past that we feel reasonably sure about. The instant perennial text dislodges the narratives of history, and therefore those who read it understandably feel a kind of freedom to participate in the dislocation. Yet the classic is exactly not ahistorical—it belongs to the history of the classic.

The most surprising occurrence while visiting the city, though, was seeing *The Wall Street Journal*'s fulsome online review. I feel certain that McKay would be as amazed as I was that a, if not *the*, media symbol of American capitalism published such a sensitive, insightful appraisal of his Black anarchist fiction. *Romance* is "gorgeously seamy," says reviewer Sam Sacks, "an unshackled and bitingly funny melodrama."[35] It is "as heady and bewitching as the scene of a Vieux Port dance floor."[36] Happily schlepping a hefty stack of *WSJ* copies around the Village and then finally sitting down in a café and realizing that I'd blown about twenty bucks on a batch of the wrong issue—the issue

[33] McKay, *A Long Way*, 193.
[34] Holcomb and Maxwell, "Introduction," in McKay, *Romance in Marseille*, xxxvii.
[35] Sam Sacks, "Review of *Romance in Marseille*," *Wall Street Journal* (February 21, 2020). Online.
[36] Ibid.

that carried the review would appear in a few days—brought home to me how the old roles of permanence and transience have swapped places.

A major lesson of *Romance*'s precipitate and unexpected rise is that the online manifestation has become the primary script while the print version has taken the back seat as the secondary text. Because the online version appeared first and is, in most instances, permanent, and the print version was, depending on the newspaper or magazine, relatively more transitory, the online version is, in the present age of digital reproduction, the closest that print and digital cultures have to permanence. *Like a classic*. This principle came about in a particularly interesting way with respect to the appearance of *Romance*. On the day of its release, as the paperback version was not to be found online, Amazon's scheme to keep sales afloat was to "gift" the Kindle edition to any consumer who'd ordered and had to wait for the paperback.

In view of its cosmopolitan character, it is fitting that word of *Romance* spread across the globe, with notices materializing in the UK, Italy, Greece, India, Australia, New Zealand, and beyond, including McKay's homeland, Jamaica. *The Gleaner*, where McKay published his earliest poetry, issued an editorial stating that the novel should stir a national discussion of homophobia in Jamaica: "More than seven decades after McKay's death and 91 years after he began writing his novel, the logic of a 156-year-old buggery law, which encroaches on the rights of the individual, diminishes the humanity of a large segment of [Jamaica's] citizens and might have caused him to be jailed, isn't sustainable."[37] McKay's statement in defense of the incinerated "Color Scheme," "I make my Negro characters yarn and backbite and fuck like people the world over," thus takes on a broader, deeper significance.[38] With its disabled African protagonist and LGBTQ ensemble, jaunty merchantmen and *les dockers noirs*, and female and male Black and white sex workers, *Romance in Marseille* went global. Almost like a salubrious virus.[39]

Romance and Disability

Molly Young's "Vulture" review for *New York* magazine touches on a profound truth about the release of the Penguin Classics *Romance in Marseille*.[40] She imagines two readers: one who has read the prefatory and supplementary materials; and another who, as I was wont to do when I was a young Penguin Classics reader, leaves past the critical materials and simply reads the novel, maybe reviewing the supplementary resources sometime later. Some young and even not so young readers are likely to

---

[37] "Claude McKay's New Relevance to Jamaica," *Gleaner* (February 13, 2020). Online.
[38] McKay, letter to Arturo Schomburg, June 1925.
[39] Though, not all salubrious. At the time of writing, one dodgy outfit in Italy has released a pirated translation, and the McKay estate, once again aroused, is obliged to prevent it if possible. Assuming legitimate renditions in other languages propagate, translating *Romance in Marseille* will lead to yet another phase of simulacra replicating from the original. It remains to see how many versions of *Romance* will spread across what becomes, one hopes at the time of writing, a post-pandemic world.
[40] See Young, "The Best New Novel."

prefer skipping the critical apparatus and reading the novel to have a *pure* experience. The reader who wades through our accompanying materials, however, is experiencing the novel amplified, and therefore an expanded and more expansive version of the text. In any case, no reader comes to *Romance in Marseille* in a chaste reading state, and, for that matter, no virtuous version of the novel exists or ever did.

By May 2020, *Romance* had become available to readers in the UK, spawning by July three of the most interesting responses, and all either explicitly or obliquely reflecting on the popular media reaction to the Penguin Classic. Highlighting the Vieux Port setting, the radical *Jacobin*'s critique hints at the favorable popular reception by pointing to the narrative's quixotic implications: "McKay sets out a vision for an unrealized, and perhaps unrealizable, working-class internationalism: one that values individual expression as much as solidarity."[41] Later in July, Penguin UK boosted *Romance* as its "Book of the Week," with a short essay by *Afropean: Notes from Black Europe* author Johny Pitts, who concludes with this sobering insight: "In the end, *Romance in Marseille* is timely because it reminds us of our secret pleasures and desires, our imperfections and idiocy, and, in all its messiness and ambiguity, of the blur and beauty behind our 'personal brands.'"[42] How instructive that by summer, UK intellectuals would turn the lens on how the culture of book consumption, both domestically and internationally, has shaped the novel's contemporary exhibition. By summer 2020, the media response to the novel also participated in casting its contemporary aura. A mere five months after its domestic release, *Romance*'s journey through the culture of print had already become both a story about the Penguin Classic itself and a narrative about its media and popular reception.

The most incisive commentary appears in the same high summer month in *The Modernist Review*. Laura Ryan pins down the dual character of the text, its historical import apace with its contemporary resonance, articulating a key insight:

> Indeed, the "new" works [*Romance, Barracoon* etc.] distort our conceptions of contemporaneity, seeming to embody what Ernst Bloch called the "simultaneity of the non-simultaneous." They appear to us at once as old texts with a particular history—time capsules unearthed and poised to reveal some past mystery—yet they also emerge as strikingly fresh, novel works: the New Negro made "new" once again eight or nine decades on.[43]

With its radically contradictory depiction of the past, *Romance* warps "our conceptions of contemporaneity" by dropping in suddenly like a drone, if a historically disabled

---

[41] Conrad Landin, "When Harlem Renaissance Novelist Claude McKay Decamped for the Port of Marseille," *Jacobin* (July 2, 2020). Online.

[42] Johny Pitts, "Claude McKay's *Romance in Marseille* shows how human truths have been erased from history," penguin.co.uk (July 2020). Online.

[43] Laura Ryan, "The 'Late' Modernism of Claude McKay's *Romance in Marseille*," *The Modernist Review* (July 3, 2020). Online. I'm happy to add that I served as guest reader for Laura Ryan's 2019 dissertation, School of Arts, Languages and Cultures, University of Manchester, UK.

one, on our social discourses, the object's message being that our assumptions of how people lived nearly a century ago are inadequate and unreliable.

Romance may be thought of as disability itself. It challenges received notions of stability and verticality, of the *wholeness* of our critical crucible. The novel opens with a comment on the merging of the emancipated imagination with colonial bestiality, how a literary art may rise from the persistent butchering of Black bodies: "In the main ward of the great hospital Lafala lay like a sawed-off stump and pondered the loss of his legs." In other words, where to go from here, and how to go there? The narrative leads the way—if at times haltingly, groping in the blackness. In the end, Lafala, offstage, has skipped out back to Black Africa thus leaving Aslima in the lurch, an eventuality that compels the black *Carmen*'s murder at the hand of her Corsican pimp, Titin (129–30). Anticipating Afro-pessimism and Black self-abnegation by nearly a century, the text asks how an art may be fashioned from the modern world's mutilation of the Black body. The creation itself must reflect disfigurement and death.

One ultimately may say that our role with this disabled novel, a document that lay immobile for nearly ninety years, was to encourage it to step forward, however unsteady it may be, into the present print cultural arena. And then witnessing the media and public readings and re-readings of *Romance in Marseille* has led the Penguin Classic toward being no longer primarily an archival vestige but a reflection of a discrete history that is surprisingly resonant. A model Black modernist text, *Romance* is simultaneously a historical document *and* a contemporary work of art, suited for its role in today's age of simultaneous mechanical and digital reproduction. The release of and reception to the novel reveal, also if by faltering steps, that McKay, though little known to the mainstream, played a role in shaping the world we inhabit today and the symbolic order, the language, we use to understand it—the most compelling definition of the term *intertextuality*.

Black Literatures Matter: A New Critical Morphology Emerging from the Wake?

Meanwhile, by late March another version of the novel already had begun to surface. The first glimpse I had that the world was going to spin off its axis transpired when the Q interview was postponed for a few days because the CBC show suddenly had to cover the newly developing Coronavirus news. But *Vanity Fair*'s March 25 listing of the Great Depression text as one of its "Great Quarantine Reads" sums up *Romance*'s next reception phase.

The *Romance* audiobook, vividly read by actor Dion Graham, gets a mention in an early April Bookriot.com piece starkly titled, "How Audiobooks Are Getting Me through COVID-19."[44] The proliferation of audio versions of perennials or any literary

---

[44] Laura Sackton, "How Audiobooks Are Getting Me through COVID-19," *Bookriot.com* (April 7, 2020). Online. Graham reads though the thirty-eight-page introduction and eleven-page "Note on the Text" before going on to the novel.

texts raises a whole new set of complex questions about print culture, beginning with the crucial detail that an audio book is not a text. I'm not sure what to think about a reader, for lack of a more precise term, not bothering to read *Romance* and instead listening to a kind of podcast version of it. (I hasten to say that I'm not talking about a disabled user of the audio text, a reader who is vision impaired). The audiobook reader isn't a reader; she or he is a listener, not engaging with the written word but with the verbalized and performed text. Imagine if I were reading this essay to you now. What relationship would you have with the printed word? But I think I understand why someone enduring a plague lockdown would rather hear than read a book, as I believe this impulse comes from the same pandemic culture impetus to re-watch favorite films and TV series. Reading is a solitary activity, and under certain conditions it may be a lonely one.

In advance of Mother's Day, *New York* magazine's "The Strategist" recommended *Romance* as a popular, online-accessible gift suggestion for offspring who had the sense to observe the early hunker-in-place orders. But I believe that the most eloquent print (and digital) cultural product was a *Los Angeles Review of Books* conversation with Bill Maxwell and me, conducted by West Coast LGBTQ activist Eric Newman.[45] I don't mean that I was especially articulate. I refer to the fact that toward the end of the colloquy, the three of us tackle the grim question of how *Romance*'s portrayal of characters barely existing at the peripheries of global capitalism potentially would resonate with the new reality for a new lost generation. When the pandemic became our essential social existence, the response to and therefore the character of *Romance in Marseille* pivoted with the new global imperative. The untold ruin against which *Romance* had shored—I'm thinking of it stacked up beside other Black perennials in the Strand Bookstore—was the coming scourge, and the Penguin Classic took on the dubious celebrity of becoming a plague text.

How bitterly eloquent that a lethal virus arrived right on *Romance*'s heels. That is, just as the novel was going viral. *Romance in Marseille* is truly a "Great Quarantine Read." A once slumbering tale of Black disability and demise is now a "woke" voice that speaks volumes to the present, seemingly capable of pivoting like a dancer, if still carrying the trauma of its decades-long immobilization, with each epochal turn. Meanwhile, the ever-mutating diadem death virus, likewise seeming to come out of nowhere, enters the world as the bestial Real, assailing human bodies with a vengeance just for being alive, bringing debility and fatality. Together, McKay's historical text and the pandemic see eye to eye in reminding us that all conclusions must be understood to be provisional. It's therefore necessary to accept that today's print culture must read McKay's regained Harlem Renaissance novel through a scraped lens, blurring one's focus on the blitzed landscape that concurrently trails behind and looms before us, the narrative that insists on never coming to an end: the struggle of the disenfranchised against oppressive ideologies, the reckless menace

---

[45] See Gary Edward Holcomb and William J. Maxwell, "Claude McKay in Our Time: A Conversation with Gary Holcomb and William J. Maxwell on 'Romance in Marseille,'" *Los Angeles Review of Books* (October 23, 2020). Online.

of inevitable global capitalist collapse at the expense of those it exploited, and certain bereavement owing to the brutish indifference of a ruthless Hegemon. I say this because the present often seems to be little more than the past unresolved—if, granted, simultaneously disintegrating, both necessarily and regrettably. Inspired by both McKay's text and the response to it is my growing awareness that what's needed now is a new critical morphology of print that must emerge from the pandemic wake, where the reader must accept that the author's experience inexorably plays a role in limning the disabled critical subject.

5

The Real Productivity: Creative Refusal and Cultish Tendencies in Online Print Journal Communities

Michelle Chihara

Recently, a group of friends and I were sharing survival strategies in the year of the global Covid-19 pandemic. Those of us with full-time work we could do from home were privileged, and we knew that. We still found it almost impossible to make a living while frantically trying to replace the social and academic structures of classrooms for our kids during the slow-moving crisis known as "distance learning." Some friends acquired Panda Planners, a trademarked paper planning system that recently partnered with Rocketbook to make one's planning uploadable via digital tablets and erasable pens. Print trends like this one, which combine journaling and therapeutic artistic practices with online communities, have driven a large segment of print sales in recent years. And self-help trends like this one capitalize on social problems. People need to get by. The tagline for the Panda Planner is "You deserve to thrive," and the system promises "scientifically designed tools" to help you be "present with the people who matter most" and develop "deeper connections."[1] These goals seemed worth a twenty-five-dollar risk in 2020 (Figure 5.1).

In text conversations, my friends discussed the fact that uploading to Panda Planner's digital interface would mean one could digitally search last month, almost like Googling inside your own memories. But while combining paper and pen note-taking with digital search was appealing, we shared a suspicion that the Panda Planner might add both surveillance and labor to our days. One friend reminded the group that we should not imagine that a new planner would render us fully efficient. "The goal is not to become someone who never has problems managing s*&t. Too high a goal!" she said. A new system is just "a way to trick yourself for a little while."

Both the Panda Planner and the system that I use, the Bullet Journal TM, are print-based methods of getting by. They help prioritize, clarify, and organize complicated lives. They're also ways of tricking yourself for a little while. Bullet Journals—or BuJo

---

[1] Panda Planner website, https://pandaplanner.com/.

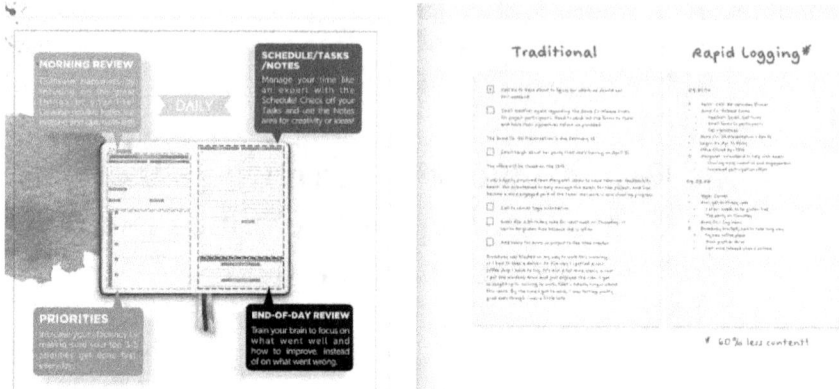

Figure 5.1 Images from Panda Planner (pandaplanner.com) and Bullet Journal (bulletjournal.com) websites, December 2020.

to insiders—in particular have been adopted by a significant online community who share digital images of their paper-based habits, connecting dedicated practitioners in a variety of aesthetic sub-groups who create and share "spreads" online (Figure 5.2). The trademarked company created by Bullet Journal's creator, Ryder Carroll, does not sell paper journals but does sell an app that allows people to upload and archive their BuJo. His website touts the ostensible benefits of paper journaling based on neurological research about the benefits of mindfulness and creativity.[2] These commitments link the inner state of being present, or mindful, to the outer state of working efficiently, or what might be known online as hustle. As practices that promise inner peace, these print trends are "digital detox" systems meant to treat technological overload in the gig economy. As practices that arose in a period where individual workers need to brand themselves online while managing multiple gigs and projects, these trends capitalize on impossible neoliberal pressures.

The BuJo was a Silicon Valley-created self-help trend online that has also materially shifted the media ecology in which people consume and circulate print books. They are a print genre which constructs and circulates an aesthetics of narrative self-presentation. As habit-trackers meant to manage what they measure, BuJo are not unlike Benjamin Franklin's diary, which inspired Gretchen Rubin's 2009 *Happiness Project*. They thus fit within the world of positive and behavioral psychology and the publishing output of *The Happiness Industry*.[3] With their indices, calligraphic quotes, and reading lists, they share features with sixteenth-century commonplace books, as instruments "for redistributing text so as to ensure maximal retrievability and optimum

---

[2] Bullet Journal website, http://www.bulletjournal.com.
[3] See Daniel Horowitz, *Happier?: The History of a Cultural Movement that Aspired to Transform America* (New York: Oxford University Press, 2017), especially 177–81. See also William Davies, *The Happiness Industry: How the Government and Big Business Sold us Well-being* (New York: Verso, 2015).

Figure 5.2 Google Image search results for "Bullet Journal December Spreads," December 2020.

application."[4] They plug into practices of social distinction that fetishize the book as an object, while circulating images that help journalers feel more peaceful and productive. They carry strands of print culture's emergence from books of piety and text-networks that evolved long before computers, invoking and absorbing cultural contradictions around Protestant performances of disinterested, virtuous hard work and the promise of rewards in this world.[5] Straddling the line between private diary and public ploy for online self-branding, between mindfulness and hustle, they don't carry a specific politics. But BuJo do provoke questions, ultimately, about what journalers believe they are working toward. Print journaling communities online can, sometimes, open out onto wider horizons about what it means to live a productive life.

An interest in mindfulness, in the early 2000s, rose up both as a means of soothing stress under the cult of productivity and as a means of managing one's time efficiently within that cult.[6] Both Buddhist-inspired gurus and hustle culture motivational speakers have fanned out from Silicon Valley across the nation and the internet.[7] In *Dissent*, Laura Marsh called the interest in mindfulness the "coping economy," where

---

[4] Ann Moss, "The Politica of Justus Lipsius and the Commonplace-Book," *Journal of the History of Ideas* 59, no. 3 (1998), 423.
[5] For a complete account of the novel's emergence as a genre from the media ecology that included books of piety, along with text-networks and dynamics of confession and vulnerability, see Jordan Alexander Stein, *When Novels Were Books* (Cambridge: Harvard University Press, 2020). I also use the term "media ecology" as Stein defines and elaborates it.
[6] Ron Purser and David Loy, "Beyond McMindfulness," *Huffington post* 1, no. 7 (2013), 13.
[7] For example, Andy Puddicombe, the Buddhist monk and CEO of the venture funded startup Headspace. For hustle culture, see Sarah Kessler, "GaryVee Is Still Preaching the Hustle Gospel in the Middle of a Pandemic," *Medium* (August 11, 2020). http://www.medium.com/. Online.

meditation rooms at GM lulled workers into being more peaceful about layoffs.[8] Ron Purser called the "neoliberal cooptation" of Buddhist practices "McMindfulness," where meditation was weaponized in the name of optimization, "refashioned as performance enhancement methods in alignment with institutional goals, whether it's a corporation or the military."[9] When the source of the stress is not politicized, the mind called to #alwaysbehustling can use Eastern-inspired techniques to calm down on demand, or to Rise and Grind with equanimity.

The contradiction between always being peaceful and always hustling is inherent in this form of capitalist neoliberal subjectivity, which individuals must by necessity internalize. In order to survive one or two or three gigs, sometimes without daycare or grocery stores, one must manage one's time and adopt a "sleep when you're dead" attitude, to some extent. Whatever tool allows people to cope, whether it's a paper planner or a guided meditation, cope they must. In this capitalist context, the slow but steady decline in the practice of sitting quietly with a paper book has been offset by the sale of journals and notebooks, mostly in service of tracking personal time.[10] Amidst the unprecedented amplification of a media- and data-centric form of capitalism—what Sarah Brouillette has called the "creative economy," or what Nick Srnicek calls platform capitalism, or what Jennifer Odell calls the attention economy—the neoliberal subject is distracted, sleep deprived, and overwhelmed.[11] McKenzie Wark wonders if this new regime of precarity and technological production isn't even capitalism any more, but something worse.[12] Whatever the master narrative, the rhythm and pace of human survival in the contemporary moment produces a living longing for pauses, for analog experiences with a different temporality, as well as for community and human connection.

The Panda Planner and the Bullet Journal promise productivity, but they also index a certain ambivalence around hard work. They promise to save time and labor, to help people work better but not longer. They also threaten to waste time. The online aesthetic excesses of BuJo influencers provoke regular accusations of gimmickry. Created to make people efficient, BuJo's elaborate decorations look feminine, slow, and unnecessary. Suspicious (often male) commentors on Reddit have looked at the drawings and Japanese stickers and asked, does this really work? Are there "any actual

---

[8] Laura Marsh, "The Coping Economy," *Dissent* (Winter 2018). http://www.dissentmagazine.org/.
[9] See Liza Featherstone, "How Mindfulness Morphed from Ancient Spiritual Practice to Big Business: An interview with Ron Purser," *Jacobin Magazine*, December 6, 2019. Web.; Ronald E. Purser, *McMindfulness: How Mindfulness Became the New Capitalist Spirituality* (London: Repeater, 2019).
[10] According to market research firm The NPD Group, US consumers spent $210 million on unruled spiral, composition, graphing and other notebooks in 2017–18. "Bullet Journaling Trend Lifts Sales of Notebooks and Writing Instruments, Reports NPD" Press Release, *NPD Group* (June 26, 2018). http://www.npd.com/.
[11] Sarah Brouillette, *Literature and the Creative Economy* (Stanford: Stanford University Press, 2014); Jenny Odell, *How to Do Nothing: Resisting the Attention Economy* (Brooklyn: Melville House, 2019); Nick Srnicek, *Platform Capitalism* (Malden, MA: Polity Press, 2017); Shoshana Zuboff, *The Age of Surveillance Capitalism: The Fight for a Human Future at the New Frontier of Power* (New York: PublicAffairs, 2019).
[12] McKenzie Wark, *Capital Is Dead: Is This Something Worse?* (New York: Verso, 2019).

business leaders" who use it?[13] As Sianne Ngai writes, in *A Theory of the Gimmick*, the gimmick "indexes a bigger wrongness in the way a society goes about valorization as such."[14] The bullet journal is a device to save labor, an outgrowth of a cult that seeks to intensify work. And yet it appears as "doing too much and yet also not enough work," and in this, it indexes the wrongness of how work is valorized, it both "attracts and repels us."[15] BuJo are devices which provoke aesthetic judgments and encapsulate and instantiate profound problems in capitalism. In their online community of amateur artistic production, bullet journals are efficiency tools that also cultivate resistance to the cult of productivity, a line of flight toward something else, or part of what Odell calls the "creative space of refusal."[16]

A short YouTube video called How to Bullet Journal, promising "an analog system for the digital age," was viewed more than 11 million times in the five years after it was posted in 2015.[17] Carroll, the consultant and designer who made it, speaks openly about an early diagnosis of attention deficit disorder, and says he wanted to tame his unruly mass of post-it notes. Using a blank paper journal with 5 mm dot grids, a pen, and a simple set of symbols, he promised a means of taming and disciplining the mind and the task list. Like BJ Fogg, the tech company consultant and habit industry behavioral researcher at Stanford, Carroll first promoted his technological services by warning of technology's dangers.[18] Technologically induced feelings of overwhelm and distraction were harming us. He provoked digital anxieties and then, on YouTube and in the name of capitalist productivity, offered a soothing solution. Bullet journaling went on to launch a massive, multi-million dollar trend that spurred a chunk of growth in the office supplies industry.[19]

Carroll specifically calls BuJo a "mindfulness" practice and the marketing industry categorizes bullet journaling with digital detox trends like coloring books geared for adults.[20] There is little clarity in the popular press around what is happening to print,

---

[13] Reddit thread, "Anyone Who's Highly Successful and Using BuJo Method? Anything They Do Differently?," https://www.reddit.com/r/bujo/comments/cpk32g/anyone_whos_highly_successful_and_using_bujo/

[14] Sianne Ngai, *Theory of the Gimmick: Aesthetic Judgment and Capitalist Form* (Cambridge: Harvard University Press, 2020), 45.

[15] Ibid., 56.

[16] Odell, *How to Do Nothing*, xxi.

[17] "How to Bullet Journal," YouTube (May 21, 2015). https://www.youtube.com/watch?v=fm15cmYU0IM.

[18] See mostly his website, http://www.bjfogg.com, but also Brian J. Fogg, *Tiny Habits: The Small Changes That Change Everything* (New York: Houghton Mifflin Harcourt, 2019).

[19] According to the marketing data firm NPD, "guided journaling" sales rose 40 percent in 2018, and the bullet journaling "craze" in particular drove up sales of notebooks and writing instruments, particularly among women. Guided journals bridge "the coloring book phenomenon" with BuJo and "other organizationally based journaling activities." See "Bullet Journaling Trend Lifts Sales of Notebooks and Writing Instruments, Reports NPD" Press Release, *NPD Group* (June 26, 2018) and "Guided Journal Sales Rose 40 Percent in 2018 the NPD Group Says," *NPD Group* (May 13, 2019). http://www.npd.com/.

[20] Ryder Carroll, *The Bullet Journal Method: Track the Past, Order the Present, Design the Future* (New York: Penguin, 2018), 19.

besides a great deal of death-of-print anxiety, but it's clear that digital detox is a growing force. The fate of the literary novel as a genre and locus of meaning remains, as it was in the seventeenth and eighteenth centuries, bound up in a media ecology shaped both by commercial pressures for certain forms of expression *and* by the pull of all that is being lost—cubicles, physical stores, small businesses, print sales, and sustained attention itself.[21] Media scholars have written extensively on the changing landscape of genre in the neoliberal era.[22] Meanwhile, articles about the death of the e-book and the return of print, the end of genre, or the victory of crime thrillers and podcasts all cycled through the headlines during the years of BuJo's rise. In 2015, adult coloring was a major part of Barnes & Noble's retail business. The CEO bet big on it, but this particular trend, it turned out, was not creative enough. Coloring was subsumed into a much larger turn toward flexible self-authoring, or "adult creative expression." Books with pre-given outlines failed to produce gift sales in the next holiday season; the CEO was ousted.[23] Meanwhile, the wider trend includes printed books like bullet journals, guided journals, and guided sketchbooks, while encompassing writing instruments, and other art supplies.

In mid-July of 2019, many of *Publisher's Weekly*'s headlines detailed losses in print sales, and the end of paper textbooks. E-readers and new types of digital tablets and stylus are still changing, creating constant shifts in what might count as a writing implement, an archive, or an artistic practice.[24] At the same time, before the global pandemic, *Vox* reported that independent shops for print books, in the UK and the United States, had been opening new stores.[25] Vox attributed this to the independent stores' social role in their brick-and-mortar communities, as well as to Instagram—where the visual circulation of images of books and bookstore events, like the circulation of BuJo spreads, was part of an "indie" brand that fetishizes paper books as lifestyle objects. While the future of print remains uncertain, the backlash against digital anomie, isolation, and immateriality is likely to play a major role in preserving the physical affordances of paper.

All of this consumer activity skews heavily toward women, in a period also marked by poverty wages, wage theft, and increasing numbers of underpaid and feminized workers.[26] These are gendered trends emerging out of the rubble of previous industrial

---

[21] For how the emergence of the novel was affected by the subtraction of books of piety from the market, again see Stein, *When Novels Were Books*, 155.

[22] See Lee Konstantinou, ed., "The 7 Neoliberal Arts," *Post45* (August 31, 2020) and Jeremy Rosen, ed., "Ecologies of Neoliberal Publishing," *Post45* (April 8, 2020). http://post45.org/, among others.

[23] Daphne How, "Coloring books, Adele leave Barnes & Noble hanging at the holidays," *Retail Dive* (January 6, 2017). http://www.retaildive.com/; and Alexandra Alter, "Barnes & Noble CEO Ronald Boire Steps Down," *New York Times* (August 16, 2016). http://www.nytimes.com/.

[24] For example, the reMarkable tablet or the RePaper tablet that sync print note taking or drawings with digital reproductions. See http://www.reMarkable.com.

[25] Nisha Chittal, "Instagram is Helping Save the Indie Bookstore: Stores like Books Are Magic and the Last Bookstore are benefiting from love on #bookstagram," *Vox* (December 19, 2018). http://www.vox.com/.

[26] See Leigh Clare LaBerge, "The Effective Turn: Affect, Gender, and the Wages of the Labor Film," *Post45* (January 10, 2019). http://post45.org.

orders, however, not out of gendered essences. In the early twenty-first century, a massively unequal platform economy rewarded a few male-dominated "unicorn" companies for hoarding billions of dollars of venture capital based on their ability to continue exploiting a reserve army of contingent laborers.[27] For decades, American workers increased their productivity but watched their wages stagnate, while the uppermost income brackets reaped the gains.[28] In 2020, most American households were staggering under heavy debts, taking on multiple gigs for inadequate pay, and struggling to survive. In the face of all this, at the beginning of his book about the Bullet Journal Method TM, Carroll cites a slight decrease in worker productivity in the US economy and implicitly lays the blame at workers' feet. He asks, "Maybe our rapidly evolving technology that promises us near-limitless options to keep us busy is not, in fact, making us more productive?"[29] Most workers in the United States had no job security; large numbers faced compounding problems around hyperexploitation.[30] But Ryder Carroll thought maybe the problem was that the Internet was distracting people, and Bullet Journals were the solution.

Of course, on one level, Carroll was right. Technology plays a role in a media regime which undermines the collective capacities that make political change possible. The artist Jennifer Odell documents a technology-obsessed culture looping in fruitless cycles of intense emotion and anxiety, "people caught up not just in notifications but in a mythology of productivity and progress, unable not only to rest but simply to see where they are."[31] Unable to create space in their own thoughts or to connect with the physical immediacy of their bodies in space, people become cut off from compassion for each other and then unable to do the work of collective thinking and planning that makes up activism. The social body that "can't concentrate or communicate with itself is like a person who can't think and act."[32] In the face of constant distraction, immediate gratification, and the atomized nature of online media, paper and pen offer sustained attention. They give access to the mental state that psychologists call flow.[33]

Digital detox trends emerge out of a popular and historically specific recognition of the need to take conscious retreats, gather the self, and restore our capacity for solitude. In *Reclaiming Conversation: The power of talk in a digital age*, Sherry Turkle references

---

[27] For the exploitation of digital labor in particular, see Veena Dubal's work, for example: Veena B. Dubal, "The Drive to Precarity: A Political History of Work, Regulation, & Labor Advocacy in San Francisco's Taxi & Uber Economics," *Berkeley J. Emp. & Lab. L* 38 (2017), 73. For income inequality trends, see https://www.pewsocialtrends.org/2020/01/09/trends-in-income-and-wealth-inequality/.

[28] Productivity Pay Gap at the Economic Policy Institute, https://www.epi.org/productivity-pay-gap/.

[29] Carroll, *Bullet Journal Method*, 17.

[30] For an account of the spirit of capital in this moment, see Annie McLanahan, ed., "Issue 1: Deindustrialization and the New Cultures of Work," *Post45* (January 10, 2019). https://post45.org/.

[31] Odell, *How to Do Nothing*, xiv.

[32] Ibid., 81.

[33] For example, see Anne E. Dickerson, "The Power and Flow of Occupation Illustrated Through Scrapbooking," *Occupational Therapy in Health Care* 12, no. 2–3 (2000), 127–40; and Pam A. Mueller and Daniel M. Oppenheimer, "The Pen Is Mightier than the Keyboard: Advantages of Longhand Over Laptop Note Taking," *Psychological Science* 25, no. 6 (2014), 1159–68.

Thoreau's analysis that society needs one-, two-, and three-chair conversations.[34] Turkle was one of the first people to see the potential and the possibility inherent in social networked technologies. She has now come full circle to warn society of the losses we face. The first chair is solitude. "Solitude does not necessarily mean being alone," Turkle writes. "It is a state of conscious retreat, a gathering of the self. The capacity for solitude makes relationships with others more authentic. Because you know who you are, you can see others for who they are, not for who you need them to be. So solitude enables richer conversation. But our current way of life undermines our capacity for solitude."[35] In Turkle and Odell's understanding, an embodied return to physical place and face-to-face conversation carries a fundamental politics, almost a pre-politics, in the sense that calm self-governance provides individuals with the psychic space to face uncertainty, governance, and the needs of the group (potentially still a necessary skill in a democracy).

These writers suggest that a different quality of attention might, in fact, encourage individuals to find their sense of purpose in something other than capitalist value. A different quality of attention, produced and guided collectively, might bring about more powerful and imaginative groups. Pressing material realities demand collective action and probably sacrifice on the part of individuals who will need to share a sense of what they're working toward. Neoliberal capitalism's answer to all problems remains the market itself, based on individuals who internalize the model of the human subject as entrepreneur, the self who plans and cares and labors to invest in self-optimization. It's an impoverished model, but especially in the face of intractable and diffuse problems, this model of the self provides a focused sense of purpose, however cruelly optimistic.[36] Suggesting that people *cease* to think of themselves as entrepreneurs doesn't give them options. Artists and scholars like Odell and Turkle suggest that people with the lived and authentic ability to be alone, people who carry a rooted understanding of human and bio-regional interdependence, might be a necessary precursor to new strategies for a shared sense of meaning and human connection—strategies that aren't #alwaysbehustling.

Print products that promise productivity emerge out of hustle culture's extreme drives to work, harnessing cultish energies for capitalist ends, but it's important to recognize that those cultish energies tap into wider social longings for a sense of purpose. At the other end of the coping economy, on the more aggressive edge of the cult of productivity, hustle culture seemed both impossible and impossibly strong, in the early twenty-first century—a form of neoliberal capitalism's biopolitical control, on steroids. Even as work became more grueling and precarious, the allure of endless hustle only seemed to get more intense. As steady jobs disappeared, workers were increasingly encouraged to see themselves as monads of human capital moving seamlessly among projects, always one self-perfecting tip away from success. At

---

[34] Sherry Turkle, *Reclaiming Conversation: The Power of Talk in a Digital Age* (New York: Penguin, 2016).

[35] Ibid., 46.

[36] See Lauren Berlant, *Cruel Optimism* (Durham: Duke University Press, 2011).

WeWork, the multibillion "tech" company that subleased office space to independent contractors, rented office space was sold as a complete hustle-based lifestyle and worldview. In one WeWork building, even the cucumbers floating in the water cooler were carved with mottos: "Don't stop when you're tired. Stop when you're done."[37] WeWork's brand promised productivity and a sense of purpose and belonging. Not only would you have an aesthetically pleasing place to be, with cucumber water, but when you stepped through the doors you wouldn't ever want to stop working.

Like so many Silicon Valley promises, WeWork was smoke and mirrors, a toxically masculine con job that ensnared global tech investors right up to the moment its IPO failed spectacularly and the company dissolved into air. Such investors had made a great deal of money by betting on platforms, as innovations in labor exploitation. But WeWork didn't really have a platform and it didn't really have a new method of exploitation, in fact, it promised a brick-and-mortar service. The WeWork CEO was tall and had good hair. But his charisma does not explain why a scheme built on subletting office space was so compelling to so many. That's because the vision that WeWork peddled was not focused on its core business, commercial real estate, but on a more nebulous and transformative "work experience." WeWork promised space to breathe, inside what the CEO called "a capitalist kibbutz," with a sense of community.[38] A kibbutz is a community organized around shared religion and shared values. The WeWork hype promised transformative culture, it implied that WeWork work would be imbued with a special something. Hard work performed within its chic spaces would pay off in more than money; autonomous work would deliver collective meaning. WeWork's business model promised that bringing freelance workers together in a nice space, plus vegan lattes, would release profits from the heavens. This was nonsense. But inside the longing for work to be a place that you never want to leave is a longing for life to be more meaningful than your day job. The live-to-work impulse carries within it an impulse to live *for* something.

WeWork, Panda Planners, and BuJo all carried the promise of replacing boring cubicle days, organized and supervised by someone else, with self-directed time that lets you "do what you love."[39] Hustle culture gave focus and discipline to the flexible worker's inner manager. For the laborer with multiple duties, and no steady income, self-help and hustle culture internalize management theory, such that the population desperately seeks to perfect itself on its own dime. The neoliberal subject, responsible for everything in her life, takes on both the need to dream big (Ryder Carroll asks, *what do you want?*) and the intense pressure to be efficient and plan (*what have you done to get it?*). Like the Bullet Journal, WeWork promised the entrepreneurial self a streamlined space and a community, a shared practice that would make everyone

---

[37] This is a real thing that happened, reported in Erin Griffith, "Why Are Young People Pretending to Love Work?," *New York Times* (January 26, 2019). http://www.nytimes.com.

[38] Amy Chozick, "Adam Neumann and the Art of Failing Up," *New York Times* (November 2, 2019). http://www.nytimes.com.

[39] WeWork website from 2013, see https://web.archive.org/web/20140110054321/https://www.wework.com/.

more productive and focused. At WeWork, it came with foozball and a coffee maker. But bullet journals promised to combine contemplation with a system for tracking and controlling each task and every day.

The cult of productivity, or the dominant and culture-wide hangover from the Protestant work ethic, is what Kathi Weeks describes as "productivism." In *The Problem with Work: Feminism, Marxism, Antiwork Politics and Postwork Imaginaries*, Weeks makes clear that the issue with work "is not just that it monopolizes so much time and energy, but that it also dominates the social and political imaginaries."[40] We have trouble, in these United States, separating ourselves from the idea that waged work should be our calling and that our work should rank us reliably against other humans. Our inner and our outer lives are wrapped up in work. Given this, management theory folds the critique of alienation into itself. It re-inducts workers into creating value for employers by making work more engaging, by building meditation rooms or gamifying the boring parts.[41] Weeks also articulates the ways in which Marxist, feminist, and socialist movements—including those to which she is indebted—can get caught up in productivism, or in seeing bad work as the problem and better work as the only answer. The anxiety produced by economic uncertainty in a society haunted by the religious idea that God's elects are productive can produce both an ascetic and "ritualistic" devotion to the cult of productivity.[42]

Precisely because they appear virtuous, efficient, and motivated by something beyond naked self-interest, BuJo influencers fit well into these ascetic Protestant dynamics. At the Christian website *Redeeming Productivity* a woman named Emily Maxson wrote about solving her "crisis of productivity," that was also a "crisis of character," with the Bullet Journal: "I was failing to steward faithfully the things which God had entrusted to me. It was sin." BuJo helped her "shake off the mental chaos" and get back to "glorifying God through faithful and diligent work."[43] In *Redeeming Productivity*, the Protestant work ethic combines with an Enlightenment model of mind-body dualism that is endemic to a particular brand of modern evangelicalism, where a rational Christian mind can and should control the body's irrational impulses. Particularly when material rewards seem hard to come by, this ascetic and ritualistic devotion to loving your work provides an alternative sense of reward.

This ritualistic devotion functions within and outside of Protestantism itself. In hustle culture, in Silicon Valley, in the entertainment industry, the workaholic

---

[40] Kathi Weeks, *The Problem with Work: Feminism, Marxism, Antiwork Politics, and Postwork Imaginaries* (Durham: Duke University Press, 2011), 36.

[41] For more on management theory folding the critique of alienation into itself, see Weeks, *Problem with Work*, 105–6.

[42] Ibid., 45–6.

[43] Emily Maxson, "How I Use the Bullet Journal Method to Steward My Attention," *Redeeming Productivity* (March 3, 2019), https://www.redeemingproductivity.com/. Let me be clear that while there is significant BuJo and white Christian overlap, it has been taken up by a diverse set of groups. Many Asian and Asian American fans of Japanese calligraphy and paper products follow it. BuJo spreads responded to the Black Lives Matter protests in 2020. And groups who would not at all respond to evangelical overtones, including a professional dominatrix who made a "Bullet Journal for sex workers" video, are also common.

impulse connects *doing what you love* and loving your work to an ascetic strain of committing the entire self to labor.[44] Within evangelicalism, a martyred giving-over of the self to work in the name of the Lord connects with a righteous indignation in the name of Christianity, *tout court*. *Redeeming Productivity* exists inside the ecosystem of a megachurch whose pastor saw California's pandemic restrictions on gathering as an attack on his right to worship. He is part of what one writer called a Christian martyrdom movement that gave "a sense of solemnity and purpose" to the forty-fifth president's victory and to the evangelical community's willingness to put everything on the line for their political choices.[45] Living-to-work, or putting all of your mental and material resources on a single leap of faith, is the flip side of being ready to die for work. The cult of productivity connects at different point with both ascetic and martyred impulses.

Academia is not exempt from these dynamics. The "mind-over-matter work ethic" is generally "inhumane for everyone it ensnares," it "obscures and rationalizes academia's austerity crisis."[46] In the face of demands that knowledge production justify itself in instrumentalized market terms, many academics internalized a labor-of-love work ethic that is particularly hard on sick and disabled people. For people struggling to force their bodies past healthy limits, for women carrying more of the labor of social reproduction, or for other precarious groups, it can be harmful, ableist, or abusive, to suggest that they might have been able to thrive in academia if only they had loved it more, organized their lives better, or hustled harder.

In the absence of long-term contracts, at a time when jobs have become more and more tenuous and abusive, the cult of productivity has gotten stronger through these martyred dynamics. The "privatization of stress" at the turn of the twenty-first century pushed society away from asking, as a collective, "how has it become acceptable that so many people, and especially so many young people, are ill?"[47] And yet illness may also connect people with moments where they are forced to imagine themselves outside of the wage relation. In the life of an individual, illness can force a step back from work. Illness itself often results from injustice, but it carries no inherent politics. Like other forms of uncertainty and obstacles to work, illness can bring interruptions, a necessary pause. And pauses may be the necessary condition for the kind of contemplation that allows individuals to shake off the cult of productivity, to ask: Wait, what was it all for?

---

[44] For academia, see Francesca Coin, "When Love Becomes Self-Abuse: Gendered Perspectives on Unpaid Labor in Academia," in *Feeling Academic in the Neoliberal University*, eds. Yvette Taylor and Kinneret Lahad (New York: Palgrave Macmillan, 2018), 301–20. For the entertainment industry see John T. Caldwell, "Stress Aesthetics and Deprivation Payroll Systems," in *Behind the Screen: Inside European Production Cultures*, eds. Peter Szczepanik and Patrick Vonderau (New York: Palgrave Macmillan, 2013), 91–111. Discussions of Silicon Valley are widespread, but see for example Byung-Chul Han, *The Burnout Society* (Stanford: Stanford University Press, 2015).

[45] Peter Manseau, "The Christian Martyrdom Movement Ascends to the White House," *The New Republic* (June 5, 2020). https://newrepublic.com/.

[46] Liz Bowen, "The Job Market Is Killing Me," *Post 45* (February 24, 2020). https://post45.org/.

[47] Mark Fisher, *Capitalist Realism: Is There No Alternative?* (Washington: Zero Books, 2009), 19.

At the turn of the twenty-first century, shifts in the flows of global finance and manufacturing created what Lauren Berlant, via Hardt and Negri, calls a "labile labor environment." Read: no more cubicles and single-job careers. With less and less economic security for more and more people, some middle-class workers "saw labor as a system that could be gamed on behalf of forging a more satisfying life" while "others opted out of a live-to-work ideology altogether." This was part of an "affective shift toward valuing lateral freedoms and creative ambitions over strict upward mobility."[48] In this same history, it's also clear that while steady jobs declined, workers were no longer rewarded for loyalty to particular organizations. They thus learned to value flexibility, creative ambition, and the ability to be their own boss. This freedom only intensified their need for internalized discipline. What powered this discipline was an intensified commitment to a sense of calling. When you feel in charge of your own destiny, you are even more inclined to feel responsible to it.

Bullet journals, and other tools for creative ambition and the optimized self, come along when this affective shift away from steady jobs and toward personal calling hits up against the hard and frantic reality of needing to earn to survive. Print culture has long existed at the intersection of practices that mediate social distinction, leisure, and mental discipline.[49] As an aesthetic pursuit navigating these dynamics, the BuJo re-packages discipline to feel like escape, but it also explicitly asks people to pause. Ryder Carroll writes: "Mindfulness is the process of waking up to see what's right in front of us. It helps you become more aware of where you are, who you are, and what you want."[50] Bullet journaling walks right up to an ethical question and asks about deeper motives. It creates a spiritually adjacent space that can then cut right or cut left, pushing people either toward a compassionate Eastern practice with ascetic strains or toward other more Protestant cult of productivity gurus.

There is no inherent class or race politics in paper or in digital detox, and the pressure individuals put on themselves, within punishing capitalist systems, will certainly not be lifted by pen and paper alone.[51] Insisting on heavy print books can be ableist and a form of pernicious nostalgia. But the appeal, and the power, of both hustle culture and mindfulness practices lie not only in their instrumental abilities to make money or to help us cope, but also in their ability to connect daily practices and disciplines around work with profound questions about why we do the work we do. Weeks makes specific political demands: for a universal basic income and shorter working days. She calls for these demands as rallying points on a broader utopian horizon that opens out onto visions of life postwork. Thus, while stronger unions and more pay are important (they are!), as political demands they can remain stuck inside the terms of the wage relation. She sees a refusal of work as a first step in

---

[48] Berlant, *Cruel Optimism*, 193.
[49] See Deidre Shauna Lynch, *The Economy of Character: Novels, Market Culture, and the Business of Inner Meaning* (Chicago: University of Chicago Press, 1998).
[50] Carroll, *Bullet Journal Method*, 20.
[51] See Jennifer M. Silva, *Coming Up Short: Working-Class Adulthood in an Age of Uncertainty* (New York: Oxford University Press, 2013).

transformative social change. A postwork imaginary must find ways to value human relations outside of the wage relation, rephrasing what are we working toward as a question about who we are together, beyond work. In order to move toward broader social change around these questions, the broader ethical and ultimately spiritual context that grounds the ritualistic aspects of daily practice must be part of the conversation.

As artists and cultural producers focused on presenting an authentic and self-directed self, BuJo influencers promote the connections between reflexivity and flexibility in what Sarah Brouillette calls the "creative economy." In this neoliberal regime, a "fundamentally ahistorical conception of creativity" is seen "as the natural expression of an innate opposition to routine and to management."[52] Mindfulness and adult creative expression, like the figure of the author, promise to help uncover an authentic expressive self, apart from market imperatives. And yet this self is also imagined as necessary in order to better function on that same market. BuJo influencers are, like authors, figures for the valorized mental laborer. At the same time, a resistant potential remains in noticing that an authentic creative self is hard to find and doesn't always pay off. This is illustrated particularly well by one BuJo influencer and anti-capitalist author, a young woman named Rachael Stephen who wrote an anti-capitalist novel called *Flux* in 2013, majored in philosophy, and according to her YouTube videos and website, failed to find a steady white collar job.[53] She worked as a barista for a while before she committed to full-time to gig work and influencer videos. In 2019, she posted a video about "seven mistakes" she was making in her BuJo, a standard influencer trope.[54] She has thirty thousand followers and her video was viewed almost four hundred thousand times, putting her in the middle range of influencers in this space. After she details her seventh mistake, the video cuts to a buddy of hers who makes anti-capitalist documentaries. He asks her how she can go from an "anti-capitalist diatribe" to giving productivity advice. Isn't she being hypocritical?

Stephen replies that her eighth mistake is the mistake that underpinned all her other mistakes. She had been using the bullet journal with an incorrect sense of purpose. When she came at it from an "entirely productivity-based mindset," she was just beating herself up for not getting everything done. She says that the goal of achieving and making money might seem "innocuous to almost everyone," because the assumption across society and productivity advice is that success and personal productivity are universally desirable and aligned. But Stephens questions this received wisdom. She describes her epiphany: "Creating profit and succeeding" were no longer her top priority. The bullet journal was a tool to help her get by. She saw that it was important not to beat herself up for wanting to get by. But productivity was not her primary purpose in life.

---

[52] Brouillette, *Literature and the Creative Economy*, 6.
[53] See Rachael Stephen, https://www.rachaelstephen.com/.
[54] Rachael Stephen, "What I was doing wrong in my bullet journal," *YouTube* (June 12, 2019). https://youtu.be/mIy5RnDuIGk. All quotations.

Here she is worth quoting at length:

I switched from being just another person trying to hack the system for their own personal success and snag a bigger slice of the pie, to wanting to change the whole system. So that we didn't have to compete for slices of pie anymore. (This is dumb! There's plenty of pie! Share the pie, god damn it! #THERE'S PLENTY OF PIE #BUT FIVE PEOPLE OWN ALL OF IT)[55]

Before, my bullet journal had started to feel heavy as lead, just like this thing I was dragging around that was stressing me out, and every time I looked at it I got more stressed out. But then it went to something really kind of magical.

And it became more than that, it became more than just a hamster wheel for endless productivity. Instead, it really became a place to declutter my mind, to help me prioritize what I'm doing and why I'm doing it, to be more mindful of how I spend my time—yes, to organize my responsibilities and the things I have to do to survive. But also, to claw back some space outside of work to balance work and this crazy thing called Not Work—life—having fun—and even activism!

When I let my bullet journal grow in this way, and I stopped using it against myself as this kind of productivity whip, it really started to become fun and light in a way it hadn't been in a long time. It really became this little haven in my everyday life, this little comfy cozy place that I could go to collect my thoughts and gain clarity and be silly and doodle. It finally started really working for me, really making me less stressed, making me less overwhelmed and just improving my life

Figure 5.3 Rachel Stephen, "what I was doing wrong in my bullet journal," *YouTube* (June 12, 2019). https://www.youtube.com/watch?v=mIy5RnDuIGk.

[55] Ibid.

in this whole new way. So, I guess, you can see the real productivity was ... the class consciousness we made.

In order to survive in this capitalist system, we meet the demands of waged work. Quiet, safe havens that create space for who we are outside the wage relation don't force anyone to think beyond it, but they hold the potential to facilitate such thinking. As one anti-racist activist and Zen priest put it: "Without inner change, there can be no outer change. Without collective change, no change matters."[56]

Inner work, like the work that people do by pausing to journal, relates to outer work. In their focus on sustained attention, intention, and community, print detox trends like the bullet journal emerge out of a symptomatic and collective need to pause. They are attempts to counterbalance the very real neurological and psychological effects of the screens. The need for solitude and a gathering of the self is familiar to many religious practitioners. It may be more foreign to Silicon Valley, which then "innovates" secular and instrumentalized versions of what others might call ritual and prayer. The bullet journal creates daily habits, and its aesthetic aspects ritualize and to some extent sanctify those routines. In print, away from the screens, the blank dot grid asks journalers to listen to their own larger intentions, using that sense of purpose to structure each day. It then offers a digital archive of this practice.

Fastidious flexibility may not by itself have a class politics, but it echoes the intentionality of Occupy Wall Street's endless remaking of systems. Jedediah Purdy wrote, of the "anarchist lending system" in Zuccotti Park, that the catalog said "nothing about the library's present holdings except what has been there," and was thus "an instantly obsolete memorial produced by tirelessly fastidious people who refuse to turn their fastidiousness into a rule for anyone else. It sits at the meeting-place of the database, the civic institution, and public art."[57] This could also describe the print-based bullet journal community online.

Occupy Wall Street and the mic check were nothing if not inefficient.[58] The movement's critics derided its lack of bullet points—Occupy refused lists of demands—but the daily liturgical practice of amplifying speakers by having everyone repeat their words, as a group, line by line, felt transformative for many participants (including me). As Purdy wrote, "What's most striking is to see those who disagree sharply, and palpably dislike and mistrust one another, reciting each other's attacks. Even when the speaker was agitated, an audible care governed the phrasing, as if the anticipated echo of the crowd and the memory of other voices in one's own mouth dissolved the ordinary narcissism of oratory."[59] It's true that the mic check was not

---

[56] Reverend angel Kyodo Williams, Lama Rod Owens, with Jasmine Syedullah, *Radical Dharma: Talking Race, Love, and Liberation* (Berkeley: North Atlantic Books, 2016), 209.

[57] Jedediah Britton-Purdy, "Observations from Occupy Wall Street," *fieldwork* blog (October 11, 2011). http://jedfieldwork.blogspot.com/2011/10/observations-from-occupy-wall-street.html.

[58] See Meredith Hoffman, "Protestors Debate What Demands, if Any, to Make," *New York Times* (October 16, 2011). https://www.nytimes.com//.

[59] Ibid.

a specific redistributive demand. But Occupy's forms nevertheless had a politics, including the mic check's form of analog conversation and profound listening. Many of those who were marked by their time in Occupy went on to continue to participate in other activist movements. The inner and outer work they did there was influenced by the free-floating library and the mic check. That work connected many people to a sustaining sense of purpose, outside of the wage relation.

The bullet journal, like the mic check, invites people into aesthetic communities that emphasize creative credit, respect, and shared resources. Neither BuJo nor the Panda Planner will, by itself, change the world, but the form of the bullet journal connects the pause and its inner work with a wide range of communities, some of whom are well-positioned to notice the failure of capitalist promises. In its most highly decorative instances, BuJo is unquestionably a gimmicky performance that bleeds easily into a feminized gender discipline around making one's life look pretty. The fetishized spreads become a competitive pastime in their own right, which are indeed unlikely to make "actual business leaders" more efficient through line drawings of snowflakes. But actual business leaders probably aren't the ones who need the help getting by. The range of December drawings registers both an aesthetic longing for pure efficiency and the distance the BuJo community has traveled away from a pure dedication to efficiency, anyway. Ngai writes that the gimmick is the "objective correlative" of the ambiguity at the heart of late capitalist technological regimes.[60] In that ambiguity lies collective potential and the seeds of creative refusal.

In the intensity of social commitments to productivity lie the seeds of cultish tendencies. Racialized and gendered vectors push lines of flight within these practices to break in different directions, along different kinds of vulnerability to different types of gurus. I can't give you an estimate for how many BuJo fans, like Rachael Stephens, became aware through BuJo that the real productivity is the collective consciousness we make. I can only say that I use my own dot grid journal and my meditation practice to connect with a sense of purpose in living for more than work—to pause and consider our interdependence, outside of and beyond the wage relation. That's the real productivity.

#Share the pie, god damn it.

---

[60] Ngai, *Theory of the Gimmick*, 55.

Part Two

Archives, Exhibits, Images, and Sounds of Print Culture

6

Hold Still: Coming Undone Reading Print Culture Like a Work of Art

Monica Huerta

Few forms of print culture in the nineteenth century became as ubiquitous as suddenly as *cartes de visite*, tiny photograph cards which typically measured about two and one-eighth by three and a half inches.[1] As Saidiya Hartman put it of another kind of small photograph, their "tiny size announces [their] minor status."[2] In the United States, *cartes de visite* were introduced around 1859 and saturated the photographic marketplace within about a year. These photo cards—made into keepsakes and souvenirs—were enmeshed in an Anglo-Atlantic history of bourgeois cultural practices. These practices involved exchanging social graces in the event of parlor-visit missed connections—that is, of leaving your "visiting card" when the person you meant to visit was not then at home. At the same time, these photo cards came to encompass a wide range of social and symbolic uses. For example, nineteenth-century celebrities employed the relatively inexpensive mementos as a publicity tool, anticipating how trading cards in the twentieth century—of sports figures and Garbage Pail Kids alike—would become a passion for hobbyists. Many photographers, like New York's well-known nineteenth-century celebrity photographer Napoleon Sarony, turned reliable profits by making *cartes de visite* for the theater's burgeoning celebrities.[3] One account notes that just one firm was making about 3,600 of these cards depicting celebrities every day.[4]

As a mechanism of exhibiting social grace *and* as a form of publicity that helped to generate modern notions of celebrity, *cartes de visite* bridged intimate relations with economic and political ones: depictions of Civil War battles were kept in albums alongside more quotidian scenes of beloved family and ancestors. These were just some of the strategies and practices for keeping close when far. This is also the representationally

---

[1] They were originally put forward in 1854 by French photographer A. A. Disdéri. Their larger format, cabinet cards, usually measured 4 ½ by 6 ½ inches.
[2] Saidiya Hartman, *Wayward Lives, Beautiful Experiments: Intimate Histories of Social Upheaval* (New York: W. W. Norton & Company, 2019), 24.
[3] Peter Decherney, "Copyright Dupes: Piracy and New Media in *Edison v. Lubin* (1903)," *Film History* 19, no. 2 (2007), 109–24.
[4] Robert Taft, *Photography and the American Scene: A Social History, 1839–1889* (New York: Dover Publications, Inc, 1938), 149.

dense nexus Sojourner Truth had in mind in producing her own *cartes* and larger cabinet cards, which she had made and reprinted from 1863 until her death, famously "selling the shadow to support the substance."[5] And both this amalgam of practices clustered around *cartes* as around photographs now more generally serve contemporary scholars in giving our histories depth, particularity, a sense of intimacy, and maybe more fruitfully, a way to imagine the archive as a site of intimacy for us as we write, too.

Quickly surveyed, the *cartes de visite* I analyze here, then, might seem too ordinary, too conventional for critical commentary. The *cartes de visite* of light-skinned slave children taken (sometimes bought away) from slavery into the north during the Civil War were also part of another larger political and cultural phenomenon in which Fannie Lawrence, Rebecca Huger, Rosina Downs, Charles Taylor, and Augusta Broujey became "celebrities" for being children with pale skin who were formerly enslaved.[6] Along with and aided by their *cartes de visite*, they became objects of fascination for northern publics. Several of their images, especially those taken in 1863 and 1864 in New York and Philadelphia, stand at the center of this chapter.[7] I encountered many of these images at the Schomburg Center for Research in Black Culture in Harlem, New York, but so ubiquitous were their images that there are also collections of these children's images scattered across the United States at the Library of Congress and the Historic New Orleans Collection Museum/Research Center, among others.

These were portraits of children who could have had little or glancing interest in having their portraits taken. Just the same, the images of children who had been enslaved reverberated against the active and tumultuous signifying in a public sphere fractured by the Civil War's violences; politics; stakes; narratives; and uneven, unfixed, and colonized geographies.[8] As Jasmine Nicole Cobb put it in her important book, *Picture*

---

[5] Likely among the most remarked *cartes de visite* of the period, the following are just two of the scholarly works that take up the images of the famous political figure at length and with great care, Darcy Grimaldo Grigsby, *Enduring Truths: Sojourner's Shadows and Substance* (Chicago: University of Chicago Press, 2015); Nell Irvin Painter, *Sojourner Truth: A Life, A Symbol* (New York: W. W. Norton Co., 1996).

[6] To describe just one example of this kind of celebrity: in antebellum America, Plymouth Church in Brooklyn gave other children the same opportunity as Sarah to be free by being bought out of enslavement. One such girl was Rose. Rose's story so inspired one woman in the congregation that she deposited her wedding band in the collection basket at church. Eastman Johnson's 1860 oil painting *The Freedom Ring* was inspired by this story. Patricia Hills, "Painting Race: Eastman Johnson's Pictures of Slaves, Ex-Slaves, and Freedmen," in *Eastman Johnson, Painting America*, ed. Teresa A. Carbone (New York: Brooklyn Museum of Art in association with Rizzoli, 1999).

[7] The archive with which I worked consists of various series of *cartes de visite*, primarily from the Prints and Photography Department at the Schomburg Center for Research in Black Culture in Harlem, New York.

[8] In the introduction to the edited collection *Child Slavery before and after Emancipation*, Anna Mae Duane asks "When is a child a slave?" in trying "to answer when *anyone* in the modern world is a slave." That is, in her introduction and in the collection of essays that follow, the "focus on the child—a subject of contention and continuity in pre- and post-emancipation versions of slavery—opens opportunities both to rethink how we teach and write about historical slavery and to reconsider the assumptions we bring to scholarly and activist engagements with twenty-first century abuses." While contemporary abuses lay outside the bounds of this essay, I share with Duane and the contributors the sense that the position of the child affords a way to reorient to the histories of enslavement. Anna Mae Duane, ed., *Child Slavery before and after Emancipation* (Cambridge: Cambridge University Press, 2017), 2.

Freedom: Remaking Black Visuality in the Early Nineteenth Century, "Black freedom in the United States posed immediate questions relating to home and nationality."[9] For example, the images of these "emancipated" and "redeemed" children—so the captions would describe them—participated in both fears of white enslavement and realities of the sexual violence threats built into the structure, mechanisms, and mores of enslavement. Likewise, the images functioned as emblems of abolition through some of their sentimental stagings of scenes from *Uncle Tom's Cabin*, part of the field of visual recitations and live performances in which Stowe's tale had an active and multivalent cultural life. The images also interacted with other many-times-told stories in other mediums about a nation divided, and the subjects that would or would not become full citizens.[10] The images operated as abolitionist—but not necessarily anti-racist—aspirations for the country and polity that would, presumably (though not inevitably), emerge from the Civil War.[11] Finally, for some critics, images like these aspired to give the North and the South stable post-war roles. In that way they were emblematic of nineteenth-century attempts to singularly affix both geography and time according to settler colonial logics amidst a multi-valent crisis, experienced differentially.

Given even just this brief overview, it's clear that various ideological readings can come from the cluster of images of these children.[12] If thought alongside critic Robin Bernstein's important work in *Racial Innocence: Performing American Childhood from Slavery to Civil Rights*, the ideological potential energy of these children's images was very like the "invocation of imagined children within directly opposing racial arguments... became so familiar as to appear unremarkable."[13] Bernstein might say, and rightly, that these images participated in the production of "racial innocence" even as their makers might have (or might not have) sought some other political end game, where "racial innocence" was "the use of childhood to make political projects appear innocuous, natural, and therefore justified."[14] Historian Mary Niall Mitchell has done extended archival work to give the histories of the children in these images more thick context. In *Raising Freedom's Child: Black Children and Visions of the Future after Slavery*, she argues that the children were being used by white abolitionists to imagine a domesticated—which is to say, palliative—future for a nation emancipated from slavery by "redeeming" the children born into its violent lifeways. Paralleling

---

[9] Jasmine Nicole Cobb, *Picture Freedom: Remaking Black Visuality in the Early Nineteenth Century* (New York: New York University Press, 2015), 12.

[10] For an extended discussion of performances and representations of *Uncle Tom's Cabin* in nineteenth-century America, please see Jo-Ann Morgan, *Uncle Tom's Cabin as Visual Culture* (Columbia: University of Missouri Press, 2007) and Robin Bernstein, *Racial Innocence: Performing American Childhood from Slavery to Civil Rights* (New York: New York University Press, 2011).

[11] For an account of one surprisingly anti-racist set of images of Black children by a white artist, please see Robin Bernstein, "Signposts on the Road Less Taken: John Newton Hyde's Anti-Racist Illustrations of African American Children," *J19: Journal of Nineteenth Century Americanists* 1, no. 1 (2013), 97–119.

[12] For an extended historical analysis of how ideas of white childhood in the Anglo-Atlantic and Anglo-American Revolution shifted before this mid-nineteenth-century moment, please see Holly Brewer, *By Birth or Consent: Children, Law, and the Anglo-American Revolution in Authority* (Chapel Hill: University of North Carolina Press, 2007).

[13] Bernstein, "Signposts," 3.

[14] Ibid., 33.

nineteenth-century fascination with light-skinned slaves, scholars' own interest in the images most often focuses on the obsession with these children's skin color as the main vessel for admitting, while not stating, the open secret of slavery's sexual violences.

But in this act of contextualizing through various ideological readings, it is easy to lose sight of the artifacts themselves, as though the photo cards are only the occasion for the stories for which we need evidence. (Because this is also, in an important sense, the nature of the photograph. To only "uncover" the various ideological readings of a photograph is, in fact, to lose the photograph as form to context.) The question remains, then, of how to write about this object of print culture without losing the materiality of print culture, while also not divorcing that materiality from its equally crucial symbolic work. In this chapter, I am less interested in how we can locate the occasion for various competing and overlapping ideologies in the images, than in how the objects themselves resist one of ideology's demands: that a coherent telos be present in any single reading. In all, I build on readings of the varied futurities immanent in these images, by using the geographically indeterminate signifiers in the *cartes* along with the various temporalities they call upon and interact with to question the ways critics might surrender their scholarly readings of print culture's objects to historical or political context and specifically to ideological critique.

Among Black Studies critics and theorists, the bearing of slavery's afterlives on contemporary living, writing, and critique has had urgency and purchase especially since the publication of Saidiya Hartman's masterwork *Scenes of Subjection: Terror, Slavery, and Self-Making in Nineteenth Century America* and more recently in *Wayward Lives, Beautiful Experiments: Intimate Histories of Riotous Black Girls, Troublesome Women and Queer Radicals*. In conversation with but as a departure from some of Hartman's arguments, Stephen Best's *None Like Us: Blackness, Belonging, Aesthetic Life* has recently analyzed contemporary art practices of aesthetic refusal to question the ontological assumptions that, to him, have upheld Black Studies' theories about American enslavement and its cultural, social, political, but especially critical and scholarly afterlives. In *None Like Us*, Best pushes against an impulse in African Americanist critique to see the scene of Atlantic slavery and its subjections as the site of modern political subjectivity and even ontologies that limn to notions and affective pathways of belonging on the way toward contemporary political repair. As he puts it, he is writing against "the assumed conjuncture between belonging and a history of subjection."[15] The "critical possibilities" Best posits are "by way of a kind of apocalypticism, or self-eclipse," "a historicism that is not melancholic but accepts the past's turning away as an ethical condition of my desire for it."[16] In my reading of Best, this is a dynamic version of historicism that, I think, offers more than just the absence of reparative aims. This chapter, which encounters an archive of these quotidian abolitionist texts, much more like Hartman's than Best's objects of analysis, is then a bit of an experiment.

---

[15] Stephen Best, *None Like Us: Blackness, Aesthetics, Belonging* (Durham: Duke University Press, 2019), 1.

[16] Ibid., 20.

Let's sit with Best's argument for a differently aligned mode for criticism a little longer. Best "seek[s] a critical comportment that embraces these forms of mimesis, conspires with the world in this way, and in the process bases the cases for a non-sovereign form of critical subjectivity on the idea that art thinks."[17] Best here posits an alternative mode of "non-sovereign" critique as a "snuggling up" to art, building on and borrowing from his and Sharon Marcus' work to articulate "surface reading" and queer theorists Eve Sedgwick, Leo Bersani, Lauren Berlant, and Lee Edelman, to name only a few of the scholars from which his own reading practice for art and history emerges. The task, as he puts it, is to "think like a work of art," which involves "a critical comportment" that "conspires with the world" toward a "non-sovereign form of critical subjectivity."[18] That is, he means that

> artworks perform, one way or another, an intellectual or philosophical project. The artwork, in this theory of form, points reflexively to its own internal complexity, it can be considered a reflection, not in the passive sense of a mirror image, but in the active sense of an act of thought.[19]

He seeks "to enact that undoing as a kind of reading of the artwork, not an interpretation or contextualization of it, but a description that allows one to inhabit it."[20] This chapter uses the vantage point of these *cartes de visites* and the material and affective pathways that this slice of print culture opens up to make use of Best's articulation and performance of a non-sovereign critical orientation, even as I depart from his archive of contemporary art to the very ordinary photo cards at hand.

It is worth noting that the center of gravity for literary critical conversations around reading practices is not the broad field of print culture. It is more generally literary texts and traditional art objects whose forms and surfaces obtain the kind of attention that then have given rise to theories of—and debates about—the job of reading critically.[21] That is to say, print culture is in the helpful position of having its stakes in a

---

[17] Ibid., 33.
[18] Ibid.
[19] Ibid., 34.
[20] Ibid., 37.
[21] In 2009's "Surface Reading: An Introduction," part of a *Representations* special issue, Stephen Best and Sharon Marcus give an account of their and the issue's collective encounter with "symptomatic reading" as popularized in the American academy by the publication of Frederic Jameson's *The Political Unconscious* (1981). The introduction makes clear that "These essays represent neither a polemic against nor a postmortem of symptomatic reading" (3). At the same time, the passionate debates over "the way we read now," to use Best and Marcus' phrasing that they go on to carefully parse in the introduction, have continued in various forums as though there would be a reason to come to a consensus rather than continuing, as Best and Marcus did then, to ask the question (how do we read now?) and offer various forking pathways. Recently the question of what way(s) there would be to read has taken one shape in debates around postcritique, especially perhaps as crystallized in the 2017 volume *Critique and Postcritique*, edited by Elizabeth Anker and Rita Felski. I imagine this essay inheriting some of the questions raised by these debates and offering another pathway for historical critique. Stephen Best and Sharon Marcus, "Surface Reading: An Introduction," *Representations* 108, no. 1 (Fall 2009), 1–21; Elizabeth S. Anker and Rita Felski, eds., *Critique and Postcritique* (Durham: Duke University Press, 2017).

more open field than either traditional art or traditional literature, whose importance of how we read them seems, to some, more urgent to "settle." Just like my interest in what is quotidian about these images, I want to suggest that there is potentially more space in which to decide what our contemporary relations are to these print culture objects *because* the urgency to do so has more room built into it. As critic Frances Smith Foster has put it, "In print culture studies, the problem of constructing a definitive history is compounded, for, with newspapers, magazines, and other ephemeral literature, complete data sets are rarely extant."[22] Aston Gonzalez, in his study of Black photographers in the nineteenth century, has done important work in putting photography and photographers in the context of the African American print cultures that Foster is here characterizing.[23] The counterintuitive move I'm making in this essay, then, is not necessarily in thinking of these *cartes* as part of their ecosystem within print culture *but rather* in using a reading practice Best first proposed with contemporary art in mind to try to allow these, objects, too, to undo us in the way he proposes "thinking like a work of art" might do/produce.

These *cartes*, ubiquitous as they were, are also examples of an undertheorized form precisely because they toggle between scholar's own specializations and reading practices: seeming to be appropriate for those who work with photography by way of the criticism that branches off from art historical modes and—by way of their quotidian nature—the practices of those trained to think with the ephemera, as Foster elegantly phrased it, of print culture's everyday routes. Ubiquitous, ordinary, even banal, these small photo cards are barely distinguishable in the archives, sometimes, from mounted photographic images that ended up in albums and perhaps over time have lost their pages. Their markers and conventions are such that they seem to melt into the mass of photographic objects in any repository of nineteenth-century images, notable, perhaps, only for their small-ish size and their captions—though not all *cartes* would have a caption.

My aim in importing Best's proposition for reading and thinking like a work of art expands the bounds not only of what is *known* about these images but of how we imagine our own relations to history through expanding the critical resonances of photographic images, and especially the form of the *cartes de visite*. In this chapter I'll ask first, then, whether it is possible to think like a work of art about something—like a *cartes de visite*—that is not art. Best is particularly attracted to artworks that unmake their own viewing and so their viewers in turn. I proceed with this archive of images of light-skinned slave children in this spirit, then, open to our ideological readings' being undone. Along with those readings becoming undone, so too does any easy relation with their historicity (through our viewing) become undone as well. At the same time, my readings of the images try to forge a way of relating to them without enacting the following: (1) only

---

[22] Frances Smith Foster, "A Narrative of the Interesting Origins and (Somewhat) Surprising Developments of African-American Print Culture," *American Literary History* 17, no. 4 (Winter 2005), 714.

[23] Aston Gonzalez, *Visualizing Equality: African American Rights and Visual Culture in the Nineteenth Century* (Chapel Hill: University of North Carolina Press, 2020).

encountering the ideological uses to which they were put, (2) crystalizing our own sense of the critical traditions into which these images fit, or (3) foregrounding our contemporary affective pathways to these images as though they are, themselves historical. And this "thinking like a work of art" has more than itself as the reason here.

My reason for trying to "think like a work of art" is to find still another way of relating to historical and aesthetic worlds that are ultimately irretrievable. Like Best, I am not trying to recover them in order to suture the genocidal politics of the nineteenth century with some oppositional politics of the twenty-first. But I do mean to salvage the meanings we can find and forge in these archival bits of print culture we have decided must matter to *us* somehow. These same bits may not matter in another moment, but still and yet, the children in these images—not children anymore, only tones in shapes on cardboard cards—continue to *mean* now. What I try to reencounter in these images are the linked and unstable channels of geography and time. My hope in doing so is to peer beyond the historical ontologies to which many of our historical narratives aspire—with print culture, as with many other archives.[24] I want to find something, maybe, more humble: a space for thick, open, accounting as a critical process of divestment *as itself* a kind of historical relation, seeking out precisely those relations that productively undo us in order to open out to otherwise.[25] Otherwise than the *here and now* to which these images brought us.

Here Where?

It's an all-too-familiar scene (Figure 6.1). Fannie's full, dark skirt extends to cover the ottoman on which she perches. One of her arms extends behind her and disappears into her full skirt, while the other lies gently across her lap. Her visible hand holds what seems to be a small basket of flowers. To her right, a straw hat sits on a draped piece of furniture; next to the hat, a flower. Her white stockings peek out from under her skirts and the embellished black leather shoes hold her feet snug, which she folds with the grace of a well-groomed lady. Fannie was not the first pale-skinned girl who became famous for having been enslaved. She "had her predecessors … in girls such as Mary Mildred Botts and Sally Maria Deiggs (or 'Pink')."[26] Deiggs' story was rendered

---

[24] Before publishing *None Like Us,* Best with Heather Love wrote an influential introduction to a special issue of *Representations* on the visual archive of slavery. His critique as it was emerging in that introduction inspires my turn of thought here too, as when he writes: "An existence erased always presents the possibility of recovery, but, having never existed, Anastácia refuses just that. To write her history isn't to discern who she may once have been but, paradoxically, to *understand who she is now* [emphasis added]." Stephen Best, "Neither Lost nor Found: Slavery and the Visual Archive," *Representations* 113, no. 1 (Winter 2011), 160.

[25] I've done some work trying to forge this mode and method of encountering an archive, specifically a legal one, elsewhere: Monica Huerta, "Geometry & Mechanism: Material Metaphors and the Force of Uncertainty in Legal Thought," New Literary Analysis of Law Special Issue, *Critical Analysis of Law* 5, no. 2 (2018).

[26] Mary Niall Mitchell, *Raising Freedom's Child: Black Children and Visions of the Future after Slavery* (New York: NYU Press, 2008), 52.

Figure 6.1 *Redeemed in Virginia by Catherine S. Lawrence. Baptized in Brooklyn… . by Henry Ward Beecher, May 1863. Fannie Virginia Casseopia Lawrence, a Redeemed Slave Child, 5 years of age*, created by Renowden (1863). Courtesy of Schomburg Center for Research in Black Culture, Photographs and Prints Division, *Cartes-de-Visite* Collection.

into a painting by Eastman Johnson in *The Freedom Ring*. She and her story were so well-known that *The New York Times* wrote about her return to Plymouth Church in Brooklyn to celebrate the eightieth anniversary of her being bought away from slavery by a woman who relinquished her engagement ring to the cause.[27]

[27] "Freed Slave Tells of SALE by Beecher," *New York Times* (May 16, 1927).

In the most obvious sense, this and other photographs of light-skinned slave children make use of the nineteenth-century invention of sentimentalized childhood to carry along the ideology of slavery abolition. It's possible to see these images as successful in depicting children as "priceless," "innocent," and "vulnerable." This engine for their abolitionist sentimental appeal, according to Mitchell and others, was itself in a process of re-articulation while the images would have first been circulating:

> White childhood was increasingly sentimentalized in the nineteenth century as middle-class children became separated from both the world of adults and the world of work. Instead of contributing to the family income, they became "priceless" members of the middle-class family: innocent, unproductive, and primarily the focus of nurture and attention. Images of white childhood, in turn, idealized in fiction, advertisements, and illustrations, highlighted the supposed "innocence" and "vulnerability" of white children. These sentiments were reflected, as well, in family portraiture of the middle and late nineteenth century. The soft vignettes in which both Rosa and Rebecca appeared and the image of Fanny perched on a chair, holding a bouquet of flowers, were the sorts of children's pictures that would have been familiar to most northerners.[28]

Viewing Fannie's and other images like Fannie's as emblems of this form of appeal depends, then, on the conventions and ideals of white childhood being able to work for these children. So that it is useful to remember that in the Anglo traditions of portraiture these images depend on for both their composition and symbolic meaning, the solitary white child was meant to signify "pricelessness," "innocence," and "unproductivity."

But the problem for both convention and symbolism is that Fannie was neither "priceless," "innocent" in the ways presumed by the ideologies then attaching to the term in relation to white children, nor "unproductive," nor could she be depicted as such. The first is the simplest to address: Fannie had a price; she'd been bought. The caption plainly accounts for this. The second is subtler to read against. Fannie was an "innocent" child inasmuch as we can make the claim, with the idea that developed in the nineteenth century, that (white) children are "innocent" as a matter of course. But abolitionists chose Fannie to be in a photograph precisely because her "innocence" could be put into question. What has she seen? What of slavery does she carry with her still? What does she know? She is a child, so she is safe from being thought of as a full witness, but not entirely innocent of slavery's terror. The fact of her skin color is, necessarily, a question of violence. That is, it's not violence that she's "innocent" of.

Lastly, Fannie's *cartes de visite* cannot be simplistically read as fulfilling the idea of children as inherently "unproductive" for the simple fact that she had been enslaved, made into a commodity, and already part of cycles of production. Because the legal and economic status of being enslaved passed matrilineally in the United States, her life was already, from conception, bound up in commercial logics bound to legal regimes

---

[28] Mitchell, 378–9.

of transforming reproduction into an economic function for profit of her mother's owner. Before she was even born, she was already part of economic production, that is, "productive" in that sense. Furthermore, her *cartes de visite* are themselves commodities, sold to make money for schools in the South for freemen and *not* private objects of sentiment. Because she'd been bought, because her celebrity generates funds and part of that celebrity lay in her being a child, Fannie's childhood had never been innocent of the market.[29] In these ways, nineteenth-century conventions of sentimentalized childhood fail to work in the image and undo the grounds of abolitionist's ideologies' claims to her.

A straight reading of convention also counts on Fannie's clothes and setting working together seamlessly to evoke the northern, urban middle-class home and particularly a parlor. As Cobb elegantly describes,

> The parlor as a private-public space remained open to international influence via the incorporation of material cultures, but it also signifies attempts to close off the home to foreign interests through the enactment of geographic borders… parlor occupants anxiously considered issues of belonging… as they were destabilized by the question of Black freedom.[30]

Fannie—a young person who would have signified multiple kinds of contestation—was then also depicted in a contested space. Yet, for an ideological reading of the photograph, the composition must successfully communicate that Fannie is a parlor *here*. Of course, the *here* of the photograph is not just supposed to be an urban north, but any home in the white, middle-class urban north.[31] But because of the caption, "Redeemed in Virginia," Fannie also specifically represents "fancies" come north. Historian Walter Johnson describes the New Orleans-centered trade in "fancies" as built around the idea that the ability to own a "fancy" was a measure of wealth and social status.[32] These women and children were valued as a perverse luxury item to be kept in the home, available for sexual and aesthetic pleasure of their masters.

While ideological readings of the image need the image to assert a seamless, urban, white, middle class *here*, the main caption under the photograph "Redeemed in Virginia" stops the ideological work in its tracks. I will think in a moment about

---

[29] For a subtle analysis of how Black women celebrities' experiences in the eighteenth and nineteenth centuries undo concepts from political theory like freedom, citizenship, contract, and sovereignty, please see Samantha Pinto, *Infamous Bodies: Early Black Women's Celebrity and the Afterlives of Rights* (Durham: Duke University Press, 2020).

[30] Cobb, *Picture Freedom*, 18.

[31] Mitchell writes, for example, "With each child framed in the vignettes and parlor scenes associated with white northern middle-class girlhood, these images of 'slave girls' brought antislavery into the homes, perhaps even the family photograph albums, of many white northerners." Mitchell, 379.

[32] Edward E. Baptist gives a helpful account of the term "fancies" as in "fancy maids" in relation to the speculative market in Edward E. Baptist, "'Cuffy,' 'Fancy Maids,' and 'One-Eyed Men': Rape, Commodification, and the Domestic Slave Trade in the United States," *The American Historical Review* 106, no. 5 (2001), 1619–50.

how the caption works against the ideological work the photograph aims to perform. But first, let me pause to consider the word "redeemed," especially in its attempt to delineate geography as though in this moment it were stable or singular rather than an amalgamation of contested histories, claims, and dispossession.[33] Fannie's image would have fed into three different narratives in which she stood for the "redeemed" figure. The most obvious resonance of the word mobilized the explicitly scriptural history of the word. To this end, the text that accompanies Fannie's image asserts that she was "baptized in Brooklyn, at Plymouth Church," such that her image can also read as a safely sanctified member of the body of Christ. This part of Fannie's "redemption" claimed for the North the role of "redeemer" and the South, the yet-to-be-redeemed. In this sense, the ideological momentum of the image is to create a clear role to play in these children's lives for northerners. Second, the word "redemption" implies an economic exchange: Fannie's being bought out of slavery. This reading of "redemption" uses her being bought by Northerners and brought to the North as a way of identifying the North not just as the place of freedom, but also as the place of economic security. Last, the implication of her legal freedom has perhaps the most tenuous life in the image. The suggestion is that the North has made her free. But the North has also decided what her fate looks like. Rumors could nonetheless still circulate about what Fannie really wants. But if the North is capable of deciding legal destiny, then the image also claims for the North the ability to decide what part of the South to keep, what part to "redeem," and what part to abandon as "unredeemable." The photograph could perform all this ideological work seamlessly were it not for the caption, which reads, "Redeemed in Virginia."

We are supposed to understand the *here* of the photograph to be in the North. But the geographic disjunction would be clearer, a narrative arc more clearly implied, were the caption to read "Redeemed from Virginia." In that case, Virginia would be announced as the place from which Fannie came to the *here* of the photograph. That narrative, of course, would situate the specter of sexual violence implied by Fannie's pale skin in the Virginia the photograph wants to leave in the past. If Fannie in the photograph were to be "Redeemed from Virginia," the "redemption" could read as complete. But the phrase *in Virginia* keeps *Virginia* with the photograph and necessarily calls the *here* into question, both in the sense that *Virginia* continues to have some claim to Fannie and in the sense that *Virginia* aspires to claim some of the urban north the photograph wants to evoke with that most quintessential middle-class aesthetic: those freshly tightened curls framing Fannie's face, echoing the ruffles on her freshly pressed dress. As Fannie has been *Redeemed in Virginia*, the work the photograph seeks to perform—northern urban charity bringing the child into safe-keeping, "redeeming" her from and of slavery, "redeeming" her, even, of what she's likely seen—is called into question. With this image of Fannie, the convention of the

---

[33] I would be remiss not to prompt readers toward the exciting scholarship growing where Black Studies and Indigenous Studies meet, perhaps most notably in Tiffany Lethabo King, *The Black Shoals: Offshore Formations of Black and Native Studies* (Durham: Duke University Press, 2019).

parlor setting for children's portraits, the insistence on *here* as a safe, urban, middle-class home, cannot escape the ghost of the master's house. Because she would have been a "fancy" in the South, she would have been strongly identified with just this sort of parlor while enslaved, as well. In the master's house, she would have had exactly *this* kind of aestheticized value, the value of being bought in order to be looked at. In this sense, the photographic convention of the parlor will not let geography stay put. All of which is to say that the caption actively disassembles ideology once we allow ourselves to "think like a work of art." What opens up, instead, could be called a kind of reading, but I would rather propose it as a dynamic mode of creating a relation to what's historical about the image. This way of relating to what's historical by way of "thinking like a work of art" does not presume a singular solution to the encounter with this or any photo card, but rather insists that these photo cards can continue to undo the narratives we might insist on to make our meanings of history work, while *also* asking us to move through them in order to become undone. It's that dynamic, then, of being undone by the historical, that *becomes* the encounter with these forms of print culture. But being undone can only happen through a process of moving through the remains that partially animate the meanings that seem to leap off the cards, but incompletely.

For one, the articulation of geography in these images is unsettled in at least two other ways. First, reading geography in the photographs is part of locating and articulating these children's desires. Second, geographic coding in these photographs helps proscribe a relationship between the North and these children, the South and these children, and, finally, between the North and the South in an imagined, eventual union. However, because photographic convention will not do stable ideological work, any reading of the photographs that asserts stable geography falls short of accounting for them. The images, then, do not merely "articulate" two different visions of the future, which is just another way of disappearing the image altogether into a logocentric account of the work images do. Instead, convention in the images, if thickly accounted for, thwarts any ideological reading we might impose. To think through another way of relating to the geographies embedded in these images, I turn now to images of the children in travel cloaks, en route to *somewhere else*.

The images of these children in their traveling gear, in obvious ways, and through the outright performance of travel, likewise make geographical claims, although, to tarry with them, to think like a work of art about them is to further confuse what claims they can make about geography. In Figures 6.2–6.5, Fannie, Rebecca, Charley, Augusta, and Rosa appear in the heavy, crisp clothing of mid-nineteenth-century travel. Fannie, unlike the other children, would have become a celebrity, would have made the lecture rounds on her own and not with a larger group. She would have skipped onto train seats that left her tiny feet dangling over the floor, as she traveled with abolitionists on the lecture circuit. In Figure 6.4, Rebecca, Charley, and Rosa stand side by side, Charley's feet ever so slightly in front of the two girls beside him. Rebecca lays her hand on Charley's stiff and folded right arm, Rosa clutches at his left elbow just enough so that his arm won't lay flat against his side. In Figure 6.5, of the three little girls in the group, while Augusta holds onto Rebecca, Rosa keeps her arms

Figure 6.2 *Fannie Virginia Casseopia Lawrence – a redeemed slave child, 5 years of age* – redeemed in Virginia. c.1863. Library of Congress Prints and Photographs Division Washington, DC.

Figure 6.3 *Rebecca, An Emancipated Slave from New Orleans* (1863), created by Kimball. Courtesy of Schomburg Center for Research in Black Culture, Photographs and Prints Division, *Cartes-de-Visite* Collection.

Figure 6.4 Rebecca, Charley, and Rosa. c.1863. Photographed by M. H. Kimball. Library of Congress Prints and Photographs Division, Washington DC.

Figure 6.5 Rebecca, Augusta, and Rosa. c.1863. Photographed by M. H. Kimball. Library of Congress Prints and Photographs Division, Washington DC.

to herself. Although differing in height, the three parallel embellishments at the hems of their skirt line up almost perfectly, an echo of train tracks, of roads traversed, of their own lifelines appearing in sync for the time in which these photographs would make sense for abolitionists to take.

But in all of these images of transit, though the girls are identified as "from New Orleans," the images themselves have very little to say about where they are off to. In some images, the imitation of a tiled floor, the unadorned background, distinct from the studio where Fannie's traveling portrait was taken. In Figure 6.4, a theatrical sash of fabric intrudes awkwardly but only purposefully behind her. It might, perhaps, mean to signal some theatrical *ongoingness* from her little cloak, which covers her elbows that jut out from her silhouette, posed as she is in a kind of pose that's unexpectedly defiant—against the camera, against the adults, against being taken to Virginia from the only home she'd known. So that this image, even beyond the relative emptiness of the portion of the studio where she'd been asked to take on the pose, because of the pose she's been asked to take on, there's a kind of haltingness to the image as a whole, no matter the draped accessory rising taller than Fannie on her right. No matter the insistence on her wardrobe on transit and somewhere else to be. Her poised feet, one heel meeting one instep, folds of the skirt resting thickly over the crinoline that would have made the fabric puff, ribbons and strings affixing cape, jacket, in an exaggerated mass against her chest, with no obvious moment when they would have been relaxed. The small fur cap atop her head, curls hugging the sides of her face, giving shelter to the ears that would have heard exactly how many cries and screams. And any direction that the ideology might want to give the reading—from South to North, from slavery to freedom, from Black to white—dissolves in the face of the image itself. An undecided terrain, in that there is no terrain, a directionless direction, in that this is a nowhere space (in a somewhere studio, New York). Reading these traveling images "like a work of art" then is also reading these photographs as mechanisms of ideological disappearance even as some figures (political, sentimental, gothic) do emerge for us to hold onto—before the images ask we let them go again.

Then, When?

For some critics, the images of these children come north operate as a kind of prehistory to what Laura Wexler has called the "institutional afterlife of sentimental fiction."[34] But in encountering the unstable geographies that these images produce, I want to build now on the interest in terms of futurity and afterlives. I want to delve deeper into the relationship between these images, various levels of time, and the political ideologies

---

[34] Laura Wexler, "Tender Violence: Literary Eavesdropping, Domestic Fiction, and Educational Reform," in *The Culture of Sentiment: Race, Gender, and Sentimentality in 19th Century America*, ed. Shirley Samuels (Oxford: Oxford University Press, 1992), 19.

to which we tend to surrender our critical readings of them.[35] (In another essay, there could be reason to think about what's *surrendered to* in order to buttress this more sovereign form of critical approach and recounting.) Along the way, I will make the case that pro- and anti-slavery politics each abided by notions of temporality that are incommensurable to one another.

The implied movement from South to North, from immorality to redemption, from legal bondage to legal freedom, from the master's house to the northern parlor that makes ideological readings of the photographs work depends not just on stable geography, but on stable concepts of time. The issue at hand in these images is not just one of future, but of conceiving of how time, and specifically historical, political time works. Redemption, freedom, and the location of both in the north are each concepts that, in order to make sense, need time to be at least forward moving and at most, forgetful. I move now to analyze how it is that ideas of time undergird what I see as the main incommensurability between pro- and anti-slavery ideological readings of these photographs. I then turn to another set of *cartes de visite* to think about how form works against the senses of time upon which both these pro- and anti-slavery readings rely. But first, in this section, I use an 1864 "hoax" pamphlet to think more about the shifting temporalities embedded in the political cultures in which the photographs intervene. All along, I insist that the concerns around which pro- and anti-slavery arguments were being made rested on conflicting senses not just of the social value of African American lives, but on diverging senses of the nature of time.

In 1864, even as the war seemed just about won by the Union, the elections were not sure for Lincoln. Some rumors help me foreground the importance of ideas of time to these debates. The publication of the hoax pamphlet *Miscegenation; theory of the blending of the races, applied to the American white man and Negro* in 1864 crystallized rumors that the Republican platform included calls for racial amalgamation. Curiously, the pamphlet's nameless narrator does not identify with Southerners or Northerners, abolitionists or pro-slavery Confederates. Instead, the narrator positions himself as an outsider to all viewpoints. Pamphlets like this one used the scientific register of the new term, "miscegenation," as a way of fueling racist fears of the social repercussions of emancipation. Derby Applegate describes the political climate in which the term was born:

> Hoping to exploit the racist fear raised by emancipation, several Copperhead reporters seized on an 1863 speech by [newspaper editor and abolitionist]

---

[35] Gwendolyn Du Bois Shaw's interest in the images, while different from Mitchell's, is in the vein of historical recovery that I here try to step beside. Shaw writes, "The text... reveals that Fannie's body, despite having been bought out of slavery by Catherine Lawrence, was essentially still a commodity. That Lawrence sought to protect her legal claim to the right to reproduce her stepchild's likeness photographically indicates that she was actively seeking remuneration from its sale and distribution." For Shaw, the image fails because Fannie is still not free. The photograph is proof that Fannie "was essentially still a commodity," such that, for Shaw, it is decidedly not like the kinds of self-representation other photographs of African Americans give us, and thus, less "authentic" to the subjects she wants to recover. Gwendolyn Du Bois Shaw, *Portraits of a People: Picturing African Americans in the Nineteenth Century* (Andover: Addison Gallery of American Art; in association with the University of Washington Press, Seattle, 2006), 154.

Theodore Tilton that suggested that mingling white and black blood would create a more powerful nation. They coined a new term—"miscegenation"—for the old fear of interracial sex, and then printed up hoax publications to make it seem as if antislavery Republicans were promoting "the beastly doctrine of miscegenation." By March, observed the *Brooklyn Eagle*, "All leading men and journals are ranging themselves on either side in the battle between decency and lust." [36]

The appendix of the 1864 pamphlet operates as a kind of screen for the "objectivity" performed by the unlocatable and unnamed narrator. Each of the documents in the appendix is listed as a "testimony." The appendix, in fact, even includes the 1863 speech by Tilton. The use of a legal-sounding term, like testimony, was a way of giving the documents the veil not just of objectivity, but of custom. One can think of texts like Thomas R. Gray's *The Confessions of Nat Turner* (1831) and of Herman Melville's *Benito Cereno* (1855) for using exactly this tactic of performing "legitimation."

Although a "hoax," what the pamphlet nonetheless makes clear is how much time is at the center of nineteenth-century pro-slavery political platforms.[37] The main "argument" of the 1864 pamphlet is the insistence that the "condition of all human progress is miscegenation."[38] The text uses this insistence that historical and political time work together in undeniable, singular, and inevitable ways to make statements that are meant to be received as threatening. For example, in the fourth chapter, "The March of the Dark Races Northward," the narrator asserts, "The fact may be startling, but the student of ethnology will be willing to admit that in the course of time the dark races must absorb the white."[39] Here is a logic of time (and the fear of its onslaught) that is not just about where "anti-slavery time" must necessarily lead in the future, but a framing of a temporal imperative that, because it ruled the past, gains irrefutability through the idea that all of history was written with the pen of "racial amalgamation." To make this point another way, the narrator asserts, "All the noted ancient and modern wars of Europe may be traced to the yearning of the brunette and blonde to mingle."[40] The "yearning of the brunette and blonde to mingle" that shaped European history in this telling—and so *must* shape the future—works to instill fear only through this notion of time and history. Time interpreted here as political and social history—so this story goes—if left alone, is irrefutable and endlessly repeats. Depicted this way, this sense of irrefutability and endless repetition is meant to engage and encourage readers that the "yearning" must be defied—precisely because its threat is the fact of

---

[36] *Eagle*, March 29, 1864; as quoted in Derby Applegate, *The Most Famous Man in America: The Biography of Henry Ward Beecher* (New York: Three Leaves Press, 2006), 351.

[37] Mark Smith's *Mastered by the Clock* answers historians' conscripting of the South into "natural" time as opposed to "clock" time. As Smith makes clear, "clock" time penetrated the South well before the Civil War. Mark Smith, *Mastered by the Clock: Time, Slavery, and Freedom in the American South* (Chapel Hill: University of North Carolina, 1997).

[38] David G. Croly, *Miscegenation: A Theory of the Blending of the Races, Applied to the American White Man and Negro* (New York: H. Dexter, Hamilton & Co., 1864), 16.

[39] *Miscegenation* 17.

[40] Ibid., 18.

being incontestable. The onrush of time is being constructed here as a kind of Goliath against which the pamphlet calls its readers to become many valiant Davids, swinging their slingshots in unlikely but heroic confrontation. The victory against what's been written as time's destructive march then, will be all the sweeter and worthy precisely because it's been thought of as unlikely. But this caricature of the Republicans' political platform nonetheless registers how important the idea of forward-moving time was for Republican politics—*and* how much of a threat this sense of time was to Copperheads and Confederates alike.

Just as this parody of the Republican platform imitates and distorts a Republican sense of time to create its political boogeyman, in a pro-slavery reading of the photographs these children represent the threat that race can infiltrate bloodlines and make itself invisible. But this reading misses the full sense of how the pro-slavery reading functions to produce fear. The production of fear in the reading rests entirely on ideas of time we associate with the "uncanny," or with the "spectral" in clear conflict with anti-slavery senses of time as we've parsed them so far. Daphne Brooks contends in a slightly different context that the white mulatta body reads as inherently "uncanny."[41] For Brooks, "The white mulatta's body of evidence, her figure encom(passing) the uncanny traces of the familiar and the foreign, makes the violence of his white supremacy spectacularly visible and yet disturbingly contiguous with blackness."[42] With Brooks' intervention in mind, then, pro-slavery fears of miscegenation rest on this more complicated conception of time and historicity, whereby history does not advance, but rather always returns (rather than repeats) and has more than just an affective tug on the present. The tug of history here is material, literal, perpetual.

Let's pause on the word "redemption" as one example from which to spin an articulation of what we might call "anti-slavery time."[43] On the one hand, as I discussed in the previous section, because these are children in the images, an ideological reading imagines that they have yet to be indelibly marked by having been enslaved and so read more strongly as emblems of "redemption." But this reading also assumes an interpretive transparency that I have been resisting. The hopefulness of reading

---

[41] Daphne A. Brooks, *Bodies in Dissent: Spectacular Performances of Race and Freedom, 1850–1910* (Durham: Duke University Press, 2006), 19.

[42] Ibid.

[43] Further research would likely find many versions and not just this one of "anti-slavery time," but what is important for me here is to begin to understand how certain discrete and incommensurable syntheses of time helped to create ideological conflict in mid-nineteenth-century United States. This analysis adds to a conversation that has been happening for some time in slavery and nineteenth-century studies, from Walter Johnson's work on narrativity and temporality in terms of scholars' accounting of slavery, to David Blight's now-canonical *Race and Reunion*. Both of these lines of inquiry—how historiographical framings of the slave trade conscript temporalities that do not align with colonial archives, and how important memorialization becomes in the post-Civil War moment—stand to be elucidated by an interest in how ideologies variously configure the relationship between past, present and future. David Blight, *Race and Reunion: The Civil War in American Memory* (Cambridge: Harvard University Press, 2002).

childhood as overlapping conceptually with ideas of redemption rests, instead, on an idea of time where the past can be left behind, like a material object, a photograph, let's say. *Only* according to an idea of time where the past can be left safely as though in a material "elsewhere" can pronouncing these subjects "redeemed" make the fullest sense. Even as the vocabulary around the extinction of slavery changes, it mirrors this belief in forward-moving time.

In the later photographs, the vocabulary shifts from the question of "redemption" to the question of "emancipation." This shift is in part about the changing vocabulary of enslavement's political extinction in the United States. The difference, at first, signals these later photographs as more explicitly political. For example, if we were looking for a telos that marked time in the use of two words, we might say that the discourse around freeing enslaved African Americans moved from more overtly spiritual to more overtly political ways of describing these subjects' relationship with the law. But both words tap into a sense of time that crosses between and even aspires to connect political and spiritual temporalities. That is, for "redemption" and "emancipation" to work, spiritual clocks and political clocks have to be set to work together and only toward an idea of the future. And this kind of overlapping metaphysics of time creates a sense of the future by way of underscoring its *difference* from and so its *incommensurability* with the past.

While the temporality implied by both "redemption" and "emancipation" ask us to think in terms of a connection between spiritual and political time where both move forward to make an anti-slavery politics conceivable, a *Harper's Weekly* article about our young subjects suggests anti-slavery politics also frames the relationship of Black families to post-war freedom in terms of their place in time. Many scholars foreground how abolitionists used the dissolution of family by enslavement's many crimes of property (as legalized theft and kidnapping) in the transatlantic circulation of anti-slavery ideas. The *Harper's* article that accompanies a woodcut of the freedmen, women and children from New Orleans makes explicit, in a way that articles about Fannie do not, that these children were not just brought out of slavery, but away from their relatives and kin.

Rebecca, for example, "was a slave in her father's house, the special attendant of a girl little older than herself," where her "mother and grandmother (to whom the [*Harper's*] writer had spoken) live in New Orleans, where they support themselves comfortably by their own labor." Unlike Rebecca,

> Rosina had a father [in the Confederate army] while her mother, "a bright mulatto, lives in New Orleans in a poor hut and has hard work to support her family." And of Charles, readers learned: "three out of five boys in any school in New York are darker than he. Yet this white boy has been twice sold as a slave. First by his father and 'owner', Alexander Wethers, of Lewis County, Virginia, to a slavetrader named Harrison, who sold [him and his mother] to Mr. Thornhill of New Orleans."[44]

---

[44] "White and Colored Slaves," *Harper's Weekly* (January 30, 1864), 71.

For one, the *Harper's* writer provides these details to prove to doubtful readers that they had, indeed, been enslaved. But the article prompts readers not just to account for their families, but to interpret those families as the reason these children were in danger, either because of their father's station and role as their master, or because of the economic instability of most freed people in the South. In these various ways, the families of these children get relegated not just to the South, but also to a sense of the past whereby it can be left as though it is merely disposable matter in space and not a condition of and afterlife in the present. That is, an anti-slavery reading of these stories rests on the idea that vexed blood relationships needn't prohibit the entry of these young subjects into full citizenship. At the same time, the assertion of this temporal logic that holds the North as an unproblematic "redeemer" rests on the obliteration of the familial ties that bound these children to their complicated families.

On the other hand, a pro-slavery reading of the photographs was not capable of imagining that interracial families could be left in the past. Instead, behind a pro-slavery reading of the photographs is the idea that the subjects' ability to "pass" would continue to perpetuate interracial families. But if we "think like a work of art" in the ways that I have been suggesting about these images would allow for the time of viewing, in which an onlooker decides how to read the form and those familial ties in terms of the temporalities they might imply, either as past (as in the possibility of being left elsewhere) or as perpetual. Seen this way, a photograph, even a *cartes de visite*, does not necessarily have to only be an emblem for pastness (as in Barthes' sense of the "that happened") but can also become a form of radical presence, an object that demands a decision, while creating another slice of spacetime in which the decision hasn't yet been made.

Lastly, I want to ask how the citizenship imagined for these children (and viewers) by these photographs relates to the conflicting senses of political, historical, and spiritual time as I've been able to read them in the hoax pamphlet. The photographs that most readily make claims to citizenship are those in which the children appear with American flags. One image from 1864 especially opens out onto questions of citizenship, and the possibilities of a new and unified nation. In another *cartes de visite*, Rebecca kneels under the stars and stripes. The caption reads "Oh! How I love the old flag!" This image could be seen as a critique of the nation that had not treated these children as deserving of "swaddling" or care. Or, in a move that Mitchell and Bernstein anticipate, this image could *also* produce the kind of "racial innocence" that could only imagine light-skinned faces for citizens. But reading Rebecca and the flag this way, what exists is only the interplay of categories: childhood, emancipation, and race. As I've been arguing, in the formal attributes of these images, and in reading them like "a work of art" it is possible to see some other possibilities at work. A closer reading of Rebecca's photograph with the flag elucidates the slippage.

In Figure 6.6, Rebecca crouches at the foot of the flag, her dress engulfing her slight frame under its circumference.[45] Unlike the image of her from 1863 where she kneels in

---

[45] In the Library of Congress prints & photograph collection, there are several versions of this image of Rebecca with a flag taken at Charles Paxson's studio. Indeed, there is an entire series of the children, grouped, draped in an American flag. I've chosen this image of Rebecca to discuss because it is the one where she most emphatically takes on the (given?) pose.

Figure 6.6 "Oh! How I Love the Old Flag," Rebecca, a Slave Girl from New Orleans. c.1864. Created by Charles Paxon. Library of Congress Prints and Photographs Division, Washington DC.

posed prayer, in 1864, she has learned to emulate more subtle emotion for the camera. In the 1863 images, her face is quintessentially, conventionally stoic. To hold a pose for at least ten seconds (the minimum amount of exposure time then needed), she would have had to have held her face in as relaxed a position as possible. However, the later image called for more simulation than that. Imitating supplication, Rebecca turns her eyes upward to the flag, and, the visual metonymy is obvious, to the heavens at one and the same time. She tilts her head slightly to the right, heightening the performance of earnestness. The phrase asserted, "Oh! How I love the old flag" secularizes the more obviously Christian supplicant. The placement of the flag indicates the flag (nation) is just as ready to embrace the young subject, but needs her aspiration. Rebecca must—and does not—bow before the flag in order for the conceptual circle to close. Her mouth remains closed, but the caption "Oh! How I love the old flag" asserts an exclamation. The cry, we are supposed to understand, is her thoughts. The disjoint between the caption, whose punctuation asserts an exclamation, and her closed mouth locates the photograph in some other slice of time and, therefore, keeps the object in temporal limbo where it does not yet fulfill either the ideological goals of an anti-slavery reading or feed pro-slavery fears.

Undone (A Conclusion)

This chapter has tried to "think like a work of art" about *cartes de visite* of formerly enslaved children—even as the cards themselves do not make the claim to *art*—in order to find their internal ideological incoherence. To use these images to arrive "nowhere" has been my way of trying to take on Best's proposition for a different posture for criticism. At the same time, gathering insight from Hartman's method of "close narration," although not reproducing that narration, I've nonetheless sought a way of describing these images and the possible worlds toward which they point (toward which there's no arriving) as something we might nonetheless relate to, in the conceptual space and critical practice of being undone by them again and again. I've argued that certain formal elements keep these images from being entirely legible either by a pro- or anti-slavery politics, such that the related questions of the efficacy of sentimental discourse in politics, the circulation of bodies as emblems, and the unstable reach of bloodlines and geographies around a nation remain open even as the children held in them hold still. Likewise, I've argued that the ideological work of the photographs depends not just on the fact that the subjects are children, but on competing ideas of temporalities at work in them. I have suggested that pro- and anti-slavery politics diverge most consequentially not only on questions of African American freedom and agency, and Anglo-American responsibility to soon-to-be-formerly-enslaved subjects, but on conceptions of how time works and has varied effects. In the throes of the Civil War, one of the most important points of contention was not just about what kind of country or countries would survive the historical, immediate, and ongoing carnage, but about how to tell, understand, and live in competing political notions of time. "Thinking like a work of art" with these ephemera of print culture, then, has helped make explicit that Americans in the mid-nineteenth century were deciding over and again how historical, political, and spiritual times work even as they might have adopted an ideology, a politics, and both sympathetic and parasitic relationships to and with children who could seem like and yet unlike themselves.

Which is all to say, if we allow historical images and bits of print culture's ephemera to keep undoing the ideological holds they likewise and nonetheless (incompletely) might conjure, these images and bits might keep undoing *us*. Having become undone, as a continual critical practice, it becomes possible to continue to reinvigorate the grounds for choosing to make these or any other objects of print culture matter to the present. This is not a question of relevance. This is a question of being willing to give over our critical practice to what Best describes as a non-sovereign mode. That mode would be another form of historical relation toward which to aspire.

7

Engraving Class: Gender, Race, and the Pictorial Politics of the 1877 General Strike

Justin Rogers-Cooper

In a pamphlet published more than two decades after 1877, the Black anarchist and author Lucy E. Gonzalez Parsons revealed she first became interested in the "Labor Question" during the "great railroad strike of July 1877."[1] Somewhat surprisingly, then, in the *Life of Albert R. Parsons*, Parsons cites the 1874 police riot in Tompkins Square Park as a precursor to the 1877 strike. Describing how the "suffering unemployed poor of New York city [sic] determined to meet in Tompkins square January 13, 1874, to appeal to the public by bringing their attention to the spectacle of poverty,"[2] she relates how New York police brutally beat demonstrating crowds of men, women, and children. Like with July 1877, for Parsons the winter of 1873–4 was also a turning point in the history of the "Labor Question"—even though it didn't involve striking wage workers.

To better grasp Parsons' crucial history of the "Labor Question," we must look again at 1877 with fresh eyes. Far from a conflict over wages and working conditions, for Parsons "the great railroad strikes of 1877 aroused the people to realization [sic] of the actual conflict between capitalism and organized labor (Socialism)."[3] The strike on the railroads, then, was actually a "conflict" over capitalism. Like the riot in Tompkins Square, the riots of 1877 emerged from indiscriminate attacks by police and militias on crowds full of hungry men, women, and children. Parsons' attention to the 1877 strike's gendered violence against waged and unwaged persons demands we further reinterpret the synchronized uprisings and rebellions first triggered by the railroad workers. Unlike traditional historians who focus on male railroad unions and prior industrial strikes to explain July 1877, Parsons adds to our understanding of why the 1877 strike transformed from a railroad blockade into synchronized urban uprisings involving entire families, neighborhoods, industrial workers, and

---

[1] Lucy E. Parsons, "The Principles of Anarchism," in *Lucy Parsons: Freedom, Equality, & Solidarity*, ed. Gale (Ahrens Chicago: Charles H. Kerr Publishing Company, 2004).
[2] Lucy E. Parsons, *Life of Albert R. Parsons with Brief History of the Labor Movement in America* (Chicago: Mrs. Lucy E. Parsons, 1889), VII.
[3] Ibid., XVI.

unemployed rioters. By locating the Tompkins Square police riot as an event within a serial narrative that climaxes in 1877, Parsons helps us understand the general strike as class war for survival, but also pushes us to see it as a heterogeneously gendered conflict. As Kim Moody emphasizes, "capitalism in Gilded Age America created not only the giant machine-driven factories but also strings of sweat shops, gangs of day laborers, armies of the jobless, growing numbers of underpaid home workers, and countless unpaid homemakers."[4] Following Parsons and Moody, I argue in this chapter that it's only by attending to the strike's gender that we can fully grasp why it went "general," but that doing so also leads us to see the strike's racial and ethnic politics in new ways, too.

Further, representations of the strike in the period's visual culture help us look alongside, and sometimes past, the male railroad workers who began the strike. If for Parsons the strike fomented a "realization" about capitalism and socialism in the United States, we might better understand that realization by reconsidering it through aesthetic perspectives wrought with such tensions. Parsons' framing is a starting point for my inquiry into the spectrum of images—specifically the woodcut engravings appearing in periodicals and monographs—that illustrated the strike. Just as the 1870s depression had already altered the perception of capitalism in the United States (and especially the railroads, their capitalists, and workers), the 1877 general strike irrevocably altered how many perceived and understood violent class conflict. This chapter thus will attend to the pictorial politics of the 1877 general strike in terms of the gendered depictions of strikers and rioters, and in turn elaborate on the ways those gendered representations also depended on racialization to make claims about class conflict, particularly through attention and inattention to facial features and details. By examining the print culture around the general strike, I will demonstrate how race and gender complicate perceptions of the strike's class conflicts and its multiform layers of class consciousness.

In this respect, I will build on the important work of Joshua Brown, who contrasted the visual representations of the strike in *Harper's Weekly* and *Frank Leslie's Illustrated Weekly*. Assigning special significance to the woodcut engravings in *Leslie's*, Brown claims the images mark a "move toward realism" in the periodical's depiction of working-class subjects, in part from the "conflicting demands of a broad and increasingly diverse readership," including those from the working class and others that sympathized with strikers.[5] It's worth noting that the major monographs published on the strike soon after largely reproduced images from *Leslie's*, including J.A. Dacus's *Annals of the Great Strikes* (1877), Edward Winslow Martin's *The History of the Great Riots and of the Molly Maguires* (1877), and Joel Tyler Headley's *Pen and Pencil Sketches of the Great Riots* (1882). By extending Brown's foundational claims about transformations during the strike in the "efficacy of social typing [that] relied on a widely shared cognitive map," I

---

[4] Kim Moody, *Tramps and Trade Union Travelers: Internal Migration and Organized Labor in Gilded Age America, 1870–1900* (Chicago: Haymarket, 2019), 15.

[5] Joshua Brown, *Beyond the Lines: Pictorial Reporting, Everyday Life, and the Crisis of Gilded Age America* (Berkeley, CA: University of California Press, 2006).

will reconsider the "physiognomy in the representation" in *Harper's* and *Leslie's*, as well as the unique engravings found in Allen Pinkerton's *Strikes, Communists, Tramps, and Detectives* (1878). Further, I will also attend to images that appeared in London and Paris, including *The Illustrated News of London*, *The Pictorial World*, *Le Monde Illustré*, and *L'Illustration Journal Universel*.[6] I will show how reproduced pictorial images published in London reinforced sympathies with the railroads found in *Harper's*, while modified engravings published in Paris succeeded in depicting the strike's Black participants (notably, as the US periodicals failed to do so). By viewing the 1877 general strike through transnational print culture, this chapter will thus consider Brown's "realist turn" in transatlantic context by attending the ways American racial, gender, and class politics bifurcated across the English Channel.

My claims in this chapter therefore span the majority of non-photographic images produced about the 1877 general strike, and will emphasize the contested realizations of the strike through intersecting categories of race, class, and gender. In particular, I want to think carefully about the constructions and erasures of blackness and white masculinity, and the performance of rioting women, in tension with the move toward "realism," particularly in terms of facial features. I argue that gendered racialization of the strikers as *general* strikers, and especially depictions of women and children, shows why the strike belongs to more than one history—that is, not just "class conflict," but also women's work and Black Reconstruction. Images of the general strike made women's insurgent militancy visible, but through technologies of racialization that depended on the militancy of both male and female strikers and rioters. Indeed, even for European immigrants and settlers, the images reveal how white citizenship was contingent on respectable class performance or lack of militancy, and how insurgent acts could make rioting white citizens vulnerable to forms of state violence routinely applied to Chinese, indigenous, and Black subjects.

The Drama of the General Strike

The financial crisis of 1873 followed a period of unsustainable growth and over-speculation in railroads and their stocks, and afterward the United States fell into a depression whose effects persisted until the end of the nineteenth century.[7] Following the failure of the Jay Cooke & Company bank due to overinvestment in the Northern Pacific Railroad, the panic in credit markets rippled into the US economy during an era when railroads were the economic engine of capitalist expansion. The immediate effect of their failures cascaded into disaster for ordinary people. Nearly a half-million workers lost employment in rolling mills, machine shops, foundries, and related

---

[6] Ibid., 167.
[7] Michael Roberts writes that the depression lasted "1873–97," and regards the period between 1873 and 1876 as a "slump." Michael Roberts, *The Long Depression: How It Happened, Why It Happened, and What Happens Next* (Chicago: Haymarket, 2016), 5. Allan Nevins, *The Emergence of Modern America, 1865–1878* (Chicago: Quadrangle Books, 1971), 291–2.

industries.⁸ The crisis led almost immediately to mass unemployment, particularly in northeastern cities like New York and Chicago. By the summer of 1877, average wages had fallen between 25 and 60 per cent, while food costs dropped only 5 percent; workers spent up to 60 percent of their wages on food, however.⁹ Labor unions collapsed along with thousands of businesses, as did, if temporarily, public demands for an eight-hour working day. The number of national unions fell from thirty to nine.¹⁰ In addition to mass unemployment, the wage labor that was available was increasingly part-time, and wages fell along with prices as severe deflation set in. The specter of mass unemployment gave way to fears of the "tramp evil" as unemployed men wandered in search of jobs, living off the land and turning to theft for survival.¹¹

The collapse of the economy sparked more than just the shock of *laissez faire* capitalism, however. The subsequent emergence of new movements among the working classes for material security, employment, and food heralded a new era of working-class revolt. Demonstrations in New York, Chicago, and Boston during 1874–5 ushered in years of "demands for outdoor and indoor relief."¹² As Lucy Parsons recounts, displaced and unemployed workers and their families demonstrated for their survival, and those demonstrations were important precursors to the general strike.

The trigger for the initial strike in July 1877 was a 10 percent pay cut on the Baltimore & Ohio Railroad, which triggered a small strike by workers at Camden Yards on July 16, 1877. They were soon followed by workers of the Baltimore & Ohio in Martinsburg, West Virginia. The cut came amidst rate wars by the railroad corporations engaging in "shoddy operating practices and continuous wage cuts," and in the context of a pooling agreement by four trunk lines to set traffic, regulate stock, and reduce wages.¹³ Many of the railroads were still profitable and paying dividends on stock, including the Baltimore & Ohio, yet firemen working on that railroad had seen their monthly wages drop from $55 in 1873 to $30 in 1877.

The drama of the strike was a national and then transnational story from its inception. Violence erupted in Martinsburg when William Vandergriff attempted to halt a strike-breaking train protected by the West Virginia militia and was mortally shot. An engineer in Pittsburgh articulated the perspectives of the strikers, their families, and the rioters: "It is a question of bread or blood."¹⁴ Many "identified with their long-standing grievances," and workers, families, communities, and unemployed masses soon converged in cities like Pittsburgh and Chicago.¹⁵ Newspapers quickly connected workers in one city with those in another. Events and actors in Martinsburg were soon known to readers all over the nation. Indeed, strikers in Westernport, Maryland, issued

---

⁸ Nevins, *Modern America*, 299.
⁹ Robert Bruce, *1877: Year of Violence* (Chicago: Ivan R. Dee, Inc., 1989), 19; Bruce, *1877*, 19.
¹⁰ Phillip S. Foner, *The Great Labor Uprising of 1877* (New York: Pathfinder, 1977), 29.
¹¹ Nevins, *Modern America*, 301.
¹² Ibid., 299.
¹³ David Burbank, *Reign of the Rabble: The St. Louis General Strike of 1877* (New York: Augustus M. Kelley, 1966), 9. Foner, *1877*, 33.
¹⁴ Michael A. Bellesiles, *1877: America's Year of Living Violently* (New York: New Press, 2010), 155.
¹⁵ Ibid., 153.

a manifesto on July 20th printed by the *Reading Daily Eagle* in Pennsylvania the next day, entitled "WE SHALL CONQUER OR WE SHALL DIE."[16] The print culture of the general strike helped facilitate what would become a synchronized rebellion.

The drama occurring in Martinsburg was overtaken and transformed by events in Baltimore. As crowds stoned a militia heading to repress the strike, the militia fired on them, wounding forty and killing at least eleven, including the fourteen-year-old newsboy Willie Hourand. Meanwhile, on July 19 workers on the Pennsylvania Railroad struck for their own reasons; three days earlier, general superintendent Robert Pitcairn issued a new policy stating all eastbound trains to Altoona would be double-headers—a "laborsaving device."[17] Not coincidently, news from Maryland and West Virginia coincided with the strike on the Pennsylvania, and "strikers began using the same tactics developed on the Baltimore & Ohio."[18] On July 21 in Pittsburgh, the arrival of militia troops from Philadelphia brought a "vast assemblage of men, women, and children to the Outer Depot" near the Union Depot where the troops stood.[19] The troops then marched on the crowd with fixed bayonets, stabbing several demonstrators. The crowd stoned the troops, who returned fire. They killed at least twenty people and wounded at least twenty-nine. News of the massacre spread quickly, and that night rioters burned the roundhouse where the troops retreated, much of the surrounding area, and thousands of train cars. During the destruction, hundreds of "men, women, and children broke into the cars and carried off everything they could get their hands on."[20] This moment of rioting, looting, and incendiarism would become a major focus of visual reproduction and description.

Newspapers carried the news of the confrontations in Martinsburg, Baltimore, and Pittsburgh across the country and delivered the drama in stark terms, describing it as a "civil war" and accusing strikers of communism.[21] They devoted numerous front-page columns to events.[22] It was a crisis containing drama full of blood and fire. Extra editions exclaimed death and alarm, with "spreading of excitement by rail and by sensational news stories."[23] The headline on Monday's *New York World* blared, "RIOT OR REVOLUTION?"[24] Crowds of people stood next to newspaper and telegraph offices eager for telegraphed notifications, while others in sites like Little Rock, Raleigh, Kansas City, and Cincinnati gathered in public spaces to discuss news.[25] The strike swept through many cities and states, and the news on July 23 detailed a range

---

[16] Foner, *1877*, 52, 293.
[17] Ibid., 67.
[18] Ibid.
[19] Ibid., 73.
[20] Ibid., 76.
[21] Bruce, *1877*, 135–6. Also see Justin Rogers-Cooper, "Downfall of the Republic! The 1877 General Strike and the Fictions of Red Scare," *Canadian Review of American Studies* 36, no. 3 (2016), 386–408.
[22] Bruce, *1877*, 159.
[23] Ibid., 160, 223.
[24] Ibid., 226.
[25] Ibid., 160.

of fighting in Harrisburg, Cincinnati, Philadelphia, Buffalo, Albany, Columbus, and beyond.[26] A major eruption of violence occurred in Chicago, where Albert Parsons and other leaders of the Workingmen's Party demanded a "nationwide general strike for the eight-hour day and for a 20 per cent increase in wages."[27] Violent police confrontations with strikers and crowds began on Wednesday July 25 and continued into the next night.

The battles in Baltimore, Pittsburgh, and Chicago dominated the news, but major episodes of violence and sabotage occurred in dozens of other cities and towns. Over two weeks, at least 100,000 workers in fourteen states led the uprising against railroad corporations, particularly in industrial cities and towns along the nation's east-west trunk lines, among them Boston, Pittsburgh, Baltimore, Chicago, Columbus, Cincinnati, St. Louis, Toledo, Louisville, Buffalo, Galveston, and San Francisco. With police and militias unable to contain the insurgent crowds—particularly following indiscriminate murders of protesters and strikers—President Rutherford Hayes declared the strike an insurrection and deployed almost half the US Army. Most newspapers called for "the most brutal form of repression" against them.[28] Between half and two-thirds of the nation's freight sat on the tracks, at a moment when rail transport was the primary infrastructure of commerce, travel, and economy.

By its conclusion, there were hundreds of casualties and deaths, millions of dollars in property damage, and dueling apprehensions about what the strike meant. Kim Moody contends that the general strike "awakened both capital and labor to the reality of class conflict."[29] For the ruling class and its sympathizers, the strike portended the necessity of repressing the dangerous classes by any means necessary. In terms of synchronicity, scale, and participation, what transpired was also the "country's first national strike," and as a social insurgency it can be compared to the Pullman Strike of 1894, the protest wave of 1967, and the rioting following Martin Luther King, Jr.'s assassination in 1968.[30] One of the strike's first historians relates that as "an entirely spontaneous outburst of labor discontent, it has never been paralleled on such a large scale, in the United States," and in terms of worker militancy the contention arguably still holds.[31] In several cities, white and Black workers joined together, and immigrant workers of various nationalities also acted in concert, including large numbers of Irish, Bohemian, German, and English communities. The widespread rioting for which the strike became infamous, particularly in Baltimore and Pittsburgh, occurred after militia massacres of civilians and should be understood as retaliations for those killings. The riots in Chicago, Baltimore, Pittsburgh, and elsewhere, in fact, are notable both for widespread participation by women and because female casualties helped catalyze retaliatory violence by working-class crowds.

---

[26] Ibid., 222.
[27] Ibid., 243.
[28] Foner, *1877*, 228.
[29] Moody, *Tramps and Trade Union Travelers*, 24.
[30] Bill Barry, *The 1877 Railroad Strike in Baltimore*, Self-Published, 1.
[31] Burbank, *Reign of the Rabble*, 8. Also see Bellesiles, *1877*.

The strike is also notable for the contradictions it revealed: some workers and intellectuals framed the strike as a gender and racial crisis, especially in terms of white masculinity. Perhaps the most famous example is Lucy Parsons's husband Albert, a printer and leading English-speaking member of the Social-Democratic Party in Chicago (later renamed the Social Democratic Party of America). Albert Parsons was a candidate on the Workingmen's Party ticket in 1877, and in a widely circulated speech during the strike, he called upon the "grand army of starvation" to recognize "men" as the "backbone of the country," demanding support for the "brothers" in a fight over "our wives and children" (for this Parsons was fired and received death threats).[32] Other strikers and leaders, including the Executive Committee of the Workingmen's Party in St. Louis, allowed the pressures of anti-Black racism to precipitate the strike's collapse there, as documented by David Roediger and David Burbank. In San Francisco, white nationalist rioters weaponized the strike against the Chinese community; indeed, the absence of images depicting anti-Chinese murders and attacks on Chinese communities typifies what Edlie L. Wong calls "the dialectic of black inclusion/Chinese exclusion" in the late nineteenth century.[33] The uprising of multiracial and multiethnic working-class crowds of waged and unwaged men, women, and children, however, largely shared the conviction that their immiseration and desperation was undeserved and collectively felt. Most united in a demand for "a living wage," and by the belief that they deserved to live, whether working or not—a norm not assured in an era of social Darwinism.[34]

The Periodical Context

Many realizations inspired by the 1877 general strike emerged in print culture. Indeed, in George S. Schilling's contribution to Lucy Parsons' biography, one of the leaders of the Social-Democratic Party elaborates how the general strike "secured us the public ear" even as "the press and pulpit, with but few exceptions, declared that it was the work of communist agitators."[35] However prejudicial most capitalist newspapers were to working-class values, narratives of strikes and riots in nineteenth-century print culture contributed to what Moody calls the "class conscious subculture of opposition," especially with the labor press: Between 1863 and 1873, there were 120 labor papers, and by the 1880s the labor press was "at its height."[36]

---

[32] "One of the Inciting Causes," *The Inter Ocean* (Chicago, IL), Wednesday July 25, 1877, 3.
[33] David Roediger, *Towards the Abolition of Whiteness* (New York: Verso, 1994), 105. Burbank, *Reign of the Rabble*, 168. Edlie L. Wong, *Racial Reconstruction: Black Inclusion, Chinese Exclusion, and the Fictions of Citizenship* (New York: New York University Press, 2015), 4.
[34] Bruce, *1877*, 15–16.
[35] George S. Schilling, "History of the Labor Movement in Chicago," *Life of Albert Parsons*, XVIII. Schilling earlier affirms that the influence of the Social-Democratic Party in Chicago, of which Albert Parsons was a leading orator, "was very limited until the great railroad strike of 1877." Parsons, *Life of Albert Parsons*, XVII.
[36] Moody, *Tramps and Trade Union Travelers*, 42, 45.

So while the 1870s depression inaugurated a new generation of class conflict that exploded vividly in 1877, the general strike also crystalized competing representations within print culture about contested norms of race, class, and gender. While most narratives of class conflict during the 1870s depression circulated as narrative reporting in capitalist and labor newspapers, daily and weekly pictorial periodicals such as *The Daily Graphic, Harper's Weekly,* and *Frank Leslie's Illustrated Newspaper* gave readers and audiences visual ways to comprehend class conflict generally and the 1877 general strike in particular. The diffusion and revision of class conflict and class actors into visual print culture had meaningful implications for how the general strike was both realized and remembered.

While newspapers played a major role in communicating news about labor and strikes, daily and weekly periodicals were also important and established mediums for communicating news in general. *Frank Leslie's Illustrated Weekly* appeared in 1855, and Harpers Brothers created their own pictorial weekly two years later. *Leslie's* focused on news with an eye toward sensationalism, and at first "teetered on the edge of respectability."[37] Meanwhile, *Harper's Weekly* was modeled on *Harper's Monthly*, which began in 1850 and aimed at a genteel, literary, and respectable readership, and considered the "leading American illustrated paper of its day."[38] Both illustrated weeklies first played a "partisan and influential role in constructing narratives" of the Civil War, and their cultural influence remained intact afterward.[39] During the war, too, both published wood engraved depictions of violent events and subjects, including the New York City Draft Riots of 1863.[40]

The pictorial politics of action sketches had been refined prior to the general strike, then. As Joshua Brown writes, the power of *Leslie's* and other illustrated weeklies lay in their "rapid visualization of the topical and in its transformation of news into a detailed pictorial narrative provided by a new type of journalist, the artist-reporter or 'special artist.'"[41] Such special artists would gather information, either in person or by reconstructing news through telegraph or testimony. Sometimes skilled draftsmen would add details for certain subjects. The Civil War proved that pictorial reporting could address rapidly changing events; during the war, "sketch artists could offer the readers of periodicals 'action images' of soldiers on the march, in camp, and even in combat."[42] This applied to strikes and riots, too. Further, while action sketches in periodicals were

---

[37] Brown, *Beyond the Lines*, 40.
[38] "Harper's Weekly," *The News Media and the Making of America, 1730–1865,* American Antiquarian Society, https://americanantiquarian.org/earlyamericannewsmedia/items/show/124. Accessed June 18, 2020. "HarpWeek," New York Public Library, https://www.nypl.org/collections/articles-databases/harpweek. Accessed June 18, 2020.
[39] Eleanor Jones Harvey, *The Civil War and American Art* (New Haven: Smithsonian American Art Museum, Yale University Press, 2012), 5.
[40] Ibid., 206.
[41] Brown, *Beyond the Lines*, 33.
[42] Kristen M. Smith, ed., *The Lines Are Drawn: Political Cartoons of the Civil* War (Athens, Georgia: Hill Street Press, 1999), xi.

obviously not allegorical political cartoons, they did require a compression of complex events into single moments that simultaneously functioned metonymically (a single moment standing in for larger events) and selectively (the sketch artist, followed by the engraving and printing team, selected one point of view out of many to curate complexity). The superiority of action sketches over still photography during the Civil War remained true in 1877, since slow-shutter photography required still subjects and access to darkrooms; further, no photographs of the 1877 general strike appeared in any periodicals of the period because such technology did not yet exist.[43]

The lengthy process of producing woodcut engravings helps to explain the temporal lag between an event and its visual representation in print. The pictorial sketches of the 1877 general strike, unlike relevant images from stories about it in the newspaper, appeared at least a week after the events they depicted. In fact, *Leslie's*, *Harper's*, and *The Daily Graphic* skeches appeared in August, after the strike ended. Even the New York *Daily Graphic* worked on several days of delay—although published as a daily paper, its first sketches of Baltimore appeared on the Tuesday, July 24 cover, some four days after the riot. Delays meant illustrated periodicals sometimes ran reference images in place of action sketches; for example, the August 4 edition of the British illustrated weekly *The Graphic* ran a five-panel page titled, "The Railway Strike in the United States—Views on the Pennsylvania Railway," that contained a lovely view of Lake Erie, a view of Harrisburg bridges spanning the Susquehanna, a scenic landscape of greater Pittsburgh and its railway terminus, and a detailed blueprint drawing of the roundhouse where rioters "Besieged" troops.[44] Readers would have adapted these images into narratives of the strike.

The delays in publishing sketches from the strike both in the United States and abroad effectively memorialized events of strike as they were reported. This conflation of news with memory was reinforced by the large numbers of *Leslie's* images that later appeared in illustrated books on the strike. Since the images were often composites and compressions of events in the first place, their power arises from an ironic temporal tension: they are action sketches and historical illustrations. Especially given the scale of the strike and its attendant violence, the expression of periodical images as historical narrative would have formed something like an instant archive.

That archive, however, revealed clear political choices. Brown rightly identifies the less innovative images came from *Harper's*, which he describes as opting for "distant, panoramic views of mass destruction and milling crowds."[45] The August 11 edition of *Harper's* devoted nine images to the 1877 general strike, for example, with six showing aspects of the violence in Pittsburgh. The often-reproduced cover, showing the militia firing on workers against a deep-set urban street perspective, actually drew from a

---

[43] Ibid., xi. Notably, the photographers S. V. Albee and J. R. Riddle produced stereograph sets of the riot's aftermath in Pittsburgh.
[44] *The Graphic*, vol. XVI, no. 401, August 4, 1877, 117.
[45] Joshua Brown, "The Great Uprising and Pictorial Order in Gilded Age America," in *The Great Strikes of 1877*, ed. David O. (Stowell, Urbana: The University of Illinois Press, 2008), 43.

photograph by Daniel Bendann.⁴⁶ As Brown and others have observed, part of what distinguishes the *Harper's* images from *Leslie's* (and other print culture representations of the general strike) is the periodical's emphasis on panoramic landscape and long views of urban landscapes (Figure 7.1). There are few faces, few characters, and few

Figure 7.1 D. Bendann, "The Great Strike—The Sixth Maryland Regiment Fighting Its Way Through Baltimore." *Harper's Weekly* (New York) vol. 21, no. 1076 (August 11, 1877).

⁴⁶ Daniel and David Bendann were German-Jewish immigrants known for their "elegant photographic backgrounds," for which they patented a system for selling negatives for other studios' background shots. "Daniel Bendann," peoplepill.com, https://peoplepill.com/people/daniel-bendann/. Accessed July 14, 2020.

individuals. Likewise, inside there are two half-page images: one of the locomotive blockades in Martinsburg, and one showing the burning of the Lebanon Valley Railroad Bridge. The opposite page includes a sketch of Pittsburgh Union depot on fire. Two pages later, two panoramic images depict the burning of Pennsylvania buildings and rail cars, and crowds looking over the smoking ruins. Other engravings focus on the burned roundhouse and a funeral winding through nearby ruins. The images are strangely elegant and picturesque, yet devoid of urgency. While a few women and children appear in the Martinsburg sketch, we only see their backs; the working-class population is essentially faceless. Such facelessness signifies obvious ideological investments, but also a lacuna within the *Harper's* imagination about *who* belonged to the working class.

The final full-page illustration is perhaps the most revealing: it contains a panel of four scenes with a middle circular frame showing "Pittsburgh in the Hands of the Mob." The top scene shows a mass of people carrying away goods from looted train cars, while the bottom reveals yet another depiction of the smoking ruins around the Pennsylvania Railroad business and machine shops. The middle left panel provides a close-up of the crowds raiding the train cars, and the middle circular window shows a crowd outside a gun store. This aforementioned final panel on the "Mob," however, stands out in two ways: although minimally sketched, we do see working-class men, women, and children carrying away goods from a train car. The other reason the "Mob" panels appear singular comes from their representation of working-class agency that—however criminal-looking to *Harper'* readers—revealed the underlying motives for the strike against wage cuts in the first place—that is, the need for food and other necessities of life. Nonetheless, *Harper's* did not feature any close-up engravings of faces. The strikers and rioters are a blurry mass.

Despite these limitations, these initial Harper's images came to define the strike's associations in visual culture and typify many illustrations into the present (for example, the Pittsburgh *Post-Gazette* would use one of *Harper's* burning roundhouse images to illustrate its centenary article on the general strike in 1977).[47] Furthermore, *Harper's* images informed the reception of the strike in England. In the August 25 edition of *The Pictorial World* of London, the two panoramic images from the August 11 *Harper's* are reprinted at half-size, and run vertically on one page with minor modifications to artist attribution, caption, and title. Likewise, the August 18 edition of *The Illustrated London News* reproduced two images from the August 11 *Harpers*: a cropped version of the cover image showing the Sixth Maryland Regiment firing on the rioters in Baltimore, and the burning of the Pittsburg roundhouse under the title "The Railway Riots in America."[48] In its August 18 edition, however, *The Pictorial World* ran two large widely reproduced images of the Baltimore militia battle and the Martinsburg strike from the August 4 *Leslie's*; the *Leslie's* image of Martinsburg also appeared in at least one French pictorial periodical.[49] These reproductions largely affirm

---

[47] Clarke Thomas, "The Pittsburgh Railroad Riot of 1877," *Post-Gazette*, Wednesday July 20, 1977, 6.
[48] *The London Illustrated News*, vol. LXXL, No 1988, Saturday August 18, 1877, 161.
[49] *The Pictorial World*, August 25, 1877, 405. *The Pictorial World*, August 18, 1877, 388.

Harper's aesthetic of working-class facelessness, suggesting an overlapping ideological investment—perhaps not surprisingly, given the enormous sums of English capital invested in American railroads.

In the second of the two issues devoted to the strike, the August 18 *Harper's* deviates from representing strikers as faceless. Set beside scenes from cavalry missions against the Nez Perce in the inside pages, in the upper panel we see a chaotic fight between workers and police in Turner Hall in Chicago, and orderly troops firing on rough-looking workers nearby at the Halsted Street Viaduct below. Both half-page scenes are medium shots, with faces visible in profile and in the foreground. It would be difficult to describe the scene in Turner Hall as realistic, but the workingmen in the corner of the Halsted Street Viaduct have recognizable expressions of anger, and their features and postures are brightly lit compared to the dark, far-off clump of firing soldiers.

Figure 7.2 E.A. Abbey, "The Frenzy, and What Came Of It," *Harper's Weekly* (New York), Vol 30, No 1077 (August 18, 1877).

The realist turn Brown observes in *Leslie's* is arguably visible on the issue's cover, however, although not in an action sketch (Figure 7.2). In the large picture drawn by Edwin Austin Abbey (1852–1911), a prominent illustrator of the period who specialized in literary and historical themes, a male worker sits on stacked railroad blocks, his foot perched on a broken train wheel. He leans his head on his hand, staring off into the distance in front of the smoking ruins of the Pittsburgh roundhouse. His wife cries into his leg, her face buried in her arm, while she holds a young child with her other. Behind them is the faint outline of a dead body, while near them sits a smoking pistol, presumably fired into the Philadelphia militia. Titled "The Frenzy, and What Came of It," the still life serves as *Harper's* editorial allegory on the strike's meaning. In contrast to Samuel Gompers, Lucy Parsons, and others who felt hope from the strike, for *Harper's* it only accomplished destruction and death, and its victims included railroad workers and their families. Yet the most visible feature in the image is the worker's face: his pensive, sullen expression sharply stands out against the dark, smoky backdrop. This expression and his surroundings beg the question: what next?

Whatever the paternalistic comment intended by Abbey and *Harper's*, the worker is rendered serious and sober, not atavistic or criminal. Further, his face is neither caricature nor cartoon. Not incidentally, the skin of his hand and face are the lightest—and whitest—shades of the image's complexion. As this working-class male face comes into focus, then, he becomes a perverse shade of white. Remarkably, while he might or might not resemble a German or Irish type, his features mostly signal white respectability. When *Harper's* did render a striker's face visible, then, it chose a prominent sketch artist to compress the strike's many actors into one: a white male laborer.

Yet this act of selection was also an act of erasure. It placed the employed white male "breadwinner" at the center of the struggle to survive the long depression. At the moment when the white worker and his family become visible, the unwaged mother—his wife—buries her face in her hands. The female rioter visible at the margins of the "Mob" image, too, recedes as the liberal imagination transfigures her back into tragic domesticity, sobbing and homeless. This signification portends one future of labor politics, one in which craft unions of mostly white male laborers organized nationally into institutions like the American Federation of Labor, while also concealing the multiracial and multiethnic crowds of men, women, and children who actually participated in the strike. Perhaps ironically, the condensation of the strikers into a white male echoes speeches by socialists like Albert Parsons, who also frame the strike as a crisis of masculinity for the working breadwinner.

Harper's decision to bring the face of the white male railroad worker into close-up belies its larger political project. The cover image is notable not only for its realistic allegory, but because it's legibly fictional. It registers differently than the action sketches, too, because such sketches were frequently accompanied by highly influential political cartoons. These cartoons had significant cultural power and helped shape interpretations of the sketches, and also arguably anchored a periodical's politics. Such cartoons drew from the tradition of the English vehicle *Punch*, began in 1841 and featuring artists such as John Leech, who was an influence on prominent US cartoonists such as Thomas Nast of *Harper's*, William Newman and Matt Morgan of *Leslie's*, and Joseph Keppler of *Puck*.[50] Like action sketches, political cartoons drove circulation and demand, and by 1860 *Leslie's* circulation reached 160,000 and *Harper's* 100,000; furthermore, "each copy had many readers."[51] This remained true in the 1870s, when Nast's success famously increased *Harper's* circulation through iconic representations of "Boss" Tweed in New York.[52] Along with Allen Pinkerton, Nast was staunchly anticommunist and equated "nineteenth-century trade unionism with Communism," too.[53] In part, Nast's anticommunism reflected anxiety among white propertied classes about a "fear of violent social revolution" activated by the 1871 Paris Commune.[54] Nast's infamous personification of communism as a grim, animated skeleton in the years following 1877 captured such anti-radical feelings inspired by the general strike. Such class anxiety and racial chauvinism permeated many of the strike's images, especially those in Pinkerton's book.

As Joshua Brown has contended, some of *Leslie's* cultural power arose from resisting the impulse to caricature strikers and rioters as one-dimensional figures of evil. This representational spectrum is worth stressing because the cover engraving on the August 18 *Harper's* is reminiscent of Nast, but it's not obviously disparaging of the white male laborer. While the editorial cover image and the action sketches inside ultimately serve different purposes, then, they share an implicit orientation toward genteel liberal politics. During the strike, *Harper's* respectable racial masculinity opens to the white male worker while simultaneously advancing an anti-labor politics: this concession announces what W.E.B. Du Bois would call the "psychological wage" of white labor during Jim Crow.[55]

Striking and Racial Performance

Harper's might have been the most respectable periodical interpreting the strike, but it was far from the only one, much less the most innovative one. In terms of simply visualizing events beyond Pittsburgh, Chicago, and Baltimore, *The Daily Graphic's* coverage of the strike on August 9 provides an important supplement to our knowledge

---

[50] Morton Keller, *The Art and Politics of Thomas Nast* (New York: Oxford University Press, 1968), 5. Allen Nevins and Frank Weitenkampf, *A Century of Political Cartoons: Caricature in the United States from 1800 to 1900* (New York: Charles Scribner's Sons, 1944), 15.

[51] Keller, *Thomas Nast*, 7.

[52] Thomas Nast St. Hill, *Thomas Nast: Cartoons and Illustrations* (New York: Dover), 1–2.

[53] Ibid., 124. In this respect, Nast's work resembled John Hay's anti-labor novel about the 1877 general strike, *The Bread-Winners*, originally serialized in *The Century* in 1883–4.

[54] Keller, *Nast*, 245. Also see Philip M. Katz, *From Appomattox to Montmartre: Americans and the Paris Commune* (Cambridge: Harvard University Press, 1998), 161–83; and J. Michelle Coghlan, *Sensational Internationalism: The Paris Commune and the Remapping of American Memory in the Long Nineteenth Century* (Edinburgh: Edinburgh University Press, 2016), 2–3, 5, 10, 24, 83.

[55] Du Bois, W.E.B. *Black Reconstruction* (New York: Harcourt, Brace, and Company, 1935), 598.

of the strike in print culture. Rarely reproduced or cited, *The Daily Graphic* was an illustrated evening paper published on Park Place in New York.[56] The first American newspaper with daily illustrations, the *Graphic* ran from 1873 to 1889 with a peak circulation of 10,000. Perhaps due to the strike's violence having ended, the August 9 cover featured eight illustrations of soldiers stationed at Kingston, Wilkesbarre [*sic*], Plymouth, and Scranton. Notable for focusing on Army guards called into action by President Hayes, the images contain only the most basic shading, with the exception of the central panel depicting a night patrol on the Lehigh Valley Railroad. While detailed, the images are mostly lines and outlines, and the facial features of the soldiers, when visible, are mostly straightforward and unemotional.

By contrast, *Leslie*'s circulated two newspapers about the strike on August 4, one regular edition and one "Railroad Riot Extra." These images were likely the first action sketches of the strike to appear in weekly periodicals. The regular edition cover used a multi-panel strategy, showing five pictures depicting the rioting in Baltimore. The caption attributes them to "Our Special Artists," and describes "Scenes and Incidents of the Conflict Between the Sympathizers with the Strikers and the Fifth and Sixth Maryland Militia."[57] In one, a woman struck holding a brick falls over a rioter laying in the street. Around her men are being struck or fighting. A boy chases a girl toward a crowd of battling men. In the next panel, a crowd of onlookers watch as a worker and gentleman carry a dead body on a stretcher, a bloody shirt covering its head. In the central panel, a well-dressed gentleman leads a barrage of workers throwing bricks against the militia, some of whom are falling and fallen. In the bottom left square, a crowd of rough-looking men attack a militia soldier, while in the bottom right a gentleman and worker lead a crowd of arsonists setting fire to Camden Street Station.

These multi-panel views are revealing for three reasons. First, they depict broad class-based violence, representing, for example, cooperation between well-dressed gentlemen and workers dressed in laboring clothes, signifying widespread support for the strike by the middle class. Second, the images focus on anti-militia attacks and violence, and not strikers or rioters. Finally, the images do not exclusively show men. Women and children are present in two panels, and children are active agents, holding brickbats or stones. Tellingly, in the top left panel a woman holding a brick has been struck from behind, perhaps by a bullet. In front of her, children surge toward the fighting crowd. By showing women and children as active agents and victims of violence, the images reveal the strike's general uprising. Although these panels are much less reproduced than the large full-page illustrations inside, one of those illustrations shows a well-dressed middle-class woman being helped up by a suited man (the Maryland Sixth Regiment firing on "The Mob" on the corner of Frederick and Baltimore Streets); next to her, a young boy flees the violence. The other full-page, often-reproduced scene shows workers on the Baltimore & Ohio dragging

---

[56] One reason *The Daily Graphic* might be infrequently cited likely reflects its lack of comparative social status, the quality of images due to its daily production schedule, and possibly the accessibility of its archives.

[57] *Frank Leslie's Illustrated Newspaper*, New York, August 4, 1877, 365.

strike-breakers from a locomotive. Although we don't see women or children here, it's significant that this is the *only* sketch of the strike and railroad workers in all the panels. *Leslie*'s coverage of riots and militia confrontations signals why July 1877 was much more than a railroad blockade.

Published simultaneously with the regular edition, the cover of *Leslie*'s "Railroad Riot Extra" further centers our attention on rioting and not on the strike itself. In a single large image spanning most of the page attributed to John Donaghy, we see the Pennsylvania roundhouse burning from the perspective of an overlooking hill; in the foreground we see three clusters of people with their backs to us, including two women and one man holding a gun. This image is significant in part because the "Extra" edition focused on strike and riot-related actors and subjects in the other images.

Indeed, the "Extra" edition of *Leslie*'s is remarkable for the range of subjects and locations it depicts. Inside, we find twenty-two different images of the strike, including scenes from Baltimore, Hornellsville (New York), Newark (Ohio), Newark (New Jersey), Pittsburgh, Philadelphia, and New York City. One entire page of panels shows scenes from the Seventh Regiment in New York City, with various representations of drilling, resting, loafing, and eating—the latter notable because two Black servants are serving food. These are the only Black figures in the strike's representations in the United States, despite the fact that Black people participated in multiple cities. Further, only five scenes actually show train tracks, railroads, or trains: a "mob" attacking a train at Hornellsville, Philadelphia police clearing a "mob" from the tracks, a "mob" pulling an engineer from a train in Newark (Ohio), rioters soaping the train tracks near Hornellsville, and, in an enormous central panorama, the Philadelphia militia firing on the "mob" in Pittsburgh near 28th street. Nearly all the images show a clash of strikers or rioters against police, soldiers, or militia. In terms of faces, the index of images mostly avoids close-ups with a few exceptions—here, not all that dissimilar from *Harper*'s.

These observations deserve attention due to their relevance to existing scholarship. Joshua Brown claims *Leslie*'s pictorial politics transformed working-class representations during the strike: it "marked a sea change in … representation of American labor and set it apart from the rest of illustrated press."[58] Whereas previously *Leslie*'s rendered its presentation of laborers through the "distancing function" of antebellum ethnic types ("exoticized, sometimes buffoonish, sometimes menacing"), Brown argues that during the strike *Leslie*'s experimentally moved away from reliable facial and ethnic types because such "social typing … could not work in representing situations in which readers might, in effect, recognize themselves."[59] Brown stresses, too, that *Leslie*'s made a distinction between the legitimate "rights" of the railroad worker and the "Communistic element."[60] This distinction led to differences in how workers might be represented against rioters, who were associated with tramps and communists. We can see this distinction in the cover image from *Harper*'s discussed above.

---

[58] Brown, *Beyond the Lines*, 162.
[59] Ibid.
[60] Quoted in ibid., 161.

What Brown leaves implicit is crucial, then, to how periodicals represented the general strike, particularly through faces. They did so through strategies of visual typing that racialized rioters as ethnic communists but rendered railroad workers as white. As Brown observes, the faces present in the "Extra" edition are rendered through realist typing. During the discursive transformation taking place, whiteness became contingent on the performance of "respectable" striking as opposed to the "criminal" act of rioting. One image encapsulates just this distinction. In one of the inside frames of the first sketches, "An Armed Mob Marching to the Scene of Action in Pittsburgh," two figures stand in front of an armed crowd of workers, including a gentleman raising an American flag (Figure 7.3). On the left is a triumphant looking, clean-shaven

Figure 7.3 "Pennsylvania—An Armed Mob Marching to the Scene of Action in Pittsburgh," *Frank Leslie's Illustrated Newspaper* (August 4, 1877).

young man with short hair, a white cap, and a loose-fitting collared shirt tucked into clean white breeches and knee-high black boots. Compared to the others present, his statuesque pose, fashionable clothes, and able-bodied form suggest a muscular and healthy whiteness. By contrast, to his left is an adolescent male, barefoot with torn clothes and tapping a drum. His face is askew, revealing a stub nose with two large nostrils—perhaps he suggests "the physiognomy ... of the 'lowly' Irish."[61]

Yet with the exception of the large panorama at the periodical's center, the drummer boy is arguably the most visible face in the sketches. He's also one of the few characters who looks directly into the viewer's eye. The intimacy and expression combine with racialized social typing to command the viewer's gaze, and the visual markers of his youth, poverty, and possibility of his Irish "physiognomic signs" function as signifiers of stereotyped blackness.[62] Ironically, the image evokes a racialized intimacy in tension with the "distancing function" such physiognomic signs imply. The ironic intimacy of racialization presents a contradiction: we are drawn *toward* the strangeness of the rioter. In the other *Leslie*'s edition, children participate in the riot but are characterized with features suggesting sympathetic norms. Here, the child's racialization emphasizes the contingency of his whiteness. The racialized boy has no other family present, either—in other images, we can find mothers and relatives nearby. Here, the orphaned working-class child defies the realist turn, and his "unreality" reveals the cultural aporia of the general strike itself. As we saw on the *Harper*'s cover, the worker as father can perform respectable whiteness; yet here in *Leslie*'s, the unwaged orphaned child rioter cannot.

One of the reasons *Harper*'s and *Leslie*'s pictorial strategies around class and race remain significant are due to just these politics of realism and unreality. *Leslie*'s realist turn matters not just because working-class representations transformed during 1877, but because the contradictions of representing the general strike capture larger contradictions of US racial capitalism at this moment. These contradictions make visible the racial and gendered composition of the United States' working-class, and with implied corresponding politics of cooperation and stratification. For example, despite the political collapse of Reconstruction during the 1870s, white and Black workers cooperated, and developed respect for women's right to work through the Knights of Labor. Kim Moody writes that the growth of the Knights of Labor "really began in the wake of the 1877 railroad strike," and he emphasizes how the rise of Knights' assemblies was "proof that American workers were not adverse to unionization, striking, or class-based politics despite the racial and ethnic divisions and tensions of the era."[63] Mark Lause also pointedly contends that "the hard times that had begun in 1873 moved desperate wage earners of all sorts to resort to versions of mass strike inaugurated by African Americans to secure emancipation."[64] Indeed,

---

[61] Ibid., 153.
[62] Ibid., 169.
[63] Moody, *Tramps and Trade Union Travelers*, 117.
[64] Mark Lause, *The Great Cowboy Strike: Bullets, Ballots, & Class Conflict in the American West* (New York: Verso, 2017), 250.

Black and white workers cooperated during the general strike in West Virginia, Missouri, and other sites. Many casual students of the period might also be surprised to learn that the interracial cooperation of the Knights reproduced the egalitarian politics of the Industrial Brotherhood, began in 1874 and modeled on the National Grange, and which admitted both African Americans and women.[65] Later, many African Americans joined the Knights, especially in Arkansas and Texas—during the purported collapse of Reconstruction.[66] Such interracial cooperation overlayed multiethnic mutual aid in urban immigrant neighborhoods during the 1877 general strike.[67] The emergence and consolidation of interracial working-class solidarity during and after the 1877 general strike reveals a racial dialectic at work. Moreover, it becomes a late episode in what Peter Linebaugh and Marcus Rediker call the "lost history of the multiethnic class that was essential to the rise of capitalism and the modern, global economy."[68] This long history stares back at us in the "Black" features of the orphaned Irish drummer boy.

The intimate "blackness" of the drummer boy also connects the general strike to African American labor beyond the rise of the Knights. For one, the general strike erupted in the wake of the Hayes-Tilden presidential election controversy, and the victor Hayes famously conceded a policy of home rule for southern white supremacists. This conciliation often marks for many the conclusion of postwar Reconstruction.[69] The near simultaneity of the general strike and the *political* concession by northern liberals like Hayes to New South apartheid, however, isn't merely incidental. As Eric Foner has aptly argued, the northern United States had experienced its own "social transformation" after the Civil War—one he calls the "North's reconstruction."[70] John B. Jentz and Richard Schneirov argue that events in post-Civil War Chicago, including the general strike, should be conceived "in the rise to national dominance of capitalism" that includes the "context of Reconstruction, which is commonly viewed by historians

---

[65] Ibid., 27.
[66] Ibid., 146.
[67] Stuart Hall poses ethnicity "in an uneasy and unresolved relationship" to race and nation. Stuart Hall, *The Fateful Triangle: Race, Ethnicity, Nation* (Cambridge: Harvard University Press, 2017), 85. That indeterminacy in racial and ethnic discourse speaks to how both operate as sliding signifiers that "organize the great classificatory systems of difference that operate in human societies." Hall, *The Fateful Triangle*, 32–3. The mark or badge of race are "*signifiers of difference*" that function materially through a "naturalization effect." Hall, *The Fateful Triangle*, 39, 58. Hall toggles between race and ethnicity to the point of contending race as "historically specific," and calling ethnicity a "perfectly good term" to refer to the cultural differences that form a "distinctive area of difference." Hall, *The Fateful Triangle*, 82, 83.
[68] Peter Linebaugh and Marcus Rediker, *The Many-Headed Hydra: The Hidden History of the Revolutionary Atlantic* (New York: Verso, 2012), 6.
[69] To understand the role the railroads played in this post-1877 conception of Reconstruction's slow death, see R. Scott Huffard Jr., *Engines of Redemption: Railroads and the Reconstruction of Capitalism in the New South* (Chapel Hill: The University of North Carolina Press, 2019), 3. Also see Moody, *Tramps & Trade Union Travelers*, 53. 1877 actually marks the beginning of the end of Reconstruction: the 1896 *Plessy v Ferguson* decision and the 1898 Wilmington coup are better critical markers to understand the consolidation of Jim Crow racial capitalism.
[70] Eric Foner, *A Short History of Reconstruction* (New York: Harper Perennial, 1990), 199.

as a Southern question."[71] After the 1873 crisis, the need to sustain corporate profits with cheap labor had bipartisan support. Both reconstructions—north and south—would necessitate extermination; in 1877, such repression was almost sequential.[72]

The blackness of the drummer boy also reminds us that the racialization of working-class labor though new racisms necessarily accompanied police repression—even among European immigrants. Protestant nativism and xenophobia emerging after the 1871 Paris Commune consolidated such new racisms during the long depression, and "the concept of a labor revolution instigated by foreigners really crystalized during the sudden, wild fury of the railroad strikes of 1877."[73] *The Nation* typified the anti-labor press, equating strikers with immigrants and defining them as racial aliens, differentiated by "blood" not culture.[74] Such "nativist thinking," as Matthew Frye Jacobson contends, was therefore not delimited to anti-Black racism nor fully absolved by legal whiteness.[75] As he relates, "race and racial difference … distinguished not only whites, blacks, Asians, and Latinos from one another, but also Hebrews, Celts, Slavs, Finns, Italians, Teutons, Magyars, and Anglo-Saxons."[76] The "modern American alien" performed as an abnormal body, signifying otherness and exception culturally, and even as Beth Lew Williams sees that alien as a "principal result of anti-Chinese violence," the legal and cultural technologies of "alienation" against the Chinese and others became contingent instruments of repression against the "alienated" working-class insurgents.[77] Even as the white nationalist press characterized the general strikers as savages in a colonial discourse, the visual "alienation" of racialized strikers speaks to "key questions over the status or role that racialized migrants play within white settler colonialism [which] often remain unasked or avoided".[78] Racial tensions became visible

---

[71] John B. Jentz and Richard Schneirov, *Chicago in the Age of Capital* (Urbana: University of Illinois Press, 2015), 242. While Jentz and Schnierow rightfully place events in Chicago during 1877 within the context of Reconstruction, their claim that capitalism rose to national dominance during this period implies that the antebellum slave economy wasn't capitalism. As R. Scott Huffard Jr. writes, among others, we should "see the Old South as a site of capitalist disaster," too, and the "New South not as an aberration, but as a function of untrammeled capitalism." Huffard, Jr., *Engines of Redemption*, 5. Also see James S. Allen, *Reconstruction: The Battle for Democracy 1865-1876* (New York: International Publishers), 207–15; and Peter Camejo, *Racism, Revolution, Reaction, 1861-1877, The Rise and Fall of Radical Reconstruction* (New York: Pathfinder, 1976), 175–87.

[72] See Justin Rogers-Cooper, "Class Wars: Race, Class, and Violence in the Long Gilded Age," *Critical Sociology* (October 2020), https://doi.org/10.1177/0896920520968258.

[73] John Higham, *Strangers in the Land: Patterns of American Nativism 1860–1925* (New York: Atheneum, 1963), 30–1.

[74] Richard Slotkin, *The Fatal Environment: The Myth of the Frontier in the Age of Industrialization*, Norman: University of Oklahoma Press, 1994, 495.

[75] Matthew Frye Jacobson, *Barbarian Virtues: The United States Encounters Foreign Peoples at Home and Abroad, 1876–1917* (New York: Hill and Wang, 2000), 61.

[76] Ibid., 69.

[77] Beth Lew-Williams, *The Chinese Must Go: Violence, Exclusion, and the Making of the Alien in America* (Cambridge: Harvard University Press, 2018), 7. Lew attributes the construction of the legal category of "alien" to anti-Chinese violence that preceded the creation of the legal category. This category arguably proved capacious enough to become a disciplining technology for radical anti-capitalists, as with anarchists later in the century.

[78] Slotkin, *The Fatal Environment*, 480; Iyko Day, *Alien Capital: Asian Racialization and the Logic of Settling Colonial Capitalism* (Durham: Duke University Press, 2016), 19.

among some strikers—including its socialist vanguard—in ways that define the other side to the aforementioned racial dialectic. David Roediger and David Burbank have written about the ambiguous anti-Black politics among the mostly German leaders of the St. Louis Executive Committee, which led the strike there. Their hesitancy to embrace black strikers portended one future of white working-class racism, but that future wasn't inevitable nor even necessarily imminent after 1877 for the American working classes as a whole.

Rioting and Gender Performance

Representations of working-class subjects in the 1877 general strike depend on distinctions between striking workers and rioting aliens. Such symbolic compression signals a wider spectrum of silences, erasures, and distortions. Most periodicals emphasized events in Pittsburgh, for example; the *Daily Graphic* is one of few periodicals to depict scenes in Louisville and Altoona.[79] Scenes from other cities are absent, such as St. Louis. Yet the representation of *who* participated in the strike and riots, and *how* their racialized and gendered representations produced public knowledge, further complicates how the 1877 general strike was constructed and remembered. Part of this complication stems from how quickly the strike spiraled into riots activated by police and militia repression, not wage cuts. As David O. Stowell describes, the strike triggered "crowds of strikers and urban residents with no wage relationship to the railroads, stopping trains, battling police, and, much to the alarm of railroad workers, attacking railroad property."[80] Many who formed crowds to stop trains, stone militias, and observe the strike were women and children, some with relationships to railroad workers. While contemporaneous accounts and historians have noted women's actions in Baltimore, Pittsburgh, and Chicago, Stowell describes how they were present even in cities like Buffalo. Moreover, they "carried clubs and uttered threats as loudly as men."[81] Their presence testifies to why Lucy Parsons calls the strike the "realization" of a world-historical conflict between capitalism and socialism: it was a racial and *gendered* class conflict.[82] The strike was general because enormous numbers of working-class people of different genders—waged and unwaged—protested for their own survival, and they believed agents and symbols of capitalism to be their enemy.

Print culture and pictorial texts represented class conflict as a gendered affair, too, and not just a racialized one. On the one hand, many male workers and Lucy's husband Albert agreed with Samuel Gompers that the "rebellion was a declaration of protest

---

[79] See *The Daily Graphic*, "Scenes of the Railroad Riots at Pittsburgh and Altoona, PA, Last Sunday," vol. XIV, 1; and *The Daily Graphic*, "Scenes of the Railroad Riot at Louisville, KY., Last Tuesday," Monday, July 30, 1877, 1.
[80] David O. Stowell, *Streets, Railroads, and the Great Strike of 1877* (Chicago: University of Chicago Press, 1999), 69.
[81] Ibid., 123. The quote is taken from the *Buffalo Express*.
[82] Parsons, *Life of Albert Parsons*, VII.

in the name of American *manhood* against the conditions that nullified the rights of American citizens. The railroad strike of 1877 was the tocsin that sounded a ringing message of hope to us all" (italics mine).[83] Gompers' royal we ("to us all") subtends his claim about "manhood" with different effects. In one respect, we might repair his conception of manhood beyond men—as a gendered performance of militancy, rather than an expression of essential identity. On the other hand, Gompers intended his remark to echo Parson's Chicago speech, when he claimed the strikers as "brothers" fighting for their "wives and children."[84] A strike fought *for* wives and children would have surprised some of the women and children fighting *with* male workers and rioters.

Indeed, women and children supported the strike in manifold ways, and representing their actions became sites of contradiction in pictorial terms. In Hornellsville, New York, striking workers of the Erie railroad mobilized their community to slow down trains to enforce the blockade: "Men and women from the town, workers and supporters, soaped the rails for a quarter of a mile up Tiptop Mountain, one of the steepest grades in New York."[85] In a significant picture of the event that would be reproduced in Joel Tyler Headley's *Pen and Pencil Sketches of the Great Riots*, Edward Winslow Martin's *The History of the Great Riots and of the Molly Maguires*, and J. A. Dacus's *Annals of the Great Strikes*, a central figure on the railroad tracks faces away from the viewer while directing three men soaping the tracks, as two crowds of male bystanders watch (Figure 7.4).[86] The figure wears a bandana over long hair, and has a checkered shirt tucked into pants; her sleeves are rolled up. In nearly every image of a woman depicted in pictorial texts of the strike, they are wearing a dress. Here, however, the female figure directing the soaping performs some stereotypical details of femininity—the bandana, figure, and body shape—while also signaling traditional male attire (checkered button shirt and pants). Our inability to see the figure's face reinforces the indeterminacy of gender. Here, the striker becomes gender queer; like the drummer boy, the image delimits the public imagination of class and gender performance. Further, gender becomes contingent upon the respectability of class performance and anti-capitalist militancy.

The queering of women's gender identity in relation to their riotous performance during the strike becomes more politically legible in Allen Pinkerton's cartoonish account in *Strikers, Communists, Tramps, and Detectives*. Unlike the other monographs

---

[83] Samuel Gompers, *Seventy Years of Life and Labor: An Autobiography*, ed. Nick Salvatore (Ithaca: ILR Press, 1984), 47.

[84] Albert Parsons, "Module 05: Industrialization and Its Discontents: The Great Strike of 1877: Evidence 17 Speech of Albert Parsons, July 23, 1877," The Digital History Reader (Virginia Tech University), https://www.dhr.history.vt.edu/modules/us/mod05_industry/evidence_detail_17.html. Accessed June 17, 2020.

[85] Bellesiles, *1877*, 162. Foner writes the "strikers' wives had prepared buckets of soft soap, and the men had liberally slathered it all over the rails for a quarter of a mile up the hill." Foner, *1877*, 98.

[86] "Rioters Soaping the Track." J.A. Dacus, *Annals of the Great Strikes In the United States* (Burt Franklin: New York, 1969), 290; "Rioters Soaping the Track of the Erie Railroad, Near Hornellsville," Edward Winslow Martin [James Dabney McCabe], *The History of the Great Riots* (New York: Augustus M. Kelley, 1971), 229; "New York: Rioters Soaping the Track at Hornellsville," J.T. Headley, *Pen and Pencil Sketches of the Great Riots* (New York: E.B. Treat, 1969), 392.

Figure 7.4 "Rioters Soaping the Track," reprinted in J.A. Dacus, *Annals of the Great Strikes in the United States* (Burt Franklin: New York, 1969), 290.

mentioned above, Pinkerton published his own images of the strike. In "Women Leading a Mob in Baltimore," rioting Irish women are racialized as caricatures with extreme anti-Black social typing, excessive of the kind present in *Leslie*'s drummer boy (Figure 7.5). Richard Slotkin brilliantly recounts how the periodical press of the 1870s cast militant urban workers and the insurgent poor as an "inversion of racial order," even portraying women's charity to the poor as a "reversal of sexual roles."[87] The inversion of racial and sexual order occurs in Pinkerton's image simultaneously. The most visible female figure has animalistic features of stereotypically anti-Black racism, with large, muscular arms and other bodily features opposite a diminutive and delicate Victorian femininity. Similarly, when ruling class periodicals and reporters encountered militant Bohemian women rioting in Chicago, they described them through similar gender reversals: "reporters' descriptions of the ensuing altercation reflected their dismay at behavior that blatantly violated the norms of middle-class womanhood."[88] The anti-communist project of 1877 was inseparable from a cultural politics of gender conformity and white supremacy.

Ironically, some images of the strike reset women's militancy back within domesticated frameworks of sympathetic femininity. One of the largest and most

---

[87] Slotkin, *The Fatal Environment*, 342.
[88] Jentz and Schneirov, *Chicago in the Age of Capital*, 207.

Figure 7.5 "Women Leading a Mob in Baltimore" in Allan Pinkerton, *Strikers, Communists, Tramps, and Detectives* (London: G.W. Carleton & Co., 1882), 194.

dramatic panoramas in *Leslie's*, a two-page inset in the center of the August 4 extra edition, demonstrates this reversion to conventional gender tropes. The drawing "Pennsylvania.—The Railroad Riot at Pittsburgh—The Philadelphia Militia Firing on the Mob," depicts perhaps a dozen women in working-class and middle-class dresses, along with at least six children—including two prominently visible babies, two girls, and two boys. In contrast to other images of women in Baltimore and elsewhere, here the women are depicted as ladies and mothers, and they face the viewer as they flee the militia's attack. Their facial expressions are full of sadness and terror. Their features are not distancing, but recognizable and, for the most part, white—that is, only a couple contain any trace of racial typing. Significantly, they are not rendered as militant actors, but passive bystanders fleeing sudden violence. Their innocence and virtue secure a whiteness rendered more visible by their clean clothes and proximity to children. In the August 18 *Leslie's*, similar figures speak with police as they attempt to recover "Property Stolen by the Mob," further reinforcing the contingency of gender performance on militancy and domesticity.[89]

Importantly, the racial and gender pictorial politics of the 1877 general strike shift outside the United States. Placed in transatlantic perspective, the *Leslie's* images

---

[89] "Pennsylvania.—Pittsburgh Policemen Recovering Property Stolen by the Mob in the Recent Riots," *Frank Leslie's Illustrated Newspaper* XLIV, no. 1, 142, August 18, 1877, 409.

dominated. Unlike English periodicals, the August 18 edition of the French illustrated weekly *Le Monde Illustré* created its own engravings and sketches "d'aprés les documents américains [from American texts]."[90] Many images clearly modify action sketches from *Leslie's*, including a stunning modification of the drummer boy's Irish features into an angry black child—a transformation which may reveal how French artists interpreted the facial features in *Leslie*'s, and which possibly reflects *Leslie*'s ambiguous intentions. Similarly, the French illustrated periodical *L'Illustration Journal Universel* modified several sketches from US periodicals, including *The Daily Graphic*. In a *Daily Graphic* cover sketch from July 26 depicting a "Debauch of Stolen Whiskey" (a theme also depicted in *Leslie's*), a drunken man stands over a whiskey barrel, his arms spread out like a scarecrow, spilling a drink. In the *L'Illustration* version, the well-dressed couple directly toast the drunken man, who smiles hoisting a glass (Figure 7.6).[91] The French engraving renders the "Pillage" less as a criminal escapade than as a party including men and women from different social classes. We can guess English and French periodicals aimed at a similar middle-class of readers, and such scenes possibly appealed to their own working- and middle-class readers.

One picture in *Le Monde Illustré* stands out, however. In a novel image by M. Ferdinandus ("desain de") looking down on Pittsburgh during the burning of the roundhouse and surrounding structures, masses of people are grouped on hills across the background [image 7 here]. In the foreground, people have bags, luggage, and parcels, presumably looted from train cars. In contrast to images in *Leslie's* and *Harper's* that equate looting with criminality, *Le Monde Illustré* depicts mostly women and families, resting and relaxed. In the center of the frame is a playful dog. Significantly, the right-hand side of the picture appears to include a Black family, including a proud-looking Black boy. While separate from other people in the foreground, including two women near sacks of flour and trunks of goods, their visibility is strongly suggestive. The outdoor scene of domesticity and recuperation suggests an exceptional solidarity, and a rioting multi-racial class where women and Black people were visible and respectable. The compelling disjunction between the destruction in the background and persons in the foreground further signals the riot wasn't the fault of depraved communists, but a jubilee allowing for the subsistence of the poor.

The fact that the most sympathetic and racially inclusive image of the strike appeared in Paris contrasts with the London reproductions. More crucially, *Le Monde Illustré* better represented the multiracial solidarities and possibilities of the 1877 general strike better than those in New York, including *Leslie's*. In part, the French vision of the strike betrays an optimism about class power and socialist solidarity evocative of the 1871 Paris Commune, an event typically rendered in the United States as an orgy of savage communist violence (particularly, indeed, during the 1877 strike). Notably,

---

[90] M. Ferdinandus, "Étas-Unis. – Pittsburgh.—Les grèves du chemin de fer de Pennsylvanie—Pillage et incendie des dépôts du Railroad et des maisons environnantes," *Le Monde Illusté*, Tome XLI, Paris: Direction et Administration 21, no. 1062, August 18, 1877, 105.

[91] "Pillage Des Tonneaux De Liqueur Contenus Dans La Gare Aux Marchandises," *L'Illustration Journal* 70, no. 1801, September 1, 1877, 133.

Figure 7.6 "Pennsylvania.—The Railroad Riot at Pittsburgh—The Philadelphia Militia Firing on the Mob," *Frank Leslie's Illustrated Newspaper* (August 4, 1877).

the French images treat the black participants with the same sympathy as other strikers and rioters, and emphasize the rebellion as an occasion of relief and even joy. The Parisian ability to imagine a "Black realism" in 1877 doesn't just point to US failures to perceive its own uprising, but also may reveal a romanticism about American racial politics, especially in light of events in St. Louis and San Francisco.

Yet the French images reinforce how women and children were important actors in the general strike, underlining why Lucy Parsons narrated the 1877 rebellion out of the police riot in Tompkins Square Park in 1874. Significant numbers of women and children were wage workers, too, especially in Pittsburgh and Chicago, two of the strike's epicenters. In this respect, the general strike's visual culture demonstrates what Alice Kessler-Harris calls the "central importance of locating women within the paradigm of class power relations."[92] Even more, locating women at the center of the 1877 general strike points to the indeterminacy of women's waged and unwaged relations to industrial capitalism in 1877. As Silvia Federici has observed, women's waged and unwaged work was critically entangled into the late "19th century, when

---

[92] Alice Kessler-Harris, *Gendering Labor History* (Urbana and Chicago: University of Illinois Press, 2007), 7.

the responses to the rise of socialism, the Paris Commune, and the accumulation crisis of 1873 were the 'Scramble for Africa' and the simultaneous creation in Europe of the nuclear family, centered on the economic dependence of women to men."[93] Federici's claim reminds us that the large number of women who participated in the strike acted in their own interest against the railroads, but also that their militancy was aimed at capitalism's increasingly strict gender norms, too. In the ambiguous and indeterminate visual ideations of racial identity and gender performance in the pictures of the general strike, we find that representations of femininity simultaneously reported women as working-class agents of power and also as domestic and sentimental figures in need of protection. As in other periods of US cultural wars and red scares, accusations of anticapitalism are inseparable from moral panic over sexuality and white nationalist paranoia.

The instability inherent in representing the different racialized and gendered populations that rose up in July 1877 is thus difficult, and likely one reason why the largest national strike in United States history has faded so far in the cultural imagination of the twenty-first century. Yet this difficulty also arises from the fact that the insurgents themselves appear to fundamentally queer many of the social norms associated with racial citizenship and gender performance. This is perhaps why they now remain largely unclaimed and forgotten, including by many on the left.

---

[93] Silvia Federici, *Caliban and the Witch: Women, The Body and Primitive Accumulation* (Brooklyn: Autonomedia, 2014), 17.

8

Sounding: Black Print Culture at the Edges of the Black Atlantic

Kristin Moriah

The archives of Black print culture call out to us in unexpected ways. They are quite self-consciously resonant. In places that house artifacts and ephemera of Black print culture we find material that forms the basis of contemporary scholarly analyses and historiographies of the Black press. But we are also confronted by the way those texts continually revert to their own sound and livingness. I have been struck by the way that the pages of nineteenth-century Black newspapers present us with vital records of Black life and Black people, even as Black voices were systematically excluded from mainstream society and the advancements of Reconstruction were slowly dismantled. To be more precise, the way that the cataclysmic low point in Black American life sometimes referred to as the Nadir coincided with the rise of audio-recording technology produced discordant results. Print is an important node in this arrangement. For many African Americans, newspapers represented the first point of access or exposure to sound recording technology, through reports about new forms of audio technology and reportage about sonic events.

Perhaps, to some extent, all writing is meant to reflect sound or the spoken word, but our understanding of the terms and our expectations of written language have changed over time.[1] Sound archivist Patrick Feaster explains,

> *Phonography* belongs to a family of interrelated terms—including *phonograph, phonographic,* and *phonogram*—that combine the Greek *phonē* (sound, voice) with *graphē* (writing) or the related *gramma* (something written) and are usually glossed in terms of "sound writing" or "voice-writing." This terminology is generally understood as referring not simply to writing about sound as subject matter but the writing of sound—that is, to the project of embodying the transient motion or perception of sound itself in writing as enduring objects.[2]

---

[1] This sentence also appears in a recent article, where it is expanded upon differently. See Kristin Moriah, "On the Record: Sissereta Jones and Black Feminist Recording Praxes," *Performance Matters* 6.2 (2020): 26–42.

[2] Patrick Feaster, "Phonography," in *Keywords in Sound*, eds. David Novak and Matt Sakakeeny (Durham, NC: Duke University Press, 2015), 139.

Feaster's explanation is important here because it lays a groundwork for understanding the hybrid nature of sound and the ways in which our understanding of sound recordings is inextricably linked to text and visual culture. It is also helpful to recall the fact that one of the predecessors to the phonograph was the phonautograph, an instrument meant to "transduce sound" rather than recreate the "perception of sound."[3]

For example, the phonograph was invented by Thomas Edison in 1877, and by 1878, Black newspapers were cracking wise about it. In the pages of the *Weekly Louisianan*, we find the following joke in a syndicated humor column: "Phonograph is feminine gender because it talks back."[4] This is a play on technology and grammar, which is itself the science of the word. The voice of the phonograph is unraced in its original context. But what if the voice of the phonograph was a Black woman? Or, as Ralph Ellison has put it, what if we slipped the yoke and changed the joke?[5] Feminine objects are free-floating linguistic signifiers that can occupy the imaginations of all readers, but the placement of the sexist joke within the pages of a Black southern newspaper calls forth a potentially racialized dimension. The syndicated joke takes us back to the nebulous early days of phonography in which recording technology was not yet stamped as white or masculine. The phonograph complicated previously existing gendered sound binaries. As Adrianna Cavarrero explains, "feminized from the start, the vocal aspect of speech, and furthermore, of song, appear as antagonistic elements in rational, masculine sphere that centers itself, instead, on the semantic," or "to put it formulaically: woman sings, man thinks."[6] The vocal aspect of public speech was even more vexed for Black readers, who were neither categorized as man nor woman, nor human. The reduction to ephemeral vocality produced a context in which new ways of establishing personhood were denied to Black people, including performers, even while gender roles were further entrenched. Thus the phonograph required a precise approach to sound recording that was at odds with stereotypes of the feminize. Early attempts to record Black sound, or to crystalize and officialize phonic emissions, were one way of masculinizing Black vocality and entering it into the audible realm of the white mainstream and its listeners. The process of phonography becomes even more complicated when we consider the intimate relationship between sound, text, and body. Voice and text compete for meaning although they are not easily separated. As such, as Alexander Weheliye notes, "the voice, even more so than writing, represents the pure interiority and the proper domain of the sovereign human subject."[7] And yet, until relatively recently, it was only as a written language, or a record, that the voice could be archived or transcend time and space. The sovereignty represented by the voice was fragile and always temporal for the marginalized subject.[8]

---

[3] Jonathan Sterne, *The Audible Past: Cultural Origins of Sound Reproduction* (Durham, NC: Duke University Press, 2003), 31–2.

[4] "Humorous," *Weekly Louisianian* (November 30, 1878), 1. *Readex: African American Newspapers* (Accessed February 12, 2021).

[5] Ralph Ellison, "Change the Joke and Slip the Yoke," *Partisan Review* 25, no. 2 (1958), 212–22.

[6] Adriana Cavarero, *For More Than One Voice: Toward a Philosophy of Vocal Expression* (Stanford, CA: Stanford University Press, 2005), 6.

[7] Alexander G. Weheliye, *Phonographies: Grooves in Sonic Afro-modernity* (Durham, NC: Duke University Press, 2005), 27.

[8] These last few sentences also appear, and are expanded upon differently, in Moriah, "On the Record," 31.

Here, and elsewhere, I have considered what it means to record sound in the absence of the artifact of the traditional phonograph record.[9] My work has drawn me toward Black press coverage of Black performers who traveled abroad during the period known by various turns as the Red Decade and the Nadir. In the late nineteenth century, technological advancements in the world of sound and music, coupled with other reports about Germany's politically progressive nature, created an arena in which Germany was understood as a desirable destination for African American performers traveling to the European continent. German innovation contributed to a context in which the location of Black performance and spectatorship was highly politicized, as was the matter of listening. By way of contrast, Berlin sounded different from America, and musical performance resonated differently there. I mean this in both a practical and figurative sense. Unsurprisingly, turn-of-the-century African American concert singers were barred from fully experiencing the many acoustical innovations that America had to offer. Space, race, and sound emerge as prime concerns for Black performers during this period. These mutually constitutive elements of performance were highly politicized in the African American press. For example, in 1895, only months after the highlights of her European tour were announced in Black newspapers all over the United States, opera singer Sissieretta Jones was invoked in W.C. Wright's article "Indignities Imposed." In the article, Wright explained to readers of *The Cleveland Gazette*,

> The greatest indignity imposed on our people at the south to me seems to be that of riding in "Jim Crow" cars. A "Jim Crow" car is an ordinary car with a partition in the center; one half is used as a smoking apartment by white passengers, some of whom are very filthy. An Afro-American cannot go into the same depot waiting room with the whites, no matter how well he may be dressed. A separate lunch counter is run for the benefit of Afro-American travelers.[10]

Implicit in W.C. Wright's report is an understanding of the ways segregated travel had practical ramifications for Black performers, people who traveled for a living. Some of the most successful Black entertainers of the day avoided these indignities and impediments to mobility by using their own private train cars. To whit, Marta Effinger argues that the Black Patti Troubadors used their own private train cars specifically to avoid white hostility while traveling west in the United States.

Discriminatory public indignities made their way into news reports about Black experiences in the concert hall, too. Reading African American newspapers, we gain a sense of the ways in which segregation in public spaces tainted the world of musical

---

[9] In point of fact, the earliest known set of vocal recordings by an African American were made by George Washington Johnson in the 1890s. Johnson "had a special talent for whistling and for laughing songs, a curious type of repertoire in which the singer laughed in time with the music" (Brooks 1). His signature "Laughing Song" was recorded for New York's Metropolitan Phonograph Co., Columbia, and Edison. Sales of that record reportedly reached 50,000 copies (Brooks 2005).

[10] W. C. Wright, "Indignities Imposed," *The Cleveland Gazette* (June 15, 1895): 1.

performance. In "Indignities Imposed" Wright also spoke out against segregated concert halls, particularly the space that readers of Carl Van Vechten's *Nigger Heaven* (1926) would become familiar with during the Harlem Renaissance, the upper balcony reserved for Black patrons. Wright noted,

> A place is set apart in the top galleries of the theaters for our people, where circus seats are provided. This section is not patronized by the best of our people. The manner in which some conduct themselves, however, causes the managements to so place all Afro-Americans, which is certainly unfair and wrong. It is true some Afro-Americans act more like monkeys than human beings. Madam Sissieretta Jones, while in the south, was not patronized by the leading Afro-Americans, because they were compelled to go up in the loft when she sang in that section.[11]

Southern segregated seating practices may have differed from those of Northern venues like Cleveland's Euclid Avenue Opera House, but segregated performance spaces were certainly not limited to the South.[12] Reports like Wright's came hard on the heels of news of Jones's success abroad and were meant to highlight the injustices of American racism faced by the Black elite. What did it mean for African American audience members to have to go to the top galleries and experience compromised forms of listening? How did these compromised listening experiences shape the way African American performers were received domestically? How did they influence the ways African American performers framed themselves? How can we discern these multiple meanings and experiences of Black performance from the print culture archives that remain?

These reported experiences are a window into cultural practices of listening in the African American community and provide another lens through which we can understand the impact of international performance for Black artists. In Wright's article, we see how receptions of performances by artists like Sissieretta Jones were used as a barometer of social tolerance in the African American press. We also see the ways in which segregated seating sections were connected to questions of class and merit within some segments of the African American community. Racist listening practices were considered unjust by elites like Wright because they prevented Jones's "leading" fans from hearing her properly. They forced upwardly mobile African Americans into close quarters with people they felt themselves to be superior to. Wright's editorial suggests that the Black elite deserved more because they could afford to pay more, in spite of their color, not simply because all people deserved to hear good music. But for those who could swing it, there were ways to avoid these unpleasantries, including travel. Temporarily sidestepping these controversies through their work in European cities like Berlin, African American performers created different kinds of listening experiences than those available to them in the

---

[11] Ibid.

[12] *Cleveland Gazette* notices suggest that the local African American community made frequent use of the hall, one of the leading performances spaces in the country at the time.

United States. They also succeeded in making their work in those exclusive spaces available to wider audiences through print.

International performance venues acted as laboratories for these experiments in sonic transcription, with Germany emerging to the forefront as one of the most significant sites for sound preservation in the late nineteenth century. Written reviews made her work almost equally accessible to audiences Black and white around the world. Furthermore, readers could use these reviews to imagine and approximate her sound. Black women who performed art music were formally excluded from early phonographic recordings, but they and their work continued to exist in relation to it. This argument becomes clearer in light of Louis Chude-Sokei's propositions about the mechanics of the Black female body and its connection to sound. Discussing the implications of the relationship between race, technology, and sound at the beginning of the modern era, Chude-Sokei writes that "blacks were linked to technology and new techniques, which also established links between race and that other significant twentieth-century sign of otherness, the machine."[13] In Chude-Sokei's estimation, the minstrel and the robot were doubles and reflections of one another in nineteenth-century culture. While many scholars have written of the relationship between the Jazz Age and mechanization, including, famously, Adorno, Chude-Sokei finds that this relationship preceded that time period. In fact, it directly overlaps the period in which African American women like Sissieretta Jones made their way onto the stage. Chude-Sokei notes that "the nineteenth century was when contemporary meanings of technology would begin to congeal, as would the current meanings of race and culture" and that "as a system, the plantation was a precursor to the regimentations and formal, time-driven depersonalizations known as Fordism and Taylorism."[14] This understanding of the relationship between the Black body and the machine extended to the very beginnings of American mass entertainment, when naive audiences thought Joyce Heth, the star of P.T. Barnum's early empire, was a machine.[15]

I refer to the way Louis Chude-Sokei attempts to draw connections between Black performance, automata, and the phonograph in order to reinforce my own argument about the relationship between Black women and phonography, and how print culture subtended this linkage. Chude-Sokei argues that the automata, which expressed a loss of certainty about what it means to be human for European audiences, evolved into the phonograph in both technical and cultural senses. Like minstrels, anthropomorphized machines threatened to supplant white male labor and authority. Thus, Black performance, including Ida Forsyne's aforementioned Topsy dance, was a spectacle of the lack of reason and a demonstration of other than humanness. In

---

[13] Louis Chude-Sokei, *The Sound of Culture: Diaspora and Black Technopoetics* (Middletown, CT: Wesleyan University Press, 2015), 32.

[14] Ibid., 36–7.

[15] Barnum experienced early success displaying Joyce Heth "(advertised as George Washington's 160-year-old nurse) in 1835" (Brooks and Ertan). Louis Chude-Sokei and Uri McMillan have explored the relationship between this moment and larger phenomenon of embodiment and automation in American popular entertainment.

Sokei's schema, there is a linkage between Negro dolls and automata, which exist as masks of each other. Again at the turn of the century, ventriloquism and masquerade become increasingly prominent properties of technology. Furthermore, "there was a general belief that Black voices had a tonality better represented by the new medium."[16] Given this slippage between the Black female body in performance and the machine, I suggest that there are a number of ways in which we can understand Sissieretta Jones's relationship to textual records of her voice through sound technology, particularly phonography.

Five years after Sissieretta Jones made her stage debut, visitors to the 1893 Columbian World's Fair in Chicago were introduced to the phonograph in its elaborate electricity building, and phonograph parlors began to appear in major American cities. This technological turn was groundbreaking for racialized performers. In *Phonographies: Grooves in Sonic Afro-Modernity*, Alexander Weheliye explains that "the invention of the phonograph at the end of the nineteenth century offered a different way to split sound from the courses that (re)produced them, thus generating a new technological orality and musicality in twentieth-century Black culture."[17] Theodor Adorno, convinced of the potential of the writing that emerges from the curve of the gramophone needle, wrote that "as music is removed by the phonograph record and the realm of live production, and from the imperative of artistic activity and becomes petrified, it absorbs into itself, in this process of petrification, the very life that would otherwise vanish."[18] Adorno's treatise suggests that there is an essential, ephemeral quality to sound that is only present in recorded form. And yet, in spite of this rich theoretical work, I believe that our frameworks for understanding how Black women intervened into such discourses using limited means remain insufficient.

This analysis relies on an interdisciplinary approach to textual evidence of sound and an understanding of the complexities of these reviews within their historical context. The multidimensional nature of sound, and its ability to be read across genres, mediums, and spaces, is key here. In the words of Roshanak Kheshti, I work from the understanding that "sound form is a hermeneutical tool; a wavy and reverberant materiality, it reflects, is productive of, and also engenders through resonance."[19] Europe was a place where the mechanical tendencies of Black women's sound were made manifest and manipulated on stage and in print. In spite of being on the margins of mainstream audio production, Black women performers used the foreign stage to perfect their sound and make sound a visible aspect of their stagecraft. In doing so, they produced new ways of interpreting the world and making it bend to their will. In Berlin, Germany, and the rest of Central Europe, Black women made sound visible through image and text, contributing to narratives of Black culture and diaspora.

---

[16] Chude-Sokei, *Sound of Culture*, 51.
[17] Weheliye, *Phonographies*, 19.
[18] Theodor W. Adorno, "The Form of the Phonographic Record," trans. Thomas Y. Levin, *October* 55 (Winter 1990), 59.
[19] Roshanak Kheshti, *Modernity's Ear: Listening to Race and Gender in World Music* (New York: New York University Press, 2015), 111.

9

"A Traveling Exhibition": Magazines and the Display and Circulation of Art in the Americas

Lori Cole

When Marcel Duchamp's *Fountain* (1917) was rejected by the Society of Independent Artists for its first annual exhibition, it was instead featured in a photograph taken by Alfred Stieglitz in the May 1917 issue of *The Blind Man*, a magazine that Duchamp edited along with Henri-Pierre Roché and Beatrice Wood. Artists like Duchamp, in their roles as editors, were able to control the distribution and display of their artwork. The magazine in this case functioned as the only site of display for the object, albeit in reproduction, enabling its wider circulation and its afterlife. The same year, 1917, American artists Stuart Davis and H.J. Glintenkamp founded the portfolio magazine *Spawn*, which they deemed a "traveling exhibition." A magazine devoid of text that simply offered the art it featured for sale, *Spawn* radically reimagined the magazine as a kind of gallery. Across the Americas, editors explored various ways magazines could supplement or supplant exhibitions, circulating artwork to larger audiences. For instance, *La Pluma* (1927–31), based in Uruguay, recreated local exhibitions and salons in a designated section of the magazine. Such publications amplified the sometimes limited local infrastructure for exhibiting art, while elevating the importance of the magazine as a site for display.

Editors frequently circulated new artwork in their publications, while simultaneously mounting physical exhibitions of art, which worked in concert with their magazines. *Camera Work* (1903–17), founded by Stieglitz, functioned in tandem with its gallery, known by its address at 291 Fifth Avenue simply as "291," while the *Little Review* (1914–29) established a corollary gallery and treated issues of the magazine as catalogs for two of its larger shows. Editors of the Cuban *Revista de Avance* (1927–30) and the Chilean *Mandrágora* (1938–41) organized exhibitions of avant-garde art for local audiences that at once replicated and expanded the work on view in their publications. While *Revista de Avance* showcased a local avant-garde that it broadcast transnationally, the Chilean group, by contrast, integrated their own work into an international movement, Surrealism, through their exhibitions. The flexibility of periodicals allowed editors to strategically select, display, and circulate art in a wide variety of formats. Magazines also allowed editors to rhetorically frame their physical exhibitions—by printing manifestos, advertisements, reviews of the shows, as well as through strategic layouts of artwork—to fundamentally transform both exhibition-making and the magazine as a medium.

Structured thematically around the magazine's different intersections with the reproduction and display of art, this essay begins by offering a brief overview of magazines' relationship to sites of exhibition in the Americas in the early twentieth century, before considering four case studies that explore the elasticity of the periodical and its various imbrications with art: *La Pluma*'s dedicated exhibition section, *Mandrágora*'s exhibitions of Chilean Surrealism, the *Little Review*'s magazine-as-exhibition catalog, and *Spawn*, a magazine that functioned as a circulating gallery. These examples demonstrate the malleability of the magazine as a site of artistic creation and a mode of contextualizing and displaying art. Moreover, they demonstrate the fluidity between editorial, artistic, and curatorial practices, an insight which reverberates later in the century, when artists used the magazine to circumvent an increasingly commercial artworld, and as an artistic medium itself.

Magazines as Sites of Display in the Americas

Magazines played a critical role in supporting new forms of artmaking in the early twentieth century, when there were few museums and only select gallery spaces that displayed avant-garde art in the Americas. In the late nineteenth and early twentieth centuries both commercial and coterie publications exploded in growth, while museums were slower to emerge.[1] In the United States, the Museum of Modern Art was established in 1929, the Whitney Museum of American Art in 1931, and the San Francisco Museum of Modern Art in 1935. In Latin America, museums for modern art were built even later: 1948 in Brazil, 1956 in Argentina, 1962 in Colombia, and 1964 in Mexico.[2] As a result, magazines—and their accompanying exhibitions—were typically the first spaces to promote, circulate, and display emergent forms of art.

Tellingly, it was a magazine, *Forma: Revista de artes plásticas* (1926–8), in Mexico City that announced the need for a "museo de arte moderno americano" (Museum of Modern American Art) in 1927, a rallying cry echoed in the magazine *¡30-30!*,

---

[1] See: *History of the Mass Media in the United States: An Encyclopedia*, ed. Margaret A. Blanchard (New York: Routledge, 1998); Theodore Peterson, *Magazines in the Twentieth Century* (Urbana, IL: University of Illinois Press, 1964); Kirsten MacLeod, *American Little Magazines* of the *Fin de Siècle: Art, Protest, and Cultural Transformation* (Toronto: University of Toronto Press, 2018); Steven Heller, *Merz to Emigré and Beyond: Magazine Design of the Twentieth Century* (New York: Phaidon, 2003); Jorge Schwartz, *Las vanguardias latinoamericanas. Textos programáticos y críticos* (Mexico City: Fondo de Cultura Económica, 2002); Ivonne Pini and Jorge Ramírez Nieto, *Modernidades, vanguardias, nacionalismos: análisis de escritos polémicos vinculados al contexto cultural latinoamericano, 1920-1930* (Bogotá, DC: Universidad Nacional de Colombia, Vicerrectoría Académica Editorial, 2012).

[2] Néstor García Canclini, *Hybrid Cultures: Strategies for Entering and Leaving Modernity* (1995), trans. Christopher L. Chiappari and Silvia L. López, expanded ed. (Minneapolis, MN: University of Minnesota Press, 2005), 56.

Órgano de los pintores de México the following year (Figure 9.1).³ *Forma*, published by the Ministry of Public Education and the National Autonomous University of Mexico under the direction of the painter Gabriel Fernández Ledesma, claimed to be the "first of its kind" in terms of the types and quality of its reproductions, and

Figure 9.1 "El museo de arte moderno americano," *Forma: Revista de artes plásticas* (Mexico City) vol. 1, no. 3 (1927): 21, featuring Gabriel Fernández Ledesma, *Primera Comunión* (First Communion), 1925. Printed with the permission of Mauricio Bidault Fernández Ledesma.

³ "El museo de arte moderno americano," *Forma: Revista de artes plásticas* (Mexico City) 1, no. 3 (1927), 21–2; Carlos Román, "Un museo de arte moderno mexicano," *¡30- 30! Órgano de los pintores de México* (Mexico City), no. 1 (July 1928), 2–3; Fernando Leal, "Fundación de un museo de arte moderno en Michoacán," *¡30-30!, Órgano de los pintores de México*, (Mexico City) 2, no. 2 (August 1928), 2.

to provide "the only history of the important Mexican art movement in our time."[4] Its subtitle "Painting, Printmaking, Sculpture, Architecture, Popular Expressions" indicated the range of material it included. Alongside the reproduction of such work were a variety of texts, some of which, art historian Harper Montgomery argues, "resembled extended exhibition wall texts or catalogue entries" while other reproductions had no accompanying texts, "a technique unprecedented in Mexico."[5] The magazine reported on local exhibitions and included questionnaires on painting, sculpture, and architecture, so that, as it claimed, "the public will have the chance to find out, without limitations, the general concept—right or wrong— about our artistic affairs."[6]

In its third issue *Forma* outlined its plans for a museum to display "current modern art," including work by children and anonymous artists. After amassing a collection of Mexican art, the magazine explained, it would then shift its focus to include work from across Latin America. *Forma* called upon artists to donate work to the museum, describing it as a place "for artists" that would eventually be run by "the nation." Artists responded enthusiastically "with the donation of some works that we published in this issue," *Forma* reported. It is notable that the vision for this museum was articulated, anticipated, and essentially replicated in print, formulating what Montgomery deems a "utopian project."[7] The magazine, she argues, worked on "constructing an audience of middle-class readers and cultivating its taste so that it could appreciate the visual and material values of Mexican art that the envisioned museum would display."[8] *Forma* reproduced four works intended for the museum captioned "Property of the Museo de arte moderno americano," emphasizing its regional span and commitment to its vision.

As evidenced by the example of *Forma*, magazines were important venues not just to display new forms of artmaking, but as national and regional canon-building institutions, and were at the forefront of shaping and promoting such canons. In the early twentieth century the notion of "America" or "American art" was in flux while Europe was seen to be in decline. Fraught conversations about the nature of what constituted American art played out in magazines. In Latin America these debates occurred through responses to questionnaires such as "What should American art be?" issued by *Revista de Avance*, or to the "meridian debate," which prompted magazines across Latin America to assert an autonomous Latin American sensibility, while in North America conflicts over regionalism versus abstraction, and other claims to national art, occurred in print, all alongside the display and dissemination of

---

[4] *Forma* (Mexico City) 2, no. 6 (1928) reprinted in *Forma, 1926–1928* (Mexico City: Fondo de Cultura Económica, 1982), 313. All translations are by the author unless otherwise noted.

[5] Harper Montgomery, "Revolutionary Modernism: A 'Museo de arte moderno americano' Rehearsed in Print in Mexico City, 1926–1928," in *Art Museums in Latin America: Structuring Representation*, eds. Michele Greet and Gina McDaniel Tarver (New York: Routledge, 2018), 227.

[6] "Encuesta," *Forma* (Mexico City) 1, no. 1 (1926) reprinted in *Forma, 1926–1928* (Mexico City: Fondo de Cultura Económica, 1982), 15.

[7] Montgomery, "Revolutionary Modernism," 234.

[8] Ibid., 223.

artwork.⁹ Magazines showcased radical new experiments with typography and design, new forms of media, such as photography, and new avant-garde movements, serving as vehicles to consolidate and telegraph burgeoning artistic and ideological identities.

In both North America and Latin America, editors used their magazines as platforms to promote and enact an idea of "American art" that could compete with and displace that of Europe; yet, there were clear material differences in putting out a magazine or mounting an exhibition in different parts of the Americas, with heightened geopolitical stakes. In the United States magazines were trying to determine what constituted a national art in conversation with the international. For instance, *Contact* (1921–3; 1932), founded by William Carlos Williams and Robert McAlmon, declared in 1920: "We will be American, because we are of America," but they add "we will adopt no aggressive or inferior attitude toward 'imported thought' or art."¹⁰ That issue includes the essay "Mickey Mouse and American Art" by Diego Rivera, and elsewhere Williams explains how Spanish helped him form what he called "the American idiom" in which he wrote.¹¹ Similarly, in response to a *Partisan Review* questionnaire issued in 1939 on American writing, the critic Harold Rosenberg notes, "America can be known only through the perspective of international culture."¹² Some of these assertions seem to be co-opting Latin American (or European) art as part of an assimilative model of North American culture.

However, some Latin Americans also had a trans-American vision. In 1921 the Mexican artist David Alfaro Siqueiros spearheaded *Vida-Americana*, which, though published in Barcelona, self-identified as a "North, Central, and South American avant-garde magazine." In its manifesto Siqueiros called for the development of a "new American art" based on the "synthetic energy" of Latin America's pre-Columbian civilizations.¹³ The lone issue of *Vida-Americana* also included articles on baseball,

---

⁹ For the "meridian debate," see Juan E. De Castro, "The Intellectual Meridian Debate and Colonialist Nostalgia," in *The Spaces of Latin American Literature: Tradition, Globalization, and Cultural Production* (New York: Palgrave Macmillan, 2008); Marcela Croce, ed., *Polémicas intelectuales en América Latina: Del "meridiano intelectual" al caso Padilla (1927–1971)* (Buenos Aires: Ediciones Simurg, 2006); Vanessa Fernández, "A Transatlantic Dialogue: Argentina, Mexico, Spain, and the Literary Magazines That Bridged the Atlantic (1920–1930)," Ph.D. diss. (UCLA, 2013). For questionnaires, Lori Cole, *Surveying the Avant-Garde: Questions on Modernism, Art, and the Americas in Transatlantic Magazines* (University Park, PA: Penn State University Press, 2018). For American art magazines: Virginia Hagelstein Marquardt, "Art on the Left in the United States, 1918–1937," in *Art and Journals on the Political Front, 1910–1940*, ed. Virginia Hagelstein Marquardt (Gainesville: University of Florida Press, 1997), 215–46.

¹⁰ William Carlos Williams and Robert McAlmon, "Contact," *Contact* (New York), no. 1 (December 1920), 1.

¹¹ Jonathan Cohen, "Introduction: Into the American Idiom: Poems from the Spanish," in William Carlos Williams, *By Word of Mouth: Poems from the Spanish, 1916–1959*, ed. Jonathan Cohen (New York: New Directions, 2011), xxi.

¹² Harold Rosenberg, Response to "The Situation in American Writing," *Partisan Review* (New York) 6, no. 4 (1939), 48.

¹³ David Alfaro Siqueiros, "Tres llamamientos de orientación actual a los pintores y escultores de la nueva generación americana," *Vida-Americana: Revista norte, centro y sudamericana de vanguardia* (Barcelona), no. 1 (May 1921): 2–3, trans. as "Three Appeals for the Current Guidance of the New Generation of American Painters and Sculptors" by Laura Pérez, *Inverted Utopias: Avant-Garde Art in Latin America*, eds. Mari Carmen Ramírez and Héctor Olea et al. (New Haven, CT: Yale University Press, 2004), 458–9.

Brazilian music, Mexican journalism, and artwork by Diego Rivera, Marius de Zayas, and Joaquín Torres-García. Rivera himself wrote in a 1934 booklet *Portrait of America*: "I have always maintained that art in America, if some day it can be said to come into being, will be the product of a fusion between the marvelous indigenous art which derives from the immemorial depths of time in the center and south of the continent... and that of the industrial worker of the north."[14]

Yet typically, as in the case of *Forma*, Latin American magazines fiercely differentiated Latin America from the United States. In *Forma*, "American," Montgomery points out, was "wielded... as an anticolonial descriptor that explicitly excluded the United States."[15] The magazine "conceived of a museum of modern art as an oppositional institution designed to resist top-down models of Pan-Americanism, as well as to redefine art," reminding us that in Latin America, the avant-garde was often invested in building institutions and audiences, rather than contesting them.[16] Similarly, in response to the questionnaire "What should American art be?" the Venezuelan historian and poet Rufino Blanco Fombona remarks, "we are not talking about the Yankees," while one of the magazine's editors maintains that "Yankee imperialism" is a "common enemy" uniting Latin Americans.[17]

The term "American" itself was debated, particularly in Latin America, since other designations—such as Pan-American, Hispanic American, Inter-American, South American, Native American, and Indo-American—were burdened by colonial histories.[18] As Argentine writer Pablo Rojas Paz notes in his response to the "meridian debate":

> Many have concocted long, terrible names for us—North America invented Pan American; France came up with Latin American; Spain created the term Hispanic American. Each of these names, though thinly disguised as an overture to harmonious relations, is actually an expression of its creator's frustrated imperialist designs.[19]

---

[14] Diego Rivera and Bertram Wolfe, *Portrait of America* (New York: Corvici-Firiede, 1934), 19.
[15] Montgomery, "Revolutionary Modernism," 223.
[16] Ibid., 224.
[17] Rufino Blanco Fombona, Response to "¿Qué debe ser el arte americano?" *Revista de Avance* (Havana) 2, no. 29 (December 15, 1928), 361; Francisco Ichaso, "Balance de una indagación," *Revista de Avance* (Havana) 4, no. 38 (September 15, 1929), 264.
[18] The term "Pan-American" was originally used by Simón Bolívar in his "Jamaica Letter" of 1815 to indicate pan-Latin American unity, but was then co-opted by the United States for ideological and commercial reasons. Simón Bolívar, "Carta de Jamaica (1815)," in *Simón Bolívar: Escritos Políticos*, ed. Gabriela Soriano (Madrid: Alianza Editorial, 1990), 61–84; Robert Alexander González, "Introduction: Entering Pan-America," in *Designing Pan-America: US Architectural Visions for the Western Hemisphere* (Austin, TX: University of Texas Press, 2011), 4; The term "Latin America" emerged from France in 1862 to advance the interests of Napoleon III. Héctor Olea, Mari Carmen Ramírez, and Tomás Ybarra-Frausto, "Resisting Categories," in *Resisting Categories: Latin American and/or Latino? Critical Documents of 20th Century Latin American Art*, vol. 1, eds. Héctor Olea, Mari Carmen Ramírez, Tomás Ybarra-Frausto, María C. Gaztambide, and Melina Kervandjian (Houston, TX: The Museum of Fine Arts, Houston International Center for the Arts of the Americas, 2012), 42.
[19] Pablo Rojas Paz, "Imperialismo baldío," *Martín Fierro* (Buenos Aires), 4, no. 42 (June 10, 1927), trans. Tony Beckwith in *Resisting Categories*, 284.

What these magazines demonstrate is how authors and artists at the time self-consciously negotiated ideologically freighted nomenclature to assert regional or national autonomy. Magazines' decisions of how to display art—and which artists to feature—were part of this calculus, as they worked to cultivate and advocate for "American" art.

Circulating Artwork in Reproduction: *La Pluma*

Editors innovated both the magazine and its display of art in an effort to promote new national artistic identities. Reflecting such an effort, the Uruguayan *La Pluma: Revista mensual de ciencias, artes, y letras* (The Pen: Monthly Magazine of Science, Art, and Letters), while not exclusively an art magazine, was exemplary in its display of art. It dedicated a section to art, frequently titled "Exhibition," accompanied by commentary. Founded by the critic Alberto Zum Felde, the monthly magazine published a total of nineteen issues, each typically over 100 pages. It covered developments in politics, science, and literature, notably publishing work in Spanish translation by Apollinaire, Whitman, and Dickinson, as well as presenting Mexican and Peruvian literature, the Brazilian avant-garde, and the work of Uruguayan poets and critics Emilio Oribe, Fernán Silva Valdés, Luis Alberto Sánchez, and Ildefonso Pereda Valdés.[20] Its incisive critical texts on poetry, art, and politics included José Carlos Mariátegui's "Nativismo e indigenismo en la literatura americana" and a Spanish translation of Le Corbusier and Ozenfant's "Modern Painting."[21] These features, together with its commitment to showcasing art, helped bolster a Uruguayan artistic identity and local art institutions while introducing readers to international developments.

Zum Felde's opening editorial outlines *La Pluma*'s dual purpose: to document the "national mentality" along with "intellectual movements" around the world.[22] He calls this the "double imperative of our *rioplatense* reality," namely, to project Uruguayan intellectual activity outward, and to draw material from the outside in, in a kind of "intellectual immigration."[23] As scholar Gloria Videla de Rivero notes, Zum Felde's statement "underscores the cultural problematic for Latin American countries: the desire to investigate and strengthen the 'national being'" while noting the need to "be attentive to the intellectual movement of the world."[24] *La Pluma*, Zum Felde asserts,

---

[20] "La Pluma," Biblioteca Digital Hispánica, Biblioteca Nacional de España, http://bdh.bne.es/bnesearch/biblioteca/La%20Pluma%20(Montevideo)/qls/0004485919;jsessionid=8B3B576EC99DD5749CC2425B5D21AAD3. Accessed May 31, 2020.

[21] José Carlos Mariátegui, "Nativismo e indigenismo en la literatura americana," *La Pluma* (Montevideo) 1, no. 1 (August 1927), 41–3; Edouard Jeanneret (Le Corbusier) and Amédée Ozenfant, "La pintura moderna," *La Pluma* (Montevideo) 1, no. 1 (August 1927), 117–24.

[22] Alberto Zum Felde, "Programa: Declaración de principios de La Pluma," *La Pluma* (Montevideo) 1, no. 1 (August 1927), 7.

[23] Zum Felde, "Programa," 9.

[24] Gloria Videla de Rivero, "Poesía de vanguardia en Iberoamérica a través de la revista 'La Pluma' de Montevideo (1927–1931)," *Revista Iberoamericana* 48, no. 118–19 (January 1982), 341.

would be "open to all collaboration" of whatever aesthetic or ideological orientation.[25] The magazine was aimed at middle-class Uruguayan audiences, as well as likeminded readers throughout Latin America and the Hispanophone world. It was distributed throughout Uruguay, and also in Spain, Argentina, Paraguay, Portugal, Panama, Peru, Colombia, Guatemala, El Salvador, Chile, Cuba, Ecuador, Brazil, Venezuela, Puerto Rico, and Mexico.[26] Like many of its print contemporaries, *La Pluma* drew from and reinforced its close relationships with a Latin American periodical network, with which it shared artwork and authors. Its display of artwork reflected these relationships.

What distinguishes *La Pluma* from other magazines of the era is the quantity and quality of its reproductions of art, as well as its mode of display, which replicated local work on view in its recurring "Exhibition" section. Featured art took the form of engravings, both in black and white and in color, some of which were removable inserts, as well as reproductions of drawings, oil paintings, sculptures, and etchings. *La Pluma*'s first issue in August 1927 included a "Salón de Otoño" (Autumn Salon) followed by a Spring Salon two issues later. While the magazine included the work of international artists—Picasso, Chagall, André Derain, Diego Rivera, and Hugh Ferriss—it typically "exhibited" Uruguayan artists, such as Petrona Viera, Carmelo de Arzadun, and Ricardo Aguerre. The May 1928 issue, for example, included three "exhibitions," introduced by a decorative title page announcing "Arte Nacional" (National Art). The exhibitions that followed were "Expocisión de 'La Casa del arte,'" of work by Uruguayan artists Petrona Viera, Domingo Bazzurro, María A. Álvarez, Rafael Barradas, Guillermo Rodríguez, and Manuel Carbajal on view at an institution newly formed in Montevideo to support the visual and performing arts; "Salon de 'La Giralda,'" a selection of work from a gallery of the same name; and "Exposición Pesce Castro," a monographic show of the work of the Uruguayan landscape painter.[27] Such inclusions helped both local and distant audiences visualize the "national mentality," which Zum Felde describes.

The exhibitions were accompanied by texts that contextualized the artwork and Zum Felde's investment in it. For instance, Zum Felde introduced the "Expocisión de La Casa del arte," citing the exhibition of "prudently selected paintings, sculptures, ceramics, and tapestries" as a representative selection of contemporary Uruguayan art. This expansive range of media—a mix of fine and applied arts—is the basis for a modern national aesthetic, a position reinforced on subsequent pages, where Zum Felde juxtaposes a relief by Delia Demicheli and a painting by Guillermo Rodríguez (Figures 9.2 and 9.3).[28] The "overall impression" the exhibition yields, he writes, is that of introducing a visiting foreigner "who would like to know the artistic culture

---

[25] Zum Felde, "Programa," 8–9.
[26] "La Pluma: Puntos para la venta," *La Pluma* (Montevideo) 3, no. 10 (February 1929), 2.
[27] "Arte Nacional: Expocisión de 'La Casa del arte,'" "Salon de 'La Giralda,'" and "Exposición Pesce Castro," *La Pluma* (Montevideo) 2, no. 6 (May 1928), 35–49.
[28] Delia Demicheli, "Bajorrelieve" and Guillermo Rodríguez, "Escenas Camperas," *La Pluma* (Montevideo) 2, no. 6 (May 1928), 50.

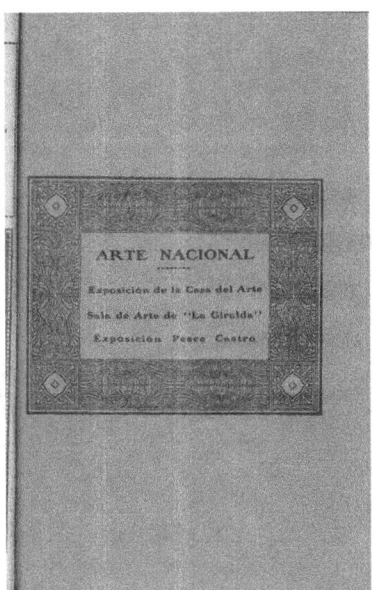

Figure 9.2 "Arte Nacional: Expocisión de 'La Casa del Arte,'" "Salón de 'La Giralda,'" and "Exposición Pesce Castro," *La Pluma* (Montevideo), vol. 2, no. 6 (May 1928): 35. Courtesy of The Library of the University of California, Berkeley.

Figure 9.3 Delia Demicheli, "Bajorrelieve," and Guillermo Rodríguez, "Escenas Camperas," *La Pluma* (Montevideo), vol. 2, no. 6 (May 1928): 50. Courtesy of The Library of the University of California, Berkeley.

of the country."[29] The magazine facilitates such an experience: one or two works are reproduced on each of the following pages, surrounded by ample white space, creating a framework to contemplate the work free from surrounding text.

The centrality of the exhibition sections was further reinforced by artwork, texts, and advertisements included throughout the magazine. Notably, Zum Felde reiterates his support for La Casa del Arte in the "Noticiario" section later in the same issue, urging Uruguayan artists and writers, led by "their spirit and patriotic duty," to materially and morally support this new institution.[30] The issue also contains a color insert of a Petrona Viera painting, several full-page and half-page reproductions of her drawings, and an accompanying analysis of her work.[31] The gallery "La Giralda" advertised in the page following the art section, showing the feedback loop created between physical gallery spaces and *La Pluma*.

Reflecting on the magazine's commitment to forging a national canon, Zum Felde observes that "on its pages... appear the signature of the majority of the country's writers, and graphic reproductions of the work of almost all its artists." Such a program fulfilled the magazine's mission to "faithfully reflect in its pages the intellectual and artistic movement of the Republic, while being an organ that transmits to the country the intellectual and artistic movement of the world."[32] By reproducing such artwork, *La Pluma* amplified local institutions, circulating the artwork they displayed and contextualizing it within a broader national and international framework. In doing so, Zum Felde demonstrates how a magazine, through its display of art, can consolidate a national visual canon and telegraph it to audiences both at home and across borders.

Editors as Curators: The *Mandrágora* Group

While Zum Felde broadcast Uruguayan art and ideas to the world by reproducing exhibitions in print, other editors across the Americas mounted physical exhibitions of artworks that complemented or served as extensions of their editorial projects. In New York, *Camera Work* and the gallery 291 worked in tandem, as did the short-lived magazine *291*, a bolder experiment in print and typography, with the Modern Gallery.[33]

---

[29] Alberto Zum Felde, "Exposición de 'La Casa del arte,'" *La Pluma* (Montevideo) 2, no. 6 (May 1928), 43. "La Casa del arte" was a cultural center created by the Uruguayan minister of public education in 1928 to promote the production of a national art. It held exhibitions of work by Pedro Figari, Rafael Barradas, and José Cúneo, among others, while also supporting music and theater.

[30] Alberto Zum Felde, "Noticiario," *La Pluma* (Montevideo) 2, no. 6 (May 1928), 147.

[31] Petrona Viera, *Recreo*, 1924 (oil on canvas; 86 x 90 cm); Luis Eduardo Pombo, "Los dibujos de Petrona Viera," *La Pluma* (Montevideo) 2, no. 6 (May 1928), 119–29.

[32] Alberto Zum Felde, "Nuestra Primera Etapa," *La Pluma* (Montevideo) 3, no. 12 (June 1929), 5.

[33] For *Camera Work*, see Sarah Greenough, "Alfred Stieglitz, Rebellious Midwife to a Thousand Ideas," in *Modern Art and America: Alfred Stieglitz and His New York Galleries*, ed. Sarah Greenough (Washington, DC: National Gallery of Art, 2002); For *291*, see Lori Cole, "'What Is 291?' Iterations of an Avant-Garde and Its Legacies," *Journal of Avant-Garde Studies*, 1, no. 1 (2020), 1–31.

In Cuba, *Revista de Avance* launched and promoted the first exhibition of avant-garde art in Havana in 1927, printing the artists' work in its pages.[34] Both the Stieglitz Circle and *Revista de Avance* had national aspirations. Stieglitz, for instance, was focused on cultivating an artistic community in the United States, titling his exhibitions "Younger American Painters" in 1910 and "Seven Americans" in 1925, and naming his gallery An American Place in 1929.[35] *Revista de Avance* wanted to forge both a Cuban avant-garde and a broader *arte americano*, celebrating the "artists of the new generation, who... fight to incorporate our art into the great undertakings of our time without neglecting... its essential Cubanism."[36]

Like *Revista de Avance*, most Latin American print communities were formed in explicit opposition to US imperialism and European colonialism. By contrast, the *Mandrágora* group of Chilean poets hoped to bring Surrealism, a European movement, to Chile. Surrealism had been known in Chile since the translation of selections of Breton's manifesto in 1925 by the artist and critic Sara Malvar. It was also transmitted by the poet Vicente Huidobro, who had moved to Paris in 1916, and who directly rebuked the Surrealist practice of automatic writing in his *Manifestes* of 1925.[37] *Mandrágora* included a poem by Huidobro in its first issue.[38] Subtitled "Poetry, Philosophy, Painting, Science, Documents," *Mandrágora* (1938–42) published seven text-heavy issues, whose contents foregrounded the values of chance and the irrational. The magazine featured French Surrealist touchstones such as Rimbaud, Breton, and Alfred Jarry, as well as work by its founding editors, the Chilean poets Teófilo Cid, Enrique Gómez-Correa, Jorge Cáceres, and Braulio Arenas. *Mandrágora*, or "mandrake," Arenas later reflected, "came directly from Surrealism."[39] Other Latin American magazines, like *Amauta* (1926–30), debated and documented Surrealism and its revolutionary political language, but ultimately

---

[34] The "Exhibition of New Art" was held May 7 to May 31, 1927 at the Association of Painters and Sculptors, an artist-run organization in Havana.

[35] "Younger American Painters" was on view at 291 from March 9 to 21, 1910. "Seven Americans" was held at the Anderson Galleries March 9–28, 1925.

[36] Los Cinco, "Exposición de arte nuevo," *Revista de Avance* (Havana), 1, no. 4 (April 30, 1927), 70, trans. and quoted in Luis Camnitzer, *New Art Cuba*, 2nd ed. (Austin, TX: University of Texas Press, 2003), 103.

[37] André Breton, "Manifiesto del Suprarealismo," trans. Sara Malvar, *Notas de Arte* N°39. *La Nación*. (Santiago, 23 March 1925); Jason Wilson, "Coda: Spanish American Surrealist Poetry," in *Companion to Spanish Surrealism*, ed. Robert Harvard (Suffolk, UK: Tamesis, 2004), 255; See also Esther Sánchez-Pardo, "Vicente Huidobro and William Carlos Williams: Hemispheric Connections, or How to Create Things with Words," in *International Yearbook of Futurism Studies, Vol. 7. Special Issue: Latin America*, eds. Mariana Aguirre, Rosa Sarabia, Renée M. Silverman, and Ricardo Vasconcelos (Berlin: Walter de Gruyter, 2017), 182–206.

[38] Vicente Huidobro, "De Cuando a Cuando," *Mándragora* (Santiago de Chile) 1, no. 1 (1938), 5.

[39] Braulio Arenas interviewed by Ștefan Baciu in *Surrealismo latinamericano: Preguntas y respuestas* (Valparaíso, Chile: Ediciones Universitarias de Valparaíso, 1979), 35 trans. and cited in Dawn Ades, "Surrealism in Latin America," in *A Companion to Dada and Surrealism*, ed. David Hopkins (Hoboken, NJ: John Wiley & Sons, Inc., 2016), 182.

championed aesthetic autonomy.⁴⁰ By contrast, *Mandrágora* more closely resembled the short-lived Argentine periodical Qué (1926 and 1930), which was inspired by Surrealism to forge a new literary language. For Arenas, who went on to edit *Leit Motiv* (1942–3), Surrealism catalyzed new forms of producing and displaying art. He, along with Cáceres, organized a series of exhibitions in 1941, 1943, and 1948 that became increasingly international in scope and strategically aligned with the international movement while displaying Chilean art.

Surrealism provided *Mandrágora* with an oppositional stance, allowing it to bypass the colonial legacy of Spain and to distance itself from its Latin American peers. One editor, Enrique Gómez-Correa, describes being "totally disconnected from the poetry of our country, and in general, from the poetry of American nations," and instead found "a nexus of continuity with other literatures, especially European."⁴¹ Despite the group's interest in Surrealism, *Mandrágora* asserted its own aesthetic agenda, promoting what the editors called "*poesía negra*" ("black poetry"), which literary scholar Melanie Nicholson defines as "an esoteric worldview in which the occult forces of language are the primary instrument for revealing hidden truths (or in psychoanalytic terms, the unconscious)."⁴² Arenas, however, felt that the group did not affiliate strongly enough with Surrealism and chose to start the more explicitly Surrealist *Leit Motiv*, which he announced in the sixth issue of *Mandrágora*. *Leit Motiv*, a "bulletin of facts and ideas" drew on relationships with the same Chilean authors as the previous publication. Its first issue includes an automatic drawing by Arenas on the front cover and a Spanish translation of Breton's partial third manifesto. Its second and final issue was more visually dynamic, featuring reproductions of art by Roberto Matta and Man Ray.

Alongside these publications Arenas and Cáceres organized a series of exhibitions. First, they showed their own objects, collages, and drawings in an "Expocisión Surrealista" held at the Biblioteca Nacional in Santiago de Chile (December 22–December 31, 1941). In the accompanying catalog, Gómez-Correa links the work of *Mandrágora* to the art on display, writing "those who have started from poetry have

---

[40] For more on *Amauta* see *The Avant-Garde Networks of* Amauta: *Argentina, Mexico, and Peru in the 1920s*, eds. Beverly Adams and Natalia Majluf (Austin, TX: Blanton Museum of Art, 2019); Harper Montgomery, *The Mobility of Modernism* (Austin, TX: University of Texas Press, 2017); For Surrealism in Latin America, see Melanie Nicholson, *Surrealism in Latin American Literature: Searching for Breton's Ghost* (New York: Palgrave Macmillan US, 2013); Michele Greet, Chapter 9 "Exploring Surrealism," in *Transatlantic Encounters: Latin American Artists in Paris Between the Wars* (New Haven, CT: Yale University Press, 2018). For Surrealism and magazines, see Lori Cole, "Reimagining Surrealism through Journals," in *Surrealism beyond Borders*, eds. Stephanie D'Alessandro and Matthew Gale (New York: The Metropolitan Museum of Art, 2021), 44–8.

[41] Enrique Gómez-Correa, "Notas sobre la poesía negra en Chile," *Mandrágora* (Santiago de Chile) 2, no. 3 (June 1940), 2. For more see Sergio Vergara, *Vanguardia literaria: Ruptura y restauración en los años 30* (Concepcion, Chile: Ediciones Universidad de Concepción, 1994), 209–10; Klaus Meyer-Minnemann and Sergio Vergara Alarcón, "La revista *Mandrágora*: vanguardismo y contexto chileno en 1938," *Acta literaria*, no. 15 (Concepcion, Chile, 1990): 51–70; Ana Borges-Rodríguez, "El grupo chileno Mandrágora y la 'facción surrealista' de *Gaceta de arte*: un estudio comparativo," Thesis (Universidad de Chile Facultad de Filosofía y Humanidades, Departamento de Literatura, 2006).

[42] Nicholson, *Surrealism in Latin American Literature*, 67.

been charged with translating into the visual certain ineffable zones of thought that *poesía negra* (black poetry) has incorporated into its best conquests."[43] In his catalog contribution Arenas reinforces the group's relationship to Surrealism, writing that although "in America they proclaim the death of this movement," he defends what he calls "Surrealist experiments" for confronting "our social and economic environment" and concludes with the rallying cry: "Let's open the doors. Listen to all: our struggle has begun. I am in excellent physical and mental condition. Let our enemies shoot soon. That they reward our excellent marksmanship."[44] Such adversarial language underscores how Arenas saw the group's work as a provocation to Chilean culture.

There is evidence that the exhibition did incite a backlash. Citing an anonymous negative review of their 1941 exhibition in the Chilean newspaper *El Siglo*, Arenas and Cáceres launched a single-issue *Boletín Surrealista* (December 29, 1941), a four-page 14.5 × 13.5 cm sheet magazine, carrying an essay titled "International Surrealism." In it, Arenas and Cáceres note the success of their exhibition, which drew "thousands of people." They denounce the review, claiming that the author "has no idea what Surrealism is" and falsely "believes that, because one has not gone to Europe, they can't be a Surrealist." They counteract such a position with a fierce defense of international Surrealism, and their own participation in it, writing: "All ideas, especially those that are belligerent at this time, have gained international content. Everything is tested internationally. In that respect, Surrealism moves controversially; and thus Surrealist groups have appeared in America (in Peru, Mexico, the United States, and Chile), with uncontrollable force, which have suffered the same attacks."[45] Such a defense suggests precisely how each iteration of Surrealism remakes it as their own, justifying Arenas and Cáceres's affiliation with the movement.

Arenas and Cáceres's instinct to put out a magazine to defend their exhibition demonstrates the inextricability of their curatorial and editorial projects. Particularly in the context of Surrealism, artists frequently mounted exhibitions, which can be seen as an extension of their artistic practice. For Arenas and Cáceres, their editorial and curatorial activities allowed them to showcase their work and to contextualize it for audiences. They next organized a Surrealist Soirée at the Rosenblatt Gallery on June 28, 1943, which was advertised in *Leit Motiv*. It once again featured Chilean artists: Arenas and Cáceres, but also the painter Roberto Matta and the photographer Erich G. Schoof, the latter of whom also documented the exhibition for the magazine. The press release anticipated the participation of the artists Nemesio Antúnez and Gabriela Rivadeneira as well, but they are not listed in the announcement in *Leit Motiv*, and likely were not included in the end. Moreover, the "gallery" was a furniture store, run

---

[43] Enrique Gómez-Correa, "La Poesia Negra y Collage," in *Expocisión Surrealista* (Santiago de Chile: Biblioteca Nacional, 1941), 3.

[44] Braulio Arenas, "Vida del Surrealismo," in *Expocisión Surrealista* (Santiago de Chile: Biblioteca Nacional, 1941), 1–2, 4.

[45] Braulio Arenas and Jorge Cáceres, "El Surrealismo Internacional," *Boletín Surrealista* (Santiago de Chile) 1, no. 1 (December 29, 1941), 1.

by a poet affiliated with the group, and the exhibition was quite modest in scale.[46] The photograph documenting the event, printed in the magazine, in many ways amplified and prolonged the existence of the show.

Much larger in scale and ambitious in scope was the International Surrealist Exhibition that Arenas and Cáceres organized at the Dédalo Gallery in Santiago, which ran from November 23 to December 4, 1948. The exhibition featured work by more than a dozen international artists, including: Hans Arp, René Magritte, Toyen, Wifredo Lam, Jacques Hérold, André Masson, Matta, Madelaine Novarina, Victor Brauner, André Breton, Arshile Gorky, Salvador Dalí, Óscar Domínguez, Leonora Carrington, and Yves Tanguy, alongside works by Arenas and Cáceres. The accompanying catalog published reproductions of select images, a checklist, essays by Braulio Arenas and Teófilo Cid, as well as poems by Arenas, Cid, André Breton, Jorge Cáceres, Benjamin Péret, and Enrique Rosenblatt.

The show was notable for its radical installation, a hallmark of Surrealist exhibitions. It included a darkened hallway filled with chairs, on which lay plates and cutlery. The hallway was crisscrossed with string and at the end of it sat a nude masked mannequin donning a sign that said "Please Touch"; such exhibition design was drawn no doubt from Duchamp's labyrinth of string covering the 1942 "First Papers of Surrealism" show in New York and echoed Duchamp and Enrico Donati's 1947 catalogue *Prière de toucher* (Please Touch). Elsewhere in the Chilean exhibition was a mannequin, painted black, with a poem by Breton written on it in white paint, reminiscent of the proliferation of mannequins at the International Surrealist Exhibition in Paris in February of 1938.[47] The Chilean exhibition also included decapitated dolls, cages filled with bells, and toy animals. The show received a great deal of attention in the press. As Cáceres reported in a letter to André Breton, the "highly successful" show attracted "an immense audience that was struggling to enter the gallery with so much noise" that the police "decided to install three men in front of the entrance."[48] While such novel exhibition design exceeded the magazine's capacity to reproduce art, like *Leit Motiv*, the show animated Surrealism for local audiences and put work by international

---

[46] *Leit Motiv* (Santiago de Chile), nos. 2–3 (December 1943), announcement for "Soirée Surrealista"; Soledad Novoa Donoso, "Escrituras sobre un fantasma," in *Papeles Surrealistas: Dibujos y pinturas del surrealismo en las Colecciones del MBNA* (Santiago de Chile: Museo Nacional de Bellas Artes, 2013), 24–5. See also Teodosio Fernández, "Pintores para la literatura hispanoamericana de vanguardia," *A través de la vanguardia hispanoamericana*, eds. Manuel Fuentes and Paco Tovar (Tarragona, Spain: Publicacions URV, 2011), 757–69.

[47] "First Papers of Surrealism" was held in New York (October 14–November 7, 1942) and the "Exposition Internationale du Surréalisme" in Paris (January 17–February 24, 1938). See Adam Jolles, *The Curatorial Avant-Garde: Surrealism and Exhibition Practice in France, 1925–1941* (University Park, PA: Penn State University Press, 2013), Lewis Kachur, *Displaying the Marvelous: Marcel Duchamp, Salvador Dalí, and Surrealist Exhibition Installations* (Cambridge, MA: MIT Press, 2001); Elena Filipovic, "Surrealism in 1938: The Exhibition at War," in *Surrealism, Politics, and Culture*, eds. Raymond Spiteri and Donald Lacoss (London: Ashgate Publishing, 2003), 179–203.; Marcel Duchamp and Enrico Donati, *Prière de toucher* (Please Touch), 1947 was the exhibition catalogue for "Le Surréalisme en 1947". I thank Bruce Altshuler for this reference.

[48] Letter from Jorge Cáceres to André Breton, December 9, 1948, quoted in Donoso, 25.

practitioners in dialogue. For artist-editors like Arenas and Cáceres, Surrealism gave them an oppositional framework in which to position their work on view and in print.

Magazine as Exhibition Catalog: *The Little Review*

As in the case of the editors of *Mandrágora*, Jane Heap, an American artist-editor, used the relationships she established through the magazine she coedited, *The Little Review*, to run a gallery and to stage large-scale exhibitions of avant-garde art. Heap ran the Little Review Gallery from roughly 1924 to 1927 and launched two exhibitions outside of the gallery, the International Theatre Exposition of 1926 and the Machine-Age Exposition of 1927. Unlike the exhibitions mounted by *Camera Work*, *Revista de Avance*, or the *Mandrágora* group, for these major exhibitions, issues of the magazine served as exhibition catalogs. While magazines and catalogs are closely aligned genres—reproducing artwork, accompanying texts, and situating readers vis-à-vis physical displays of art—they are infrequently collapsed into a single object and, in this case, introduced two exhibitions that were radical in terms of both the objects they included and their mode of display. The catalog-as-magazine reproduced a curatorial process that juxtaposed art with non-art objects and circulated a version of the exhibition experience to subscribers.

Founded by Margaret Anderson in March 1914 in Chicago, the *Little Review*'s motto was "Making No Compromise with the Public Taste" and it was a premiere venue for avant-garde literature, publishing American writers such as Ezra Pound (who served as the magazine's foreign editor starting in 1917), Sherwood Anderson, Gertrude Stein, Djuna Barnes, Jean Toomer, and Ernest Hemingway. In 1917 the magazine moved from Chicago to New York. Best known for serializing Joyce's *Ulysses* from 1918 to 1920, the magazine was put on trial for obscenity, and convicted and fined in 1921. In 1916 Heap, an artist, became coeditor of the magazine and updated the magazine's design and included reproductions of art by Hans Arp, Giorgio de Chirico, Charles Demuth, Hannah Höch, El Lissitzky, Kurt Schwitters, László Moholy-Nagy, and writing by Apollinaire, Breton, and Tristan Tzara.[49] She declared that the *Little Review* featured "the foremost artists in Europe. In fact, we have unostentatiously presented all of the new systems of art to America… about twenty Isms, in the last few years."[50] Indeed, as early as 1921 the magazine produced issues focusing on single artists, such as the Brancusi number (Autumn 1921), Picabia number (Spring 1922), and Juan Gris number (Autumn 1924). In 1922 the magazine declared (in all caps): "The *Little Review* is an advancing point toward which the 'advance guard' is always

---

[49] Susan Noyes Platt, "Mysticism in the Machine Age: Jane Heap and the *Little Review*," *Twenty One/ Art and Culture* 1, no. 1 (1989), 29. See also Jayne E. Marek, "Reader Critics: Margaret Anderson, Jane Heap, and the *Little Review*," in *Women Editing Modernism. "Little" Magazines and Literary History* (Lexington, KY: University Press of Kentucky, 1995), 60–100.

[50] Jane Heap, "Notes on Contributors," *The Little Review* (New York) 12, no. 1 (Spring–Summer 1926), 1.

advancing."[51] When Anderson moved to Paris in 1923 and Heap became the *Little Review*'s sole editor, she shifted its focus even more toward avant-garde art.

Heap showed artwork that she received for the magazine at the Little Review Gallery, which was housed at 66 Fifth Avenue, including that of Brancusi, Picabia, Man Ray, Joseph Stella, Tristan Tzara, Kurt Schwitters, Hannah Höch, Hans Arp, and Theo Van Doesburg.[52] As Anderson writes about Heap, "She made it [the *Little Review*] the American mouthpiece for all the new systems of art that the modern world has produced, from the German expressionists and the Russian constructionists to the French sur-réalistes... where the painting, sculpture, constructions, and machinery of these groups were exhibited."[53] The gallery functioned as "an adjunct to the magazine and a gathering place for intellectuals" according to scholar Susan Noyes Platt. Hart Crane corroborates this view of the gallery in a letter he wrote to Heap in 1926, calling it a "rendezvous of talent, galaxy of wit."[54] Heap kept the magazine and gallery running on her own, with little assistance or financial support. The exhibitions "were barely publicized even in the pages of *The Little Review*" and were infrequently reviewed.[55] Heap did have additional support, however, for her two larger exhibitions, the International Theatre Exposition of 1926 and the Machine-Age Exposition of 1927. The accompanying issues of the magazines functioned as exhibition catalogs, whose design mirrored the work on view.[56]

While in Europe in 1925 Heap met Frederick Kiesler, a visionary architect, designer, and writer who had curated the "International Exhibition of New Theatre Techniques" in Vienna in 1924 as well as the Austrian section of the "International Exhibition of Modern Industrial and Decorative Arts" at the 1925 Paris Exposition. Heap invited him to reproduce his theater exhibition in New York, the bulk of which he brought with him in January 1926, to which he added American designers. The two of them oversaw the International Theatre Exposition, which ran from February 27 to March

---

[51] *The Little Review* (New York) 8, no. 2 (Spring 1922), 33 cited in Dickran Tashjian, "From Anarchy to Group Force: The Social Text of *The Little Review*," in *Women in Dada: Essays on Sex, Gender and Identity*, ed. Naomi Sawelson-Gorse (Cambridge: MIT Press, 1998), 268–9.

[52] Group exhibitions included Ossip Zadkine, Lett Haines, Cedric Morris, Nicolai Granovsky, Pavel Tchelietcheff, Charles Demuth, John Storrs, and Henry McFee. In 1927 the Gallery moved to 24 West Fortieth Street, and then closed later that year when Heap moved to Paris. Platt, 32. See also Linda Lappin, "Jane Heap and Her Circle," *Prairie Schooner* 78, no. 4 (Winter 2004), 5–25.

[53] Margaret Anderson, *My Thirty Years War: An Autobiography* (1930) (New York: Horizon Press, 1970), 265.

[54] Hart Crane letter to Jane Heap, 1926, cited in Platt, 32.

[55] Platt, 32. Two exceptions that Kristina Wilson notes are "New Photography Employs No Lens," *New York Times* (January 6, 1924): 6 and "Art: Exhibitions of the Week," *New York Times* (March 29, 1925): sec. X, 11. Wilson, fn 28, 223.

[56] Heap had also planned an "International Exposition of New Systems of Architecture," possibly with Kiesler that never materialized. The show planned to include "the most recent developments in new systems of building, city plans, urbanism, time space construction—by the most vital architects in America, Austria, Belgium, France, Germany, Holland, Italy, Poland, Russia, etc.— organized by 'The Little Review,'" circular quoted in Barnaby Haran, "Constructivism in the USA: Machine Art and Architecture at *The Little Review* Exhibitions," in *Watching the Red Dawn: The American Avant-Garde and the Soviet Union* (Manchester, UK: Manchester University Press, 2016), 32–3.

15, 1926.[57] The exhibition was enormous and required a great deal of planning. As Heap notes in correspondence with her mother, "My theatre show will take up 25 cubic meters—20 models, drawings of sets, costumes, masks, photographers etc. that will cost hundreds of dollars to bring over? But we will charge admission, sell Little Reviews—and a catalogue."[58] It was held at the Steinway building at 113 West Fifty-Second Street, and featured 1541 elements from over 100 exhibitors from at least a dozen countries, and ranged from set designs, costumes, and props, as well as work by Léger, Picasso, Tzara, Hans Richter, and Rafael Barradas.[59] Kiesler's radical installation methods and the scale of the show drew extensive press coverage; one historian calls it "one of the most important theatrical exhibitions ever mounted in America."[60]

The catalog opens with a list of the show's many collaborators and a manifesto-like text from Kiesler announcing "the theater is dead." It includes twenty-three articles by an international array of playwrights, artists, and critics, along with more than seventy photographic reproductions of plays, costumes, set designs, and film stills.[61] The essays cover the Swedish Ballet, French theater, a manifesto by the Paris-based American musician George Antheil, and "Gas: A Theatrical Experiment" by artist Louis Lozowick on a stage set he designed. A checklist was interspersed throughout, published in different orientations that required the reader to swivel the page to read it. Published in a revised version as *The Little Review*'s Winter 1926 "Theatre Number," the magazine retained Kiesler's typography and the choice to present texts printed in different directions and sizes and included the essays by Hans Richter, Léger, Prampolini, and Kiesler (Figure 9.4).[62] Moreover, because the catalogue was delayed, the winter issue of the *Little Review* served in its place. Below the table of contents, Heap claimed ownership over the exhibition, stating:

> The idea for an International Theatre Exposition, New York, 1926, originated with me, in Paris, last summer. Tristan Tzara advised me to invite the cooperation of Friedrich Kiesler, director of the Theatre Exposition of the city of Vienna, 1924, and famous theatre-architect… in the organization of the project… I alone am responsible for contents, format and printing of Catalogue and *Little Review*.[63]

---

[57] The exhibition was supported by the Theatre Guild, the Provincetown Playhouse, the Greenwich Village Theatre, and the Neighborhood Playhouse.

[58] Letter, Jane Heap to her mother, July 15, 1925, in *Dear Tiny Heart: The Letters of Jane Heap and Florence Reynolds*, ed. Holly A. Baggett (New York: New York University Press, 2000), 106.

[59] It included work from Czechoslovakia, Yugoslavia, Romania, Hungary, Sweden, Poland, the USSR, France, Holland, Germany, Belgium, and the United States. Platt, 33–4.

[60] Jeanne T. Newlin, "Part of the Cosmos: Kiesler's Theatrical Art in America," in *Frederick Kiesler* exh. catalog, ed. Lisa Phillips (New York: Whitney Museum of American Art, 1989), 88 cited in Alan Golding, "*The Little Review* (1914–1929)," *The Oxford Critical and Cultural History of Modernist Magazines, vol. 2 North America, 1894–1960*, eds. Peter Brooker and Andrew Thacker (Oxford: Oxford University Press, 2012), 83. Platt, 34.

[61] Haran, "Constructivism in the USA," 28.

[62] Platt, 34; *The International Theatre Exposition*, eds. Frederick Kiesler and Jane Heap (New York: Little Review, 1926), https://dizbi.hazu.hr/a/?pr=iiif.v.a&id=10859 and *The Little Review* (New York), "Theatre Number," 11, no. 2 (Winter 1926).

[63] Jane Heap, *The Little Review* (New York), "Theatre Number," 11, no. 2 (Winter 1926), table of contents.

Figure 9.4 The "Theatre Number" of *The Little Review* (New York), vol. 11, no. 2 (Winter 1926). Photo: Beinecke Rare Book and Manuscript Library, Yale University.

In addition to claiming ownership over the exhibition (despite acknowledging the help of Kiesler and Tzara)—and recirculating it on her terms to her subscribers—Heap also advertised her gallery on the back cover, declaring it "the only gallery in America devoted entirely to the new movements in the arts."

Even before she had launched the International Theatre Exposition, Heap had already laid the groundwork for her second large show on machine-age aesthetics. As early as 1922, she wrote that the artist "must affiliate with the creative arts in other arts, and with constructive men of his epoch; engineers and scientists etc … The *Little*

Review has long been working on a plan to promote this idea, and to bring the artist into personal contact with the consumer and appreciator." [64] In 1923 Heap published Fernand Léger's "The Esthetics of the Machine," which "celebrated engineering principles as more vital than traditional painting."[65] Heap reiterated her interest in the marriage of arts and industry the following year, showcasing work by Russian Constructivists, whom she identified as "engineers of art" and noting that "something very interesting could be written about the Machine as a religious expression as great if not greater than the great cathedrals."[66] Later that year Heap published Enrico Prampolini's essay "The Aesthetic of the Machine and Mechanical Introspection in Art," which she later reprinted in the catalog for the Machine-Age Exposition.[67] Heap saw the need for the artist and engineer to join forces, a synthesis which would form the spiritual expression of the age. While such impulses were legible internationally, as evidenced by the geographic range of artists included in the exhibition, machine aesthetics had particular resonance in the United States.[68] Moreover, the suggestion that art could extend beyond traditional media like painting and sculpture paralleled the increasingly flexible and iterative space of the magazine, as re-imagined by editors like Heap.

Heap announced the magazine's plans for the "Machine-Age Exposition," in 1925, indicating that the show would be held later that year (although it was not actually mounted until 1927). Her vision foregrounded industrial objects, noting, "The Exposition will show actual machines, parts, apparatuses, photographs and drawings of machines, plants, constructions etc., in juxtaposition with paintings, drawings, sculpture, constructions, and inventions by the most vital of the modern artists."[69] By pairing art with industry, she reiterated her support for their spiritual synthesis, announcing, "THE MACHINE IS THE RELIGIOUS EXPRESSION OF TODAY."[70] She suggested that there was great interest in the show: "All of the most energetic artists, both here and in Europe: painters, sculptors, poets, musicians are enthusiastically organized to support this exposition, the Engineers are giving it their

---

[64] Jane Heap, "Independents, etc.," *The Little Review* (New York) 9, no. 2 (Winter 1922), 22.
[65] Fernand Léger, "The Esthetics of the Machine: The Manufactured Object, the Artisan and the Artist," *The Little Review* (New York) 9, no. 3 (Spring 1923), 45–9; Part II was published in *The Little Review* (New York) 9, no. 4 (Autumn–Winter 1923), 55–8. Platt, 29.
[66] Jane Heap, "Comments," *The Little Review* 10, no. 2 (Autumn–Winter 1924), 22. Platt, 31.
[67] *Broom* (1921–4) first published Enrico Prampolini, "The Aesthetic of the Machine and Mechanical Introspection in Art," trans. E.S., *Broom* 3, no. 3 (October 1922), 235–7. It was reprinted in *The Little Review* (New York) 10, no. 2 (Autumn–Winter 1924–5), 49–51 and again in the Machine-Age Exposition catalog, *Machine-Age Exposition* (New York: Little Review, 1927), 10.
[68] See Henry M. Sayre, "American Vernacular: Objectivism, Precisionism, and the Aesthetics of the Machine," *Twentieth Century Literature* 35, no. 3 (Autumn 1989), 310–42; Wieland Schmied, "Precisionist View and American Scene: The 1920s," *American Encounters: New Approaches to American Art and Literature*, ed. David C. Miller (New Haven: Yale University Press, 1993), 47–59; Gail Stavisky, "Reordering Reality: Precisionist Directions in American Art, 1915–1941," in *Precisionism in America, 1915–1941*, ed. Diana Murphy (New York: Abrams, 1995), 12–39.
[69] Jane Heap, "Machine-Age Exposition," *The Little Review* (New York) 11, no. 1 (Spring 1925), 22–4.
[70] Ibid., 22.

interested cooperation."[71] Heap amended this essay for the Machine-Age Exposition catalog two years later, demonstrating the continuity of her thinking.[72]

When it was finally held, from May 16 to May 28, 1927, the Machine-Age Exposition brought together "architecture, engineering, industrial arts and modern art" to demonstrate the "inter-relation-inter-influence of architecture, engineering, industrial arts, and modern art."[73] It showcased over 300 objects from seven countries, including light bulbs, a tractor, a coffee grinder, machine guns, and a meat slicer, which were installed alongside paintings, sculptures, and photographs.[74] Many architectural models, drawings, and photographs were also included.[75] The juxtaposition of fine art and equipment suggested, as art historian Kristina Wilson writes, that the "machine was so powerful that old standards of representation could not capture it—modern forms and sensibilities alone were sufficient."[76] The *Little Review* helped bring together and showcase these experiments. Heap collaborated with groups in Brussels, Russia, Austria, and France as well as artists like Duchamp, Man Ray, Charles Sheeler, Alexander Archipenko, and Charles Demuth, many of whose work was on view and included in the catalog/magazine.[77]

Held at 119 West 57th Street in a large warehouse space adjacent to where the International Theatre Exposition had been, the installation of the Machine-Age Exposition possessed a "physical theatricality" which Wilson compares to an automobile showroom or department store, noting its "carnival-like atmosphere."[78] "The exhibition acted as a kind of enormous machine itself, immersing visitors in its raw factory space and surrounding them with unusual-looking objects," she observes.[79] A contemporary reviewer, Herbert Lippmann, corroborates this assessment, noting the impact of the space and installation on the reception of the work:

> The setting of this exposition itself had significant form. This was the unpainted white plaster finish of walls, columns, beams, girders and floor slabs of an unpartitioned office floor of a common type of building erected for commercial

---

[71] Ibid., 24.
[72] Jane Heap, "Machine-Age Exposition," in *Machine Age Exposition* (New York: *Little Review*, 1927), 36–7.
[73] Platt, 36.
[74] Ibid., 35–6.
[75] Perhaps these were the objects that Heap had hoped to include in the unrealized International Architecture Exposition. Haran, 35.
[76] Kristina Wilson, "Spiritual and Material Gods in the Machine Age," *The Modern Eye: Stieglitz, MoMA, and the Art of the Exhibition, 1925–1934* (New Haven, CT: Yale University Press, 2009), 159.
[77] This included paintings by Charles Demuth and Van Doesburg, sculptures by Archipenko, Pevsner, and John Storrs, and decorations by Gabo and Hans Arp. Haran, 35.
[78] Wilson, 180–1. She notes that "some have assumed that the site was Steinway Hall, opened in 1925 at West 57th Street, but because there are no contemporary sources that place the exhibition at Steinway Hall (and because 119 is not a part of the Steinway property), this seems not to have been the case." Wilson, fn 9, p. 221.
[79] Wilson, 179.

renting. An amusing touch was the use of ordinary tin pails inverted as reflectors in the place of lighting fixtures.⁸⁰

Beyond the installation, the array of industrial objects on view was exceptional. The show, he notes, included "radio sets, valves, gears, propellers, metal cupboards, ventilators, aeroplanes, diving apparatus, rifles and machine guns, slicing machines, harvesting implements, scales, gas manufacture, piano frames, motor car designs and electric light bulbs," whose display suggested its kinship with art.⁸¹ As Lippmann states, the objects "stood about like the pieces at a sculpture exhibition, on pedestals of a sort, numbered and catalogued."⁸² As for architecture, there were photographs of raw sulfur storage plants in Germany, a church in Poland, new Bauhaus architecture, Hugh Ferriss's model for a glass skyscraper, Raymond Hood's Radiator Building, and Arthur Loomis Harmon's Shelton Hotel.⁸³ The show garnered the most press of any exhibition the magazine had produced.⁸⁴

Like the exhibition, the catalog's cover, by Léger, presents a Constructivist machine, and the ensuing texts celebrate architecture and industrial design (Figure 9.5). It announces itself as a "catalogue" even though it includes advertisements and resembles a magazine and was circulated as a supplement to the *Little Review*. It lists the exposition committee, artists' committee, and then a checklist, organized by country, interspersed throughout the catalog with reproductions of art and texts, much like that of the Theatre Exposition. It opens with a "Foreword: Architecture of this Age" by Hugh Ferriss, asking, "May we find, in this age of the Machine, tendencies which are more than local to America? The fact is that exhibits are appearing from all parts of the world which unanimously assault a certain accepted convention of Beauty."⁸⁵ This theme is revisited in Enrico Prampolini's "The Aesthetic of the Machine and Mechanical Introspection in Art," which had previously been published in the *Little Review* and culminates in a manifesto.⁸⁶ It is followed by Alexander Archipenko's "Machine and Art" and Louis Lozowick's "The Americanization of Art," as well as essays on French and Russian architecture. The texts are not only thematically linked but are also dynamically integrated with reproductions of photographs of buildings, costume designs, architectural models, sculptures, and machines. In total, the catalog contains nine essays and forty-five illustrations, many of which are drawings and photographs of industrial architecture.⁸⁷ In this way, the impulse toward the synthesis

---

[80] Herbert Lippmann, "The Machine Age Exposition," *The Arts* (New York) 11, no. 6 (June 1927), 325.
[81] Ibid.
[82] Ibid.
[83] Platt, 35–6; Haran, 35–7.
[84] It was reviewed in the *Arts*, the *Masses*, the *Christian Science Monitor*, the *New Yorker*, the *New York Times*, and the *New Republic*. Haran, 35; Wilson, fn 32, p. 223.
[85] Hugh Ferriss, "Foreword: Architecture of This Age," in *Machine-Age Exposition* (New York: *Little Review*, 1927), 6.
[86] Enrico Prampolini, "The Aesthetic of the Machine and Mechanical Introspection in Art," trans. E.S., *Machine-Age Exposition* (New York: *Little Review*, 1927), 10.
[87] Haran, 37.

Figure 9.5 Fernand Léger, *Machine Age Exposition* (New York: *Little Review*, 1927). © 2021 Artists Rights Society (ARS), New York/ADAGP, Paris. Photo: Beinecke Rare Book and Manuscript Library, Yale University.

of the machine and modern art was replicated in print, as was its imbrication in an American context.

Heap centralizes the importance of this aesthetic in her catalog contribution, a revised version of her 1925 essay. In it, she cites the significance of the engineer who will "make a union with the architect and artist."[88] As Wilson notes, there was a shift in Heap's attitudes from celebrating machines as art objects to "promoting machines

---

[88] Heap, "Machine-Age Exposition," *Machine Age Exposition*, 36.

as machines, first and foremost. In their engineering and functional efficiency they were exemplary, but unintentional, models of artistic expression."[89] Heap thought, Platt notes, that "by understanding the workings of the machine, the artist could utilize that structure to create a meaningful art for the new spiritual age."[90] By printing and circulating the exhibition catalog as the magazine—available at the show and to its regular subscribers—the *Little Review* demonstrates the seamlessness of its curatorial and editorial concerns and the capaciousness of the magazine to withstand a formal reinvention as a catalog, functioning as a corollary to an exhibition, as well as a site of display for new forms of artmaking.

"A Traveling Exhibition": *Spawn*

Although groundbreaking magazines like *The Little Review*, *La Pluma*, and *Mándragora* reimagined the display and circulation of artwork in and beyond the magazine, they never dispensed with the separation between magazine and exhibition as different physical entities. However, Stuart Davis and H.J. Glintenkamp collaborated on a magazine that was in fact a gallery, circulating reproductions of artwork, which were for sale, in a portfolio. *Spawn* offered an intimate physical encounter for the reader with artwork. Both Davis and Glintenkamp worked for the *Masses* (1911–17), and their own cooperatively run journal operated like the socialist monthly, with which they had become disenchanted. Artistically and politically progressive, the *Masses* featured artwork by John Sloan, George Bellows, Rockwell Kent, and Reginald Marsh. Despite championing artistic freedom, the *Masses* weathered internal conflicts over the display of art.[91] In March 1916, Sloan led a strike in favor of artistic integrity, arguing that the insertion of captions under drawings compromised the artwork for the sake of legibility.

Many of the artists featured in both the *Masses* and *Spawn* were part of the Ashcan School of realism, founded by the artist Robert Henri, who often drew quickly on site what they observed in urban environments. As Davis described, "We were encouraged to make sketches of everyday life in the streets, the theater, the restaurant, and everywhere else."[92] In doing so, art historian Robert Hunter explains, "These artists ... purposefully attacked conventional values and taste ... in both the style and the content of their work."[93] Often described as "unfinished," the sketchy drawings frequently satirized the wealthy and drew attention to the working poor. Readers unaccustomed

---

[89] Wilson, 166.
[90] Platt, 38.
[91] See Lori Cole, "'What Is the Matter with Magazine Art?' On Censoring the *Masses*," *Art Practical* 6, no. 4 (May 2015).
[92] Stuart Davis quoted in Karen Wilkin, "Stuart Davis: The Cuban Watercolors," *Latin American Art* 2, no. 2 (Spring 1990), 40.
[93] Robert Hunter, "The Rewards and Disappointments of the Ashcan School: The Early Career of Stuart Davis," in *Stuart Davis: American Painter*, ed. Lowery Stokes Sims (New York: Metropolitan Museum of Art, 1991), 38.

to such quick, realist sketches dismissed Davis's drawings as "decadent art."[94] Yet much of Davis's work was exhibited in galleries and re-circulated in magazines, even those publications that derided his work.[95] Davis was keenly aware of the print cultural landscape, as evidenced by his June 1913 cover of the *Masses*, in which two women huddle beneath oversized hats under the caption "Gee, Mag, Think of Us Bein' on a Magazine Cover!" Drawn in sickly blue and green crayon lines, the women served as an antidote to the "cover girls" typical of commercial magazines. The provocative cover elicited a great deal of press.[96] A critic for the *New York Evening Mail* deemed it the "best magazine cover of the year."[97] Such work suggests that Davis was self-reflexively reimagining the limits of the magazine, even before starting his own.

Before starting *Spawn*, Davis, Glintenkamp, and the artist Gar Sparks created a one-sheet proto-Dadaist parody of a magazine called *The Bla!* in 1916 (Figure 9.6). The words "published sometimes by Stuart Davis and G.S. Sparks" were written on the top righthand corner, mocking a magazine's periodicity.[98] It consisted of the program from Stravinsky's ballet *Petrouchka* overlaid with a cacophony of drawings, musical notations, and scrawled texts, signed with "Words and Music by Sparks, Glintenkamp, Davis."[99] Despite being slight and irreverent, *The Bla!* garnered a review in *Bruno's Weekly*, which reprinted it and declared that "it out-stieglitzes Mr. Stieglitz's '291.'" "See what you can make of it," the review prodded.[100] Even more so than *291*, *The Bla!* combined text and image, forming a frenzied scrawl of typographical markings that required the reader to reorient it to try to decipher it. By identifying an illegible single page of overlaid text and image titled an exclamatory nonsense word "a magazine," Davis and his collaborators playfully upended a reader's expectations, demonstrating the medium's elasticity and anticipating Dadaist experiments with print.

The artists' ability to garner press for their mischievous experiment also indicated their savviness and familiarity with mainstream print culture. Under the provocative headline, "Magazine Guaranteed to Be Free from the Remotest Suggestion Even of a Single Idea," the *Evening Mail* commented on *The Bla!* as follows:

> Magazines there have been in plenty to exploit this idea or that idea. But we have now in our midst the magazine without any idea at all. Stuart Davis, the editor,

---

[94] *Harper's Weekly*, no. 58 (October 11, 1913), 30–1 cited in Hunter, 38.

[95] For instance, *Harper's Weekly* published six drawings by Davis between August and September 1913. Hunter, fn 37, p. 44.

[96] Oliver Herford, "Pen and Inklings," *Harper's Weekly* (New York), no. 58 (September 6, 1913), 28. The cover was also mentioned in the *New York Globe* (May 24, 1913).

[97] Franklin P. Adams, "Always in Good Humor," *New York Evening Mail* (May 22, 1913), 10 quoted in Hunter, 39.

[98] *The Bla!* no. 1 (1916).

[99] *The Bla!*, no. 843, *Stuart Davis: A Catalogue Raisonné*, vol. 2, eds. Ani Boyajian and Mark Rutkoski (New Haven: Yale University Art Gallery, 2007), 409.

[100] "Books and Magazines of the Week: *The Bla*," *Bruno's Weekly* (New York), vol. 2 (February 6, 1916): 437. Jay Bochner speculates that the magazine began when the three of them "defaced a news column about the Ballets Russes" and calls it a "triple superimposition of handwriting over drawing over printed text." Jay Bochner, "dAdAmAgs," in *Making Mischief: Dada Invades New York* (New York: Whitney Museum of American Art, 1996), 16.

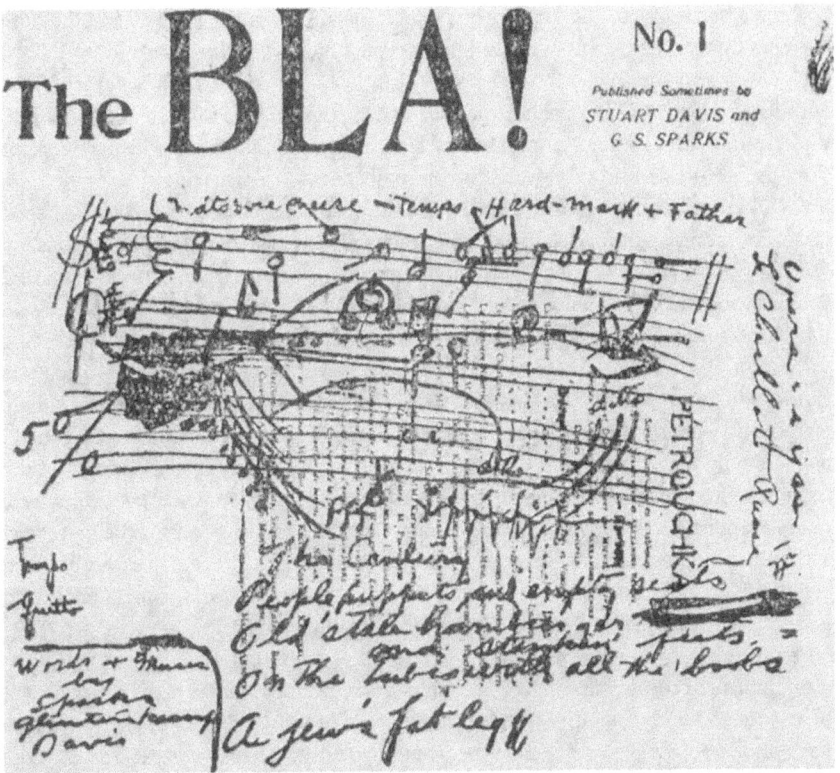

Figure 9.6 *The Bla!*, no. 1 (1916). © 2021 Estate of Stuart Davis/Licensed by VAGA at Artists Rights Society (ARS), NY.

insists that nothing having the slightest idea attached to it can pass through the editorial desk. He submits Volume I, No. I to prove that the editorial aspirations have been achieved … Subsequent numbers will appear whenever the editors find a theme sufficiently free from all taint of an idea.[101]

The point of the project was to draw attention to what constitutes a magazine, here defined as "a single idea," and then to withhold it. Part of the appeal of *The Bla!* for the *Evening Mail* was how it undercut self-serious avant-garde publications. The review describes *The Bla!* as being produced in reaction to the editors being "bored with too much futurist art." The article then describes "some futurist artists, who spent over

---

[101] "Magazine Guaranteed to Be Free from the Remotest Suggestion Even of a Single Idea," *Evening Mail* (February 17, 1916) quoted in *The Bla!*, no. 843, *Stuart Davis: A Catalogue Raisonné*, 409.

two and a half hours trying to make out what it meant ... were told they were all wrong and that this magazine was something that even a futurist couldn't make out."[102] Both the editors and the reviewer were poking fun at high art and at those exasperated with it. *The Bla!* playfully pushes the idea of what constitutes a magazine to a limit, undermining expectations for periodicity, length, legibility, affiliation with a movement (or even an "idea"), and yet it was still nominally deemed a magazine.

While clearly a provocation, *The Bla!* did seriously demonstrate the editors' interest in collaborating on innovative print experiments. Next, in 1917, largely in response to the artist strike at the *Masses*, Davis and Glintenkamp formed the portfolio magazine *Spawn*, whose manifesto announced, "It has no axe to grind or propaganda to propound. Its sole purpose is to reach an audience of picture lovers." It is, "in short, a traveling exhibition."[103] Unlike the *Masses*, which artists had felt privileged text, particularly captions, over artistic integrity, *Spawn* eliminated both captions and text and simply featured artwork. Published in three monthly issues between January and March 1917, *Spawn*'s only text consisted of a set of four poems and a story in the opening of the issue, and a mission statement on the back cover of the third issue. Its covers were made of rough brown paper devoid of images, overlaid in black text for the first issue, a shimmering golden orange for the second, and blue for the third. Each was between eight and ten pages and either opened like a booklet, in the case of the first and second issues; in the third, the recipient pulled the images out from an envelope (Figure 9.7).

Although it diverged from the *Masses* in terms of its presentation of artwork, *Spawn* was "published co-operatively by the contributors," noting, "*Spawn* is the embodiment of an idea and is co-operative in the strictest sense of the word. Each man pays for his page and is absolutely responsible for what goes on it." *Spawn* was described in the *Masses* as "A new magazine—an experiment in freedom. No editor! A group of artists, each of whom pays for his own page, and puts what he wants to on it."[104] In fact, *Spawn* barely identified as a magazine at all. As it states, "*Spawn* is a magazine in name only; its real object is the publication in portfolio form of reproductions of drawings and paintings of artists." Instead it functioned as a circulating gallery, announcing that "the originals of all contributions are available and prices can be had upon application."[105] Through *Spawn*, Davis and the other contributors showcased artwork that they could distribute and sell themselves. As for subscribers, *Spawn* could "be bought on the newsstands for a quarter or subscriptions may be sent to 401 Park Avenue, East Orange N.J."[106] Such a model radically diverged from that of a traditional commercial gallery or a standard magazine.

Spawn contained reproductions of drawings, oil paintings, and watercolors presented in an array of styles. In Davis's *Forty Inns on the Lincoln Highway*, words connect disparate pictorial segments, comprising a frenetic, humorous take on urban

---

[102] Ibid.
[103] *Spawn*, no. 3 (March 1917): back cover.
[104] "Spawn," *Masses* (New York) 9, no. 5 (March 1917), 41.
[105] *Spawn*, no. 3 (March 1917): back cover.
[106] "Spawn," *Masses* (New York) 9, no. 5 (March 1917): 41.

Figure 9.7 *Spawn*, vol. 1, no. 3 (March 1917). © 2021 Estate of Stuart Davis/Licensed by VAGA at Artists Rights Society (ARS), NY.

life. Charles Demuth's *In Vaudeville,* a watercolor, reflected the new urban world of entertainment. Others were figurative, such as Elias Goldberg's drawings of nudes, while the work of Alfred French and Engelbert Gminska was more abstract. Each was a new or very recent piece by the artists. As a cooperative gallery, the work *Spawn* featured was intended to be sold. Indeed, many of the works are now in the collections of major museums; *Forty Inns on the Lincoln Highway* is now at MoMA and Glenn O. Coleman's work was collected by the MoMA and the Whitney.[107] Even if a reader did not purchase the original work, the pages of the magazine each contained an individual

---

[107] *Forty Inns on the Lincoln Highway*, 1916, https://www.moma.org/collection/works/37442; Glenn O. Coleman's *Election Night* included in *Spawn* was later made into a lithograph dated 1928, https://www.moma.org/collection/works/73494, and given to the Whitney in 1931, https://whitney.org/collection/works/3801; Glenn O. Coleman, *A Chinatown Balcony*, 1910, https://whitney.org/collection/works/12234.

piece of art, which one can imagine subscribers removing and displaying as editioned artworks in a gallery. Davis and his associates repurposed the mail—and the magazine as a form—as a means to cluster together works, for sale, on their own terms.

Conclusion: Art and Magazines

Spawn, like many other magazines of the era, can be seen as an extension of Davis and his collaborators' artistic practice.[108] Editing a magazine allowed artists like Arenas, Cáceres, and Davis to put their work in conversation with that of their peers and to control and display its circulation (and in the case of *Spawn*, its sale). Much as galleries were spaces to gather, so too did the site of the magazine replicate relationships, reinforcing the magazine as a community formation, while at the same time advancing aesthetic agendas. These magazines, despite their ephemerality, outlasted many more tangible exhibitions of their work. Moreover, such magazines offered visibility to new art practices across the Americas in the early twentieth century, and their flexibility allowed for innovations in the presentation of art. As art historian Samuel Bibby argues, magazines are themselves "active agents in the making of art-historical meaning, as opposed to functioning as mere documents of the past."[109] By positioning the periodical as an alternative exhibition space and as an inventive and interactive form, these early-twentieth-century artists and editors worked to expand the ways in which visual art is incorporated into the form of the magazine.[110]

Moreover, these exhibitions led to the institutionalization of much of the art that these magazines displayed. Magazines like *La Pluma* reinforced the importance of local institutions like La Casa del Arte, bolstering them through its exhibition section. While a magazine like *Spawn* started as an irreverent side project, the work it featured is now part of the collections of the Whitney and MoMA. *The Little Review*'s exhibitions influenced Alfred Barr, Jr., who saw them as a professor at Wellesley and soon thereafter became the founding director of MoMA.[111] Barr called the Little Review Gallery a place to "always find something interesting."[112] Barr's early shows at MoMA reflected the influence of Heap: an exhibition of modern architecture in 1932, a display of theater art in 1934, and a "Machine Art" exhibition in 1934, in whose catalog Barr made a reference to the *Little Review* exhibition.[113] While *Forma*'s vision for a Museo

---

[108] Karen Wilkin, "Davis as Illustrator," in *Stuart Davis: A Catalogue Raisonné*, eds. Ani Boyajian and Mark Rutkoski (New Haven: Yale University Art Gallery, 2007), 51–3.

[109] Samuel Bibby, "'The Assemblage of Specimens': The Magazine as Catalogue in 1970s Britain," *British Art Studies*, no. 14 (November 2019), https://www.britishartstudies.ac.uk/issues/issue-index/issue-14/assemblage-of-specimens. Accessed January 16, 2020.

[110] Gwen Allen, *Artist Magazines: An Alternative Space for Art* (Cambridge, MA: MIT Press, 2011), 3.

[111] Marek, "Reader Critics," 94.

[112] Platt, 39. See Rona Roob, "Alfred H. Barr, Jr.: A Chronicle of the Years 1902–1929," *New Criterion* 5, no. 11 (Summer 1987), 1–19.

[113] Platt, 36–9; Haran, 43; Sybil Gordon Kantor, *Alfred H. Barr, Jr. and the Intellectual Origins of the Museum of Modern Art* (Cambridge, MA: MIT Press, 2002), 303–6.

de arte moderno americano was not realized, magazines compensated, at times even catalyzing museum collections established later, demonstrating the canon-building function of even the most experimental publications.

While many periodical communities in the Americas in the early twentieth century turned to magazines due to a lack of infrastructure for displaying modern art, by the later half of the century, magazines became a cite for "dematerializing" the art object, for artist-editors to circulate work on their own terms, and to circumvent an increasingly commercial art market.[114] Experiments such as Phyllis Johnson's *Aspen: The Magazine in a Box* (1965–71), whose themed issues included postcards, flexidiscs, film reels, and flip books by artists such as Warhol, William Burroughs, and Yoko Ono, or William Copley's *S.M.S. (Shit Must Stop)* (1968), also a collection of editioned art objects, reflected the legacy of a magazine like *Spawn*, while Seth Siegelaub's *July/August 1970*, a trilingual forty-eight-page exhibition produced as *Studio International*'s July/August 1970 issue, replaced the exhibition with a magazine that functioned as its catalog, like Heap's repurposing of the *Little Review*.[115] Following *Mándragora*, Latin American Surrealist publications such as *Ciclo* (1948–9), *A Partir de Cero* (1952–6), and *Boa* (1958–60) proliferated, while the Argentine artist Edgardo Antonio Vigo's *Diagonal Cero* (1962–9) offered a mix of art and concrete poetry that played with the materiality of the magazine.[116] Such contemporary print experiments were indebted to periodicals such as *La Pluma*, *Mandrágora*, *Little Review*, and *Spawn* and their accompanying curatorial activities. Editors across the Americas were exploiting the magazine's tactility, materiality, portability, and ephemerality as a means to convey art and ideas in conversation with sites of exhibitions. By harnessing print culture as an alternative means of producing and distributing art, these editors expanded their communities, forged innovative approaches to art's display, and demonstrated new possibilities for activating the magazine as a medium, ideas that were renewed by artists and editors in the ensuing century.

---

[114] See Allen, *Artist Magazines*; Lucy Lippard, *Six Years: The Dematerialization of the Art Object from 1966 to 1972* (Berkeley, CA: University of California Press, 1997); Alexander Alberro, *Conceptual Art and the Politics of Publicity* (Cambridge, MA: MIT Press, 2003); Luis Camnitzer, *Conceptualism in Latin American Art: Didactics of Liberation* (Austin, TX: University of Texas Press, 2007).

[115] See *Aspen*, http://www.ubu.com/aspen/; *S.M.S.*, http://sms.sensatejournal.com/?cat=7; *July/August 1970*, https://primaryinformation.org/wp-content/uploads/2017/05/studiointl4.pdf

[116] *A Partir de Cero*, https://www.ahira.com.ar/revistas/a-partir-de-cero/, *Boa*, https://www.ahira.com.ar/revistas/boa/, *Ciclo*, http://americalee.cedinci.org/portfolio-items/ciclo/, *Diagonal Cero* http://caevediciones.blogspot.com/p/diagonal-cero.html.

10

Comics in the Archive: Approaches to the April 1956 Newsstand

Rebekah Walker and Daniel Worden

Comics studies is a vibrant field, and its establishment as an academic research area has been accompanied and sometimes spurred on by the growth of comics archives and collections in major museums and libraries. This expansion of research collections has already led to a windfall of new scholarship in recent years—scholarship that has rewritten comics history, often providing different accounts of the medium, its creators, and its social and political contexts than the conventional histories of American comic books that have been written by industry insiders, fans, and collectors. In what follows, we detail how we sought to make one of our institution's comics archives usable as a print culture studies resource that makes visible a representative piece of comics history and offers a teaching archive for the undergraduate classroom.

Making archives and periodicals available for research is a collective undertaking, so we are writing as both a digital librarian (Rebekah Walker) and a comics studies scholar (Daniel Worden). We worked together on this project and alongside a lot of other archivists, librarians, photographers, staff assistants, and students, and we hope that our two perspectives and sets of expertise have blended together here to demonstrate how much can be accomplished through collaboration. While we ultimately want to convey what we learned about comics and print culture in this essay, we also wish to emphasize here how important it is and has been to us to advocate for institutional support of archival research projects. Getting the resources to even begin the work that follows required a lot of labor, from grant writing to digitization workflow meetings. All of that work and more led to this essay, but is not necessarily visible within it. Acknowledging this reality is necessary as we try to envision a better environment for studying and teaching our cultural history. We now turn to a capsule of history of comic books as a periodical form in the United States and then focus on how one particular comic book and our particular comic book archive can both be read in relation to comics history.

Comics as Print Culture

Comic books appeared on US newsstands in the 1930s. Staplebound periodicals that looked much like the pulp magazines that immediately preceded them, comic books offered low-cost visual narratives to a mass readership. Notably, comic books arrived on newsstands before television brought moving pictures into most American homes, but just barely. Widely recognized as the first superhero, Superman first appeared in *Action Comics* #1, published by Detective Comics Incorporated with a cover date of June 1938. Less than a year later in April 1939, the Radio Corporation of America (RCA) broadcast a president on television for the first time, Franklin Delano Roosevelt speaking at the New York World's Fair.[1]

In the 1930s and 1940s, comic books were immediately accessible to a mass readership; for example, National Comics, Superman's publisher, was printing around 5 million comic books per month by 1943, when they began reporting to the Audit Bureau of Circulations.[2] While comic books were immediately available in an affordable format on American newsstands, television underwent a longer period of basic research and development to bring costs down for the common household. *Action Comics* #1 in 1938 had a cover price of 10 cents, while in 1939, RCA's tabletop TT-5 television set cost $200 (and it required a separate console radio for sound).[3] As televisions became more affordable and more common throughout the 1940s and 1950s—by 1955, half of American households owned televisions—the mid-century comic book industry found itself in crisis, as sales sharply declined.[4] Indeed, one way to think about comic books is to think of them as a short-lived publishing fad, a pulp-magazine-sized form of visual narrative that emerged at around the same time as television and that was quickly eclipsed when television sets became affordable commodities. Comic books thrived for about twenty years on American newsstands,

---

[1] It is an interesting point of comparison to note that *Action Comics* #1 had an initial print run of about 200,000, according to every popular news story about that collectible issue. In 1939, when FDR was broadcast on television, there were about 200 television sets in the New York City area capable of receiving the transmission. Jeremy M. Norman, "RCA Introduces of Regularly Scheduled Electronic TV Broadcasting in America," *History of Information*, https://www.historyofinformation.com/detail.php?id=4219.

[2] This data is available through Brooks Hefner and Ed Timke, *Circulating American Magazines: Visualization Tools for U.S. Magazine History*, https://sites.lib.jmu.edu/circulating/. National Comics Group's data is available at https://osf.io/rm6u9/.

[3] It might be useful to put these media costs in context. According to the 1940 census, the average income in the United States was $1,368. Details about early RCA television prices and models can be found in Richard Brewster, "Early Electronic Television: RCA TV Development: 1929–1949," *Early Television Museum*, http://www.earlytelevision.org/rca_story_brewster.html.

[4] Scholarly histories of comic books can be found in many works, including Jean-Paul Gabilliet, *Of Comics and Men: A Cultural History of American Comic Books*, trans. Bart Beaty and Nick Nguyen (Jackson: University Press of Mississippi, 2010); Charles Hatfield and Bart Beaty, eds., *Comics Studies: A Guidebook* (New Brunswick: Rutgers University Press, 2020); and Shawna Kidman, *Comic Books Incorporated: How the Business of Comics Became the Business of Hollywood* (Oakland: University of California Press, 2019). Histories of television include Gary Edgerton, *The Columbia History of American Television* (New York: Columbia University Press, 2009), and Michelle Hilmes, ed., *The Television History Book* (New York: British Film Institute, 2003).

from the mid-1930s to the mid-1950s, before they became just another old print form, surviving in an increasingly televisual late twentieth century.

The comic book's short-lived, mid-century prominence has meant that most histories of American comics are structured by a scrappy resentment and a poignant nostalgia—in most accounts, comics are characterized as an inherently democratic artistic medium because of its economically low barrier to entry and openness to "low" cultural forms, as well as a medium that was tragically robbed of its former glory by the forces of 1950s conformity, both economic and social. Yet this focus on comics as a new, even insurgent media form of the twentieth century, overlooks the medium's connection to the longer history of printing. Even today, new comic books bear direct evidence of the long history of printing in their emphasis on the bordered panel and the individual page as discrete units. Much like early books, comics use both image and text, a common practice throughout the history of printing.[5] Comics stand out today as emblems of print history, rather than its transgressive other, and indeed, comics comprise a sector of the publishing market that is actually growing in a twenty-first-century literary marketplace struggling to find space on digital platforms.[6] Yet for all of their long historical resonances, comics are also an extension of modern, mechanically reproducible art forms such as film and photography, alongside which comics emerged in the nineteenth and twentieth centuries.[7] Comics are both a modern continuation of the tradition of illustrated (or illuminated) books and an upstart medium that thrives on immediate production and consumption. Accordingly, comics evoke a dual nostalgia for both pre-modern cultural forms and the kitschy commodities of our more recent childhoods.[8] Comics evoke the artisan traditions of calligraphy, caricature, engraving, and illustration as well as the "pop" plastic materials of postwar US culture.[9] Owing in part to this conjuncture, which sutures nostalgia for US culture's immediate past to the enlightened tradition of textual production, nostalgia has determined much of comics culture.

---

[5] For example, scholars have often worked on the connections between medieval manuscripts, sacred texts, and comics. See, for example, Chris Bishop, *Medievalist Comics and the American Century* (Jackson: University Press of Mississippi, 2016); Ann D'Orazio, *Neither Surrogate nor Complement: The Long Life of Visual Narratives* (The University of New Mexico: Proquest, 2017); Assaf Gamzou and Ken Koltun-Fromm, eds., *Comics and Sacred Texts: Reimagining Religion & Graphic Narratives* (Jackson: University Press of Mississippi, 2018); Martha Rust, "It's a Magical World: The Page in Comics and Medieval Manuscripts," *English Language Notes* 46, no. 2 (2008), 23–38.

[6] For an account of comics in relation to contemporary digital and print cultures, see Aaron Kashtan, *Between Pen and Pixel: Comics, Materiality, and the Book of the Future* (Columbus: Ohio State University Press, 2018).

[7] For a history of comics that emphasizes technological and formal connections to other media forms, see Jared Gardner, *Projections: Comics and the History of Twenty-First Century Storytelling* (Stanford: Stanford University Press, 2012).

[8] For a history of children's comics, see Gwen Tarbox, *Children's and Young Adult Comics* (New York: Bloomsbury, 2020).

[9] For accounts of comics as both evocative of print-making traditions and embedded within modern plasticity, respectively, see Hillary Chute, *Disaster Drawn: Visual Witness, Comics, and Documentary Form* (Cambridge: Harvard University Press, 2016), and Scott Bukatman, *The Poetics of Slumberland: Animated Spirits and the Animating Spirit* (Berkeley: University of California Press, 2012).

If you imagine a superhero comic book from the late 1950s—an unironic, benday-dot speckled, four-color sequence of images with over explanatory, hokey word balloons and a hermetically sealed world of childish good versus ridiculous-yet-harmless evil—it evokes both a childish fancy and a sense of aesthetic appreciation. Indeed, "Silver Age" superhero comics, published from roughly the mid-1950s to the early 1970s, provided the visual template for both a multibillion-dollar industry of licensed superhero products and an expansion of contemporary art, as comics imagery was widely employed by a range of Pop and contemporary artists from Joe Brainard and Roy Lichtenstein onward.[10]

Comic books from the "Silver Age" period, then, connote both the charge of a nostalgic artifact from a simpler popular culture environment and the emergence of a billion-dollar transmedia industry. We think it is important to keep this complexity in mind when looking at comics as print culture, for we must view the printed pamphlet both as a commodity from its historical moment and as a work of expressive, mass-produced art. *Detective Comics* #230, published in April 1956 by National Comics Publications, now known as DC Comics, is one example of the many comics that match the sketch of the "American comic book" that we've provided here (see Figure 10.1).[11] Merely looking at *Detective Comics* #230's cover, the crisp lines and four-color printing evoke a sleek, modern style, and the cover art, which depicts the Mad Hatter poised to remove Batman's cowl—no one's life is at stake here—is just goofy. It's a wonderful example of how comics capture currents in cultural history, like the emergence of the youth consumer market in the 1950s, symbolized through both the Mad Hatter's criminal fetish and Bruce Wayne's playboy lifestyle. Enmeshed as they are at the intersections of artistic experimentation, industrial production, and immediate audience response, comic books represent reality through embodied symbols, walking and talking metaphors that we know as "superheroes." On the cover of *Detective Comics* #230, the cultural context of the Silver Age can be read in the cover's overall design as well as its intentionally silly, yet morally instructive narrative.

---

[10] For an array of fine art inspired by superhero imagery, see Alejo Benedetti et al., *Men of Steel, Women of Wonder: Modern American Superheroes in Contemporary Art* (Fayetteville: Crystal Bridges Museum of American Art/University of Arkansas Press, 2019). A concise history of superhero comics is Marc Singer, "Superheroes," in *Comics Studies: A Guidebook*, eds. Charles Hatfield and Bart Beaty (New Brunswick: Rutgers University Press, 2020), 213–26. For accounts of comics and their relationship to the art museum, see Bart Beaty, *Comics Versus Art* (Toronto: University of Toronto Press, 2012) and Kim A. Munson, ed., *Comic Art in Museums* (Jackson: University Press of Mississippi, 2020).

[11] Nostalgia saturates appreciations of the comic book, and that nostalgic feeling has been important to the revaluation of a devalued medium such as comics. Indeed, the object of nostalgia has shifted according to generation and aesthetic—while the art comics figures Jules Feiffer and Art Spiegelman explicitly looked back to Golden Age comics for inspiration, artisanal yet nonetheless mainstream comics artists like Mike Allred and Darwyn Cooke evoked the clean designs of Silver Age superhero comics (and animation), and contemporary artists like Michael Fiffe and Ed Piskor have made work that makes reference to the 1980s and 1990s explosion of superhero art. These artist's influential styles contribute to the creation of a kind of stylistic shorthand for different historical periods in comics illustration, and these stylistic shorthands, perhaps most explicitly in the case of artists like Mike Allred and Darwyn Cooke, are often much more stylized than their original counterparts.

Figure 10.1 Cover of *Detective Comics* #230. National Comics Publications, April 1956. Stephen Neil Cooper Synchronic Comic Book Collection. Cary Graphic Arts Collection, Rochester Institute of Technology Libraries.

Detective Comics #230 is one of the 201 comic books that comprise the Stephen Neil Cooper Synchronic Comic Book Collection at the Rochester Institute of Technology's Cary Graphic Arts Collection. RIT's Cary Graphic Arts Collection is a library devoted to graphic communication history and practices, and the Cooper Collection was the first of what has become a number of comic book collections in its holdings. In both comics culture and periodical studies, the comic book as a material artifact is of paramount significance; yet outside of specialized research collections, comic books can be prohibitively expensive for scholars to purchase as objects of study. In comics culture, issues of Silver Age superhero comics like *Detective Comics* #230 are valuable objects, graded by collectible appraisal firms like the Certified Guaranty Company (CGC) and sealed in protective plastic "slabs." The collectibles market around comics values "mint condition" of print artifacts so highly that collectors seal their valuable comic books in these slabs to preserve the print object, as the simple act of turning an old comic book's pages can cause creases to form along staple bindings, thus eroding its value on the comics market. In periodical studies, scholars have emphasized the importance of the periodical as a whole object, including paratexts like editorial notes, letters columns, advertisements, and other material like the public service announcements common in 1950s comic books.[12] In reprint editions of comics, just as with text-based literature, the "text" itself is fundamentally changed—the comics themselves are typically recolored in reprint editions, and their paratextual materials are removed.[13] Indeed, *Detective Comics* #230's cover story, "The Mad Hatter of Gotham City," was reprinted as recently as 2014, in a DC Comics collection titled *Batman: The TV Stories*, owing to the story's similarities to the first storyline involving the Mad Hatter in the 1966 *Batman* television series. Yet, that story appears in isolation from the other materials in *Detective Comics* #230, offering only a partial view of comics history.

"The Mad Hatter of Gotham City" story in *Detective Comics* #230 is less than half of the content in the comic book—the twenty-eight-page comic book contains the twelve-page Mad Hatter story, as well as a six-page Martian Manhunter story, four pages of advertisements, a two-page humor comic titled "Casey the Cop," a two-page prose story about detective work, and a one-page public service announcement from the National Social Welfare Assembly featuring a boy named Binky who learns that "It's Fun to Belong!"[14] While "The Mad Hatter of Gotham City" story is the most substantial portion of this comic book, these other materials in the print artifact provide contextual information about audience, editorial intent, political and social ideologies, and even how comics figure into an aspirational vision of the self. For example, in *Detective Comics* #230, the main heroes' financial, intellectual, and physical gifts are in effect advertised to comic book readers through body building guidebooks, correspondence courses, and money-making opportunities (one advertisement in

---

[12] For an account of how editorial and advertising materials can contribute to a revision of literary history, see Robert Scholes and Clifford Wulfman, *Modernism in the Magazines: An Introduction* (New Haven: Yale University Press, 2010). Work across print culture and periodical studies also uses this idea as a methodological premise. For examples, see the work published in the academic journals *American Periodicals*, published since 1991, and *Journal of Modern Periodical Studies*, published since 2010. The term paratext was initially used to describe the print ephemera in books, yet is also useful as a way of thinking about the different kinds of materials in periodicals. See Gerard Genette, *Paratexts: Thresholds of Interpretation*, trans. Jane E. Lewin (New York: Cambridge University Press, 1997).

[13] For example, Zoë Smith's account of how pre-digital coloring processes determined the representation of racial difference in comics demonstrates print technology's significance to comics history. See Zoë Smith, "4 Colorism: The Ashiness of It All," *Inks* 4, no. 3 (Fall 2020), 340–56.

[14] "Binky Says 'It's Fun to Belong!,'" *Detective Comics* 230 (April 1956), np. The Grand Comics Database identifies the creators of this comic as Jack Schiff (script), Win Mortimer (pencils and inks), and Ira Schnapp (letters). See https://www.comics.org/issue/12777/.

Detective Comics #230 asks and demands: "Do You Want Spending Money? Sell these popular Patriotic and Religious Mottoes"). A more perverse model of aspiration is also apparent in the story, if we connect the Mad Hatter story itself, about a collector turned criminal, to the advertisement on the comic's back cover for rare stamps and a stamp collectors' guide. This advertisement encourages the very activity of collecting that the Mad Hatter embodies, an impulse to collect turned extreme. The paratexts, then, can complicate, expand, and inform the meanings in the Mad Hatter feature story, as even the question of readerly identification can be partially inflected by paratexts. Rather than merely viewing the comic book as a container for particular stories which are reproducible through anthology collections and transmedia adaptations, we argue that comics should be regarded as objects of study in and of themselves, as material artifacts that coalesce creative labor and corporate strategy, works of art that are fundamentally commercial and industrial.

While some independent, underground, and mainstream comic books are now available in their entirety through scholarly databases, there is no digital archive of original mainstream comics, and it is unlikely that such an archive will be possible because of copyright restrictions.[15] If we are going to teach comics as a print medium, we must make the print artifact available. As a digital librarian and a comics studies scholar, we believe that acknowledging and even methodologically foregrounding the collaborative processes of acquiring, touching, cleaning, scanning, storing, cataloging, transferring, posting, viewing, tagging, annotating, scraping, mining, extracting, analyzing, and summatively reading our objects of study is worthwhile, as that kind of stewardship labor is often invisible in scholarship that takes the accessibility of primary sources for granted. Part of what makes comics studies so exciting is also what makes it so difficult—it can be hard to get your hands on historical comics because they're so culturally significant as to be really expensive, but so culturally ephemeral as to be absent from most major print holdings in research libraries.

In *Breaking the Frames: Populism and Prestige in Comics Studies*, Marc Singer argues that comics studies should reorient itself around the study of history "as both method and discipline... a process for sorting through the archives of the past, organizing their contents into narratives, and evaluating the claims those narratives make for their accuracy and explanatory power."[16] We believe that a necessary component of that process is the comic book itself, and in this chapter, we will discuss how we made our print copy of *Detective Comics* #230 available to student readers. We will

---

[15] ProQuest's Alexander Street currently offers two comics archives, one focused on Underground and Independent Comics (https://search.alexanderstreet.com/comx) and another on Archie Comics (https://search.alexanderstreet.com/com3). Two of the largest publishers in American comics, DC Comics and Marvel Comics, do offer their own paid digital subscription services that provide access to an archive of their comics. But, the DC Comics and Marvel Comics services feature selective, retouched, and recolored reprint materials, almost always excluding any paratextual materials, rather than complete scans of original comic books. The community-supported Digital Comics Museum (https://digitalcomicmuseum.com/) hosts a large archive of comic books that are now in the public domain.

[16] Marc Singer, *Breaking the Frames: Populism and Prestige in Comics Studies* (Austin: University of Texas Press, 2018), 30–1.

also read *Detective Comics* #230 in relation to comics history and visual culture, and then moving beyond the individual print artifact, we will detail how we worked with a group of undergraduate students with the larger comics archive to which our copy of *Detective* #230 belongs. By beginning with one exemplary text and then zooming out to a wider archive of comic books sold on US newsstands that month in 1956, we hope to demonstrate the sliding scales of analysis available with a print culture archive.

Looking Backward and Forward through *Detective Comics* #230

Detective Comics #230's cover alone delivers the absurd scenarios we have come to associate with Silver Age superhero comics, alternately one of the most maligned and celebrated types of American comic books. Constrained by the censorious Comics Code Authority, *Detective Comics* #230's main story about the Mad Hatter's eponymous fixation represents the imposed silliness and lackluster narratives that relegated American comic books to subcultural status from the 1950s to the 1980s. Under the Comics Code Authority, implemented in 1954 by many comics publishers in the United States to protect the industry from both an impending economic collapse due to overproduction and public concern about the effect of comic books on juvenile delinquency, comic book narratives could depict crime as neither compelling nor practical. The "General Standards" of the Comics Code begins with these two rules:

1. Crimes shall never be presented in such a way as to promote distrust of the forces of law and justice, or to inspire others with a desire to imitate criminals.
2. No comics shall explicitly present the unique details and methods of a crime, with the exception of those crimes that are so far-fetched or pseudo-scientific that no would-be lawbreaker could reasonably duplicate.[17]

The cover of *Detective Comics* #230 certainly satisfies these two criteria. The Mad Hatter's modus operandi is decidedly anarchic yet without any substantive critique of "law and justice." As he announces early on in the comic, "some people collect paintings... stamps... old cars... but I, Jarvis Tetch, collect **hats!**" (emphasis in original).[18] The Mad Hatter's criminal impulse is not outside of social norms at all—he is an eccentric collector, modeled on the familiar big-game hunter of jungle adventure genre stories but with a domestic twist—nor is his plan for winning Batman's cowl anything but "far-fetched," per the Code's designation. It begins with a failed lasso abduction at the Green Derby Cafe, moves through a sequence wherein the Mad Hatter impersonates a sculptor at work on a statue of Batman, and then concludes with a chase sequence

---

[17] Code of the Comics Magazine Association of America, Inc., 1954, https://www.visitthecapitol.gov/exhibitions/artifact/code-comics-magazine-association-america-inc-1954.
[18] "The Mad Hatter of Gotham City!," *Detective Comics* 230 (April 1956), 12. The Grand Comics Database identifies the creators of this comic as Bill Finger (script), Sheldon Moldoff (pencils), and Charles Paris (inks). See https://www.comics.org/issue/12777/.

involving Batman's newly radioactive cowl. The clear morals to the story occur at the end. The villain is defeated by his own compulsion, when Batman punches the Mad Hatter into his prized wall of hats and Robin quips, "Looks like the Mad Hatter's hobby has finally gone to his head!" Then, in the final three panels of the story, the Mad Hatter is escorted off to prison by two police officers, as Bruce Wayne's hat blows in front of him on the sidewalk. Ironically, the Mad Hatter thinks, "Too bad Batman's headgear didn't come to me that easily! Instead, all the wind brings me is an ordinary hat!"[19] In this final conclusion, the Mad Hatter's own disregard for the "ordinary" marks his real failure. The nonconformist villain is arrested, as the plain-clothed Bruce Wayne and Dick Grayson look on. The heroic duo accomplish the containment of criminal and vigilante activity, to use Alan Nadel's theme for Cold War American culture.[20] Batman and Robin in this Silver Age incarnation protect the "ordinary," even as they clearly exist outside of the boundaries of any kind of "ordinary" life. In this way, as the Code perhaps imagines, the Mad Hatter story in *Detective Comics* #230 engages in some fun escapism, while also disciplining its young readers into a moral economy that polices and punishes excessive, transgressive, and unordinary behaviors and identities as "criminal."

Yet, as much as these kinds of silly superhero stories anchor comics in a juvenile subculture, *Detective Comics* #230 is also strikingly beautiful. It's not classically beautiful, and it's not soothing to look at. But, the bold linework and the sharp color contrasts on the cover endow the image with a crispness that evokes mid-century modernism. This is unlike the more ornamental mastheads of earlier cartoon periodicals. *Puck* magazine's masthead, for example, was in a calligraphic engraving, evoking the handwritten even in a mechanically reproduced, otherwise typeset periodical.[21] By contrast, *Detective Comics* and nearly every comic book on American newsstands at that moment had a masthead title that was less organic and Romantic than technical and abstract. The straight lines, mechanical coloring, and paste-up consistency of these titles lend the comic an inherently modernist feel. Comics offer a brightly colored, escapist modernism, a synthesis of experimental aesthetics with consumer plastics.

In *Detective Comics* #230, then, two narratives about comics history converge. The comic book is, on the one hand, an example of comics' subcultural status, an experimental and popular medium laid low by Cold War censorship. Comics, in this narrative, is an unfairly censored and restricted artistic and literary medium, and the simple superhero story in *Detective Comics* #230 registers just how steep the decline was, in terms of narrative complexity, from the "Golden Age," before the Comics Code's implementation, to the mid-1950s, when the medium is effectively

---

[19] Ibid.

[20] Alan Nadel, *Containment Culture: American Narrative, Postmodernism, and the Atomic Age* (Durham: Duke University Press, 1995).

[21] For an account of how organic and natural linework in the comics medium connotes a sense of intimacy, see Hillary Chute, *Graphic Women: Life Narrative and Contemporary Comics* (New York: Columbia University Press, 2010) and Jared Gardner, "Storylines," *SubStance* 40, no. 1 (2011), 53–69. For an account that considers the history of race in relation to these traditions, see Rebecca Wanzo, *The Content of Our Caricature: African American Comic Art and Political Belonging* (New York: New York University Press, 2020).

censored.[22] On the other hand, *Detective Comics* #230 is evidence of how mid-century superhero comics partook of modernist art and design practices, providing a visual iconography for Pop Art, graffiti, and a wide range of art practices that incorporate comics and comics icons. In this narrative, *Detective Comics* #230 is one of many examples of the comics style that would become increasingly ubiquitous in global culture, through licensing deals and Hollywood blockbusters, as well as in art and literary culture, as comics accrue legitimacy following the erosion of modernism's high/low divide.

At the risk of overemphasizing the importance of any one periodical among its peers on the newsstand, *Detective Comics* #230 is an emblem of both the wreckage and the promise of the comics medium. It is both victim of unwarranted bias, perpetually undervalued as legitimate art, and an art form that has defined large swaths of American popular visual culture.[23] These two characterizations of the medium—comics as a perpetual shame of popular culture and comics as a newly legitimized artistic medium—usually travel together in comics studies. Many of us have staked out "comics studies" as a field both by celebrating the medium's complex histories and by adopting the hierarchical values of both comic book collecting and academia in the formation of a comics canon, one that singles out "great works" that are worthy of reprinting, collecting, and archiving from the vast range of comics materials. Indeed, collectors have created the major bibliographies and databases for comic book research, and as superheroes loom large in comics collecting, superhero comics tend to be well annotated by fans on online databases like the *Grand Comics Database*.[24] Yet, as Bart Beaty and Benjamin Woo have pointed out in their *What Were Comics?* project, comics scholars often make assumptions, unsupported by any data, about which comics were "popular" in the twentieth-century United States.[25] What might feel exemplary for us

---

[22] For an influential account of Golden Age comics as representing a period of creative flourishing, cut short by the implementation of the Comics Code, see Jules Feiffer, *The Great Comic Book Heroes* (Seattle: Fantagraphics, 2003). The role of the Comics Code in the comics industry's reconfiguration in the 1950s is now the subject of scholarly debate, as the Comics Code may have been just one factor among many, including the rise of television, oversaturation of the newsstand marketplace, and disruptions in print distribution chains for the decline in comics publishing in the mid-1950s. For this broader account of the Golden Age and the comics industry's history, see Kidman, *Comic Books Incorporated*.

[23] In American periodical culture, the legitimation of comics can be seen nowhere more clearly than through the fact that in 2005, even the *New York Times* entered into the newspaper comics market, over 100 years after the *New York World* and the *New York Journal* helped to popularize the form in the United States in the 1890s. The *New York Times*'s inaugural "Funny Pages" feature was described by the editors as an attempt "to reflect the tastes of a new century" in 2005. See "The Funny Pages," *New York Times Magazine* (September 18, 2005): 1.

[24] See the Grand Comics Database, https://www.comics.org/.

[25] The *What Were Comics?* digital project website is http://www.whatwerecomics.com/. See also Bart Beaty, Nick Sousanis, and Benjamin Woo, "Two Percent of What?: Constructing a Corpus of Typical American Comic Books," in *Empirical Comics Research: Digital, Multimodal, and Cognitive Methods*, eds. Alexander Dunst, Jochen Laubrock, and Jenina Wildfeuer (New York: Routledge, 2018), 27–42. For accounts of the comics canon and the methodological difficulties of studying comics history, see Bart Beaty and Benjamin Woo, *The Greatest Comic Book of All Time: Symbolic Capital and the Field of American Comic Books* (New York: Palgrave, 2016) and Singer, *Breaking the Frames*.

and for our students—Batman, Superman, Wonder Woman, etc.—may in fact be a minor tradition within a comics medium composed of a much wider variety of genres. Indeed, recent work in comics studies has focused on the important yet often neglected genres of children's, horror, romance, teen comedy, and Western comic books, even as other work in comics studies has begun to approach superhero comics through more varied theoretical and methodological frameworks.[26] These works have helped to expand the kinds of things we can study, and the kinds of research questions we can work through with our students. For example, we might look at *Archie* for a formal cartography of teen comedy, or Dell's Disney comics for evidence of mid-century consumerism. How about the *Rawhide Kid*, initially published in the 1950s by Atlas Comics and one of the Jack Kirby and Stan Lee collaborations that would lead to the development of Marvel Comics's line of superhero characters? Any single comic book could figure into a typical history of comics. *Detective Comics* #230 is more immediately resonant with comics history than another artifact from this archive may be, but a more ambitious scope would consider comics more holistically as a publishing system. In comics studies, though, much of the data needed to answer our basic questions about the publishing system has yet to be created or made accessible, so collaborative research projects are necessary to work on both primary source material and analysis. Working collaboratively, we may be able to produce a different version of comics history, a story about how this visual medium operates as a network, system, and structure.

Thinking of comics as a publishing system has become a priority of recent comics studies scholarship. Scholars have sought to use data analysis, industry history, and periodical studies methodologies to emphasize how creative and professional networks as well as market and regulatory forces have shaped the medium's history.[27] So, while *Detective Comics* #230 is just one comic book, the copy of the comic book housed at RIT's Cary Graphic Arts Collection is part of an unusual synchronic archive, a collection created to reflect the variety of the 1956 comics newsstand.

---

[26] Recent works on comic book genres include Bart Beaty, *Twelve-Cent Archie* (New Brunswick: Rutgers University Press, 2015); Sidney Heifler, "A History of Romance," *Panel x Panel* 36 (2020), 4–46; David Huxley, *Lone Heroes and the Myth of the American West in Comic Books, 1945–1962* (New York: Palgrave, 2018); Tarbox, *Children's and Young Adult Comics*; Qiana Whitted, *EC Comics: Race, Shock, and Social Protest* (New Brunswick: Rutgers University Press, 2019). Recent work on superhero comic include José Alaniz, *Death, Disability, and the Superhero: The Silver Age and Beyond* (Jackson: University Press of Mississippi, 2014); Ramzi Fawaz, *The New Mutants: Superheroes and the Radical Imagination of Comics* (New York: New York University Press, 2016); Anna Peppard, ed., *Supersex: Sexuality, Fantasy, and the Superhero* (Austin: University of Texas Press, 2020).

[27] There is a range of work that falls under this banner, from network-focused analyses to social science-oriented studies of fan culture. For a range of these approaches, see Neil Cohn, ed., *The Visual Language Reader* (New York: Bloomsbury, 2016); Alexander Dunst, Jochen Laubrock, and Janina Wildfeuer, eds., *Empirical Comics Research: Digital, Multimodal, and Cognitive Methods* (London: Taylor and Francis, 2018); Margaret Galvan, "Archiving *Wimmen*: Collectives, Networks, and Comix," *Australian Feminist Studies* 32, no. 91–2 (2017), 22–40; Benjamin Woo, *Getting a Life: The Social Worlds of Geek Culture* (Montreal: McGill-Queen's University Press, 2018).

A Synchronic Archive

The Stephen Neil Cooper Synchronic Comic Book Collection is a distinctive snapshot of mainstream comics publishing in the United States. The collection contains 201 comic books and a single issue of *Mad* magazine bearing cover dates of March or April 1956. Like many comics collections, this archive began with a childhood memory. When he was eleven years old, Stephen Cooper was sitting on a New York City bus with "the latest issue of my favorite science fiction magazine":

> I was reading a story about a guy who was getting larger and larger, and still larger, until he grew so incredibly colossal that the enormous planets of the solar system simply passed through him. What? My pea-sized brain struggled with this cosmic-sized vision. I put up some rational resistance, but finally my imagination surrendered and the concept of atomic expansion on such an enormous scale broke through. This fantastic idea permanently blew my mind and I was never to be the same little boy again.[28]

Cooper grew up, graduated with a degree in photography from RIT in the late 1960s, and now works as a photographer and fine art framer in New York City. Thirty years after that formative comic book moment in 1956, Cooper turned back to comics as a collector.

In a fortuitous moment, Steven Cooper rediscovered the story that had so impressed him in 1956. When he was collecting comics stories about trips to the moon, he purchased *Strange Adventures* #230 (1971), a sixty-four-page collection of reprints, including his treasured "shrinking man" story. In the reprint volume, Cooper found a citation for its original appearance, in *Strange Adventures* #67 from April 1956. "Search for a Lost World!" tells the story of an alien scientist, Vern Aiken, who expands in size.[29] Aiken leaves his home world of Shandar to investigate strange happenings, which, he learns when he expands to the size of earthlings, have been caused by atomic bomb explosions in the United States. He then searches, and finds, his home planet of Shandar in a handful of gravel. The story concludes as Aiken shrinks back down to "infinite smallness, back to the world in an atom of Earth."[30]

A dedicated comics collector, Cooper decided that this one story in this one issue of *Strange Adventures* wasn't enough to satisfy him. He set out to track down every title on newsstands at that time in April 1956 "in order to fully recapture the comic book Zeitgeist of that momentous day in my life!"[31] Cooper proceeded to compose a catalog of every US comic book that would have been published in April 1956, as well as comics published once every two months that appeared in March 1956. His research was

---

[28] Steve Cooper, "The Odyssey of a Synchronic Collector," *Comic Book Marketplace* 67 (March 1999), 34.
[29] According to the Grand Comics Database, the creators of "Search for a Lost World!" are Edmond Hamilton (script), Sid Greene (pencils), and Joe Giella (inks). See the entry for *Strange Adventures* #67 (April 1956) at https://www.comics.org/issue/12752/.
[30] "Search for a Lost World!," *Strange Adventures* 67 (April 1956), 6.
[31] Cooper, "Odyssey of a Synchronic Collector," 35.

painstaking, involving looking through the *Photo-Journal Guide to Comic Books* with a magnifying glass to locate printed months on comic book covers, and highlighting the *Overstreet Comic Book Price Guide*'s entries for comics series published during the year 1956.[32] Ultimately comprising 201 comic book issues and one issue of *Mad* magazine in as pristine condition as he could collect, his newsstand recreation was featured on the cover of *Comic Book Marketplace* magazine in 1999, with a photograph taken by Stephen Cooper that recreates the childhood joy he experienced with comics (see Figure 10.2). The Stephen Neil Cooper Synchronic Comic Book Collection was

Figure 10.2 Cover of *Comic Book Marketplace* (April 1999). Stephen Neil Cooper Synchronic Comic Book Collection. Cary Graphic Arts Collection, Rochester Institute of Technology Libraries. Courtesy of Stephen Neil Cooper.

---

[32] See Ernst Gerber and Mary Gerber, *The Photo-Journal Guide to Comic Books*, 2 vols. (Minden, NV: Gerber, 1989–90) and Robert M. Overstreet, *Overstreet @ 50: Five Decades of the Overstreet Comic Book Price Guide* (Hunt Valley, MD: Gemstone, 2020).

donated to RIT's Cary Graphic Arts Collection in 2011, where it has formed the foundation of a growing comics library and archive.[33]

It's fitting that the origin of this collection lies in a story that features a main character who is both miniscule and gigantic. The collection is a sliver of comics history—a monthly sample of mainstream US comics. Yet, it is also of wide breadth, capturing not just collectible moments, like DC's *Showcase* #1, which would re-introduce the Flash in its fourth issue, or *Black Knight* #5, with its dazzling cover by one of Stan Lee's favorite Atlas Comics artists, Joe Maneely. Indeed, the synchronic collection was designed to be a "democratic" collection, giving equal space to lesser-known and lesser-respected comics like *Andy Panda*, *First Love Illustrated*, *Little Archie*, *Roy Rogers*, and many more.

Comics History by the Numbers

With this comics archive at hand, we imagined that we may be able to glean some information about the comics industry in 1956. We were inspired by the University of Calgary's "What Were Comics?" project and its attempt to quantitatively analyze the genres, publishers, story lengths, and even use of standard page layouts of comics in the United States from 1934 to 2014. We were also equally interested in working with digital archives in the classroom, inspired in this case by the student-focused research projects in the Yale Digital Humanities Lab's "Robots Reading *Vogue*" project.[34] Our synchronic collection of comics, we thought, afforded a snapshot of the industry as a whole at a crucial time in its history, as the Comics Code Authority had gone into effect and comics' "Silver Age" was emerging. A data-based approach to this archive, then, might provide some evidence of how the transition from the "Golden Age" to the "Silver Age" of US comics occurred, in a way that certainly takes into account a classic comic book issue like *Detective Comics* #230, but that treats that comic book as merely one among the over 200 available at the newsstand.

To get started with our project, we first acquired reading copies of the Cooper Collection. Duplicating the collection with low-quality reading copies allowed us to physically work with the comic book issues in a freer manner, and RIT Libraries' digitization lab imaged them so that we could work with digital versions of the entire

---

[33] Stephen Neil Cooper Synchronic Comic Book collection, RIT Libraries Archives Space, https://twcarchivesspace.rit.edu/repositories/3/resources/990.

[34] See *What Were Comics?* at http://www.whatwerecomics.com/, and *Robots Reading Vogue* at https://dhlab.yale.edu/projects/vogue/. Many digital projects analyze text corpuses at varying levels of detail—computational analysis or large scale processing (see work from the Stanford Literary Lab: https://litlab.stanford.edu/, the Data-Sitters Club project: https://datasittersclub.github.io/site/, and the journal *Cultural Analytics*: https://culturalanalytics.org/) to close text encoding (Women Writers Project: https://wwp.northeastern.edu/, the Willa Cather Archive: https://cather.unl.edu/). These textual projects served as informative models when considering our corpus.

contents of the archive.³⁵ We then designed a project-based Digital Humanities course around the archive, during which we worked with a group of fifteen advanced undergraduates on analyzing the collection.³⁶ Compared to the intentionally grand scale of a comprehensive data-based project like "What Were Comics?" at the University of Calgary, the small scale of our archive limited the kinds of questions we could ask. Yet, that limited scope also provided some clarity. As a first step toward understanding our archive (and to create relevant data to analyze), the class as a group went about the task of completing the partial catalog of our comics, verifying the publication months, dates, publishers, issue numbers, and titles of the comics themselves. The class worked off a central spreadsheet that was populated with available information at the project's outset.³⁷ That verification work is sometimes more complicated than it may seem. DC Comics, for example, used "National Publications" and "Signal Publications" to publish different genres of comics in this period, so what appear to be separate publishers are in fact the same, though it is not clear how to note these kinds of differences and distinctions in a catalog. Moreover, students were asked to identify genres in our collection to begin to inch toward an understanding of our corpus's narrative shape.

Identifying genres meant that we were cataloging not just the bibliographic data in our comics, but also interpreting these comics as narratives. Nearly every title in our collection has clear investments in genre, so identifying genres within our archive was mostly a straightforward process.³⁸ After some class debate about whether, for example,

---

[35] Instructors and students in the course were given access to the full digitized archive of comic books, with the understanding that their access ended with the semester. After extensive discussions about copyright and providing access to part of the comic books to the public, RIT Libraries included the comic book covers in their publicly accessible digital collections. View the covers at https://digitalcollections.rit.edu/luna/servlet/s/irh44x.

[36] Useful starter resources for digital humanities teaching include: Claire Battershill and Shawna Ross, *Using DH in the Classroom: A Practical Introduction for Teachers, Lecturers, and Students*: http://scalar.usc.edu/works/digital-humanities-in-the-classroom-a-practical-introduction/index.(Digital companion to book of the same name); the *Debates in Digital Humanities* series: eds. Matthew K. Gold & Lauren F. Klein: https://dhdebates.gc.cuny.edu/; HASTAC's Pedagogy Project: https://www.hastac.org/pedagogy-project.

[37] It is important to consider the growing conversations around student labor as it relates to digital project creation. We viewed working with the students on building this catalog as a way for them to gain insight into the materials and for the class collectively to develop resources to analyze. When we did work collectively on the archive at the beginning of the semester, that work was grounded in reading our primary materials and interacting with our primary source databases. Student work in our course was self-determined, as each student created a project around their own research interests. For an introduction to the topic of students, pedagogy, labor, and the digital humanities, see Keralis, Spencer D. C. "Disrupting Labor in Digital Humanities; or, The Classroom Is Not Your Crowd," in *Disrupting the Digital Humanities*, eds. Dorothy Kim and Jesse Stommel (Goleta, CA: Punctum Books, 2018), 273–94; Katrina Anderson et al., "Student Labour and Training in the Digital Humanities," *Digital Humanities Quarterly* 10, no. 1 (2016). http://www.digitalhumanities.org/dhq/vol/10/1/000233/000233.html; UCLA's "A Student Collaborators' Bill of Rights" (June 8, 2015), https://humtech.ucla.edu/news/a-student-collaborators-bill-of-rights/.

[38] Indeed, the comics in April 1956 are typically clear in their genre signaling, and comics historians have already developed some shorthand notions of the various names for genres in comics, such as "funny animals," that we used due to their ubiquity. For an extended discussion of genres in comics, see Nicholas Labarre, *Understanding Genres in Comics* (New York: Palgrave, 2020).

Superhero comic books are a genre unto themselves or are actually a subgenre within Action, or if Teen comics like *Archie's Girls Betty & Veronica* are a distinct genre or a subgenre within Humor or even Romance, we devised a two-part genre schema that identified "primary" and "secondary" genres, drawing from fifteen options. By identifying genre in two ways, we aimed to acknowledge both the overarching genre categories in which comic books participated (categories like action and romance that have rich histories across popular media forms) and more specific genre categories that are more closely tied to the comics medium (categories like funny animal and superhero). The data visualization in Figure 10.3 shows the consolidated primary and secondary genres of the corpus as percentages using our class-created data. While our data is quite small, the precise timeframe of the Cooper Collection nonetheless provides a capsule of the comics publishing industry in early 1956. The genre count in Figure 10.3 demonstrates, for example, just how small a segment of comics publishing was devoted to superhero titles—less than 3 percent of the overall genres, and only the primary genre in ten (4.95 percent) of the comics. "Superhero" is the least common genre to appear as primary or secondary, followed by "Horror/Suspense." "Action" and "Children" are the two most common overall genres, with "Humor" and "Western" following closely behind. Figure 10.3 shows the full detailed genre counts and percentages from the total.

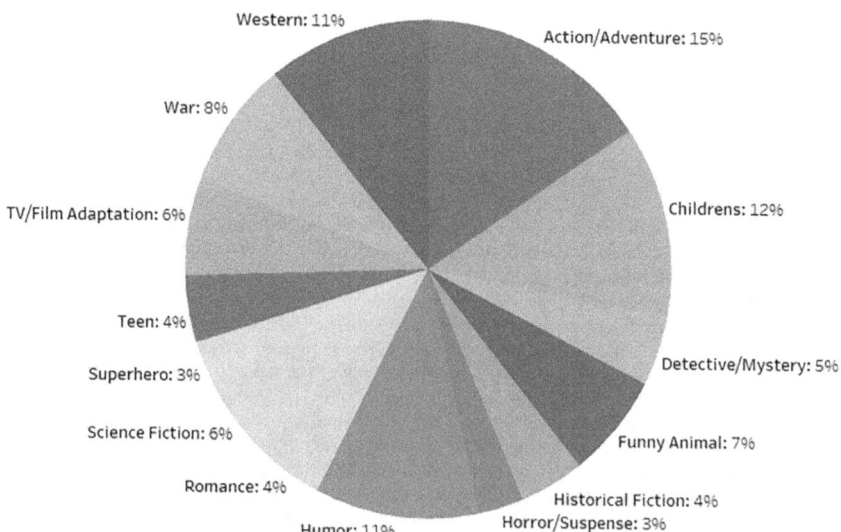

Figure 10.3 Comic book genres in April 1956, by percentage. Count of primary and secondary genres combined for overall percentages. Rebekah Walker. Rochester Institute of Technology, Spring 2019.

Likely printed in early 1956 and containing both new stories and reprints from pre-Code comics, the comics in the Cooper Collection represent an industry adapting to change. As Shawna Kidman details in *Comic Books Incorporated*:

> Most notably, the rise of television between 1949 and 1954 was corroding the audience for comic books, while simultaneously, struggles in the supply chain (between publishers, distributors, and retailers) were creating a surplus of product. Then, in the spring of 1954, a public relations crisis brought more distress... it put additional pressure on distributors and wholesalers and intensified the existing discrepancy between decreasing demand and increasing supply. The result was a crash in the market.[39]

As Kidman goes on to document, the result of this crash was "a narrowing of the field, as more than half of the industry's existing publishers and distributors closed their doors."[40] The March and April 1956 comics issues in the Cooper Collection are very much products of the industry at this moment of consolidation and transformation. At this point in comics history, publishers like DC and Dell began to "conduct business in ways that would support licensing," and indeed, there are large numbers of licensed comics, especially from Dell, in the Cooper Collection.[41] Furthermore, *Detective Comics* #230's Pop Art style is also indicative of how DC Comics would fall back on its classic intellectual properties in order to reposition itself in a new media environment. Both the past of newsstand comics and their future are visible in our snapshot of 1956.

Digital Projects

We designed our project-based "Comics in the Archive" course to involve continual work with the Cooper Collection corpus and for students to work with technologies that might enhance their analysis over the course of the semester. The course included a lot of lab time, and students were encouraged to engage with one another and their faculty and librarian instructors to explore ideas related to the corpus. Though we did not employ a co-instructor or fully embedded model, Digital Humanities and Social Sciences Librarian Rebekah Walker visited the class over ten times during the semester and worked with students to shape their final outputs. For the first eight weeks of the semester, Daniel Worden provided contextual readings and led class discussions with students about how to read the Cooper Collection comics in different contexts, emphasizing research questions that could be meaningfully explored through digital

---

[39] Kidman, *Comic Books Incorporated*, 30.
[40] Ibid., 31.
[41] Ibid.

tools.⁴² And throughout those eight weeks, Walker also led hands-on tutorials of several digital tools in class, including the data visualization tool Tableau and the digital exhibit platform Omeka to represent different approaches to analyzing the corpus and its data. The final six weeks of the semester were devoted to project work time, research collaboration, and group presentations.

Since this course was the first of its kind to be offered, we spent more time than we may otherwise have on basic bibliographic features, so that many students could pursue their projects. For example, we worked to compile creator's names, so that we could identify artists, writers, colorists, letterers, and editors; to gather page counts; to transcribe reprint records; and to cross-reference different sets of comics data with histories and interviews. The final assignment guidelines allowed students broad control over their approach to the Cooper Collection corpus, and we saw a mix of technical, artistic, and narrative outputs. While some students refined our genre and cataloging data, other students pursued archival-based projects after spending some time with the full collection. Students utilized a wide range of software and digital tools in their projects, including Tableau, Excel, Python, MATLAB, Voyant, Esri StoryMaps, and publishing tools WordPress and Dropbox Paper. The following project examples from the class demonstrate the range of research interests and cultural histories that comics touch upon:

> Boniecki: Sally Boniecki examined the average color composition and clothing style of characters across seventeen comics from the corpus that represent a wide range of genres—superhero, teen, science fiction, war, action/adventure. Boniecki identified protagonists and antagonists in these comics and created prototype outfits for protagonists and antagonists generally, as well as separated out into male and female. Figure 10.4 shows an example of one of these compilations.
>
> Lefurge: Andrew Lefurge created a wide-ranging project that looked at comics reproduction and availability of comics in the corpus, finding that only 23 percent of the series represented in the collection were "in print" at the time of the class (spring 2019) and only 16 percent of the particular issues in the corpus were readily available in print form outside of the collectibles market.⁴³ Lefurge examined genres' and publishers' relationships to availability and also created interactive

---

⁴² The class readings consisted of digital scans of the Cooper Collection comics themselves, digital scans of selected pre-Code comic books for context, and a number of essays from comics studies. As a class, we also read David Hajdu's *The Ten-Cent Plague: The Great Comic Book Scare and How It Changed America* (New York: Farrar Straus and Giroux, 2008) over the course of the semester and discussed the Comics Code's role in American comics history. Our class discussions about Hajdu's book provided a way for us to become familiar with the popular history of comics, necessary to the contextual framing of our own research questions about comics. Notable collections on comics pedagogy more broadly, by which we have been influenced, include Lan Dong, ed., *Teaching Comics and Graphic Novels: Essays on Theory, Strategy, and Practice* (Jefferson: McFarland, 2012); Susan Kirtley, Antero Garcia, and Peter E. Carlson, eds., *With Great Power Comics Great Pedagogy: Teaching, Learning, and Comics* (Jackson: University Press of Mississippi, 2020); Stephen Tabachnick, ed., *Teaching the Graphic Novel* (New York: MLA, 2009).

⁴³ Lefurge, Andrew, https://mikrowelle.github.io/cooper-comics-final/.

Figure 10.4 Female protagonist costume prototype. Sally Boniecki. Rochester Institute of Technology, Spring 2019. Used with permission. sallyjaysparrow.com.

sliders that overlay original and reprinted versions of comics to display color changes, all on a github.io website. Figure 10.5 is a screenshot of one of Lefurge's sliders demonstrating color reprints.

Sikorski: Jake Sikorski analyzed the reading levels of text from twenty-three comics from three "problematic" genres according to the Comics Code Authority (highlighted in David Hajdu's *The Ten-Cent Plague*): detective/mystery, romance, and horror/suspense. Sikorski used the Flesch-Kincaid grade level test and Flesch reading ease test to analyze the 101 stories that appear in the twenty-three books, confirming that these comics are generally addressed to a young audience (3.189 mean grade level). Figure 10.6 demonstrates the Flesch Kincaid Reading Level of books in the Cooper collection.

Figure 10.5 Screenshot of color comparison slider between original and digital reprint. Andrew Lefurge. Rochester Institute of Technology, Spring 2019. Used with permission.

Student work from the course is also highlighted on the Cary Graphic Arts Collection's digital exhibits website, alongside an exhibit that features thirty notable covers from the collection.[44]

---

[44] View the "Frozen in Time" exhibit on the Cary Graphic Arts Collection's digital exhibit site: https://cary-exhibits.rit.edu/exhibits/show/cooper-comics.

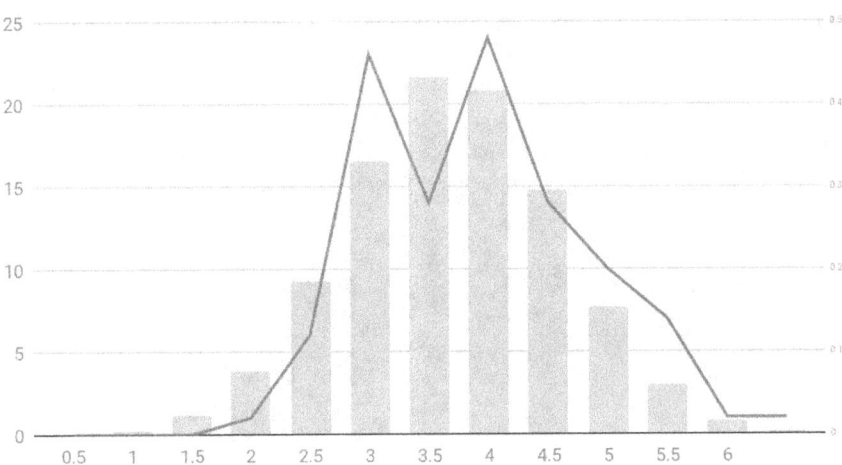

Figure 10.6 Flesch Kincaid Reading Level of books in the Cooper collection. Green bars represent the spread of the data, and the red line indicates the grade level of individual stories Jake Sikorski. Rochester Institute of Technology, Spring 2019. Used with permission.

Conclusion

We would like to conclude with a reflection on what we study, when we study comics. While his biography provides a rationale for the Cooper Collection, Stephen Neil Cooper has a unique history, too. He worked as a photographer for *High Times* magazine in the 1970s and 1980s, has completed a book of ink drawings, and has worked with comics collectors and galleries for decades. Cooper and the generations of creative workers like him have preserved comics history and transmitted the styles and conventions of comics to other media forms throughout the late twentieth and early-twenty-first centuries, and it is our hope that this archive can tell his story, too. The Cooper Collection itself tells a story of comics studies in miniature, as it begins with a private collector's childhood memory, and then evolves into a special collections archive that serves as the basis for research and teaching projects at an institute of higher education. This radiation of activity parallels the emergence and flourishing of comics studies as a teaching and research endeavor.

Acknowledgments

We would like to acknowledge the support of a Provost's Learning Innovation Grant from the Rochester Institute of Technology's Innovative Learning Institute. We also wish to thank Stephen Cooper, who is such a supportive friend and visionary thinker; the Cary Graphic Arts Collection staff: Steven Galbraith, Amelia Hugill-Fontanel, and Ella von Holtum; the Wallace Library Digitization Lab staff; Christine Lang at the School of Individualized Study; Laurie Jean-Francois for her summer work on this project; and the students in our Spring 2019 "Comics in the Archive" class: Madeleine Baum, Bryan Black, Sally Boniecki, Nic Bove, Mitchell Cartner, Michaella Colon, Tyler Hollinger, Laurie Jean-Francois, Nick Jodlowski, Lucas Kates, Andrew Lefurge, Jake Sikorski, Patrick Toy, Sherry Viggiano, and Alex Wisnieswki.

11

Icons and Archives: James Baldwin and the Practice of Celebrity

Robert F. Reid-Pharr

> *For, finally, Richard was hurt because I had not given him credit for any human feelings or failings. And indeed I had not, he had never really been a human being for me, he had been an idol. And idols are created in order to be destroyed.*
> – James Baldwin, "Alas, Poor Richard," 1961

If in some not yet fully imagined future there is ever a thoroughgoing assessment of the ideological and discursive preoccupations of our own generation's versions of African American and African Diasporic cultural studies then it will surely turn on the fact that we are a people obsessed, in more or less equal measures, with questions of both the archive and celebrity. The basic conceit of African American life is that our history has been robbed from us. Those of us most interested in questions of black memorialization, black memory, and black archives continually use a rhetoric of lack—and response to lack—to describe the ontological and epistemological quandaries strung ingloriously between the clumsy words, African and American, African and diasporic, African and modern, African and alive. One must ask if it is indeed true that in this moment, some four hundred years after the first captives of the Atlantic slave trade arrived in North America, that what most distinguishes our contemporary communities is not only the fact of our continued oppression and exploitation under racial capitalism, but also a deficit of archival evidence marking our passing and our resistance.

I suspect that few of my interlocutors will disagree with these claims, given the fact that so many of our generation's most brilliant minds have turned themselves decisively toward both the theorization of these problems and ever more clever methods of remediation. Where I push into troubled waters, however, is in my claim that celebrity and celebration are also central to contemporary African American and African Diasporic intellectual and cultural practice; indeed, it is plainly difficult to tease out where or how our undying desire to rediscover, uncover, and reinvent a presumably lost past can be distinguished from an equally palpable, if perhaps more straightforwardly coarse, fascination with what I name "the practice of celebrity." Though much of the rhetoric surrounding progressive archival practice—and its attendant print cultures—turns on the matter of the lost voices and identities of the enslaved, the defeated, the poor, and the unheralded, the actual *business* of archiving, the bread and butter matters of donations, grants, patronage, and prestige, is one in which questions of name and status are always fully central. The Martin Luther King Papers are ranged between ostentatiously affluent Stanford University and the grand King Center in Atlanta. The Angela Davis papers are available as part of the remarkable holdings of Harvard University's Schlesinger Library. More importantly for my purposes here, the James Baldwin Papers were purchased by the Schomburg Center for Research in Black Culture in 2017. This followed on the heels of the 2013 acquisition of some one hundred Baldwin letters by Yale's Beinecke Library, a purchase that augmented the institution's already impressive holdings of Baldwin's early manuscripts and juvenilia.

Here, however, I want to move slightly beyond the simple iteration of the fact that archives (and here I am primarily concerned with print archives) are largely made up of materials left by prominent individuals, and toward the idea that there is a set of structural issues that establish a clear connection between archival practices and practices of celebration. In the epigraph with which I began this essay, James Baldwin regrets that he has treated Richard Wright as an idol, a thin, two-dimensional figure, produced precisely in order to be destroyed. This admission of fault and responsibility is the continuation of a famously raucous confrontation between Baldwin and Wright in Paris after the 1949 publication of Baldwin's path breaking work, "Everybody's Protest Novel," an essay that ends with perhaps one of the most quoted paragraphs in black letters, a paragraph in which Baldwin makes an explicit connection between Harriet Beecher Stowe's 1852 sentimental classic, *Uncle Tom's Cabin*, and Wright's 1939 breakthrough work, *Native Son*. Speaking of the two novels' protagonists, Baldwin writes:

> Bigger is Uncle Tom's descendant, flesh of his flesh, so exactly opposite a portrait that, when the books are placed together, it seems that the contemporary Negro novelist and the dead New England woman are locked together in a deadly, timeless battle; the one uttering merciless exhortations, the other shouting curses, And, indeed, within the web of lust and fury, black and white can only thrust and counter-thrust, long for each other's exquisite death; death by torture, acid, knives and burning; which blinds and suffocates them both, so that they go down into the pit together.[1]

Of course, what even the most modestly gifted sophomore could tell you is that Baldwin's target here is what we might think of as the thinness of black characterization, an American tendency to read African American subjectivity between polls of suffering and rage that admit of no social or spiritual complexity. What I would add to this is the reality that both Baldwin and Wright understood, more or less clearly, the fact that the publication of this essay and the rift in the men's relationship that followed in

---

[1] James Baldwin, "Everybody's Protest Novel," in *Notes of Native Son* (Boston: Beacon P, 2012), 22.

its wake were structured by a politics of black representation, memorialization, and indeed archivization, into which the two giants were actively attempting to intervene.

"Everybody's Protest Novel" was first published in *Zero Magazine* and almost immediately thereafter in *Partisan Review*, making a twenty-five-year-old James Baldwin the first acknowledged African American to gain access to the prestigious journal. It is important to note, however, that New Orleans born Creole, Anatole Broyard, had, in fact, preceded Baldwin by a year with the June 1948 publication of "A Portrait of the Hipster," itself a clear precursor to Norman Mailer's 1957 work, "The White Negro." Broyard, however, was generally not recognized as a black person until 1996 when the fact was revealed by Henry Louis Gates in the *New Yorker*.[2] The genius of Broyard's essay, the thing that steals the breath and forces the heart to skip, is the fact that the piece is not only a form of archiving, a presentation and documentation of a new social type, but also a particularly clever commentary on the practice of cultural and racial passing. For Broyard the hipster is the jive talking, illegitimate son of The Lost Generation, who carries "his language and his new philosophy like concealed weapons."[3] He wears a white streak made with powder in his hair that works as "the outer sign of a significant, prophetic mutation."[4] He is an aficionado of Jazz, Bebob, and Marijuana who comports himself like a street corner evangelist. Yet in the end he is ruined by his own mendacity and artifice:

> The hipster—once an unregenerate individualist, an underground poet, a guerilla—had become a pretentious poet laureate. His old subversiveness, his ferocity, was now so manifestly rhetorical as to be obviously harmless. He was bought and placed in a zoo. [...] He was *in-there*... he was back in the American womb. And it was just as hygienic as ever.[5]

What is easy to hear in Broyard's sentences is the resonance of his own bitter critique of the Hipster with Baldwin's equally withering pronouncements in regard to Richard Wright's creation, Bigger Thomas. In both cases bombast gives way to sterility, while even the presumably most gritty markers of black subjectivity—poverty, bastardy, sexual prowess, popular music, marijuana, and violent confrontation—become nothing more than increasingly complex modes of masking and recategorization. For Baldwin and Broyard mid-century black subjectivity, at least insofar as that subjectivity was related to literature and popular culture, was a thing that was already knitted, worked upon, and translated such that the clever or ambitious black intellectual had seemingly no choice but to adopt a species of artificiality, a spectral second skin, if he was to be seen at all. Both men, one black, one *not* black, gained access to the exclusive/excluding pages of the *Partisan Review* by referencing a presumably necessary artificiality in American cultural life operationalized through various forms of emulation and ventriloquism. Black subjectivity, black thought, black articulation, black culture, black speech can

---

[2] Henry Louis Gates Jr., "White Like Me," *New Yorker* (June 10, 1996). https://www.newyorker.com/.
[3] Anatole Broyard, "A Portrait of the Hipster," *Partisan Review* (June 1948), 722.
[4] Ibid., 723.
[5] Ibid., 727.

only be seen once they have been properly styled, domesticated, and indeed veiled. Bigger Thomas is no more dangerous than Uncle Tom; the presumably white hipster no more threatening than a tanked-up street corner evangelist.

My intention is that the preceding comments be taken as a preamble to a discussion of that afternoon in Paris, shortly after the publication of "Everybody's Protest Novel," when Richard Wright in the company of the novelist, Chester Himes, met a young James Baldwin at a Left Bank café ostensibly in order to hash out the details of the controversy that Baldwin's iconoclastic article had provoked. Though all three men would eventually write about this iconic moment of intellectual confrontation, only Baldwin and Himes published their accounts. Wright's version, delivered as a speech on November 8th, 1960, at the American Church in Paris and entitled "The Position of the Negro Artist and Intellectual in American Society," was among the last public statements he would make before his untimely death just short of three weeks later on November 28th. The piece is now among his papers in the James Weldon Johnson collection of the Beinecke Library. Wright begins by retreating to what was quickly becoming a relatively common, even expected, procedure in the criticism of James Baldwin, a sort of shocked and sad assessment of the young writer's masculinity. "I must tell you that there existed between Chester Himes and me, on the one hand, and Baldwin, on the other, a certain tension stemming from our view of race relations," Wright offers. "To us, the work of Baldwin seemed to carry a certain burden of apology for being Negro and we always felt that between his sensitive sentences there were echoes of a kind of unmanly weeping."[6] Where the work of both Wright and Himes becomes truly interesting, however, is in their meticulous attention to the staging of the scene. The confrontation took place in Les Deux Magots café in Saint-Germain-des-Prés, a site famous less for being a place where the Parisian intellectual elite met to eat, drink, and debate their art as a place where they could be *seen* eating, drinking, and debating their art. The very structure of Parisian cafes, that unnerving turn of the tables outward so that you might watch the passing crowd watching you, is itself an indication of the essentially performative and indexical work done within them. In Paris today tours crowd the wooden tables of Les Deux Magots, sipping Sancerre, and sniffing at haphazardly prepared pain aux raisins in order to note the fact that something special once took place there, something worth noting and reiterating if never exactly reenacting.

Wright stresses in his account of the day that Baldwin came with his own audience in tow in the person of a Mrs. Putnam, wife of James Putnam, the former secretary of the US chapter of PEN international. He goes on to claim that Baldwin's abusive and outlandish behavior was, in fact, enacted precisely to establish and reiterate his stature in the eyes of his white female interlocutor. In the older writer's telling, the conversation quickly skidded outside the margins as Baldwin leaped to his feet, pointed his finger into the maestro's face, and let loose the full force of his venom.

---

[6] Richard Wright, "The Position of the Negro Artist and Intellectual in American Society," Richard Wright Papers, Box 3 Folder 41, James Weldon Johnson Collection, Beinecke Rare Book and Manuscript Library, Yale University.

"I'm going to destroy you! I'm going to destroy your reputation! You'll see!"
"What are you saying? What are you talking about?"
"I said that I am going to destroy you!" Baldwin screamed.
"Tell 'im, Jimmy; tell 'im!" the white woman, Baldwin's friend, egged him on.
"Why don't *you* tell me?" I challenged her.
"He's telling *you* for *me*," the white lady said, her face excited with a kind of sensual hate.[7]

After the episode came to a close both Baldwin and Mrs. Putnam left and a spooked Himes returned to the table. The two shocked and exhausted men then performed their post-mortem with Himes reporting that what he found most offensive was Mrs. Putnam's role in the affair.

"That was horrible," Himes sighed.
"Well, I guess it is better for it to be said openly than just thought of in private," I said.
"But he said that in front of that white woman," Chester Himes voiced the heart of his and my objection.
"That was that point," I said.[8]

In Himes's own treatment of the incident, recorded in his 1971 autobiography, *The Quality of Hurt*, he repeats many of the particulars of Wright's account while radically reworking the structure. He claims, in fact, that Wright himself wanted an audience for the confrontation. More surprising still, Himes notes that Wright not only knew Mrs. Putnam, but had reneged on a commitment to attend a cocktail party at her home that very afternoon so that he could meet Baldwin at the Deux Magots. Himes also reapportions the blame in the story, painting Wright himself as the aggressor.

Dick sat down in lordly fashion and started right off needling Baldwin, who defended himself with such intensity that he stammered, his body trembled, and his face quivered. I sat and looked from one to the other, Dick playing the fat cat and forcing Baldwin into the role of the quivering mouse. It wasn't particularly funny, but then Dick wasn't a funny man. I never found it easy to laugh with Dick; it was far easier to laugh at him on occasion. Dick accused Baldwin of showing his gratitude for all he had done for him by his scurrilous attacks. Baldwin defended himself by saying that Dick had written his story and hadn't left him, or any other American black writer, anything to write about. I confess at this point they lost me. Then suddenly a large group of people approached us. I looked up and was startled to find Mrs. Putnam among them.... It wasn't long before Mrs. Putnam and all of her friends had gotten to the heart of the argument and taken sides. All of the women and the majority of the men... took Baldwin's side—chiefly,

[7] Ibid.
[8] Ibid.

I think, because he looked so small and intense and vulnerable and Dick appeared so secure and condescending and cruel. But in the course of time they left us to go to dinner, and still Baldwin and Dick carried on while I sat and watched the people come and go... .The last thing I remember before I left them at it was Baldwin saying, 'The sons must slay their fathers.' At the time I thought he had taken leave of his senses, but in recent years I've come to better understand what he meant.[9]

It would obviously be unwise to attempt to re-adjudicate this incident at a remove of some seventy years. I will, however, repeat my contention that what is most interesting here is the fact that Himes, Wright, and Baldwin all remained so focused on the theatricality of the incident, the keen attention applied to not only cast and setting but also tone and demeanor. The confrontation between Wright and Baldwin or at least the *description* of the confrontation was imagined by the three as a work of art itself. Though the incidents of Café Deux Magots are offered to us as what Diana Taylor names "repertoire," those many lived, fleshy moments of performance in which meaning is conveyed through quotidian practices that are only infrequently understood to be important enough to be either recorded or even noted, we nonetheless have access to these embodied and presumably spontaneous incidents only through resort to the archive.[10]

Wright, Himes, and Baldwin carefully prepare their narratives. They remind us that at no moment during the disastrous encounter was there ever a lack of self-consciousness or tuition. I will add here that in his own treatment of the incident in the 1961 essay, "Alas, Poor Richard," Baldwin amplifies this point when he suggests that Wright was obsessively concerned with the need to prepare black people, particularly black intellectuals, to be seen by their white compatriots and interlocutors. Speaking of the efforts to help found the Franco-American Fellowship Club, Baldwin reports that in Wright's comments to the black Parisians assembled at the first meeting of the group, Wright apologized for the lack of white participants, claiming that Jean-Paul Sartre, Simone de Beauvoir, Albert Camus, and Wright's own wife, Ellen, wanted to attend, but "I told them that before I can allow you to come, we've got to prepare the Negroes to receive you," to which Baldwin imagined the insolent response, "Nigger, I been receiving white folks all my life—prepare *who*?"[11]

My desire here is to help in the necessary work of de-romanticizing the practice of African American and African diasporic cultural and intellectual history by narrowing the imagined divide between real life and recorded life, theater, and print. I want, that is, to play with the idea of an essentially mechanical understanding of history, one in which subjectivity is established both in the lived and somatic reality of our lives, the sensuous tickle of flesh against flesh, as well as in the naming, cataloging, and reproduction of that reality. Or to perhaps speed a bit too quickly to one of my

---

[9] Chester Himes, *The Quality of Hurt: The Autobiography of Chester Himes* (New York: Doubleday, 1971), 200.
[10] Diana Taylor, *The Archive and the Repertoire* (Durham: Duke University Press, 2003).
[11] See James Baldwin, "Alas, Poor Richard," in James Baldwin, *The Price of the Ticket: Collected Nonfiction, 1948–1995* (New York: St. Martin's/Marek, 1985), 284.

main arguments, I am convinced that what we think of as "truth" and "authenticity" are themselves essentially discursive effects, indeed forms of organization and reinterpretation. Twisting the matter even further, I would make the simple point that in the brief examination of the famed confrontation between Wright and Baldwin that I have just offered, our return and our retreat to the archive can bring us closer to the bleeding "truth," the right and wrong of the matter, only if we refuse to pay attention to the obviously rehearsed methods of storytelling that each of our protagonists deploys. I have in mind now Walter Benjamin's 1935 essay, "The Work of Art in the Age of Mechanical Reproduction."[12] It interests me here precisely because Benjamin names the fact that our increasingly sophisticated techniques of reproduction and dissemination work to produce a consuming public keenly aware of the artificiality of the objects in front of them. While they know, or at least *think* they know, that there is an original somewhere, some ancient script that might contain within itself an unblemished aura, they also understand, as a key aspect of their status as modern subjects, that the documents heralding truth and fixity that they hold in their hands are, in fact, copies, copies of copies, such that both elite and popular critical practices turn on the effort to note—and in a sense celebrate—the clumsy ruptures of logic and tearing of narrative that alert us to the "fakeness" of our materials while nonetheless encouraging the hope that there is an original truth "out there," that might be found if we could only figure out how to clear the mountains of obfuscating detritus—history, if you will—that block our path. James Baldwin's oeuvre, his reproduced and infinitely reproducible corpus, his spectral body, work ultimately to drive a need for access to the real Baldwin, the Baldwin who existed as a creature of spirit and repertoire and not solely as the two-dimensional emanation of a million television screens and a billion bits of paper. Benjamin argues that while "the presence of the original is the prerequisite to the concept of authenticity," it is the fact of its mechanized reproduction that allows "the original to meet the beholder halfway." Moreover, it is the general awareness of this process, the sense that we are continually in the presence of simulacra, the belief that we are continually being lied to, that provokes so much of the at-once corrosive *and* productive toxicity within modern American cultural life.

I should admit at this juncture that I am fully aware that the throttle is open and that we are now in the midst of a full-scaled reevaluation and celebration of the work and life of James Baldwin. And as I am myself a modern man, fitted out with healthy measures of ambition, drive, and good common sense, I have, in fact, climbed onto that wagon and attempted to commode myself, however awkwardly, alongside the rest of the band. Working within this context, I have begun the task of writing something like a biography of James Baldwin and immersed myself in his papers, hoping to discover and then announce truth. The problem with retreat to the archives, however, particularly the archives of the celebrated, is that they can never deliver you to exactly where you want to go. Every newly opened box, each rediscovered document further

---

[12] See Walter Benjamin, "The Work of Art in the Age of Mechanical Reproduction," in *Media and Cultural Studies Keyworks*, eds. Meenakshi Gigi Durham and Douglass M. Kellner (Malden, MA: Black Well Publishing, 2001), 18–40.

obscures the path to the original source. Both the archive and the archivist speak in languages not so dissimilar from the thin whine of harried university professors discovering yet again that they have gotten no closer to font, foundation, origin, or cradle than when they began. In the particular case of celebrity archives, from the first giddy touch of trembling fingers to precious text one is forced to admit the correctness of David Marshall's contention that "to a great degree, the celebrity is a production of the dominant culture," produced by "a commodity system of cultural production" with the intention of establishing and representing the common sense.[13] Nevertheless, the celebrity's audience always immediately enacts its revenge, assigning their own judgments, their own meanings, to the celebrity's always unstable personage, such that "an exact ideological fit" between the production of the cultural icon and the consumption of that same icon is rare. Or to bend Marshall's claims to the everyday practices of print culture, particularly the pen and paper archives in which I work, all of that rifling of texts and uncovering of long buried documents produces its own scarring effects. Those many tears, mis-filings, and petty thefts that are quotidian, yet always unacknowledged, parts of archival practice have the effect of reorienting even the most carefully crafted of narratives. Moreover, even when we are most moved, when the master's words spring from the page with the electricity of the gospels, we should be particularly careful. A single tear falling from the eyes of even the most committed of disciples can both stain the document and blur the ink.

Of the hundreds of persons who corresponded with Baldwin during the height of his celebrity, none was more interesting—or interested—than Alex Haley, the ghost writer of the 1965 classic, *The Autobiography of Malcolm X*, who wrote at least twelve letters to Baldwin in 1967 while he was doing research for his wildly successful 1976 novel, *Roots: An American Saga*. Baldwin meanwhile was skipping between borrowed apartments in the United States, France, and Turkey as he attempted to complete his fourth novel, *Tell Me How Long the Train's Been Gone*. What truly startles in the exchange between the two literary giants, however, is the surprising news that Haley wanted to write a biography of Baldwin, entitled simply enough, "Baldwin." In a letter dated January 14th, 1967, he wrote to "Jimmy" that his meeting with Tony Curtis to discuss the actor's playing the role of celebrity attorney, Melvin Belli, in a proposed biopic went well. He also reiterated his excitement about the idea of a biography: "And- yes, we've both much to do in between, but I find myself repeatedly anticipating the research and writing of BALDWIN. A great book. I feel it—you know?"[14]

The subject of "Baldwin," or more precisely the subject of Haley's feelings about a proposed project tentatively called "Baldwin," became a dominant theme in Haley's eager correspondence. The work was clearly meant to extend the wild success that Haley had had with *The Autobiography of Malcolm X* and that he would have with *Roots*. Even more to the point, it would reiterate and expand the celebrity status that

---

[13] See David Marshall, *Celebrity and Power: Fame in Contemporary Culture* (Minneapolis: University of Minnesota Press, 2014).

[14] Letter from Alex Haley to James Baldwin. January 14, 1967. James Baldwin Papers, Schomburg Center for Research in Black Culture, box 3, folder 19.

Baldwin achieved when his face appeared on the cover of the May 17, 1963 issue of *Time Magazine*. Haley wanted, that is, to produce an iconic text, one in which Baldwin's biography would act as a stand in for a deeper, more elemental, tale of creativity and the African American experience. Writing on January 23rd, 1967, Haley wraps Baldwin in a thick blanket of promises, compliments, and predictions about how the two will work together to finish the proposed biography:

> There isn't a project I have pending to which I feel, truly subjectively, more committed… There is, for one thing, my indelible respect that you went through <u>all</u> that it took—to blast through, and <u>make</u> it, really <u>do</u> it, which really was done for all of us brethren who write, or who purport to; we all benefited from the new-respect legacy. And then what it meant to all the rest of the brethren, generally. You know, the voice, when there hadn't really been that kind of voice, in our immediate time. Power of that pen, all of that. Already, of course you know me too well to feel I am puffing you. It's the way I feel. And this man needs chronicling. Definitively. For now, and for future when we're all gone, and those unborn now are studying us—and what happened, in the various areas, facets. And I will be very damn frank: I feel privileged that I will be the one to do it. I'm very patient, very thorough, and when I want I can write. And write of you, for you, I will.[15]

Strangely, Baldwin the prolific novelist, essayist, playwright, and critic is hard to discern in these lovely sentences. Instead, from the very first, Haley turns toward the hagiographic, a discursive mood that forces sensitive writers to push beyond "puffing" in order to create a necessary and future-oriented chronicle of the man who ushered in "the new-respect legacy." In lieu of a flat-footed discussion of the humdrum realities of years of disciplined creation, Haley focuses on a sort of ethereal not quite real conception of the grand writer. Baldwin becomes a voice powerful enough to answer the needs of the brethren, both the living and yet to be born. This is then answered late in the letter by a sort of obsessive focus on the quotidian. Haley warns Baldwin that "Gonna want to know what you ate, when you ate, where; what, when, where you wrote, and how. What you wore. <u>How</u> broke were you. Our frustrations, bitternesses, happinesses everything. Before I get done asking questions, you are going to get damn good and sick of me." That is to say, for Haley the biographic practice that he imagines is one in which the saintliness of his subject might be accessed through reference to the quality of his subject's food, clothes, finances, schedule, and everyday emotions. He wanted to do with Baldwin what he had achieved already in the *Autobiography of Malcolm X*. He wanted to announce a people's genius and grace through recourse to the lived realities of a single—and singular—individual. He wanted to establish Baldwin as an unassailable African American icon, and Haley was proudly confident that he could get the job done.

---

[15] Letter from Alex Haley to James Baldwin. January 23, 1967. James Baldwin Papers, Schomburg Center for Research in Black Culture, box 3, folder 19.

What captures and dominates my imagination now, however, is the extremely telling fact that Haley punctuates his many letters to Baldwin with not only compliments and promises, but also sometimes detailed descriptions of the archival work he was doing in preparation for the writing of *Roots*. On August 20th, 1967 Haley wrote Baldwin to congratulate him on completing the manuscript for *Tell Me How Long the Train's Been Gone* and to detail the remarkable discoveries he had made during his own research:

> Two weeks ago. I went through over 1100 itineraries of slave ships, and I found her, unquestionably—the ship that brought over my forebear Kunta Kinte. She was the <u>Lord Ligonier</u>. Built in New England in 1765, in 1766 she went to London, thence to Africa, thence to Annapolis, landing with 98 slaves alive of her 140 taken on board at James Fort, Gambia, Africa. I have by now found, or am closing in on every available minute detail about her. Have been to about every research source institution that's relevant, in Washington, Annapolis, New England, etc., and next month am going to London. The book will open on that day, July 15, 1766, she sailed from London, bound to Africa. The beginning of a sweeping black saga, Jimmy. I have got a big one baby.[16]

What is staggering, heartbreaking really, is how radically successful—and how disastrously tragic—Haley's "sweeping black saga" turned out to be. Of course, Haley did win grand critical and financial success with the publication of *Roots*. The initial reception of the 1976 novel, timed to be released during the country's bicentennial, could not have been more impressive. Telling the story of Kunta Kinte, a young man stolen from eighteenth-century Gambia and shipped to the United States where he founded a family whose multi-generational saga the novel recounts, the shock—and the promise—of Roots rested on the ways in which it helped to reframe the uncomfortable and rarely discussed history of enslavement into the dominant narratives of American culture, identity, and vibrancy. Like European immigrants African Americans could now point to a specific homeland from which they were taken as fully formed, complicated, and at times noble people with an even nobler past. The novel spent forty-six weeks on the *New York Times* best-seller list, including twenty-two in the number one position. In 1977 it was adopted into a first of its kind Emmy and Peabody Award winning mini-series, followed by a second one, Roots: The Next Generations in 1979. For his efforts Haley received both a Pulitzer Prize and a National Book Award. In both cases the book earned special citations that pointed to its awkward status, the reality that it was neither fish nor fowl, but instead half fiction, half fact, or "faction" as Haley sometimes called it.

Still, even with this bright and remarkable reception still unfolding, the serious problems with the novel were becoming increasingly apparent. Alex Haley was sued for plagiarism in the spring of 1977 by Harold Courlander, the author of a 1967

---

[16] Letter from Alex Haley to James Baldwin, August 20, 1967. James Baldwin Papers, Schomburg Center for Research in Black Culture, box 3, folder 19.

novel, *The African*, and Margaret Walker, author of the 1966 work, *Jubilee*. While the charges brought by Walker were eventually dropped, Haley was forced to pay $650,000 to Courlander, from whose earlier work he had taken large portions of the material included in *Roots*. More damaging still, Haley's claims to have traced his family lineage back to the village of Juffure in The Gambia were seriously and indeed devastatingly challenged. The head of the Gambian National Archives made it clear that the information Haley claimed to have taken from a griot, Kebba Kanga Fofana, could not be reliable both because Fofana's status as a true griot was in question and because during his stay in Juffure Haley had spent so much time telling the story of Kunta Kinte's early life and capture that he had effectively created the familial/ancestral storyline that he later heard repeated by Fofana. More important for our treatment of Haley's relationship to Baldwin, however, is the fact that Haley's keen interest in writing his hero's biography, in capturing the voice and legacy that he believed Baldwin represented, was also caught up with a need to establish a noble and triumphalist narrative of African American life and identity that though attractive was—and is—largely inaccurate.

I hope that it is clear that I do not believe that the problems so patently evident in Haley's attempt to produce a noble, or perhaps better put, usable history of the pre-colonial African American past are simply failings of a single artist. Instead, they are indicative of the especially complicated relationship of African American intellectuals to the questions surrounding history and the archives, particularly the print archives, that presumably open on to that history. I am fully open to the possibilities inherent in the practice of what Saidiya Hartman has called "critical fabulation" as long as we remain strictly attuned to the reality that part of the reason that this idea has become so appealing to us is that it gives critical/theoretical license to a fictional process that already has a very long and distinguished history. We are always making it up. We are always creating narratives of the past that serve the needs of the present. And as with Haley's production of Kunta Kinte, we are always attempting to retrieve figures from the historical record, figures whom we might celebrate in the same sense in which Christians celebrate the Eucharist by taking the host, the representation of the body and blood of Christ, into the mouth, and consuming it, thereby turning our myths and desires into useable things that might aid us in our everyday struggles for abundant life and a bit of hope for an uncertain future. I would rush to say, moreover, that I am in no way hostile to this reality. On the contrary, I recognize that these modes have been widely useful in the development of our historical and cultural studies, not to mention a vibrant sense of community and shared purpose.

What I *am* opposed to is the idea of our further obfuscating these processes. Earlier in this essay I noted that I want to encourage what I have called a mechanical understanding of historical practice. I want to focus less on naming the truth of African American life and culture and more on making obvious and plain the many complex practices that we have developed in order to move us at least one step closer to capturing that truth and establishing the beloved community. I would add to this that my actual experience of working with the massive amount of materials available within the several archival caches associated with the life and work of James Baldwin has made me increasingly suspicious about a certain reflexive mournfulness within African American and African Diasporic historical, literary, and cultural studies. The logic that our history has been robbed from us, that we are a people unmoored in time, tends to discourage actual archival research and to belittle the often heroic efforts of generations of librarians and archivists who have attempted to address just these concerns.

When the James Baldwin Papers were opened in the spring of 2017 at the Schomburg Center for Research in Black Culture, I was as bothered as anyone by the announcement that five sets of letters to Baldwin, including letters from his brother, David, would be kept closed for another twenty years. The outcry about this very serious error on the part of both the New York Public Library and the Baldwin estate was both defiant and loud, with many persons suggesting that the estate wished to keep definitive information about Baldwin's sexuality from the public. At the same time, dozens of people suggested to me that I needed to hurry with my research and writing as the archives would be flooded with individuals attempting to produce their own biographies. None of this has proven to be true. There is remarkable information in the papers about both Baldwin's sexual practice and his romantic entanglements. Moreover, while there are many persons who have used the materials at the Schomburg Archive alongside me, I have yet to encounter a single researcher who is looking systematically at them all. Or to state the matter in as blunt and flat-footed a fashion as possible, even and especially the most sophisticated of our archival and historical practices tend to be inextricably caught up with what, bending the words of Nietzsche, I will name "the will to celebration." Our most precious efforts, our struggles to recapture a forgotten past, are altogether overdetermined by highly sedimented discursive processes that push us decidedly in the direction of producing the two-dimensionality and fungibility that are the very bases of both celebrity status and the processes of celebration that I have been at pains to describe.

I will leave you then by asking what would happen, what worlds would collide, if we simply acknowledged this fact, if we noted what I take to be the simple truth that our archival practices are things that we do for ourselves, that our never-ending shifting of mountains of paper through our hands can never rectify the wrongs of our ancestors, can never allow the dead to speak for themselves. Perhaps in doing so, in treating celebrity as a social and discursive practice, we can begin the process of weaning our many peoples from the tendency to ignore their own good judgment in the favor of clumsy rhetorics of fixity, authenticity, and a thin conception of a boundaryless history. James Baldwin reminds us that "idols are created in order to be destroyed." What he failed to mention, however, was that the worshiper, the fanatic, the celebrant, and the true believer are always the first to go.

Part Three

Print Culture Studies in Practice

12

Reimagining Literary History, and Why It Matters Now

Kelley Kreitz

On a hazy morning in August at the start of an unprecedented fall 2020 semester at Pace University in New York City, I stood at the center of the Brooklyn Bridge with a group of students from my introductory Latinx literature course for undergraduates.[1] We looked up at the iconic network of cables and contemplated the lyric descriptions of "las cuerdas de acero que en forma de abanico bajan en cuatro paredes" (iron cords that descend like a fan in four walls) penned almost a century and a half earlier by Cuban writer and revolutionary José Martí in his reflection on the bridge's opening in 1883.[2] We also remarked on how striking it was that the bridge, typically crowded with tourists, was so empty. We speculated that Martí would have been just as surprised if he had magically joined us on that steamy, late-summer day, and we considered the ways in which his expectations would likely have exhibited similarities to those that my students and I had formed through our prior experiences on this bridge that neighbors what is now Pace University's Lower Manhattan campus.

Although Martí never knew the stop-and-start rhythm of walking across the bridge in a twenty-first-century crowd dominated by tourists posing with their selfie sticks, his own nineteenth-century experience of a "muchedumbre premiosa, que lleva el paso de quien va a ver maravilla" (dense throng, moving at the pace of those who go to see wonders) sounded familiar enough.[3] In addition, Martí probably would have expected,

---

[1] I use the term "Latinx" following its increasing prevalence within Latinx Studies, while recognizing the ongoing debate about when and how widely to apply "Latinx" vs. "Latina" and "Latino," as well as the critique of its Anglocentrism. In my writing and teaching, the term "Latinx"—including its instability and limits—connects current debates to the long history of notions of community and identity articulated by writers of Latin American descent in the United States. A helpful summary of the history of these terms appears in Yara Simón, "Hispanic vs. Latino vs. Latinx: A Brief History of How These Terms Originated," *Remezcla* (September 14, 2018), https://remezcla.com/features/culture/latino-vs-hispanic-vs-latinx-how-these-words-originated/. Accessed October 9, 2020.

[2] José Martí, "El Puente de Brooklyn," in *José Martí en los Estados Unidos: Perodismo de 1881–1892*, eds. Roberto Fernández Retamar and Pedro Pablo Rodríguez (Madrid: Colección Archivos, 2003), 271. Translations for this text are from "The Brooklyn Bridge," in *José Martí: Selected Writings*, ed. and trans. Esther Allen (New York: Penguin, 2002), 143.

[3] Ibid., 269, 140.

as we did, the snippets of conversation spoken in many different languages—reflecting the international character of New York City then and now—that felt conspicuously absent that morning as we walked across the bridge. We thought Martí would have missed, too, the "algazara, asombros, chistes, genialidades, y canciones" (cheering, astonishment, jokes, witticisms, and song) that surround him on the bridge in his account—an atmosphere that starkly contrasted with the stillness and quiet that we experienced in the same place on that morning.[4]

With evident admiration for its ability to showcase the human experience in myriad forms, Martí transforms the bridge into a symbol of the promise of uniting people for the cause to which he devoted his life—promoting political independence and democracy, especially in his native Cuba, which was then under Spanish colonial rule. The bridge and the people it brings together represent "la Libertad [que] es la madre del mundo nuevo,–que alborea" (Liberty, who is the mother of the new world that is only now dawning).[5] Although many of his essays written while he made New York his home-in-exile call on a hemispheric, Spanish-speaking community to participate in this dawning new world, his articulation of the future of democracy represented by the Brooklyn Bridge extends beyond the hemisphere. He represents New York City as a microcosm of a global community, including "hebreos... irlandeses... rusos... japoneses... " (Hebrews... Irishmen... Russians... Japanese), among other members of the city's immigrant and working classes.[6] This "guión de hierro" (steel hyphen) that connects Brooklyn (then a separate city) to Manhattan, Martí suggests, represents the possibility of bridging racial, ethnic, and national differences to fight for human dignity and survival.[7] It is a call for unity in a city that left its poorest residents—many of whom we might consider the nineteenth-century's essential workers—struggling to get by in the best of times and vastly more vulnerable to the calamities of the period, such as the Great Blizzard of 1888 and the economic depression that followed the Panic of 1893.

For my students and for me, as we conversed through our masks at the outset of a semester transformed by the many new adjustments to learning and living that the pandemic made necessary, the bridge became another kind of connector—between the past and the present. We thought about our desire to make sense of our personal and collective struggles in a city still grappling with a pandemic that magnified and exacerbated longstanding inequalities for Latinx, African American, and Indigenous

---

[4] Ibid., 271, 143.
[5] Ibid., 269, 141.
[6] Ibid. Perhaps most famously, Martí articulates a hemispheric identity in his 1891 essay, "Nuestra América" (Our America).
[7] Ibid., 270, 142. Martí's views on racial equality have been considered both forward-thinking for a white male of his time and also limited and problematic. On the role of Afro-Latinos, including Rafael Serra, Sotero Figueroa, and Arturo Schomburg, in organizing for Cuban independence at the end of the nineteenth century and in influencing Martí's views on racial justice and democracy, see Jesse Hoffnung Garskof, *Racial Migrations* (Princeton: Princeton University Press, 2019). I will discuss Serra and Figueroa later in this chapter.

communities in New York City and beyond.[8] And we began to see new relevance in the efforts in which Martí and his collaborators engaged as part of a long-since forgotten Spanish-language publishing community that resided in lower Manhattan in the nineteenth century whose writers, editors, and printers organized for independence in Cuba and Puerto Rico, criticized U.S. imperial designs on Latin America, and dreamed of achieving true democracy throughout the Americas.[9]

That walk across the Brooklyn Bridge—the first of a series of walks on New York City history that I created to offer my students what I considered to be the safest possible face-to-face meeting option, outside with masks—provides an introductory glimpse of the view of literary history and the future of its research and teaching that I offer in this chapter. As a contribution to this collection's commitment to rewriting literary history to emphasize networks, dialogues, and tensions over canons and major works, this chapter contemplates those possibilities based on my work as a scholar and teacher of U.S. literary studies, Latinx Studies, and the digital humanities. I am also a white woman committed to listening to and learning from Black, Indigenous, and People of Color (BIPOC) scholars and students and to being an ally in uplifting BIPOC histories and putting them in conversation with ongoing struggles for racial justice in the present. From those perspectives, I suggest here that a reimagined literary history has an essential role to play in putting the past in conversation with the present like never before. Fulfilling that role relies on continuing a shift already underway toward the very methods that this book collection contemplates: engaging archives and recognizing archival absences, looking for networks of circulation and influence that de-emphasize canonical authors and often transverse national boundaries, and, most importantly, empowering students to participate in producing knowledge about the lost or suppressed histories of the past and to draw their own connections to the present.

In what follows, I reflect on my experience of introducing students to nineteenth-century U.S.-based Spanish-language print culture to recover Latinx voices of our literary past and to contemplate the insights they provide during a semester when we also wrestled with the ongoing challenges and emerging lessons of the pandemic. I also consider other recent courses and digital humanities projects centered in Latinx Studies. Together, the examples considered herein point toward a possible future of literary studies—and humanistic inquiry more broadly—that is relevant to the various fields brought together by this book's emphasis on print culture studies as a "hybrid methodology and field of analysis [that] draws upon periodical studies, histories of the book, literary studies, American studies, art history, science and technology studies,

---

[8] On inequality and Covid-19, see Samuel Kelton Roberts et al., "Bearing Witness: The Covid-19 and Inequality History Documentation Project," Columbia University, Center for Science and Society Cluster on Race, Inequality and Health, https://bearingwitness.github.io/. Accessed October 10, 2020.

[9] On the development of this publishing community throughout the nineteenth century in New York City from the perspective of the Cuban independence movement and its various, competing ideas of the future of democracy, see Lisandro Pérez, *Sugar, Cigars, and Revolution: The Making of Cuban New York* (New York: New York University Press, 2018).

design studies, history, economics, sociology, education, material culture, visual culture, and more."[10] In conversation with recent discussions of pedagogical approaches from within the digital humanities centered on Latinx intersectional feminist praxis, Black digital humanities, and postcolonial digital humanities, I will demonstrate that this collection's conversation about research methods is also necessarily linked to transforming our pedagogy in these fields and, ultimately, throughout higher education.[11] Especially as the United States grapples with longstanding and new issues of racial injustice, such a transformation is needed to inform public debate with greater understanding of the links between the inequities of our present and the lost voices of our past.

Locating Literary History in Print and Digital Cultures of the Americas

Two keywords throughout this collection—"print culture" and the "Americas"—provide a starting point for locating, theoretically and historically, the reimagined approach to literary history that this chapter contemplates. In Latinx Studies, especially in recent efforts to recover the nineteenth-century origins of notions of Latina/o/x identity that entered into widespread circulation much later, the Americas and print culture have served as organizing frameworks.[12] They have provided the conceptual foundation for many investigations of U.S.-based Spanish-language archival materials, as scholars have recovered lost and suppressed histories of Latinx written expression, and, increasingly, employed digital humanities methods to reimagine the cultural record—including who should participate in creating it. A brief consideration of how both the Americas and print culture have operated as conceptual frameworks will elucidate the future of literary studies that this chapter proposes in relation to its foundations and to recent innovations.

---

[10] See Jesse W. Schwartz and Daniel Worden, "Introduction: Archives, Materiality, and Modernism American Culture," page 6 of this volume.

[11] See, for example, Gabriela Baeza Ventura, Lorena Gauthereau, and Carolina Villarroel, "U.S. Latinx Digital Humanities: Rehumanizing the Past through Archival Digital Pedagogy," forthcoming in *Beyond Digital Fronteras: Rehumanizing Latinx Education*, eds. Dr. Isabel Martinez, Dr. Irma Montelongo, Dr. Nicholas D. Natividad, and Dr. Angel D. Nieves; Kim Gallon, "Making a Case for the Black Digital Humanities," in *Debates in the Digital Humanities*, eds. Matthew K. Gold and Lauren F. Klein (Manifold 2016). https://dhdebates.gc.cuny.edu/read/untitled/section/fa10e2e1-0c3d-4519-a958-d823aac989eb#ch04. Accessed January 11, 2021; and Roopika Risam, *New Digital Worlds: Postcolonial Digital Humanities* (Chicago: Northwestern University, 2019. Kindle edition.) I will discuss each of these texts later in this chapter.

[12] On the history of the terms "Hispanic" and "Latina/o," see Suzanne Oboler, *Ethnic Labels, Latino Lives: Identity and the Politics of (Re)presentation in the United States* (Minneapolis: University of Minnesota Press, 1995) and G. Cristina Mora, *Making Hispanics: How Activist, Bureaucrats and Media Constructed a New American* (Chicago: The University of Chicago Press, 2014). On the more recent term "Latinx," see footnote 1.

The idea of studying literature across a hemispheric geographic expanse is, of course, not new. Within U.S. literary studies, an influential wave of scholars in the 1990s and early 2000s, including Ramón Saldívar, José David Saldívar, Amy Kaplan, and Donald Pease, articulated the need for "an interpretive framework that links the North and South Americas instead of the old and new Englands."[13] As what became known as hemispheric studies took shape within the U.S. literary field, scholars including Kirsten Silva Gruesz, Rodrigo Lazo, and Anna Brickhouse laid the groundwork for "a strong revision of literary-historical narratives of the U.S. national tradition that render the Latino presence ghostly and peripheral," which included a reclaiming of "Spanish as a literary language of the United States."[14] They also demonstrated that, while finding such lost and suppressed voices and stories might be a hemispheric undertaking, it requires archival investigations that reconstruct local or regional contexts. As Claire Fox noted in a 2006 essay, "the geographical sweep of that term [hemisphere] is so vast" that it might best be considered "a field for locating particular trajectories rather than an object of analysis itself."[15] Gruesz's *Ambassadors of Culture: The Transamerican Origins of Latino Writing* provides an illustration. She draws on a hemispheric archive of understudied texts to reveal the local dynamics of Spanish-language publishing in New Orleans, New York, and the borderlands of the Southwest and California, as well as a broader pattern of exchange between Anglophone and Hispanophone poets of the period.

Emphasis on local and regional specificity enabled by a hemispheric perspective has also propelled a more recent turn within Latinx Studies toward nineteenth-century origins of Latinx identity and cultural expression. Over the past decade, Gruesz, Lazo, and Brickhouse, along with Raúl Coronado, Laura Lomas, Marissa López, and others working within Latinx Studies, have looked to the contested space of the hemisphere as an organizing framework for their investigations of the long history of people of Latin American descent in the United States.[16] Most recently, as a result of increasing availability of archives, as well as a sense of urgent political need, scholars within Latinx Studies have demonstrated a new emphasis on border studies, especially in projects such as Sylvia Fernández's and Maira Álvarez's *Borderlands Archives Cartography*,

---

[13] Ramón Saldívar, *The Borderlands of Culture: Américo Paredes and the Transnational Imaginary* (Durham: Duke University Press, 2006), 15. Also influential from this wave of hemispheric studies are: José David Saldívar, *The Dialectics of Our America* (Durham: Duke University Press, 1991), and Amy Kaplan and Donald Pease, eds., *Cultures of United States Imperialism* (Durham: Duke University Press, 1993).

[14] Kirsten Silva Gruesz, *Ambassadors of Culture: The Transamerican Origins of Latino Writing* (Princeton: Princeton University Press, 2002), xii, xvii. Other influential studies include Rodrigo Lazo, *Writing to Cuba: Filibustering and Cuban Exiles in the United States* (Chapel Hill: University of North Carolina Press, 2005) and Anna Brickhouse, *Transamerican Literary Relations and the Nineteenth-Century Public Sphere* (New York: Cambridge University Press, 2004).

[15] Claire Fox, "Commentary: The Transnational Turn and the Hemispheric Return," *American Literary History* 18, no. 2 (2006), 643.

[16] See, for example, Marissa López, *Chicano Nations: The Hemispheric Origins of Mexican American Literature* (New York: New York University Press, 2011) and Raúl Coronado, *A World Not to Come: A History of Latino Writing and Print Culture* (Cambridge: Harvard University Press, 2013).

which have showcased the possibilities of digital humanities methods, such as digital mapping, to recover lost histories.

It is difficult to underestimate the central role played by increased access to archives of U.S.-based Spanish-language materials—especially periodicals—in enabling the turn toward hemispheric studies within the U.S. literary field, the investigations that followed of the nineteenth-century origins of Latinx writing within Latinx Studies, and the recent work in border studies that I have just described. Their development followed the field-building work that Nicolás Kanellos began with the founding of the *Revista Chicano-Riqueña*, followed by Arte Público Press in the 1970s, and continued with the indexing and archiving work undertaken through the establishment of the Recovering the U.S. Hispanic Literary Heritage initiative in 1991. In the early 2000s, through partnerships with EBSCO Inc. and NewsBank, the Recovery Project made hundreds of newspapers relevant to Latinx history from throughout the United States available online for those whose institutions can afford the subscription fee. Additional digitization efforts, such as those undertaken by the U.S. Library of Congress, which has also in recent years digitized and made accessible for free a substantial number of Spanish-language periodicals, have also vastly expanded access to archival materials.

This growing archive is invaluable both for what it contains and also for what it suggests is missing. In his introduction to *The Latino Nineteenth Century* edited with Jesse Alemán, Lazo points out that "the texts of the Latino nineteenth century come to us in pieces" through "partial, sometimes fragmented, and regularly dispersed textual remains."[17] Those archival remains serve a dual function of enabling scholars to "register the views and aspirations of people who share (or at least engage with) concerns related to bilingualism, social formation, and political organization," while also foregrounding the oversights and omissions of "U.S. literary history driven by the canonical desires of U.S. American literature and the fetishization of major writers."[18] Such omissions include the failure to prioritize the preservation of U.S.-based Spanish-language publications, as well as the notable absences due to prejudices within and outside Spanish-language communities of print, that marginalized and suppressed BIPOC and female voices.[19]

In recognition of these absences and omissions, as scholars have brought the Latino nineteenth century more fully into view, they have not merely replaced one focal point for another; instead, they have challenged the very idea of centrality. As Lazo explains, "the documents of a Latino past point as much to multiplicity and flight as they do to something that we might call heritage. In other words, they point away from a central holding and toward movement."[20] Raúl Coronado makes a similar point in

---

[17] Rodrigo Lazo, "Introduction," in *The Latino Nineteenth Century*, eds. Jesse Alemán and Rodrigo Lazo (New York: New York University Press, 2016), 1, 3.

[18] Ibid., 7.

[19] Two recent studies on Afro-Cuban and Afro-Puerto Rican leaders in New York's Spanish-language publishing community, both of which also reflect on locating Latina voices, are Hoffnung Garskof, *Racial Migrations* and Nancy Mirabel, *Suspect Freedoms: The Racial and Sexual Politics of Cubanidad in New York, 1823–1957* (New York: NYU Press, 2017).

[20] Lazo, "Introduction," 12.

his contribution to the same collection, in which he argues that "the discursive world of nineteenth-century Latina/os, [was] a world filled with texts and individuals that held competing, often contradictory, beliefs," which has been difficult to recognize through "the narrative of nation formation."[21] The challenge for literary historians, Coronado continues, is to "think against the grain, against the nation as teleology" and to work instead to "think creatively through and with the archive."[22] Because the literary field since the nineteenth century played a key role in constructing nation-building narratives, this work includes "deconstruct[ing] the category of the literary."[23] Coronado's use of the term "print culture" in the subtitle of his 2013 *A World Not to Come: A History of Latino Writing and Print Culture* provides an indication of how scholars might engage in the at once energizing and humbling work of opening up the field of possible texts beyond the boundaries of the nation and of literature. "Print culture" provides a conceptual framework for thinking outside the nation and locating investigations of Latinx lives within the hemisphere.

Just as the concept of the hemisphere has enabled scholars to locate understudied local or regional histories, print culture plays a similar role as a conceptual space that facilitates investigation of particular paths and encounters. Coronado's reflections on his method in *A World Not to Come*, for example, note the need to "strike a balance between narrating a story with its specific actors, texts, and networks of circulation, and narrating a larger history of the discursive formations to which these texts and carriers contributed."[24] Here, "actors, texts, and networks" of circulation constitute the new objects of inquiry that can provide fresh perspectives on—and also challenge—more familiar discursive formations.[25] Alemán points to a similar approach in his "Preface" to *The Latino Nineteenth Century*, when he asserts that the people of the Latino/a nineteenth century "inhabited ... a world of Spanish-language print culture, circuits, readerships, and routes that, while not at all surprising for nineteenth-century America, prove more difficult to decipher and narrate in the largely Anglophone print history of the United States."[26] At the outset of the list provided in this observation, "print culture" helps to bring into focus the more geographic- and media-specific formations that follow: "circuits, readerships, and routes."[27] These are the objects of inquiry that can help cast aside the towering authors, major works, and movements made familiar by U.S. literary history, thus making room for unfamiliar or forgotten voices and stories.

While many of the foundational efforts in Latinx Studies to uncover such print cultural formations, as I have discussed here, have resulted from traditional

---

[21] Raúl Coronado, "Historicizing Nineteenth-Century Latina/o Textuality," *The Latino Nineteenth Century*, eds. Jesse Alemán and Rodrigo Lazo (New York: New York University Press, 2016), 52.
[22] Ibid., 51.
[23] Ibid., 52.
[24] Coronado, *A World Not to Come*, 21–2.
[25] Ibid.
[26] Jesse Alemán, "Preface," *The Latino Nineteenth Century*, eds. Jesse Alemán and Rodrigo Lazo (New York: New York University Press, 2016), viii.
[27] Ibid.

humanities research methods, an increasing number of scholars in the field are also employing digital humanities methods to recover lost and suppressed voices. Such methods include visualizing communities represented by archival materials, making visible absences in the archival record, and engaging academics, students, and the public in contemplating history and its making. For example, Álvarez and Fernández's *Borderlands Archives Cartography* shows the former locations of 285 newspapers from throughout the nineteenth century that are now housed in archives on both sides of the U.S.–Mexico border. In this way, the map visualizes "the borderland as a space where different cultures co-exist under strong political, economic, and social hegemonies; as well as, a space where regions influence each other, but maintain their own identities."[28] Echoing the goals of earlier projects like Coronado's, the *Borderlands Archives Cartography* map locates lost publications and networks of nineteenth-century print culture to recover the diversity and complexity of borderlands history. As Álvarez and Fernández explain, "The richness of transnational periodical archives located along the U.S.-Mexico border region… documents borderlands communities since the nineteenth century and contradicts the idea of the region as static, a recent division, and threat."[29] Extending the ambitions of the studies discussed here, the map more explicitly puts history in conversation with "the constant and current aggressive political rhetoric that displays the geographical and ideological border between Mexico and the United States as a threat" in the present, while also showcasing archival materials on both sides of the border that invite further investigation and reflection from the map's users.[30] *Borderlands Archives Cartography* provides a glimpse of the potentiality that scholars in the digital humanities have begun articulating in a variety of ways—including "decolonizing DH," "engaging absence," and "postcolonial digital humanities"—as they have sought to correct the ways in which our digital era has reproduced the hierarchies and injustices of the past.[31]

Such revisions of our history call for rethinking the process of making history as well. In her 2019 *New Digital Worlds: Postcolonial Digital Humanities*, Roopika Risam argues, "To intervene in the digital cultural record—to tell new stories, shed light on counter-histories, and create spaces for communities to produce and share their own knowledge should they wish—is the great promise of digital humanities."[32] As in Álvarez and Fernández's description of Borderlands Archives Cartography, Risam's articulation of the promise of the digital humanities echoes the commitment to rejecting

---

[28] Maira Álvarez and Sylvia Fernández, "Borderlands Archives Cartography: About," https://www.bacartography.org/autoras. Accessed October 9, 2020.
[29] Ibid.
[30] Ibid.
[31] See Roopika Risam, "Decolonizing The Digital Humanities In Theory And Practice," in The Routledge Companion to Media Studies and Digital Humanities, ed. Jentery Sayers (New York: Routledge: 2018), 78–86 and Risam's New Digital Worlds. On "engaging absence," see Thomas Padilla's blog post "Engaging Absence," *Thomas Padilla*. https://www.thomaspadilla.org/2018/02/26/engaging-absence/. Accessed October 9, 2020.
[32] Risam, New Digital Worlds, n.p.

and finding alternatives to colonial knowledge regimes exhibited throughout the Latinx Studies scholarship considered here. Her emphasis on engaging communities to "produce and share their own knowledge should they wish" points toward the public engagement, as well as to the respect and the humility that such work requires.[33]

Risam's words provide a reminder that, once we begin to rethink literary history through lost or suppressed voices of hemispheric print culture—even just the small fraction that we can still recover through archives that themselves have been shaped by colonial knowledge regimes—it is no longer possible to maintain the same one-way flow of information from expert to audience or teacher to student. It follows that classrooms become key sites for increasing participation in the production of knowledge.

An Archival Turn in the Classroom

As traditional and digital humanities scholars redraw the boundaries of literary history and recover lost actors within those redrawn territories, an archival turn in pedagogy has begun. A selection of examples considered in what follows provides a glimpse of how scholars in Latinx Studies and the related fields brought together by this book might help shape the future of our disciplines by empowering students to find their own pathways through the vast collection that literary history becomes through access to archival texts and through the use of traditional and digital humanities research methods. Engaging students in print cultural history in this way may also help address a vital need to demonstrate the importance of humanistic inquiry within and outside of academia.

In my own experience in my fall 2020 Latinx literature course with which I began this chapter, I followed our initial session on the Brooklyn Bridge with two assignments that introduced students to archival research on Lower Manhattan's Spanish-language publishing history. First, students worked in teams to plot former sites of New York's nineteenth-century Spanish-language publications in Google My Maps. The sites included *La Revista Ilustrada de Nueva York* (New York Illustrated Magazine), where Martí's "Nuestra América" (Our America) debuted in 1891 and where Afro-Puerto Rican writer, editor, and printer Sotero Figueroa published literary criticism and poetry that pushed for attention to racial justice in a publication that centered on the views of white liberal elites.[34] Another site was *La Doctrina de Martí* (Martí's Doctrine), which Figueroa helped to found with Afro-Cuban writer, editor, and educator Rafael Serra, as a site for circulating ideas about racial justice in a future Cuban democracy. For each assigned site on the map, students investigated a series of research questions, in order to discover what has been published—and how much has not—on the sites

[33] Ibid.
[34] I have discussed the role of Figueroa's writing in *La Revista Ilustrada de Nueva York* in my "Sotero Figueroa's Editorial Roles in *La Revista Ilustrada de Nueva York, Patria*, and *La Doctrina de Martí*," *American Periodicals* 30, no. 2 (2020), 105–9.

that we visited on our tour. The idea was to invite students to situate Martí within the community in which he participated; to bring into view for students a U.S.-based community of print that is not accessible through more common teaching materials, such as edited collections; and to give students an experience of the gaps in the archive of nineteenth-century US-based Spanish-language periodicals.

Following that project, students worked individually to select and research a newspaper in English or Spanish through the *Readex Hispanic American Newspapers, 1808–1980* database. The objectives were to help students develop basic archival research skills, to gain familiarity with an understudied publication (almost all of the newspapers in the database fall into this category) relevant to Latinx history, and to invite reflection on history and its making. Students produced a short essay about their selected publication, and then participated in an online discussion with their classmates to compare notes on their findings. Many students reflected that, although the assignment had initially seemed intimidating, the project ultimately felt meaningful because it provided access to texts that enabled them to recover suppressed and subsequently understudied voices in U.S. history. One student observed a sense of loss that resulted from "not having access to many of the archives of Spanish-language press that was created in this area," particularly in relation to insights that "the Afro Puerto Rican and Afro Cuban exiles fighting for independence" might have brought to current struggles for racial justice "if we had direct access to all of their work."[35] Another student commented, "Right now more than ever, being able to assess the world we are in and study what we once were, who we are now, and who we plan to be in relevance to history is crucial."[36]

In this fall 2020 course, as well as in previous ones where I introduced undergraduate students to archival research, the results have been both unpredictable and inspiring. When I taught the same course in fall 2018, the students were so surprised by the lack of representation of many of the leading figures that they researched from New York's nineteenth-century Spanish-language press that they voted unanimously to change their final project for the course to creating new Wikipedia pages for those whose absence they thought represented the biggest gaps. That classroom initiative produced, among others, new English-language Wikipedia pages for Figueroa and Serra, which have since benefited from editing by many more contributors on Wikipedia. This kind of engagement with archives and their absences in my classes is a modest start, but I believe it provides a glimpse of the role that students might play in participating in the production of knowledge about print cultural history and in connecting the lost and suppressed voices of our past to the struggles for racial justice in the present.

Further articulation of this archival turn in the classroom comes from a February 2020 workshop sponsored by the Center for U.S. Latino Digital Humanities at the Recovering the U.S. Hispanic Literary Heritage project's biannual conference (the last time before the arrival of the pandemic that I attended a conference in person).

---

[35] LIT 211U Latinx Voices Discussion Board Post, 9/14/20.
[36] LIT 211U Latinx Voices Discussion Board Post, 9/15/20.

Gabriela Baeza Ventura, Lorena Gauthereau, and Carolina Villarroel emphasized engaging students in archival research—through combined digital and traditional methods—especially to help students "understand assumptions and prejudices embedded in various digital tools, platforms and devices; and to envision how Digital Humanities can transform our individual work practice" while also gaining insight into "the makeup, organization and inclusion/exclusion in archival practice."[37] These were the learning objectives on a syllabus shared at the workshop for a course called "From the Archive to the Digital: Introduction to Digital Humanities" designed by Baeza Ventura. As one of its central assignments, the course engages students in researching and creating their own critical editions of the Spanish-language periodical *Feminismo Internacional* (International Feminism) published in the 1920s in New York City and now part of the archival collection made available by the Recovery Project through the *Readex Hispanic American Newspapers, 1808–1980* database. The assignment models an approach to literary history that centers on giving students access to understudied materials that, in many cases, tell a different story from the history that they have encountered through writers, editors, and publications that are more prominently featured in edited collections and textbooks. This kind of collaboration with students again shows how classrooms can become sites of increasing participation in the production of knowledge by enabling investigation of the print cultures of the past. As Baeza Ventura, Gauthereau, and Villarroel explain of what they call "archival digital pedagogy," "using these archives in the classroom rehumanizes the Latinx community as students bear witness to first-hand accounts that challenge the hegemonic narrative of national history. We understand rehumanizing the past as an action that amplifies voices in Latinx collections, allowing them to take space and to speak for themselves, by providing alternate historical accounts to those that depict them negatively."[38] This is a transformative view of what the humanities classroom can accomplish, in which classrooms become laboratories for locating lost voices and new directions in Latinx Studies and beyond, with students as new partners in this work.

In a sense, such a role for the classroom builds on a historical one that, as Rachel Sagner Buurma and Laura Heffernan have shown in *The Teaching Archive: A New History for Literary Study*, is itself understudied. Based on an analysis of twentieth-century syllabi from a wide range of colleges and universities, they argue: "Literary value *seems* to emanate from texts, but is actually made by people. And classrooms are the core site where this collective making can be practiced and witnessed."[39] Sagner Buurma and Heffernan are primarily concerned with rethinking the story of the development of the

---

[37] Gabriela Baeza Ventura, "From the Archive to the Digital: Introduction to Digital Humanities" (syllabus, University of Houston, Houston, TX, 2019).

[38] Gabriela Baeza Ventura, Lorena Gauthereau, and Carolina Villarroel, "U.S. Latinx Digital Humanities: Rehumanizing the Past through Archival Digital Pedagogy," forthcoming in *Beyond Digital Fronteras: Rehumanizing Latinx Education*, eds. Dr. Isabel Martinez, Dr. Irma Montelongo, Dr. Nicholas D. Natividad, and Dr. Angel D. Nieves.

[39] Rachel Sagner Buurma and Laura Heffernan, "Introduction: A New Syllabus," in *The Teaching Archive: A New History for Literary Study*, eds. Rachel Sagner Buurma and Laura Heffernan (Chicago: University of Chicago Press, 2020, Kindle edition), n.p.

literary field in the twentieth century. They demonstrate, for instance, that New Critics produced through their teaching "an earlier incarnation of pedagogical formalism [that] differs from New Critical close reading in its transformation of the classroom into a 'laboratory' and students into teams of reader-experimenters."[40] If scholars have always, to some degree, made their classrooms into spaces where students participate in the production of humanistic knowledge, digital archives—particularly of those that provide access to the suppressed and alternate stories—vastly increase the possibilities for such participation. Those possibilities include a future where classrooms become bridges between universities and their communities.

The university where such transformative classroom experiences thrive can also foster projects that reach outside of the university through partnerships with public institutions, particularly public libraries, to explore methods of research and develop public projects that prioritize equity and access. Marissa López's *Picturing Mexican America*, founded on a partnership with digital humanities and library staff at UCLA, along with community partners at the Los Angeles Public Library, is a mobile application that enables users to access archival photos relevant to the city's Mexican American history as they navigate Los Angeles. Students play a key role in bringing academic knowledge to a public forum in this project. Undergraduate research assistants searched the library's digitized photograph collections (collecting their archival discoveries in a blog along the way) to gather the images. Graduate students and a team of designers also collaborated to develop the app scheduled for launch in 2021. The project shows how universities can play new roles as facilitators of research projects that involve students and ultimately the public in creating, as well as finding, new uses for historical findings and insights. The app invites users to look "back at the history of Mexican Los Angeles to help us understand our present and undo the systematic erasure of Los Angeles' Mexican past—in a fun way!"[41] *Picturing Mexican America* gives users the opportunity to contemplate history in relation to the present in their own neighborhoods and in the places where their daily routines take them in the city.

To a certain degree, the promise of an archival turn in the classroom—and ultimately also in the communities where its students live and learn—is one that scholars in the digital humanities have been discussing for quite a while. In their 2009 "Digital Humanities Manifesto 2.0," for example, Jeffrey Schnapp and Todd Presner reflect on the possibility of "the open, the infinite, the expansive, the university/museum/archive/library without walls, the democratization of culture."[42] In his widely discussed 2012 essay, Alan Liu argues that "the digital humanities have a special role to play in helping the humanities reach out."[43] The digital humanities, he suggests, have the

---

[40] Ibid.
[41] Marissa López, "Picturing Mexican America," UCLA, https://mklopez.humspace.ucla.edu/research/picturing-mexican-america/. Accessed October 9, 2020.
[42] Jeffrey Schnapp and Todd Presner, "Digital Humanities Manifesto 2.0," 2009, jeffreyschnapp.com/wp-content/uploads/2011/10/Manifesto_V2.pdf, 3. Accessed October 10, 2020.
[43] Alan Liu, "Where Is the Cultural Criticism in the Digital Humanities?" in *Debates in the Digital Humanities*, ed. Matthew K. Gold (Minneapolis: University of Minnesota Press, 2012), 490.

potential to "create, adapt, and disseminate new tools and methods for reestablishing communication between the humanities and the public."[44]

More recently, scholars have further articulated what such a publicly engaged digital humanities might achieve. According to Miriam Posner,

> Digital humanists have heard numerous recent calls for the field to interrogate race, gender, and other structures of power... these calls, while necessary and justified, do not go far enough. To truly engage in this kind of critical work, I contend, would be much more difficult and fascinating than anything we have previously imagined for the future of DH; in fact, it would require dismantling and rebuilding much of the organizing logic that underlies our work.[45]

In the same 2016 edition of *Debates in the Digital Humanities*, Kim Gallon makes a case for the crucial role of Black digital humanities: "Digital tools and platforms should be mobilized to interrogate and disclose how the humanities are developed out of systems of power. The black digital humanities reveals how methodological approaches for studying and thinking about the category of blackness may come to bear on and transform the digital processes and tools used to study humanity."[46] Drawing on her own work in African diaspora and postcolonial studies, Risam suggests: "The hope for change comes not from self-proclaimed acts of disruption, but from creating sustained communities of practice that foreground critiques of colonialism in scholarship."[47] In all of these scholars' accounts, the digital humanities provide a possible means of dismantling systemic racism and colonial power structures that were founded on white supremacy.

Of course, this potentiality of the digital humanities brings with it massive new challenges. As Risam notes,

> Digital humanities scholars must contend not only with the colonial hangovers from the cultural record, but also with the forces that are actively constructing the medium of the digital cultural record—the internet—as a hostile environment where universities, libraries, and the cultural heritage sector are under threat, right along with the knowledge being produced and made publicly available by them.[48]

As I revise this essay in the first week of 2021, the day after insurrectionists incited by President Trump violently attacked the Capitol, that hostile environment feels inescapable. And yet, I believe it is still productive—and more urgent than ever—to

---

[44] Ibid., 498.
[45] Miriam Posner, "What's Next: The Radical, Unrealized Potential of Digital Humanities," in *Debates in the Digital Humanities*, eds. Matthew K. Gold and Lauren F. Klein (Minneapolis: University of Minnesota Press, 2016), https://dhdebates.gc.cuny.edu/projects/debates-in-the-digital-humanities-2016. Accessed March 9, 2021.
[46] Gallon, "Making a Case for the Black Digital Humanities," n.p.
[47] Risam, *New Digital Worlds*, n.p.
[48] Ibid.

ask, among the many other questions that we are asking right now about how to ensure the future of democracy: How do we use the digital tools and humanistic methods available to us to realize the potential for a different kind of digital culture—one that pursues and extends those earlier promises articulated over a decade ago by digital humanities scholars who saw opportunities to create an engaged, informed, digital culture?

What would it look like to pursue together, across our related fields brought together in this book, goals centered on decolonizing the cultural record and advancing antiracist pedagogy? How might our disciplines work—through the methods described in this book and the programs and classes we offer—to transform our universities into true sites of revolutionary knowledge production? And what if we could model, through such work, how to combine a focus on technical skills with a commitment to recovering lost and suppressed voices and putting history in conversation with ongoing struggles for racial justice? What might that future look like if we could make our universities—starting with our classrooms—vehicles for bringing together our individual experiences, skills, and expertise to advance such topics as Indigenous and borderlands histories and worldviews; the intersections of digital mapping and community archives; and models of higher education that make racial justice and participation in the production of knowledge central goals? These are the questions that I believe scholars in the fields represented by this book need to pursue, through our research agendas and also within our own classrooms and institutions.

Futures of Humanistic Inquiry and Democracy

This chapter, initially planned as a typical research chapter and reimagined as the pandemic piled on personal and professional pressures and provided a new vantage point from which to consider the significance and the future of literary studies, has ended up as a kind of a time capsule. It is a message—which I started drafting in early fall 2020 and revised during the tumultuous first week of 2021 (and then again at various points later that same year)—to those of you who will be reading this in book form on the other side of the writing, editing, publishing, and distribution process. I am worried that we are not having the right conversations in higher education and that we are missing opportunities within the conversations that scholars in the fields represented by this book are already having. The declining revenues and pressurized budgets of 2020 (and before and after) have already exacerbated many of the problems that higher education has long been facing, including the mistaken idea that so-called "practical" or "pre-professional" tracks of learning will prepare students for a fast-changing job market, the false separation of STEM and fields of humanistic inquiry when now more than ever we need these fields to work together, and an unmet need for educational institutions to model a way of defining value beyond economic value. How might colleges and universities talk, as most other segments of the nonprofit sector already do, about social impact? How do we prepare students—all students, no matter what their major—for the economic, political, and ethical challenges of the twenty-first century? I believe that one important place to start to answer these questions is in our teaching and through shared dialogue about our teaching. My hope in writing this essay is to identify the work that many of us are already doing—that of engaging students in exploring the archival record and in finding new patterns and suppressed voices in our print cultural history—as part of a broader movement to reshape our fields and better articulate the case for the humanities within and outside our institutions.

The kind of literary history that I have tried to reimagine here supports recent articulations of the future of literary studies that have emerged since I first began writing this chapter. As Jesse Alemán notes in his contribution to *PMLA*'s May 2021 issue, literary studies—particularly the field of English in the United States—"is irrelevant if it's not confronting the questions of race, transformative justice, structural inequality, and the long legacies of coloniality that shape and define national cultures, traditions, and histories of literary production."[49] In the same *PMLA* issue, Kyla Wazana Tompkins points out that "questions of race and racism, as curricular, pedagogical, and enrollment issues, are rarely discussed in conversations and especially in documents about the state of the field, including the recent ADE report on the state of the major (ADE Ad Hoc Committee)."[50] Calling for centering these questions in rethinking of literary studies, and in the humanities more broadly, she proposes: "Let us imagine a world, for a moment, in which the courses and intellectual directions whose enrollments might actually save the entire field are given the resources to revitalize the field. For example, the fields of Black literary studies and Indigenous studies are in a state of effervescence."[51] The new Digital Ethnic Futures Consortium, an initiative at Salem State University led by Risam that received funding from the Mellon Foundation in September 2021, offers a glimpse of such a future by providing "a community for pedagogy at the intersections of ethnic studies fields and digital humanities."[52] Notably, pedagogy plays a central role in these recent articulations of the future of the literary field, as they call for learning from the struggles for true justice and democracy of the past and for facing our current ones with courage, creativity, and hope.

To return to the experience of my fall 2020 course, as my students and I met for weekly walks on the print history of New York City, putting the past in conversation with the present to gain understanding of the struggles evident on the city's streets—and through the personal experiences that we shared with each other—was very much on our minds as we visited former sites of the city's Spanish-language press. While the emptiness of the Brooklyn Bridge struck us most on that first day, as the semester wore on, we noticed many more empty store fronts, as well as increasing signs of homelessness in the city. In addition, on one memorable walk that took place the day before the 2020 presidential election, the air rang with the sound of shopkeepers boarding up some of

---

[49] Jesse Alemán, "The End of English," *PMLA* 136, no. 3 (2021), 472.
[50] Kyla Wazana Tompkins, "The Shush," *PMLA* 136, no. 3 (2021), 420.
[51] Ibid.
[52] Digital Ethnic Futures Consortium [@DigitalEthnic Futures]. "Coming soon ... " *Twitter,* September 29, 2021, https://twitter.com/DEFConsortium/status/1443225959826608128?s=20.

the storefront windows that remained out of fear of what might happen. It was a jarring reminder that our own democracy was being tested. (Little did we know at that time how much more it would be tested in the coming months.) Throughout the semester, the inequalities intensified by the pandemic combined with our heightened awareness of the fragility of our democracy made the city's nineteenth-century Spanish-language press—in which Martí, Figueroa, Serra, and others participated as part of their work to define the future of democracy in Cuba and throughout the hemisphere—a constant point of reference.

As the students became familiar—through our walks in Manhattan, digital mapping projects, and archival research—with this print community that once thrived in our own neighborhood near Pace University, they began to see how its writers, printers, editors, and bookstore owners debated, negotiated, and circulated ideas about the future of democracy and about the role that a then-expanding world of print might play in realizing that future. We considered how the editors of *La Revista Ilustrada de Nueva York* saw an increasingly interconnected world of print as an essential vehicle for bringing together "toda la grande América que fué hispana, que padeció bajo el poder colonial y que sigue padeciendo bajo sistemas que proclamamos como redentores" ("all of the great America that was Spanish, which suffered under colonial power and that continues to suffer under systems that we proclaim as redeemers.")[53] We discussed how Figueroa and Serra, with support from Martí until his death in 1895 in an early battle of the Cuban independence war that he helped to organize, built their ideas of the intertwining futures of print and democracy around a vision of racial and economic justice. That vision included, as Figueroa articulated it, "no... solamente arrojar de la Isla esclavizada al español codicioso que nos explota y nos humilla, sino hacer hoy, mañana y siempre, *revolución* en las ideas" ("not only dispelling from the enslaved island the greedy Spanish who exploit and humiliate us, but also achieving today, tomorrow, and always *revolution* in ideas").[54] We also noted repeatedly during the semester that the difficulties we faced in recovering the ideas and ambitions of New York's nineteenth-century Spanish-language press reflected both past and current biases and injustices.

The walks within a two-mile radius of the Pace campus, as well as our online discussion of them, took the place of the publications and voices that were not there to be included on the syllabus. As the walks helped us to contemplate New York City's past and present, they made us more aware that many U.S.-based Spanish-language publications are no longer or not easily available. One example we discussed was the *Gaceta del Pueblo* (People's Gazette), which we were able to learn about only from collected works of one of its contributors, Francisco Gonzalo "Pachín" Marín as, to my knowledge, no copies of the newspaper itself remain. The walks also helped us to recognize absences within the archival record of this community—not only because of what hasn't been saved, but also because the vast majority of those who had access to

---

[53] "La Revista Ilustrada," *La Revista Ilustrada de Nueva York*, (July 1887): 1. Translations are mine.
[54] Sotero Figueroa, "Por la revolución," *La Doctrina de Martí* (July 25, 1896), 2. Translations are mine.

the production of print were white, male, and elite. Near the end of the semester, one student noted the dearth of Indigenous voices in our discussions, which I committed to addressing in future semesters of the course. Another student dedicated her final project to locating nineteenth-century Latina voices and to highlighting the fact that many women who were part of the community organizing for Cuban and Puerto Rican independence in the city at the time did not have opportunities to play public-facing roles. (This project has since, with the student's permission, helped me fill a gap in available materials on nineteenth-century Latinas in New York City.) We also considered how the ideas and ambitions that we were able to access through archival materials provided lessons and hope for the future of true democracy, which we still very much needed.

As I conclude this chapter while reflecting on the past eighteen months since I began drafting this chapter in October 2020, engaging students with the hopes and dreams of New York City's late-nineteenth-century Spanish-language publishing community feels more important than ever. Martí, Figueroa, Serra, and their collaborators knew all too well that democracy is not inevitable and that its success relies on dedication, collaboration, and constant vigilance. It also requires creativity and imagination, which they brought to the publications in which they participated as they contemplated where their changing world of print might lead. In their best moments, they articulated a future of democracy and the role of media within it that has yet to be realized. Maybe the forms of participation in the production of knowledge about our past and present that we can model in our classrooms could enable us to pick up where those dreams left off to pursue the promise of true democracy that has motived writers and editors throughout the Americas for centuries.

13

Anthologizing Alternatives: June Jordan and Toni Cade Bambara's Publishing Pedagogies

Danica Savonick

Anthologies are a profoundly pedagogical genre. Because they can affordably aggregate work that was first published in different time periods and by various authors and publishers, anthologies are often used to teach American, British, or "World literature," and thus disseminate notions of national belonging and aesthetic value.[1] As Cynthia Franklin argues, anthologies "define cultural traditions" and drive decisions about "what literature teachers include in their syllabi and how they present it."[2] As such, anthologies have been famous sites of contestation, where debates over what gets to count as literature are hashed out. While anthologies are constructed explicitly for classroom use, with students as their intended audience, their making is typically removed, in Kenneth Warren's terms, from the "site" and "sight" of the classroom, reflecting a unilateral model of knowledge transmission from expert scholar to presumably novice student.[3]

One of the most popular literary anthologies, *The Norton Anthology of English Literature*, rose to prominence in the 1960s and 1970s amidst the postwar expansions to higher education. Norton aggressively marketed the anthology to its "target audience at flagship state universities, where one adoption could mean an order of 3,000 copies."[4] And yet while the *Norton Anthology* was establishing hegemony in college classrooms, marginalized writers who had been excluded from such canonical collections also embraced the form of the anthology to collect and share their writing. The social movements of the 1960s and 1970s gave rise to collections of writing by women, African Americans, Asian-Americans, and Puerto Ricans: *Black Fire: An*

---

[1] See J. Lockard and J. Sandell, "National Narratives and the Politics of Inclusion: Historicizing American Literature Anthologies," *Pedagogy* 8, no. 2 (2008), 227–54.
[2] Cynthia G. Franklin, *Writing Women's Communities: The Politics and Poetics of Contemporary Multi-Genre Anthologies* (Madison: University of Wisconsin Press, 1997), 4.
[3] Kenneth Warren, "The Problem of Anthologies, or Making the Dead Wince," *American Literature* 65, no. 2 (1993): 338–42.
[4] Sean Shesgreen, "Canonizing the Canonizer: A Short History of The Norton Anthology of English Literature," *Critical Inquiry* 35, no. 2 (2009), 303.

Anthology of Afro-American Writing (1968), *Aiiieeeee! An Anthology of Asian American Writers* (1974), *The Nuyorican Poetry Anthology* (1975), and later *This Bridge Called My Back: Writings by Radical Women of Color* (1981). In these collections, marginalized authors insisted on their collective consciousness and formalized distinct literary traditions that had been excluded from the traditional canon.[5] As Franklin argues, although these anthologies often circulated "beyond the confines of the academy... they also reflect on and issue challenges to the academy's literary centerpiece—the canonical anthology."[6]

At the nexus of these two types of anthologies—the hegemonic Norton textbook and the grassroots anthologies by writers of color—lie four anthologies edited by authors June Jordan and Toni Cade Bambara: Jordan's *The Voice of the Children* (1970) and *Soulscript* (1970) and Bambara's *The Black Woman* (1970) and *Tales and Stories for Black Folks* (1971). In contrast to canonical anthologies produced by senior scholars, Jordan's and Bambara's anthologies were all written, at least in part, by the students in their classrooms. These were not students at elite and exclusive institutions; they were working-class students of color in weekend workshops and remedial writing classrooms at public universities (specifically, the City College of New York and Livingston College). In a moment when textbooks and curricula reflected the values of a racist society, Bambara and Jordan reimagined their students not as passive readers and recipients of American literature, but as its newest authors.

This essay draws on the insights of feminist print culture studies to analyze the publishing histories of these four literary anthologies.[7] I argue that these anthologies, and Bambara and Jordan's editorial labor in producing them, were a political, activist response to the absences and inadequacies of mainstream textbooks and the selective curricula students were taught in schools. Through analysis of these anthologies and the pedagogical and editorial decisions that factored into their construction, I illustrate how Jordan and Bambara implemented an activist publishing pedagogy that challenged established hierarchies in literary and educational institutions. By attending to Bambara's and Jordan's publishing pedagogies we can better understand the classroom as a site not only for reception and dissemination of American literature but also for its production.

---

[5] Since the Harlem Renaissance, anthologies have been a means by which writers have formalized traditions of African American literature (Warren 338) and women's literature (Franklin 1). For example, Alain Locke's *The New Negro* announced the arrival of what would come to be known as the Harlem Renaissance, as anthologies like *Black Fire* and *Black Voices* heralded the arrival of the Black Arts Movement. As John Lash argues, Alice Dunbar Nelson's *Masterpieces of Negro Eloquence* and James Weldon Johnson's *Book of American Negro Poetry* also "made generations of writers and readers." (59) John S. Lash, "The Anthologist and the Negro Author," *Phylon* (1940-56) 8, no. 1 (1947), 68–76.

[6] Franklin, *Writing Women's Communities*, 4–5.

[7] See Jaime Harker and Cecilia Konchar Farr, *This Book Is an Action: Feminist Print Culture and Activist Aesthetics* (Chicago: University of Illinois Press, 2016) and Agatha Beins, *Liberation in Print: Feminist Periodicals and Social Movement Identity* (Athens: University of Georgia Press, 2017).

Black Feminist Publishing

Historically, the literary publishing industry has privileged the voices of a narrow, white, male elite. Amidst a sea of white editors serving as gatekeepers to coveted contracts, Black writers have not been afforded the luxury of focusing solely on their writing and craft. Rather, they have had to navigate and, in some instances, transform the material conditions of production and publication in and through which literature circulates. In the 1920s, some of the most influential figures of the Harlem Renaissance—Alain Locke, Claude McKay, W.E.B. Du Bois, Jessie Fauset—were also editors of literary magazines and anthologies that highlighted the writing of Black authors. While these editorial interventions resulted in some of the era's most important works of literature, Black authors continued to be subjected to decisions made by white publishers. In 1950, Zora Neale Hurston criticized "What White Publishers Won't Print," describing the ways Black authors were subject to white publishers' standards of what counts as acceptable or "authentic" Black writing. In 1965, Black poet Dudley Randall established Broadside Press to publish the work of poets such as Gwendolyn Brooks, Audre Lorde, Nikki Giovanni, and Sonia Sanchez, facilitating the rise of The Black Arts Movement. As a publisher, Randall aimed to create "a poetic space out of which black poets may create without restriction."[8]

Black women writers, in particular, have made important interventions in the material conditions that enable literary production. As the twentieth century progressed, many Black women took on positions as editors in order to address the racism and sexism of literary publishing. They were motivated by their own difficulties in publishing their writing and wanted to publish the work of their friends, colleagues, neighbors, and students as well. In 1970, Toni Morrison famously joined the editorial staff at Random House, where she published the work of writers including both Bambara and Jordan, as well as Lucille Clifton and Gayl Jones, and "helped to define two decades of African American literary history."[9] In the 1970s, the Women in Print Movement emerged as "an alternative communications circuit—a woman-centered network of readers and writers, editors, printers, publishers, distributors, and retailers through which ideas, objects, and practices flowed in a continuous and dynamic loop."[10] As Trysh Travis documents, this included such notable presses as the Women's Press, the Feminist Press, Diana Press, and Daughters, Inc.[11] And yet, many Black women writers experienced racism from these new presses and publications led by middle- and upper-class white women.[12] In 1980, Barbara Smith and Audre Lorde

---

[8] Waters, Mark V. "Dudley Randall and the Liberation Aesthetic: Confronting the Politics of 'Blackness,'" *CLA Journal* 44, no. 1 (September 2000), 111–32. Report. in *Poetry Criticism*, vol. 86.

[9] Cheryl A. Wall, "Toni Morrison, Editor and Teacher," in *The Cambridge Companion to Toni Morrison*, ed. Justine Tally (Cambridge University Press, 2007), 139.

[10] Trysh Travis, "The Women in Print Movement: History and Implications," *Book History* 11, no. 1 (September 2008), 276.

[11] Ibid., 278.

[12] As Travis argues, the women in print movement "skewed toward (though [was] not exclusively about) middle-class, white, Western experience" (292).

created Kitchen Table: Women of Color Press in order to "make visible the writing, culture, and history of women of color," often in the collective form of an anthology.[13] Kitchen Table was grounded in the idea that "freedom of the press belongs to those who own the press."[14] As Smith writes, the press was born from:

> our need for autonomy, our need to determine independently both the content and the conditions of our work and to control the words and images that were produced about us. As feminist and lesbian of color writers, we knew that we had no options for getting published except at the mercy or whim of others—in either commercial or alternative publishing, since both are white dominated.[15]

For these reasons, women writers of color have also historically undertaken the labor of editing, copyediting, proofing, binding, reviewing, publishing, marketing, and promoting their work. Reflecting upon their experiences editing the foundational anthology *This Bridge Called My Back*, Gloria Anzaldúa and Cherríe Moraga describe how they "bore the burden of the book... not only doing the proofreading and making editorial decisions, but also acting as a telephone answering and courier service, PR persons and advertisers, interviewers and transcribers, and even, occasionally, muses for some of the contributors during their sometimes rather painful 'writing blocks'" (xlv). In their roles as teachers, Jordan and Bambara voluntarily undertook this kind of additional editorial labor in order to share the voices and visions of their students. Looking back, we can understand this practice of publishing their students' writing as a form of pedagogical and editorial activism.

Student-Centered Anthologies: June Jordan's *The Voice of the Children* and *Soulscript*

June Jordan's edited poetry collection *Soulscript* (1970) has been celebrated by critics as "a poignant, panoramic collection of poetry from some of the most eloquent voices in the art." *Soulscript* responded to what Jordan felt was Clarence Major's excessive leniency in editing *The New Black Poetry* (1969) and the sense she shared with Amiri Baraka (then LeRoi Jones) that Black literary anthologies had been constrained by an imperative to protest and selected for their "sociological" rather than "literary" interest.[16] Her aim, by contrast, was "to demonstrate the existing literature of American black poets," emphasizing the literary and aesthetic value of the poems she selected. Upon publication, *Soulscript* was met with critical approbation, lauded as "an exemplary,

---

[13] Barbara Smith, "A Press of Our Own Kitchen Table: Women of Color Press," *Frontiers: A Journal of Women Studies* 10, no. 3 (1989), 11.
[14] Ibid.
[15] Ibid.
[16] June Jordan, "Letter to Milton Meltzer, January 28, 1969." June Jordan Papers, Schlesinger Library Archive, Radcliffe Institute. Box 53, folder 10.

tasteful anthology"[17] and "an enjoyable volume of thought-provoking reading."[18] Reviewers praised these poems as "the best, represent[ing] a striking convergence of the vocabulary of individual recognitions and historical immediacy."[19] Since then, it has become a foundational anthology of African American poetry.

While *Soulscript* has been deservedly praised, scholars rarely dwell on the fact that it included student writing. In fact, *Soulscript* was one of two groundbreaking anthologies Jordan edited, both of which included the writing of her students.

In 1967, Jordan, an up-and-coming writer, began co-teaching a weekend writing workshop for Black and Puerto Rican youth in New York City. The workshop was part of the Teachers and Writers Collaborative, a group of authors and educators who aimed to empower students by sharing the skills possessed by writers, such as problem solving, comfort in open-endedness, and creativity.[20] As a solution to the rote memorization approach that dominated classrooms in poor school districts, the Collaborative advocated for the elimination of grades on written work, the elimination of arbitrary rules and impositions, and a pedagogy that would nurture children's creative use of language. Under the leadership of Herbert Kohl, the Collaborative sent poets into classrooms to collaborate with passionate educators similarly invested in mending a broken system. Jordan's assigned collaborator was a white woman named Terri Bush, who taught at Sands Junior High School in Brooklyn.

In their weekend workshops, Jordan first encountered, as an instructor, students who spelled "him" with an "n" and could not distinguish a fragment from a sentence, producing in Jordan "a sense of desperation," that threatened to derail the entire undertaking.[21] In contrast to the pathologizing journalism of the time, Jordan's published diary entries depict these students not as unintelligent, but as arriving at their weekend workshops with a "history of no education" already battered by years of "shit treatment" and "despisal pedagogy" at the hands of underfunded public schools.[22] As these reflections indicate, Jordan's work belongs amidst a body of late 1960s writings that sought to explain the underperformance of Black and Puerto Rican students in New York City's public schools as the product of racist institutions and not individual deficiencies. For Jordan, the question then became, "How can you correct completely illiterate work without entering that hideous history they have had to survive as still another person who says: You can't do it. You don't know. You are unable. You are ignorant."[23] Determined not to be part of this stifling history, Jordan set about exploring other ways of being together and doing things with language that taught these young people that they are capable of action.

---

[17] April 1, 1970 Review, untitled publication. June Jordan Papers, Schlesinger Library Archive, Radcliffe Institute. Box 53, folder 14.
[18] Ingrid Tarver, Review of Soulscript, edited by June Jordan. *Alabama News*, October 4, 1970.
[19] April 1, 1970 Review.
[20] Phillip Lopate, *Journal of a Living Experiment: A Documentary History of the First Ten Years of Teachers and Writers Collaborative* (New York: Teachers & Writers Collaborative, 1979), 9.
[21] June Jordan, "'The Voice of the Children' Diaries," in *Journal of a Living Experiment*, 135.
[22] June Jordan, "The Voice of the Children," in *Civil Wars* (Boston: Beacon, 1981), 32.
[23] Jordan, "Voice," 32.

As Jordan learned through careful questioning, these students did not read books in school; instead, they were taught from a literary magazine called *Scope*, in which each short reading concluded with a set of questions to test their comprehension. By contrast, Jordan gave students poems by contemporary Black and Puerto Rican writers like Langston Hughes, Gwendolyn Brooks, and Victor Hernandez Cruz that she hoped would inspire their own writing. As Richard Flynn argues, Jordan gave students "good poetic models in order to enable them to write 'real poetry'" as part of her larger "refusal to underestimate children."[24] Each week, they would review their writings from the previous week, Jordan would offer a writing prompt, and together they would write for a while, eating snacks and listening to music. Rather than assigning essays on "those who won wars or who conquered territory,"[25] Jordan asked the children to write about what they knew: New York City, riots, love, American history, blackness, Civil Rights, Nina Simone, and their schools, which, in the words of one student, taught children that they "are slaves to teachers."[26] The first prompt was "An Introduction of Self," followed by a description of somebody else, and then, "write about 'white power' or "black power."[27]

The resulting poems bear titles like "Hands," "No Way Out," and "I am waiting." In these poems, the young authors respond to prompts such as "what would you do if you were president?" with trenchant critiques of ghetto stereotypes, settler colonialism, US imperialism, and patriarchy, made all the more powerful when we consider that their average age was thirteen. Their poems command—"put my black father on the penny,"[28]—and elegize Martin Luther King Jr. They use rhyme to urge the reader along and puzzling punctuation to stop us in our tracks. They speak to a moment of youth culture, in which young people did not accept what they were handed by authority figures and dominant institutions, but instead organized to demand what they desired. Amidst a stratified society that sought to discipline and silence these young people, poetry validated their voices and visions.

And yet, just beyond the walls of these thrilling workshops brimming with young people's poetry, journalists were describing these same students as "silent creatures... [who] didn't know the names of things, didn't know that things had names, didn't even know their own names."[29] Collaborative participants were outraged at the ways mainstream media naturalized and even exacerbated conditions of educational apartheid by depicting these students as ineducable, lazy, and intellectually disabled, destined only for vocational training. They saw that publishing their students' writing could address these racist stereotypes of illiterate urban youth by speaking to a

---

[24] Richard Flynn, "'Affirmative Acts': Language, Childhood, and Power in June Jordan's Cross- Writing," *Children's Literature* 30 (2002), 163.
[25] June Jordan, Merit Review Statement. 1993–4. June Jordan Papers, Schlesinger Library Archive, Radcliffe Institute. Box 78, folder 8.
[26] Isabel Velez, "Children Are Slaves." in *The Voice of the Children*, eds. June Jordan and Terri Bush (Holt, Rinehart and Winston, Inc., 1970), 32.
[27] Jordan, "Diaries," 135–6.
[28] Howard, "Monument" in *Soulscript*, 4.
[29] John Holt, "Introduction," in *Teaching the "Unteachable*," ed. Herbert R. Kohl (New York: The New York Review, 1967), 5.

reading public concerned with educational inequality. At the same time, Collaborative participants understood how publishing could give urgency to students' writing:

> A student will only be concerned with his own use of language, will only care about its effectiveness, and therefore try to judge its effectiveness—and therefore be able to improve its effectiveness—when he is talking to an audience, not just one that allows him to say what he wants as he wants, but one that takes him and his ideas seriously.[30]

In the late 1960s and early 1970s, educators and authors involved with the Collaborative published numerous collections of student work in genres ranging from memoirs to anthologies. As Marvin Hoffman remarked in a 1970 book review, "over the past several years, the publication of young students' writing has increased at a geometric rate."[31] While some Collaborative instructors focused on publishing the insights that they, as teachers, had learned from this program (in hopes of improving education nationwide), Jordan focused on helping her students write "real poetry," and connecting these young authors to an audience of readers.

In her earliest years as an educator, Jordan was certain of little except that binding and publishing students' work would generate enthusiasm about reading and writing more effectively than comprehension quizzes. Initially, in October 1967, this took the form of "folios," in which Jordan and Bush would type students' poems into collections they could take home, "making something they have done seem more permanent and… valuable via a kind of simple-minded, physical change of appearance."[32] Jordan refers to this potentially tedious labor of typing students' poems as "effectively pedagogic."[33] By March of 1968, the folios had transformed into a student-written and edited newspaper, *The Voice of the Children*, which became the title of their first anthology.

The Voice of the Children is an anthology of poetry authored entirely by students in Jordan and Bush's weekend workshops. Jordan and Bush's editorial style is evident in their arrangement of the poems, not chronologically or by individual author, but into five sections ("Politics, Observations, Blackness, Love and Nature, Very Personal") that highlight the conversations among them, especially, as Rachel Conrad observes, the "themes of racial politics and black identity."[34] The original cover photograph depicts

---

[30] Ibid., 8.
[31] Marvin Hoffman, "Wishes, Feelings, Dreams." *Library Journal*, October 15, 1970, 3599. Examples include Richard Lewis's *Miracles* (1966) and *Journeys* (1969), Herbert Kohl's *36 Children* (1967) and *Teaching the Unteachable* (1969), Diane Divoky's *How Old Will You Be in 1984* (1969), John Birmingham's *Our Time Is Now* (1970), Kenneth Koch's *Wishes, Lies and Dreams* (1970), and Steven Joseph's *The Me Nobody Knows* (1969), which was made into a rock musical that won the Obie Award for Best Off-Broadway Show.
[32] Jordan, "Diaries," 132.
[33] Ibid., 151.
[34] Rachel Conrad, "'We Speak to Be Heard': June Jordan, Terri Bush, and The Voice of the Children," in *Time for Childhoods: Young Poets and Questions of Agency* (Amherst: University of Massachusetts Press, 2019), 135.

a group of children, their bodies entangled, arms extended, and hands clenched tight into confident fists, radiating a sense of intimacy, pride, and power.

While anthologies are typically introduced by an editorial forward, Jordan's view of the collection appears as an afterword, letting the children speak first, and on their own terms. In the foreword titled "Ghetto," fourteen-year-old Vanessa Howard theorizes the power of stereotypes to reduce the complexity of individuals:

> Nine out of ten times when a person hears the word 'ghetto' they think of Black people first of all … Ghetto has become a definition meaning Black, garbage, slum areas. To me the word 'ghetto' is just as bad as cursing. I think they put all Black people in a box marked 'ghetto' which leaves them having no identity. They should let Black people be seen for themselves, not as one reflection on all.[35]

As Conrad argues, Howard's poem critiques "white supremacist hegemony … [and] claims for plural 'Black people' an authority over their own identities."[36]

For students who had been taught that their voices did not matter, publishing gave their voluntary weekend workshops "a sense of clearer purpose,"[37] a sense that their work with words mattered for audiences beyond the classroom. Once students knew that adults would be reading their poems, they started asking questions "about punctuation, stanzas, paragraphs, and form."[38] As Jordan writes, "they want to avoid adult errors of understanding; they want people to receive the message, and no mistake about it."[39] While contemporary debates concerned student illiteracy and error, through publishing, students learned both how narrow notions of correctness can maintain dominant power relations and how they could use those very conventions to gain adults' attention. In short, they learned the invaluable skill of writing for different audiences. In the decades to come, these kinds of real-world writing assignments would become central to the field of composition and rhetoric.

That same year, Jordan edited another anthology that included her students' writing. While *The Voice of the Children* was written entirely by students, *Soulscript* includes student poetry right alongside the work of literary luminaries such as Paul Laurence Dunbar, Langston Hughes, and Jean Toomer. As noted in her introduction, Jordan imagined the anthology as a corrective to the classroom's "typical textbook," with its omissions and distorted visions of Black Americans.

The original publication included a plain white cover dissected vertically by the bold, uppercase title, tilted sideways, prominently announcing that it was "Edited by June Jordan." In this way, Jordan used her own name recognition to draw readers to

---

[35] Vanessa Howard, "Ghetto," Jordan and Bush, ix.
[36] Conrad, "We Speak to Be Heard," 143–44.
[37] Jordan, "Diaries," 150.
[38] June Jordan, "Children and the Hungering For" *"Life Studies,": 1966–1976*, eds. Conor Tomás Reed and Talia Shalev. Lost and Found CUNY Poetics Document Initiative ser. 7. No. 3. 2017, 29.
[39] June Jordan and Terri Bush, eds., *The Voice of the Children* (New York: Holt, Rinehart and Winston, Inc., 1970), 96.

the collection. Nowhere does the cover indicate that a significant number of the poems contained therein were authored by students. And yet, archival records reveal that circulating her students' poetry was a crucial motivating force in its publication. When Jordan's publisher, Milton Meltzer, wanted to cut several of her students' poems, Jordan fought back passionately, insisting that eleven student-poets "are necessary to support my contention that children flow among the wellsprings of poetry as much as any adult."[40] As she explained to Meltzer, inclusion in the anthology would "testify to the ordinary, earnest talent of all youngsters to work towards a personal expression of language."[41]

As the publication date drew nearer, Meltzer requested, in addition to the introduction they had initially agreed upon, "a brief introductory statement... to head each of the seven sections... crutch[es] the less-equipped teachers could lean on."[42] Just as a teacher sets the stage for an encounter with a literary text, Jordan's resulting introductions frame each cluster of poems. Instead of authoritatively explicating students' poems, Jordan's introductory poems guide the reader by setting the mood. For instance, the poem introducing "Tomorrow Words Today" urges readers to listen to these young people not as a benevolent act of charity, but because our survival and flourishing depend upon it. Their poems "predict the future terms/for measuring the world/we must share."[43] The publishers also requested "a brief reading list for the back of the book—other collections the youngster or teacher could look up."[44] While these teaching resources never made it into the final published version, these remarks indicate how deliberately the anthology was created for classroom use as an effort to address the absences in existing canons and curricula. Jordan also recognized these efforts as labor and requested that this additional work be properly compensated.

When soliciting contributions from established writers, several authors like Calvin Hernton and David Henderson were "shy" and even intimidated "by the youth of their intended readers" fearing the subjects of their poems were too violent, explicit, and difficult.[45] But nothing could be farther from Jordan's view of young readers. She believed that poems like Nikki Giovanni's "NIKKI-ROSA," Gwendolyn Brooks's "The Bean Eaters," and Audre Lorde's "Coal" could offer young people the validation and encouragement they were elsewhere denied: "the view that I believe you can handle it, that there is a way and a means to creatively handle whatever may be the pain or the social predicament of your young life, and that I believe that you can and will discover or else invent that way, those means."[46] When her publishers protested the difficulty of

---

[40] Jordan, "Letter to Milton Meltzer."
[41] Ibid.
[42] Milton Meltzer, Letter to June Jordan, January 22, 1969. June Jordan Papers, Schlesinger Library Archive, Radcliffe Institute. Box 53, folder 10, 1.
[43] June Jordan, "Introduction," in *Soulscript: Afro-American Poetry* (New York: Random House, 2004 (1970)), 1.
[44] Meltzer, "Letter to June Jordan," 2.
[45] Jordan, "Letter to Milton Meltzer."
[46] June Jordan, "The Creative Spirit: Children's Literature," in *Revolutionary Mothering: Love on the Front Lines*, eds. China Martens, Alexis Pauline Gumbs, and Mai'a Williams (Oakland: PM Press, 2016), 18.

the introduction's prose given the youth of its anticipated audience, Jordan suggested they recruit three twelve-year-olds to read it and share their reactions. This response exemplifies Jordan's respect for the intellectual capacity and preferences of her young readers, and insistence that they should be making decisions regarding their learning and lives.

Both anthologies received considerable critical praise and sold well, primarily to libraries and school systems, allowing students' words to travel to classrooms as far as Houston and Albuquerque. As a result, the young poets were invited to read on local television and radio stations and at universities, and to have their writing published in *The Village Voice* and *The New York Times*. Of course, not everyone thought student poetry was worth reading. One review in *The Courier Post* claimed "the editors are the heroes of this anthology of ghetto kids poems and paragraphs,"[47] which the reviewer deems unworthy of being "listened to" (and clearly they didn't listen to Vanessa Howard's "Ghetto").

What sets Jordan's anthologies apart from other contemporary collections are their multiple aims and audiences. Jordan created the conditions for students not only to collectively refute racist depictions of illiterate children and intervene in national conversations, but also to speak *to each other* across the partitioning walls of classrooms and schools. Through these anthologies, the student-authors shared survival strategies, perspectives, and insights that could be used to navigate and contest dominant institutions. For example, in prose poems like "Sands Junior High School," Arlene Blackwell critiques the unfairly "harsh" and disinterested teachers at her school who "pin a reputation on you back ten times quicker than you earn it."[48] Another student, Michael Goode, wrote a poem "April 4, 1968," commemorating the death of Martin Luther King Jr. Goode's poem depicts King's assassination not as an isolated incident but as characteristic of a society structured by quotidian anti-Black violence:

> It's funny it's so you can't even walk out in the street anymore some maniac might shoot you in cold blood.[49]

He invites readers to honor King's legacy by continuing to ask: "What kind of world is this?" While Goode was initially invited to read his poem at Sands Junior High School's memorial assembly, administrators rescinded the offer out of fear that the poem might incite a riot.[50] While school officials feared that the poem would galvanize students, the workshop participants celebrated the power of poems that could turn justified anger into collective action.

As Blackwell and Goode's poems demonstrate, these students were writing not only for their teacher, but also for themselves, for each other, for those who deem them

---

[47] Fred Hullet, "The Voices." *Courier Post*, December 31, 1970. June Jordan Papers, Schlesinger Library Archive, Radcliffe Institute. Box 54, folder 11.
[48] Arlene Blackwell, "Sands Junior High School," in *Voice of the Children*, 31.
[49] Michael Goode, "April 4, 1968" in *Voice of the Children*, 9.
[50] Conrad, *Time for Childhoods*, 128.

illiterate, and for students potentially trapped in other classrooms who might benefit from the ways these young authors have learned to see the world. And some reviews, like Marvin Hoffman's, acknowledge the profound student-centered ethos of these anthologies. Whereas many of the era's published collections of young people's writing were little more than "coffee-table literature for adults," Hoffman praised *The Voice of the Children* as "one of the finest, most balanced representations of student thought and creativity to date... One senses in reading their work a group of young people writing for their own and each other's pleasure; the adult reader just has the privilege of listening in."[51]

In addition to drawing inspiration from the Teachers and Writers Collaborative, these experiments with publishing student writing were shaped by Jordan's efforts to counter the racism and sexism of the literary publishing industry. There are countless examples of Jordan's first-hand experiences of this: editors changing the titles of her essays without permission in ways that reinforced the very ideologies she was interrogating; a dearth of publicity surrounding her poetry, prompting her to embrace the feminist tactic of interviewing herself; her disbelief that no Black reviewers were asked to review books on racism.[52] In her journalism, poetry, and speeches, Jordan argued that mainstream US culture actively silences huge swaths of the US population, elevating wealthy, white male voices over others—showing how "free speech" is anything but free given the material and institutional conditions in which language circulates.[53] The hours she spent convincing prestigious publishers like Doubleday and Holt, Rinehart & Winston (an imprint of the publishing branch of the television network CBS) to publish her students' writing were an activist intervention to circulate their voices and visions to readers who needed them.

Kicking Open Doors: Toni Cade Bambara's *The Black Woman* and *Tales and Stories for Black Folks*

While Toni Cade Bambara is best known for her fiction, she also edited two anthologies, both of which included the writing of her students. In 1970, Bambara's collection *The Black Woman: An Anthology* was published by the New American Library as part of its Mentor Books series.[54] *The Black Woman* includes poems, stories, interviews, and essays on a wide range of subjects relevant to Black women's lives, including motherhood, activism, relations between Black men and women, educational racism, birth control, social work, poverty, and Black family dynamics. It is difficult to overstate the impact of *The Black Woman*, considered by many the first anthology of its kind. Scholars such as Robin D.G. Kelley and Patricia Hill Collins have recognized

---

[51] Hoffman, "Wishes, Feelings, Dreams," 3600.
[52] Jordan, *Civil Wars*, 25, 122, 44.
[53] Ibid., 93.
[54] Toni Cade Bambara, *The Black Woman; an Anthology* (New York: New American Library, 1970).

The Black Woman as a foundational text of Black Women's Studies.[55] Kelley describes this "landmark collection of essays" as "a kind of manifesto for black feminism, a critique of both the women's movement and male-led black politics, and a complex analysis of how gender, race, and class worked together to oppress everyone."[56] Since its publication, *The Black Woman* has inspired generations of students, activists, artists, and authors, and it continues to appear on college syllabi across disciplines to this day.[57] Despite the collection's profound impact both within and beyond universities, scholars rarely consider that this anthology was born in Bambara's classrooms. In an interview, filmmaker Louis Massiah asked Bambara "about the genesis of *The Black Woman*... How did that come about?"[58] Her initial response was only one sentence: "In 1968 I was teaching at City College in the SEEK program."

In 1965, five years prior to its publication, Bambara was hired to teach English in the new Search for Education, Elevation, and Knowledge (SEEK) educational opportunity program at the City College of New York in Harlem. While City College had a historical mandate to educate "the children of the whole people" and had long boasted of being the "Harvard of the Proletariat," it was not until 1965 that SEEK was established to address the fact that the college's student body did not reflect the diversity of the surrounding Black and Puerto Rican Harlem community. The SEEK program recruited "economically and educationally disadvantaged" students from Harlem, waived their tuition fees, provided money for books, and prepared them to matriculate at City College through remedial coursework, thus providing a pathway to college for hundreds (and later thousands) of low-income, minority, and first-generation students.

At this time, educational racism prevailed in ideas about Black and Puerto Rican students as "ineducable," "illiterate," and "culturally deprived."[59] In reality, SEEK students, like those in Jordan's writing workshops, came from underfunded schools that were left out of the city's Progressive-era education reforms. Their unpreparedness was the product of racist institutions, discrimination, underemployment, and poverty, and not individual deficiencies. At City College, Bambara taught alongside scholars of Black literature Barbara Christian and Addison Gayle, authors June Jordan, Audre Lorde, and Adrienne Rich, and composition scholar Mina Shaughnessy. There, they formed a creative community of writers and teachers committed to empowering their marginalized students and upending the status quo.

In her introductory and remedial reading and writing courses, Bambara helped students understand the ways their own educations had reflected the values of a

[55] Robin D.G. Kelley, *Freedom Dreams: The Black Radical Imagination* (Boston, MA: Beacon Press, 2008) and Patricia Hill Collins, *Black Feminist Thought: Knowledge, Consciousness, and the Politics of Empowerment* (New York: Routledge, 2015).
[56] Kelley, *Freedom Dreams*, 143–4.
[57] Open Syllabus Project.
[58] Toni Cade Bambara, *Deep Sightings and Rescue Missions: Fiction, Essays, and Conversations* (New York: Pantheon Books, 1996), 228.
[59] James Traub, *City on A Hill: Testing the American Dream at City College* (New York: Addison-Wesley, 1994).

racist society. She taught students to critique the ways that Anglo-Saxon literature is taught as "The Literature," and that White Western History is taught as "World History," overlooking "the role the African and Afro-American tradition plays in our history, our art, our culture."[60] In addition, Bambara insisted that students take an active role in shaping "the content, direction, and goals of the course." For example, in a remedial summer writing course designed to prepare students to matriculate into the mainstream City College curriculum, Bambara instead challenged them to design their own course and equipped them with the tools to reinvent the university. As in all of Bambara's courses, students conducted research from the very first day of class, experimented with different modes of storytelling, and were taught to see their learning as a collective endeavor that made an impact beyond the individuals in each classroom. Students left Bambara's courses cognizant of the gaps in dominant narratives and institutional knowledges; able to do research and seek out missing perspectives; aware that authority is not synonymous with knowledge and not always legitimate; and with the power to tell stories, rather than be told by them.

While the SEEK program is often remembered as a landmark educational opportunity program and the birthplace of basic writing, it was also a site of literary innovation, where classrooms gave rise to some of the era's most important anthologies of African American literature and literary and cultural criticism. At City College, students and faculty alike were galvanized by Bambara's classroom and campus lectures on Black literature and history, educational racism, myths and propaganda, and the need for more relevant education. One student, Francine Covington, recognized that Bambara had a perspective that was missing from mainstream media, bookstores, and curricula and confronted her: "You've been saying this, that, and the other. Why don't you do a book, dammit?"[61] This insistence was echoed by her colleague Addison Gayle, who told Bambara, "I heard you give eight talks. Why the hell don't you write them down and get them printed?"[62] According to Bambara, it was Gayle who "urged me to assemble a book on the black woman rather than run off at the mouth about it" and who helped her secure the contract for her later collection, *Tales and Stories for Black Folks* (1971).[63]

In the tumultuous year of 1968, Bambara began collecting materials for what would become *The Black Woman*. While Covington and Gayle both urged Bambara to publish a collection of her own writing, she instead chose to edit an anthology, a collective format that, in Eleanor Traylor's words, reflects Bambara's pedagogy of "gathering": bringing people together to "think deeply and act decisively."[64] To be fair, Gayle would have understood her decision. He was simultaneously compiling his own anthologies,

---

[60] Toni Cade Bambara, "Realizing the Dream of a Black University," in *Realizing the Dream of a Black University*, eds. Conor Tomas Reed and Makeba Lavan, Lost and Found CUNY Poetics Document Initiative ser. 7. No. 2. 2017, 4.
[61] Bambara, *Deep Sightings*, 229.
[62] Ibid., 229.
[63] Bambara, "Interview with Tate," 29.
[64] Eleanor Traylor, "ReCalling the Black Woman," in *The Black Woman: An Anthology*, ed. Toni Cade Bambara (New York: Washington Square Press, 2005. [Originally published in 1970, reprinted version cited here published in 2005]). Traylor's introduction starts at ix–xviii.

Black Expression and *The Black Aesthetic*, which became foundational texts of African American literary criticism. As Sean Molloy argues, Gayle's anthologies responded to the absences and distortions in the City College curriculum and included the writing of his SEEK program colleagues.[65] Bambara, however, made an even more radical decision to include the work of her City College students. If pundits were skeptical that these "new students" could withstand the rigors of a college education, little could they have imagined that Bambara's students would have their writing published in one of the most influential anthologies of the twentieth century.

Bambara explicitly envisioned this anthology for, by, and about Black women as an intervention in racist and sexist publishing practices. Years before Toni Morrison would top best-seller lists or Alice Walker recovered the work of Zora Neale Hurston, books by Black women were not readily available in bookstores, nor were they household names. Given the widely held belief, among white presses, that "there is no market for Black women's work,"[66] Bambara was determined to compile "a book that will kick the door open... so that other Black women's manuscripts could get a hearing... and prove that there was a market."[67] Though she initially planned to include writing by women in SNCC, CORE, and the Black Panther Party, she shifted focus to expedite the project. Rather than waiting for busy activists to slowly come around to the idea of publishing their writing, the collection would feature writing by Bambara's friends, neighbors, and colleagues, and local community organizers. While traditional publishing practices favor established authors with name recognition, with *The Black Woman*, "previous publication was not a prerequisite for inclusion in the project. Its featured writers included those who were known and those who were unknown."[68] With no formal training in editing, Bambara drew on insights about the material realities of Black women's lives: "All I knew in the beginning was that it had to fit in your pocket and it had to be a dollar. I didn't know anything about publishing, but I stuck to that."[69] Indeed, the collection had to be affordable and small so that women who worked long hours to provide and care for families could read it on the bus or subway and in short increments during breaks in work shifts.

When *The Black Woman* went to press in 1970, it included the writing of Black women parents, community organizers, activists like Grace Lee Boggs and Frances Beale's famous essay, "Double Jeopardy: To Be Black and Female," and even Bambara's mother, Helen Cade. Among the collection's twenty-seven authors, more than one-third were affiliated with the City College SEEK program, either as students (five) or as instructors (five). Students' contributions include personal essays on topics ranging from "Black Romanticism" to Gillo Pontecorvo's 1966 film *The Battle of Algiers*, as well

---

[65] Sean Molloy, "A Convenient Myopia: SEEK, Shaughnessy, and the Rise of High-Stakes Testing at CUNY," All Dissertations, Theses, and Capstone Projects, September 30, 2016, 196.

[66] Bambara, *Deep Sightings*, 229.

[67] Ibid., 230.

[68] Holmes, Linda Janet. *A Joyous Revolt: Toni Cade Bambara, Writer and Activist* (Santa Barbara: Prager, 2014), 45.

[69] Bambara, *Deep Sightings*, 230.

as a transcribed conversation among seven young Black women students and their friends. Some of these, such as Francee Covington's "Are the Revolutionary Techniques Employed in the Battle of Algiers Applicable in Harlem," were likely final projects from Bambara's classes. Among the students' contributions, Joanna Clark's personal essay "Motherhood" offers a particularly scathing indictment of society's abuse of Black mothers. Clark describes trying to support two children as a single mother while also attending college through the SEEK program. Her essay critiques the injustices she experienced as she is shuffled between inept institutions; the Department of Welfare, Support Court, and New York City hospitals all seem to do more harm than good. She recalls condescending doctors, flagrantly sexist "Support" Court lawyers, and an "investigator... extremely gung-ho about filling out forms" and equally as eager to "throw me off welfare."[70] Her essay indicts a culture that frees fathers from responsibility, leaving all obligations to fall on the mother, "as if... [she] went out behind a barn somewhere and knocked herself up with the nearest twig."[71] These observations are conveyed with wry, understated wit, and humor, which is astounding given how cruelly she was treated. In a moment when some Black activists considered birth control a form of Black genocide, Clark reveals the terrifying realities she faced as a young, poor, single Black mother, urging readers to develop a more nuanced understanding of the material realities of Black women's lives.

As Clark's essay demonstrates, *The Black Woman* circulated the knowledge and perspectives missing from mainstream journalism, publishing, and curricula, as well as the era's male-dominated anthologies of Black literature. In the words of Linda Holmes, "now, writers that had not been included in some anthologies edited by black men were a part of a project that created its own black female fire."[72] As Traylor writes, echoing a common refrain throughout Bambara's work, the anthology picks up where educational institutions fall short: "In this collection, we gain the pedagogy of those who think better than they've been trained."[73] As such, we can read it as a kind of grassroots pedagogical formation and means of sharing knowledge beyond the guarded gates of university walls, what Lavan and Tomás Reed call a "feminist studies open curriculum."[74] And people wanted this knowledge. As Bambara recalls, "within the second month the book came out, it went into a new edition. That book was everywhere. There were pyramids of *The Black Woman* in every bookstore."[75] According to Holmes, the book was viewed as a "literary bombshell": "In reading *The Black Woman*... black women across the age spectrum sensed a new age dawning of women exerting their power."[76] Indeed, *The Black Woman* successfully kicked down the doors and proved that there was a viable market for Black women's writing.

[70] Joanna Clark, "Motherhood" in *The Black Woman*, 75–86.
[71] Clark, "Motherhood," 70.
[72] Holmes, *A Joyous Revolt*, 45.
[73] Eleanor Traylor, *The Black Woman*, xv–xvi.
[74] Lavan and Tomás Reed, Introduction, 9.
[75] Bambara, *Deep Sightings*, 230.
[76] Holmes, *A Joyous Revolt*, xix.

The Black Woman was one of the first "multi-genre anthologies," a form that would become crucial for Black and women of color feminisms.[77] As Gilley argues, the multi-genre anthology is suited to multiple voices, styles, and genres of writing.[78] Because each writer only contributes a shorter piece, it can prove less intimidating for writers who might not have formal training and more accessible to women who have to take care of children and work long hours to support their families.[79] As Gilley writes, it was also a genre well-suited for writers whose political voices were shaped by their activism and involvement in communities: "The type of women who would be creating radical theory are more likely to be out engaging in radical praxis, organizing and protesting rather than writing alone in a room."[80] As one of the first multi-genre anthologies, *The Black Woman* helped pave the way for other collections by writers of color such as *Third World Women* (1972), *Aiiieeeee! An Anthology of Asian American Writers* (1974), *The Nuyorican Poetry Anthology* (1975), *Giant Talk: An Anthology of Third World Writings* (1975), *This Bridge Called My Back* (1981) (for which Bambara wrote the preface), *Some of Us Are Brave* (1982), and *Home Girls: A Black Feminist Anthology* (1983). As Bambara's work suggests, classrooms were sites not only where such anthologies were read, but also where they were written and produced.

In 1969, Bambara accepted a position as an assistant professor at the newly established Livingston College, a college for Black and activist students that was part of Rutgers, The State University of New Jersey. Livingston offered courses in new subjects like Afro-American Studies, provided opportunities for students to participate in college governance and decision-making, and supported many activist student organizations. There, Bambara taught a range of English courses, especially for first-year students. Reflecting on her time at Livingston, Bambara refers to it as "one of the most stunningly profound periods of my life," during which she was "thoroughly enmeshed with students and their academic and otherwise lives."[81]

Similar to her City College students (as well as Jordan's weekend workshop students), Bambara's students at Rutgers-Livingston were primarily working-class students of color from what she called "nonwriting backgrounds."[82] In order to interest them in writing, Bambara developed assignments that honored the experiential knowledge they brought to the classroom and challenged them to write for real audiences beyond just their professor. For example, one assignment asked students to reflect on their lives, extract some useful lesson from their experiences as Black students, and use writing to convey that lesson to a younger reader:

---

[77] Franklin, *Writing Women's Communities*, 5.
[78] Jennifer Gilley, "Ghost in the Machine: Kitchen Table Press and the Third Wave Anthology That Vanished," *Frontiers* 38, no. 3 (2017), 144.
[79] Chester and Pinkvoss qtd. in Gilley, 144.
[80] Gilley, "Ghost in the Machine," 144.
[81] Bambara, "Working At It," 3. There is a minor discrepancy between drafts.
[82] Toni Cade Bambara, "Interview with Claudia Tate," in *Black Women Writers at Work*, ed. Claudia Tate (New York: Continuum, 1983), 22.

Remember how you used to get all hot in the face, slide down in your seat, suddenly have to tie your shoe even though you were wearing loafers back then in fourth grade whenever Africa was mentioned or slavery was mentioned? Remember the first time the mention of Africa, of Black, made your neck long and your spine straight, made the muscles of your face go just so? Well, make a list of all the crucial, relevant things that happened to you that moved you from hot face to tall spine: then compose a short story, script, letter, essay, poem that makes that experience of change available to the young brothers and sisters on your block.[83]

Bambara's assignment treats their unique experiences as Black students as a source of vital knowledge that could be useful to others. Knowing that their words could make a difference in people's lives, students worked long hours revising and editing. This assignment resulted in midnight phone calls, "notes... outlines... rough drafts... cut-downs... editing... the search for form and metaphor." While some students chose to write "position papers for organizations in their community," others "were working at the storytelling library hour, so they wrote stories." Much to Bambara's delight the students were teaching "themselves and each other in that process of sifting and sorting, dumping, streamlining, tracing their own process of becoming," the results of which she deemed "fantastic." Together, they traveled to local elementary schools, community centers, and children's hospitals to share these lessons. After witnessing young people's enthusiastic reactions to her students' words, she decided to compile them into an anthology that could reach even broader audiences. As Bambara recalls, "I thought that the stories were great and I published them in the book."[84]

Bambara's former City College colleague Addison Gayle helped her secure a contract with Doubleday for *Tales and Stories for Black Folks* (1971): a collection of fables and parables that use animals as characters to explore human relationships and power dynamics.[85] Many, like "Little Black Riding Hood" and the "Three Little Panthers," are rewritings of classic stories inspired by the Black Power Movement. Similar to Jordan's *Soulscript*, *Tales and Stories* includes student writing alongside the work of more "seasoned writers" and "well-honed analysts" like Langston Hughes and Alice Walker. The collection is dedicated to "The Family at Home, The Family at Livingston, The Family at Large, and especially to our Young."

Bambara imagined *Tales and Stories* similar to the way that Jordan envisioned *Soulscript*: as a corrective to the lies children are exposed to in "traditional textbooks," that often reflected the values of a white supremacist society and offered few life lessons for Black children. She writes that "my students at Livingston College in New Jersey have done a change up on the nursery things so that our children can get something

---

[83] Bambara, "Interview with Tate," 22.
[84] Bambara, *Deep Sightings*, 231.
[85] At Doubleday, Bambara worked with up-and-coming assistant editor Cheryl Chisholm (Holmes 48). As they worked on the book, Chisholm was "blindsided by the structured racism she encountered at the publishing company," especially the copyeditors mistakenly "correcting" Bambara's use of Black language (Holmes 49).

for real out of the reading."[86] She describes it as a collection of "kitchen table wisdom" that honors the knowledge shared in Black families and communities through oral storytelling traditions. As Bambara notes in the introduction, these stories were designed to "instruct" and "teach" while entertaining. For instance, "The Three Little Panthers," co-authored by Bambara and her student Geneva Powell, uses the story of an assignment to teach children to recognize the thinly veiled racism that may present in the guise of benevolent integration. In their fable, a cunning teacher sends three little panthers to live in the suburbs, where they are greeted with a specious welcome. It begins: "Once upon a time, there were Three Little Panthers. They attended Freedom School, not to learn how to make their fortune, but to learn how to survive in this world."[87] Just as the Freedom Schools of the 1960s sought to address the racist omissions in mainstream textbooks and curricula, so too did *Tales and Stories*.

While the book wasn't in print for very long, it was praised by critics as "a commanding and never ambiguous assemblage that provokes introspective reading and encourages creative writing."[88] And what Bambara valued most about *Tales and Stories* was "that my students are in it."[89] Indeed, were it not for these students and her City College and Rutgers-Livingston classrooms, we would not have such important collections today.

Editing as Feminist Praxis

Considered together, Jordan's and Bambara's work suggests that publishing their students' writing in the collective format of an anthology was a form of activism that aimed to empower marginalized students and address absences in mainstream media, publishing, and curricula. In contrast to the top-down construction of traditional anthologies, which are typically produced for but not by students in the classroom, Jordan and Bambara acted on a conviction that authorship—the power to move people through language—is widely distributed despite cultural institutions that privilege the voices of a narrow, white male elite. The authors they worked with were low-income, women with families to support, people of color, and students (some as young as nine) and the editorial labor that went into these collections ranged from convincing publishers that these authors had something important to say to convincing the authors themselves. As educator-editors, they put in countless uncompensated hours corresponding with publishers, negotiating contracts, and organizing publicity events because they understood the multifaceted impact these anthologies could make in people's lives. This publishing pedagogy helped students understand the power of their

---

[86] Toni Cade Bambara, *Tales and Stories for Black Folks* (Garden City: Zenith Books, 1971), 124.
[87] Toni Cade Bambara and Geneva Powell, "The Three Little Panthers," in *Tales and Stories for Black Folks*, ed. Toni Cade Bambara (Garden City: Zenith Books, 1971), 140.
[88] "Tales and Stories for Black Folks, eds. Toni Cade Bambara," *Kirkus Review*, January 1, 1971.
[89] Bambara, *Deep Sightings*, 230.

voices; address gaps in the literary, educational, and cultural record; share survival strategies across the partitioning walls of classrooms and institutions; and call out to collectives of readers who had been ignored by publishers. Considered together, their work demonstrates the centrality of the classroom not only for the dissemination of literary anthologies, but also for their production.

For both Bambara and Jordan, these early experiences led to a lifetime of editorial activism. For example, in 1975, when Bambara and Leah Wise were tasked with editing a special issue of the magazine *Southern Exposure* titled "Southern Black Utterances Today," Bambara included the writing of students from Atlanta's local Frederick Douglass High School alongside the work of established authors like Addison Gayle and Beverly Guy Sheftall.[90] In addition, Bambara regularly chaired panels like "Dealing with Major Publishers" which "focused on strategies for writers to publish their work through mainstream presses, alternative publishers, and self-publishing."[91] Given the racism Bambara experienced throughout every stage of the publishing process—such as copyeditors changing her Black English to standard written English—Bambara implored Black women writers not to outsource publishing decisions to executives, but to get involved in the process: "Writers need to deglamorize publishing and study marketing, distributing, printing—the entire process including bookbinding."[92] Similarly, Jordan advised aspiring writers that being an author involved not only writing but "public performance, publication, and media appearances."[93] These, she argued, "are natural and necessary steps to the acquirement of power through language."[94]

For the remainder of their lives, both writers continued developing innovative teaching practices informed by their editorial activism. While term papers remained the norm across much of higher education, Jordan and Bambara continued to publish their students' writing, both in anthologies and other formats. "Do not write term papers for me," Bambara often told students, "Make sure they are useful for somebody else as well." She would suggest forms such as an individual or collaborative annotated bibliography, performance art, a short story (for radio or TV), a magazine, puppet theater, a street theater performance, a slide show, or a picture book. The one requirement was that it "can be shared with others."[95] Similarly, many of Jordan's courses concluded with collaborative, public projects such as a "Wrath Rally" and letter-writing campaign against poverty in Biafra, organized by students in her Upward Bound Class and dramatic radio productions on children's welfare and racial justice in South Central Los Angeles. In her Poetry for the People program at the University of California, Berkeley in the 1990s, Jordan trained hundreds of students to write,

---

[90] Holmes, *A Joyous Revolt*, 70 and *Southern Exposure* 3.1, "Southern Black Utterances Today," Chapel Hill: Institute of Southern Studies, 1975, 2–3.
[91] Holmes, *Revolt*, 110.
[92] Bambara, "Interview with Tate," 38.
[93] L. Muller, ed., *June Jordan's Poetry for the People: A Revolutionary Blueprint* (New York: Routledge, 1995), 8. What's quoted here is June Jordan's introduction, pp. 1–9.
[94] Ibid.
[95] Holmes, "Lessons in Boldness," 157 & Bambara, *Deep Sightings*, 231.

publish, and perform their poetry and to become educators who would go out into community centers, homeless shelters, K-12 schools, and churches to teach others to write and publish poetry, resulting in anthologies such as *Poetry in a Time of Genocide* (1993) and *Whose Country Is This, Anyway* (1995). Working with college-age students and the resources of Berkeley's campus, Jordan involved students to a far greater extent in the publication process: editing, proofing, binding, budgeting, distribution, and marketing. One semester, they published *A Revolutionary Blueprint*, a collection of reading lists, syllabi, poetry, and activities that turned the lessons of Poetry for the People into a "how to guide" for others interested in democratizing poetry. Reflecting on a course that concluded with a collaboratively authored anthology, Jordan notes that "the class was producing its own literature: A literature reflecting the ideas and dreams and memories of the actual young Americans at work."[96].

---

[96] Jordan, "Merit Review Statement."

14

Hybrid Scholarly Publishing Models in a Digital Age

Krystyna Michael, Jojo Karlin, and Matthew K. Gold

Should one want to learn more about the history of the book, Amaranth Borsuk's *The Book*, published in 2018 by MIT Press as part of its Essential Knowledge series, would be a reasonable place to start.[1] Navigating to the Amazon website to make a purchase, the reader is confronted with a choice of formats: paperback; Kindle ebook; audiobook. What, one might wonder, are the differences between these formats? Varying in material instantiation and presenting dissimilar reading experiences, to what extent do they represent the same book object? For years, scholars have argued that the publication of books on digital platforms offered the opportunity not just to present the same work in different forms, but also to move beyond the materialities of the printed book in inventive ways—essentially creating connected, but productively different, experiences for the reader.

More often than not, however, such hopes for the creative possibilities of digital publishing have been disappointing. Johanna Drucker, for instance, has argued that skeuomorphic design—a term used in media theory to explain how new technologies often include design cues that mimic the look and feel of older technologies (such as the use of folder icons on computers to organize files)—of eBooks—and even the term "eBooks" itself—too closely ties digital publications to print antecedents of the book.[2] She characterizes these platforms as "charged by a need to acknowledge the historical priority of books and to invoke a link between their established cultural identity and these electronic surrogates."[3] In Drucker's estimation, early eBooks did not fulfill their ambition to move beyond the traditional paper-based book because of their drive to maintain a connection to the reading experience and cultural authority of the

---

[1] Amaranth Borsuk, *The Book* (Cambridge, MA: MIT Press, 2018).
[2] Johanna Drucker, "The Virtual Codex from Page Space to E-space." Syracuse University, History of the Book Seminar, April 25, 2003. Presentation. www.philobiblon.com, www.philobiblon.com/drucker/. Skeuomorphs, design features that imitate another object with a similar use like the envelope that represents electronic mail, are described in the context of virtuality in N. Katherine Hayles's *How We Became Posthuman* (University of Chicago Press, 1999).
[3] Drucker, "The Virtual Codex."

conventional book form. Thus, eBooks failed to realize the novel modes of reading and thinking afforded by the web; Drucker calls for new models of digital texts that take advantage of the web's ability to assemble "textual, visual, graphic, navigational, and multimedia artifacts that are geographically dispersed in their original form" in one reading experience and to exploit the social aspects of new media to foster the "creation of an inter-subjective, social space of shared use and exchange."[4]

This tension between books as printed objects and books as digital experiences animates ongoing discussions of the present state and future possibilities of digital publishing. In this essay, we will explore how recent digital publishing platforms aim to fulfill Drucker's call for an electronic book platform that reimagines reading, but we will also complicate the idea that digital books supersede or move beyond printed books in teleological ways. In place of a model that considers print and digital publishing as inherently separate processes, and that places digital publishing as the inevitable evolutionary endpoint of the codex form, we propose—building on work done by the Manifold team—"hybrid publishing" as a model that involves concurrent print and digital editorial and publication processes. In fact, we will show that in important respects, hybrid publishing can help us reimagine the relations between print and digital publishing by aligning pre-production processes that reduce the extent to which print and digital book objects need to be produced independently. In so doing, we draw upon recent work by Jacqueline Wernimont and Elizabeth Losh that uses the model of intra-action and distributed agency to explore how the method of production—be it print or digital—acts on, or produces, new modes of reading and new readers.[5] We are also extending Jessica Brantley's insights into how the design of the codex form and the design of digital reading interfaces help determine reading practices.

In *The Book*, Amaranth Borsuk traces the standard progression of print culture from the ancient and medieval modes of distributing text through tablets and scrolls, in which the object of the text was singular, unique, and primary, to modern modes of the codex and the eBook in which the text is separated from its object, and the object is multiple, standardized, and seemingly contingent. Borsuk's account of this evolution helps us to think through the ways that "content does not simply necessitate its form, but rather writing develops alongside, influences, and is influenced by the technological supports that facilitate its distribution."[6] Specifically, in the context of hybrid publishing, we are interested in the changes Borsuk lays out that different modes of distribution wrought on the book, and on reading, as an event. Ancient and medieval scrolls were largely public objects, often shared, collaboratively annotated, and meant to be read out loud and, especially in the case of scrolls, in the order they were written. Codex books became private items, rather than shared objects

---

[4] Ibid.
[5] Jacqueline Wernimont and Elizabeth Losh, eds., *Bodies of Information: Intersectional Feminism and Digital Humanities* (Minneapolis: University of Minnesota Press, 2018). Available in a Manifold edition at https://dhdebates.gc.cuny.edu/projects/bodies-of-information.
[6] Borsuk, *The Book*, 26.

experienced publicly.[7] In the current day, hybrid modes of publishing create a kind of digital commonplace book that facilitates reading that is both highly personal—like the codex because it is remixable and can be navigated in different ways—and at the same time public, singular, and unique—like the ancient and medieval text, since there is one object that is read and annotated by multiple users. Hybrid publishing thus takes us beyond debates about the primacy or advantages of digital books or printed books because it gives us a new way to think about the historical progression whereby the digital version of the book "exceeds" the print version. Hybrid publishing instead offers an opportunity to rethink the relationship between different forms of the book. If the ancient and medieval modes of producing texts on tablets and scrolls gave primacy to the book as object, and the mass-produced codex and early forms of digital publishing treated the text as a disembodied idea that could be presented in a variety of distinct formats, hybrid publishing suggests that print and digital versions of the text can coexist and can be produced concurrently, foregrounding the differential experience of readers across varying forms. The book, then, as experienced in print and as digital object, becomes hybridized and multiplied, both connected to material form and disassociated from it, and the reader is free to engage with either or both for different ends. As the book proliferates across forms and combinations, we will show how design emerges as paramount to holding the digital object together as an object of consideration.

Situating Book History in Digital Publishing

Multiple recent movements in literary scholarship—the archival turn, new formalism, and new materialism—point to a contemporary academic refiguring of our understanding of materiality. Connecting this work to book history, "bookishness" (as explored by Jessica Pressman) can be seen to lie less in objects than in the nexus of objects and relations around a text or set of texts.[8] With Digital Humanities, Critical University Studies, and Critical Infrastructure Studies, and in connection with scholars such as Bruno Latour, Alain Badiou, Donna Haraway, Jane Bennett, and Sara Ahmed, we recognize that the connections between ideas and the structures that support those connections are as pertinent and co-productive as the ideas themselves. For our purposes, we consider what the philosophical and practical trend toward network consciousness means for "print culture," as Matthew G. Kirschenbaum has recently explored with his work on bibliologistics—the connection of book objects to the digital and material infrastructures and logistical systems that support their creation, production, and dissemination.[9] The book, in such work, appears as a nexus

---

[7] See Borsuk, *The Book*, 61, 88.
[8] Jessica Pressman, *Bookishness: Loving Books in a Digital Age* (New York: Columbia University Press, 2020).
[9] Matthew Kirschenbaum, "Bibliologistics: The Nature of Books Now, or a Memorable Fancy," *Post 45* (April 8, 2020), post45.org/2020/04/bibliologistics-the-nature-of-books-now-or-a-memorable-fancy/. Accessed July 10, 2020.

of information connected to a large, networked supply chain, rather than as a single object or end point. In this view, as Kirschenbaum argues, an understanding of books in the present moment must take into account the ecological, economic, and logistical traces that books leave as they move through the processes of creation, production, and distribution.

If books are now hyperlinked nexuses of information, as well as local repositories of resources, the notion of the book as a unit becomes unstable, its binding loosened. The book object becomes inflected with questions of logistics, aesthetics, and processes. What organization of digital materials can generate the same sense of cohesion and stability as the bound physical book? What constitutes the sameness of a text in separate forms, and what constitutes a separation of forms?

While the shift to digital involves a transition from physical paper objects to electronic objects, the shift to new platforms necessarily involves a reconception of the central object of the digital book. New platforms, shared through electronic distribution, can increase the reach of the content with greater flexibility. A print book circulates through bookstores, library systems, and personal libraries. With digital publishing, the continuity of the object shifts—the solidity of the object—becomes a matter of the files served up through different devices. Publishers approaching books with a production-oriented understanding of the complexities of print and the means of digital publication must grapple with the ways a digital book object can extend itself with hypertext and data storage without losing the sense of the persistent technology of the book. While earlier iterations of digital books attempted to achieve this stability through designs that mimicked the appearance of their physical counterparts, more recent forays into digital publishing offer designs that lend visual coherence while capitalizing on the affordances of the web. As the concept of a digital book becomes more culturally accepted, new models attempt to embrace the book across its print and digital forms.

Models of Hybrid Publishing

Over the past few decades, academic publishers have explored a range of models for publishing digital content in connection with a print book. Often, the printed text is completely separate from the digital publication. In some cases, the digital publication acts as a supplemental marketing site for the printed book; it lacks the text of the book itself, but instead contains a wide array of ancillary materials such as archival images, interview transcripts, publicity materials about the text, and an author blog. In essence, such sites serve as marketing vehicles for the printed text and do not attempt to replicate the content of the print text in explicit ways. Instead, the companion website becomes a space for sharing materials that could not fit easily in the book itself due to a range of factors, including the cost of illustrations.

Many projects published with the Scalar platform, which focuses on the presentation of multimodal narrative that can be explored in nonlinear fashion, take this approach. Scalar is a project of the Alliance for Networking Visual Culture, which is based at the

University of Southern California. The website for Scalar emphasizes a disconnection with print, describing the platform as a publishing system that is "designed to make it easy for authors to write long-form, born-digital scholarship online." Projects published with Scalar, such as Matthew Delmont's "The Nicest Kids in Town," are described as "digital companions" to printed texts. In this case, the printed version of Delmont's book was published by the University of California Press in 2012.[10] On the Scalar site, visitors can find a range of ancillary archival materials that were not included in the printed book, such as images, videos, memorabilia, and newspaper clippings. Delmont uses Scalar to help the reader explore nonlinear paths through these materials, moving from a photograph of a 1967 keynote address by Martin Luther King, Jr. at the National Association of Radio and Television Announcers Convention to an audio recording of Chuck Berry singing "Sweet Little Sixteen," all placed alongside explanatory text.

Another digital companion project is "Surfacing," a multimodal website created by Nicole Starosielski, Erik Loyer, and Shane Brennan to accompany and extend Starosielski's print book, *The Undersea Network*.[11] In "Surfacing," the authors provide a creative experience that leads readers through some of the major themes of the monograph, though they do so through interactive aural and visual elements that demonstrate some of the argumentative points of the book. A user beginning to explore "Surfacing," for example, might start on a photo of an urban space in Katong, Singapore; upon zooming out with the mouse, the user begins to see a world map of connected network cables, showing how the infrastructure that undergirds the global internet is composed of physical cables that run through particular social and political environments. This serves as a largely nontextual expansion of the points made in *The Undersea Network*, one that takes advantage of the experiential nature of the web to make an argument.

In other cases, digital publications exist without a print counterpart. Many digital humanities projects fit this model, as scholars attempt to move away from text-based arguments and the limitations of print and instead explore the possibilities of creating scholarly arguments through nontextual forms. As Stephen Ramsay and Geoffrey Rockwell argue in "Developing Things: Notes toward an Epistemology of Building in the Digital Humanities," digital humanities scholars "have turned to building, hacking, and coding as part of their normal research activity"; they "build digital libraries, engage in 'deep encoding' of literary texts, create 3-D models of Roman ruins, generate charts and graphs of linguistic phenomena, develop instructional applications, and even (in the most problematic case) write software to make the general task of scholarship easier for other scholars."[12] Increasingly, scholars creating digital projects

---

[10] Matthew F. Delmont, *The Nicest Kids in Town: American Bandstand, Rock "n" Roll, and the Struggle for Civil Rights in 1950s Philadelphia* (Berkeley: University of California Press, 2012). The website companion project for *The Nicest Kids in Town* is http://nicestkids.com.

[11] Nicole Starosielski, *The Undersea Network* (Durham: Duke University Press, 2015). The "Surfacing" project is at http://www.surfacing.in/.

[12] Stephen Ramsay and Geoffrey Rockwell, "Developing Things: Notes toward an Epistemology of Building in the Digital Humanities," in *Debates in the Digital Humanities*, eds. Matthew K. Gold (Minneapolis: University of Minnesota Press, 2012), 75–84.

attempt to have them count toward tenure and promotion processes in the academy, arguing that scholarly argument itself is not restricted to textual forms. In response, scholarly organizations such as the Modern Language Association, the American Historical Association, and the Association for Computers and the Humanities have released guidelines aimed at helping scholars evaluate digital projects for tenure and promotion.

The Association of University Presses has recently created a website titled "Ask UP" that seeks to "explain how university presses work."[13] On a page titled "The Lifecycle of a Book," the print publication workflow is described in detail, with no mention whatsoever of the role a digital publication can play in the process. And on a supplementary page, "What Is Digital Publishing," the site points out that digital publishing is "not any one thing," but then continues on to say that "One working definition is that digital publishing is the hosting and dissemination of a project entirely in the digital sphere." Digital publishing, in this view, is based on the model of the digital project that is completely separated from any print artifact. The possibility of a hybrid publication, one that results in both print and digital artifacts, is not even considered as a possibility.

By contrast to these models of digital publishing, we focus in this essay on "hybrid publishing," the creation of a combined stream of print and digital texts that sees these elements as part of a unified publishing process. As an example of hybrid publishing, we focus on Manifold, a publishing platform collaboratively created by the University of Minnesota Press, The CUNY Graduate Center Digital Scholarship Lab, and Cast Iron Coding, and supported by grants from The Andrew W. Mellon Foundation and the National Endowment for the Humanities. Manifold was designed as a specific alternative to the digital publishing models listed above; neither a supplemental companion website nor a digital project without a print counterpart, a Manifold publication is designed to present the text of a printed book in augmented digital form.

One example of the hybrid nature of Manifold is its starting point. Manifold is not an authoring platform, such as WordPress. Instead, Manifold begins with the assumption that a text has been authored elsewhere (i.e., through the editorial and production systems of a university press) and that it can afterward be "ingested" into Manifold. While a number of types of files can be ingested, including Google Docs, Microsoft Word Docs, HTML files, and markdown files, many presses ingest ePub files into their Manifold installations. The ePub—an XML-based format developed by the International Digital Publishing Forum—represents the common endpoint of a university press editorial and production process; it is created by the Press once those other processes are finalized, after which the ePub file is then sent off to the printer to create printed books—or, in this case, sent both to the printer to create a printed text and to Manifold to create a digital publication. In Manifold, the digital publication can be further enhanced with video, image, and interactive resource layers and can be

---

[13] Association of University Presses, *Ask UP: Authors Seeking Knowledge from University Presses* https://ask.up.hcommons.org/. Accessed October 26, 2021.

connected to social networks of readers and commenters. This workflow allows digital and print publications to begin with the same base layer of text, and for authors and publishers to conceive of the digital version as an organic part of the printed book, not a separate entity. By placing the beginning of Manifold at the end of the editorial and production workflow, the "fork" between a digital and print publication occurs after the text has been completed.

The experience of reading a publication on Manifold is meant to mirror the process of reading other content on the web, completing the transition of print artifact to web form and creating a hybrid publication between them. Many pieces of online publishing software use code from the Readium project to display the content of ePubs. Like the skeuomorphic projects described in the introduction to this essay, the user interface of Readium includes several visual features that attempt to replicate the experience of reading a print book, such as paginating content, creating an animated "page flip," and producing the overall appearance of a printed page on the web. With a goal of creating a web-friendly reading experience that maximizes user customization and focuses on "flowable content"—content that could be easily resized so as to be as readable on a mobile phone as it might be on a desktop—the Manifold development team, by contrast, decided to build its own reader and to embrace the web-based idea of the vertical page scroll instead of an animated page flip. In essence, Manifold, as a piece of technology, takes its visual and performative cues from the web browser rather than the printed page. This opens up an entirely new range of possibilities we will explore below for how the text is presented to readers and for ways resources like other texts, images, and websites can be presented to the reader and combined alongside the primary text.

In Focus: The Manifold Platform as a Hybrid Publishing Platform

As a hybrid publishing platform, Manifold operates in different ways for different types of publishers. For instance, when used by a university press such as the University of Minnesota Press, Manifold is administered by a small number of specialized editors who publish approved texts on it. The University of Minnesota Press indeed makes available a large number of published texts on an open-access basis. Minnesota has also experimented with the creation of iterative or in-progress publishing by which authors begin publishing on Manifold *before* the Press has put a text through an editorial or production process. This enables authors to begin to build communities of readers around their texts before the Press has officially published the text. Instead of the published text functioning as the static and finalized end point to the writing process, and the object to which its readers respond, iterative publishing allows the readers to become part of the writing process itself by offering feedback and comments while the text itself is still in the process of creation.

By contrast, Manifold is used very differently at the City University of New York (CUNY), where the CUNY Graduate Center hosts an installation for the entire twenty-five-campus system. While Manifold was originally designed for use in a press setting, users began applying it to classroom contexts, so Manifold responded by developing teaching-specific features and interfaces. The example of CUNY's instance points to the interplay between design, infrastructure, and modes of reading and writing with which we began this essay. Manifold's design inspired uses its developers had not originally conceived. Accordingly, at CUNY, Manifold operates as a more loosely organized community platform; faculty members and students are given permission to publish texts without needing to seek approval. This allows for direct publication without the intervention of an editorial or production process, thus enabling the quick and polished publication of hybrid texts such as custom course readers, and student and faculty work.

Manifold's design invites these multiple uses and this flexible and responsive development process. The main unit of organization in a Manifold instance is the project. A Manifold project consists of a homepage that contains one or more texts. The homepage is organized into content blocks that run horizontally across the page and are stacked one on top of the other. Every project has at least one content block on its homepage that appears at the top; this is called the "hero block" and generally includes the project's title, authorial or editorial information, a brief description, and an identifying cover image and background image. The hero block can also include links and "calls to action," such as buttons labeled "Start Reading," that bring the reader into the text at various points such as the first page or a table of contents. Below the hero block, the authors and editors have a wide variety of choices of content blocks that can be arranged in different configurations to suit a project's needs. These include a social media block that displays tweets about the project, a live table of contents, a texts section for projects with multiple texts, and a block where text can be added to explain more about the project. The Manifold project homepage is thus flexible enough to adapt to different publishing contexts but consistent and coherent enough to provide the reader with a sense of the project as a discrete entity and to orient the reader toward the text itself. The fact that the homepage is modular and customizable, but also scrollable, is one of the major elements that distinguishes Manifold as a digital reader from both previous readers that strove to resemble a print book and its contemporary alternatives that are organized like a website, often placing different types of data or materials on different pages. Manifold's scrollable, modular project homepage lends the project coherence even as it incorporates various kinds of media into one page.

Case Studies: Hybrid Publishing in Action

Hybrid publishing opens up new possibilities for books while maintaining ties to print publishing practices that have defined the modern book trade. Looking at key examples across a range of publication types, we aim to show in this section how publishers are producing digital book projects that open up new ways of presenting content, interacting with readers, and sharing resources related to texts. While we draw our examples primarily from Manifold, it is but one of many platforms (other prominent examples include Scalar, PubPub, Fulcrum, and PressBooks) currently used by academic publishers to create digital publications that may accompany printed books. Our examples focus on Manifold as the platform most invested in hybrid publishing as a concept, and span multiple types of publications used for various ends including the publication of research, teaching materials, archival materials, public domain texts, conference proceedings, academic journals, student writing, and a variety of handbooks and guides. In each case, hybrid publication processes allow for the creation of both print and digital manifestations of the work.

Publishing Digital Monographs

The history of Manifold as a platform serves as a case study that illustrates our understanding of the role hybrid publishing plays in the future of the scholarly monograph. In 2014, the Andrew W. Mellon Foundation began to solicit grants from members of the Association of University Presses for projects centered around the future of the digital monograph. As Donald Waters, then senior program officer for Scholarly Communications at Mellon, described the situation in his essay "Monograph Publishing in the Digital Age," the Mellon Foundation did not take the continued production of scholarship in print-based form as a given; instead, it noted that "the monograph is increasingly being challenged as a viable component of systems of scholarly communications" and questioned "what other genres are needed to disseminate knowledge in the humanities."[14] As a major funder of both humanities scholarship and digital humanities platforms, Mellon was well-positioned to help university presses and, by extension the academy, think through the future of scholarly book publishing.

Perhaps unsurprisingly, a number of university press grantees sought to find continuities between print and digital publishing rather than create different publication streams. As detailed above, Manifold was designed to take an ePub—the set of files a Press produces at the end of the editorial and production processes and sends off to printers to produce print books—as the starting point for Manifold. This allows the Press to finalize all editorial and production work before sending it off, on the one hand, to a printer to create printed books and, on the other, to Manifold to create digital versions of the text.

Manifold itself is modeled on an earlier project—the first edition of *Debates in the Digital Humanities*, edited by Matthew K. Gold and published by the University of Minnesota Press in 2012. After the print publication of the book, Cast Iron Coding and the CUNY Graduate Center Digital Scholarship Lab, in partnership with the University of Minnesota Press, worked together to create an innovative open-access interactive webtext version for the book. The original site included some of the features that are now part of Manifold, such as comments and highlights; the entire series now

---

[14] Donald Waters, "Monograph Publishing in the Digital Age," *The Andrew W. Mellon Foundation* (July 2016), https://mellon.org/shared-experiences-blog/monograph-publishing-digital-age/. Accessed October 26, 2021.

appears on an open-access basis in Manifold.[15] It includes triannual volumes such as *Debates in the Digital Humanities 2016* and *Debates in the Digital Humanities 2019*, as well as special volumes such as *Bodies of Information: Intersectional Feminism and Digital Humanities, Making Things and Drawing Boundaries: Experiments in the Digital Humanities,* and *The Digital Black Atlantic*. Drawing upon new Manifold features that allow project access to be restricted and to create private reading groups around texts, the platform is now being used to conduct peer-to-peer reviews of new volumes, a defining feature of the series.

One of the strongest examples of the hybrid publishing model being used for digital monographs is *Metagaming: Playing, Competing, Spectating, Cheating, Trading, Making, and Breaking Videogames*.[16] Published in print by the University of Minnesota Press in 2017, *Metagaming* was simultaneously released in print and in digital, open access form on the press's Manifold instance. The text of *Metagaming* explores the sensory and political economies of videogames, and its Manifold version illustrates the capacity of a digital text to bring together the multimedia artifacts such as images, videos, and links that the text engages with into the reading experience itself. Readers can, for instance, watch the trailer for a video game that is discussed in the text without leaving the browser window. Readers can download playable games from the digital book project, enabling them to test out some of the games discussed in the book. Readers experience this multimodal text in a community of other readers in two respects. First, each chapter bears the traces of previous readers in the form of highlights and annotations, and second, the homepage of the Manifold text pulls in and displays thousands of Tweets that use the #metagaming hashtag, demonstrating and providing entry into the text's active social life. *Metagaming* is a powerful example of the possibilities of hybrid publishing because it is at once a successful print monograph and simultaneously an active, shared, networked digital text that harnesses the power of the internet and its networks to fundamentally change the shape of the book.

Publishing "Iterative" Scholarship

Hybrid publishing ensures that print publication and digital publication don't have to be separate processes, but it also makes it possible to make the publication process itself more transparent. Hybrid publishing opens up the publication process to the public at earlier stages of development through iterative versioning. *The Lab Book* is one of several publications under contract to be produced in print with the University of Minnesota Press that is using Manifold to publish chapter drafts alongside other materials in process such as the notes, interviews, and sections that will go into the chapters.[17] This model lays bare the writing process and opens up the possibility of

---

[15] *Debates in the Digital Humanities*, http://dhdebates.gc.cuny.edu. Accessed October 26, 2021.
[16] Stephanie Boluk and Patrick LeMeiux, *Metagaming: Playing, Competing, Spectating, Cheating, Trading, Making, and Breaking Videogames* (Minneapolis: University of Minnesota Press, 2017). See also http://manifold.umn.edu/projects/metagaming.
[17] Darren Wershler, Lori Emerson, and Jussi Parikka, *The Lab Book: Situated Practices in Media Studies*, http://manifold.umn.edu/projects/the-lab-book. Accessed October 26, 2021.

engaging readers and receiving feedback prior to publication, thus enriching the text. It also incorporates the digital version into not just the final product, but also the process of publication.

Other book projects that are developing over time include *Going the Rounds*, which shows how hybrid texts can incorporate archival materials and digital humanities projects into both the finished published text and its conception and development.[18] *Going the Rounds* emerged out of a digital humanities project *Viral Texts*, which studies the circuits of distribution of nineteenth-century newspaper texts that "went viral" by virtue of the lax copyright laws of the period that allowed publishers to freely reprint passages of text in many different venues across the nation.[19] The authors of this collaborative project are using Manifold to publish draft chapters and archival materials, and to integrate the digital humanities methods the project draws on such as text mining, geospatial analysis, and network analysis directly into the digital version of the text itself.

Publishing Open Educational Resources and Classroom Projects

Hybrid publishing has a place not only among scholarly publishers but also within the classroom, where a range of factors—drives to reduce textbook costs; the rise of the student-centered classroom; and student publishing as a course outcome—have helped create a rich ground for digital publishing. In recent years, concern has grown about the debilitating amounts of student debt that college students walk away with after finishing their degrees. As a significant contributor to student debt, the high cost of textbooks has come under scrutiny, and the movement to build Open Educational Resources (OER) has grown. Offering the opportunity for students to read assigned materials free of cost, OER have been supported by multiple state and federal initiatives aimed at reducing student debt. Educators and librarians have embraced the OER movement; with the move to distance learning during the Covid-19 pandemic, online resources for students have become even more important, and hybrid models of publishing educational materials make new approaches and projects in the classroom possible. Enforced distance and the capsized economy make educators, publishers, and librarians that much more aware of the need for readily distributable digital resources. As scholars work from home, many see the limitations of physical resources, and as libraries hasten digitization in order to reduce in-person contact, both are recognizing the advantages of open licenses for digital dissemination. While the scale of conversion is difficult to measure, let alone predict, the changes wrought by remote learning will likely highlight advantages to a flexible, hybrid publishing model.

---

[18] Ryan Cordell, David A. Smith, Abby Mullen, and Jonathan D. Fitzgerald, *Going the Rounds: Virality in Nineteenth-Century American Newspapers*, http://manifold.umn.edu/project/going-the-rounds. Accessed October 26, 2021.

[19] Ryan Cordell and David Smith, *Viral Texts: Mapping Networks of Reprinting in 19th-Century Newspapers and Magazines* (2017), http://viraltexts.org. Accessed October 26, 2021.

Hybrid Classroom Texts

Hybrid approaches to publishing course texts open up the possibility of allowing students to benefit both from engagement with a physical print version and from an interactive digital copy. A major benefit to students of hybrid publishing is the possibility of developing workflows for the production of academic materials that incorporate accessibility from the start. The University of Washington Libraries and Press is one of several publishers that are using Manifold for OER publication, and they have focused much of their work toward building the production of an accessible version of the text into its workflow instead of adding accessibility concerns to the digital text as an afterthought. The University of Washington's Accessible Technology Services collaborated with the Manifold team to conduct a thorough review of Manifold's front and back ends.[20] The result of this ongoing collaboration is that new tools are tested as they are developed and accessibility is now a core principle in Manifold's development.

Another concern that hybrid publishing of student texts helps to address in the literature classroom is the quality and consistency of the editions students read, particularly of public domain texts that tend to have many editions of varying quality on the market. As book history scholar Robert Darnton has shown, piracy and knock offs have long been adjacent to the mutations of publishing.[21] In the contemporary framework, with the fast replication and distribution of the internet, students can find themselves in possession of poorly edited copies of public domain class texts. To ensure the integrity of texts available to students, Paul Hebert, Christina Katapodis, and Jason Nielsen—all graduate student adjunct instructors at CUNY—have developed "CUNY Student Editions," a set of standard American Literature texts for common reading and annotating on CUNY's instance of Manifold. Understanding the hybrid experience of contemporary classrooms, these instructors use the Manifold text as a shared space for reference and annotation alongside the variegated print editions that many students purchase. With a single, free, online edition, instructors can draw students together around a single version of the text with the assurance that it reflects a past version of record—especially important in a university system like CUNY, where the majority of students come from families with a combined income of less than $30,000 a year in one of the most expensive cities in the world.[22] The common digital text also provides the impetus for a teachable discussion of publication history. These editions are not meant to replace the paper copies students may purchase or borrow from a library, but instead provide a common searchable text for class discussion and collaborative annotation.

---

[20] Elizabeth Bedford, "'Open for Whom?': Accessibility and Open Access," *UW Libraries Blog* (October 22, 2019), sites.uw.edu/libstrat/2019/10/22/open-for-whom-accessibility-and-open-access/. Accessed October 26, 2021.

[21] It is worth noting that the economic and technical models of production and distribution of print and digital books are very different. The relative value a text or digital file holds is bound in cultural, legal, and moral contexts. We mention the adjacency to acknowledge the network of these forces outside the book container. For more on this, see Camarero et al. (2014) and Goertzen (2017).

[22] "CUNY Students Go for the Value," *CUNY Matters* (November 6, 2015), http://www1.cuny.edu/mu/forum/2015/11/06/cuny-students-go-for-the-value/. Accessed October 26, 2021.

In a similar vein, the University of Washington's edition of George Eliot's *The Mill on the Floss* provides students with a common digital text that acts as a corollary to the print version, but adds the element of teaching digital editing.[23] In an advanced English course taught by Professor Jesse Oak Taylor, students read their own print editions of the text and collaborated to produce a Manifold "Anthropocene Edition" with a critical introduction, annotations, suggestions for further reading, and embedded video and text resource collections. Students thus participated in producing the knowledge of the course and created a text with which future classes can contribute and engage, both at the University of Washington and at other institutions. Since students read their own print versions, but collaborated on the digital text, this activity, made possible by the hybrid model of publishing, helped to promote critical thinking about what constitutes a text, and how we think between the print and the digital in a way that choosing either print or digital materials would not.

Hybrid publishing holds the promise of shaking up industry norms surrounding the production of textbooks and other educational materials. *The American Yawp*, a massively collaborative open US History textbook, took a scholar-led approach to editing.[24] Editors Joseph L. Locke and Ben Wright brought together more than 300 American history and culture scholars to collaboratively build a history of the United States using the WordPress publishing platform. Subsequently, Stanford University Press picked up the project, publishing it under its digital projects imprint and producing print copies. Despite beginning as a digital project, *The American Yawp* follows a traditional peer-review process. This example short-circuits the traditional, top-down models of textbook development and publishing with a digital model that incorporates new modes of collaboration that incorporate more voices. It also reverses the usual relationship of print and digital text and illustrates new possibilities and workflows for the hybrid publishing of educational materials.

Hybrid Student and Community OER Projects

Increasingly, instructors are using digital platforms for projects that ask students to produce knowledge in their field as a means to sharpen digital literacy skills alongside course content. Hybrid models of publishing lend themselves to student-driven projects surrounding questions about the status and boundaries of particular texts and the printed word more generally.

Hybrid models of publishing hold great potential for the recovery of out-of-print materials. *The Negro and the Nation*, a recovery project hosted on CUNY's instance

---

[23] George Eliot, *The Mill on the Floss: An Anthropocene Edition*, ed. Megan Butler et al., http://uw.manifoldapp.org/projects/the-mill-on-the-floss. Accessed October 26, 2021.

[24] Joseph L. Locke and Ben Wright, *The American Yawp: A Massively Collaborative Open U.S. History Textbook*, Vol. 1: *To 1877* (Stanford: Stanford University Press, 2019), http://www.americanyawp.org. Accessed October 17, 2020. See also Scott McLemee, "Interview with Editors of *The American Yawp*, a Free History Textbook Published Online," *Inside Higher Ed* (March 11, 2015), https://www.insidehighered.com/views/2015/03/11/interview-editors-american-yawp-free-history-textbook-published-online. Accessed October 26, 2021.

of Manifold, is an interactive, media-rich digital version of a long-neglected text.[25] The project was developed as a course-based, student-focused collaborative project through which students collected and embedded supplementary materials that frame this primary text in different approaches to American Studies. *The Negro and the Nation* brings a text that is no longer in print back in circulation by digitizing it, fosters student engagement in the editorial process, and, because users can access images and download an ePub of the original, serves as an example of how hybrid texts can revive out-of-print texts by pointing back to the original print version.

Hybrid publishing also presents opportunities for students and community users to think critically about the status of a digital version by encouraging engagement with its otherwise discrete structures. An example of a hybrid project that incorporates the producer of the text into the means of production is *City Amplified*, a project on the CUNY instance of Manifold.[26] *City Amplified* represents a collaboration with an institution at the Graduate Center, The Center for the Humanities, which already produces a full catalog of short-run print publications including the successful chapbook series Lost and Found. As part of a public seminar about oral histories, the Center for the Humanities supported a publication of the findings. Because the group wished to make their discoveries more widely available, they published a digital version to complement the print publication; they added an outward facing digital edition to expand, not replace, the reach of the print run. The example of *City Amplified* illustrates the way hybrid publishing has the capacity to lay bare and provide access to important aspects of the final product's structure that would otherwise be obscured by publication workflows.

Hybrid Futures

If print and digital publication were at one time contesting for the same space, a focus on hybrid publishing reveals how print and digital publication can coexist in a constructive tension. Hybrid publishing takes full advantage of the possibilities of digital space, incorporating materials and interactive experiences that simply can't fit into a printed artifact. At the same time, the digital version of a hybrid text is not meant to replace the printed artifact. Readers are not faced with a binary choice between the print and the digital version. Rather, hybrid publication opens up multiple solutions for different types of problems. In the realm of education, hybrid publishing offers individual instructors a way to create accessible, high-quality, rich-media texts. In the classroom and beyond, the hybrid model provides a highly portable version of texts, making references in class or while traveling more flexible. And experience so far

---

[25] Hubert Harrison, *The Negro and the Nation*, ed. Justin Rogers-Cooper and Krystyna Michael, http://cuny.manifoldapp.org/projects/hubert-harrison-the-negro-and-the-nation. Accessed October 26, 2021.

[26] Allison Guess et al., *The City Amplified: Oral Histories and Radical Archives*, http://cuny.manifoldapp.org/project/the-city-amplified. Accessed October 26, 2021.

has shown that digital publishing can open up access without precluding print. Most readers of monographs tend not to use either the print *or* the digital version of a hybrid text; instead, they often use the print *and* the digital versions in different ways. Readers might start with the printed text and turn to the digital in order to explore resources and engage with other readers and communities through reading groups. As Jacqueline Wernimont and Elizabeth Losh might have predicted, this new method of production has inspired new modes of reading that go beyond the traditional relationship between reader and text to incorporate other forms of engagement like watching, looking, and interacting with a variety of different types of media and other readers.[27] Contrary to our expectations of the impact of technology on attention, the mode of reading that hybrid publishing affords is necessarily slow, recursive, and immersive. Engaging with the same text in two different mediums doesn't just encourage re-reading; it requires it.

Whereas previous models of digital publishing asked readers to choose either the digital or the print version, digital publication that is tied to print publication in a hybrid process creates a both/and answer to the future of scholarly publishing. Scholars, students, and readers can have the print object to hold and page through *and* have the digital interactive version at their fingertips to read and comment upon through their mobile phones. Seen through the lens of the hybrid model, digital publication becomes not the successor to print publication, but rather a partner to it, an adjacent possibility that opens a wider array of networked possibilities.

---

[27] Wernimont and Losh, *Bodies of Information*.

Notes on Contributors

Agatha Beins is Associate Professor and Coordinator of the master's program in Multicultural Women's and Gender Studies at Texas Woman's University, USA. Her book *Liberation in Print: Feminist Periodicals and Social Movement Identity* (2017) analyzes US feminist *newsletters* and newspapers published in the 1970s. She joined the Denton Black Film Festival Institute as Assistant Director in 2018 and has served as editor for the online, open-access journal *Films for the Feminist Classroom* since 2014.

Ayendy Bonifacio is Assistant Professor of US ethnic literary studies at the University of Toledo in Ohio, USA. His areas of scholarship are American literature and culture, Latinx studies, periodical studies, poetry and poetics, and the digital humanities. Bonifacio's work has been published in *American Periodicals, Prose Studies, J19*, and *American Literary Realism*.

Michelle Chihara is Associate Professor of English at Whittier College, USA, where she teaches contemporary American literature, media studies, and creative writing. Her work has appeared in *Postmodern Culture, American Literary History, Post45: Contemporaries,* and in the book *Slouching Towards Los Angeles*. She coedited *The Routledge Companion to Literature and Economics* and currently edits the Econ & Finance section in *The Los Angeles Review of Books*. In a former life, she was a reporter, and she has published fiction, nonfiction, reportage, and essays in a variety of publications.

Lori Cole is Clinical Associate Professor and Associate Director of the interdisciplinary master's program XE: Experimental Humanities & Social Engagement at New York University, USA. She previously taught at Brandeis University, the Whitney Museum of American Art, and the Museum of Modern Art, and her writing has been published in *Artforum, Cabinet, Journal of Surrealism and the Americas*, and *The Oxford Critical and Cultural History of Modernist Magazines*. She is the author of *Surveying the Avant-Garde: Questions on Modernism, Art, and the Americas in Transatlantic Magazines* (2018).

Matthew K. Gold is Associate Professor of English and Digital Humanities at the CUNY Graduate Center, USA, where he holds teaching appointments in the PhD Program in English; the MA Programs in Digital Humanities and Liberal Studies; the MS Program in Data Analysis and Visualization; and the doctoral certificate programs in Interactive Technology and Pedagogy and American Studies. He serves as Advisor to the Provost for Digital Initiatives, and he is Director of the MA Program in Digital Humanities and the MS Program in Data Analysis and Visualization. He also founded and directs the CUNY Academic Commons and the GC Digital Scholarship Lab. He edited *Debates in the Digital Humanities* (Minnesota, 2012) and, with Lauren F. Klein (with whom he has coedited the Debates in the Digital Humanities book series), coedited *Debates in the Digital Humanities 2016* and *Debates in the Digital Humanities 2019*.

Gary Edward Holcomb is Professor of African American Literature and Studies, Department of African American Studies, Ohio University, USA. He is the author of *Claude McKay, Code Name Sasha: Queer Black Marxism and the Harlem Renaissance* (2007). He is either coeditor or editor of the following: Claude McKay's circa 1933 *Romance in Marseille* (2020), *Hemingway and the Black Renaissance* (2012), *Teaching Hemingway and Race* (2018), as well as two special issues of *English Language Notes*, "Rehistoricizing Claude McKay's Romance in Marseille" (2021) and "Sexing the Left" (2015). With Brooks Hefner, he is currently coediting Claude McKay's letters for Columbia University Press.

Monica Huerta is Assistant Professor of English and American Studies at Princeton University, USA. In her critical work, she interrogates the aesthetics of power from inside the histories, afterlives, and ongoing catastrophes of racial capitalism. She is the author of *Magical Habits* (2021), and her work has appeared in *J19, Critical Analysis of Law, Women & Performance, American Literature*, and the *LA Review of Books*, among others.

Jojo Karlin (she/her) is the Digital Scholarship Specialist at New York University, USA. Previously the Manifold Graduate Fellow, she received her PhD in English from the Graduate Center, CUNY, and won the 2021 Dissertation Showcase prize for her illustrated dissertation, *Yours Sincerely, Virginia Woolf: Virginia Woolf's Poetics of Letter Writing*. She serves on the Journal of Interactive Technology and Pedagogy Editorial Collective. At NYU Libraries, she works on open scholarship and digital humanities, and has been developing her research practice of visual notetaking and conference illustration.

Kelley Kreitz is Associate Professor of English and an affiliate faculty member in the Latinx Studies program at Pace University in New York City, USA. She is also the co-founder and director of the university's digital humanities center, Babble Lab. Her research on print and digital cultures of the Americas has appeared in *American Literary History, American Periodicals, English Language Notes, Revista de Estudios Hispánicos*, and the digital mapping project C19LatinoNYC.org, and she serves on the board of the Recovering the US Hispanic Literary Heritage Project at the University of Houston.

Krystyna Michael is a Assistant Professor of English at the City University of New York, Hostos Community College, USA. She is on the development team for

Manifold, an Andrew W. Mellon funded digital publishing platform, and a member of the editorial collective of *The Journal of Instructional Technology and Pedagogy*. Michael's teaching and scholarship revolves around 19th-century American literature and writing, the digital humanities, and architecture and city space. She has published articles and reviews in *The Edith Wharton Review*, *The Journal of American Studies*, and *Postmedieval*.

Kristin Moriah is Assistant Professor of English at Queen's University in Kingston, Ontario, Canada. She is a Colored Conventions Project Teaching Partner. Her research interests include sound studies and Black feminist performance, particularly the circulation of African American performance within the Black diaspora and its influence on the formation of national identity. She is currently at work on a monograph entitled *Dark Stars of the Evening: African Americans in Berlin, 1890–1945*. Her research has been supported by fellowships from the Social Sciences and Research Council of Canada, the Rare Book School at the University of Virginia, and the Harry Ransom Center.

Robert F. Reid-Pharr is Professor of Studies of Women, Gender, and Sexuality and African and African American Studies at Harvard University, USA. He is the recipient of grants and awards from the National Endowment for the Humanities, the Humboldt Foundation, the Guggenheim Foundation, the Radcliffe Institute for Advanced Study, and the American Academy in Berlin. His most recent book is *Archives of Flesh: African America, Spain, and Post-Humanist Critique* (2016).

Justin Rogers-Cooper is Professor of English at LaGuardia Community College, USA, and a faculty member in the MA Program in Liberal Studies at the CUNY Graduate Center. His scholarship addresses the intersections of racial capitalism, gendered labor cultures, and political fictions in the long Gilded Age, with an emphasis on the 1877 general strike. He is a frequent guest on the podcast *The Nostalgia Trap*.

Danica Savonick is Assistant Professor of English at SUNY Cortland, USA. Her research focuses on twentieth-century and contemporary US literature, pedagogy, and social justice. She is currently completing a book manuscript on the teaching, writing, and educational activism of authors Toni Cade Bambara, June Jordan, Audre Lorde, and Adrienne Rich, all of whom taught at the City University of New York in the late 1960s. Her work has appeared in *American Literature*, *Modern Fiction Studies*, and *Multi-Ethnic Literatures of the U.S (MELUS)*, as well as *The Chronicle of Higher Education* and *Inside Higher Ed*.

Jesse Schwartz is Associate Professor of English at LaGuardia Community College (CUNY) in Queens, NY, USA. He had held fellowships with the Deutscher Akademischer Austauschdienst in Osnabrück, Germany, as well as the National Endowment for the Humanities in New York. He is currently at work on a project that traces the cultural responses to transnational socialism in the late nineteenth and early twentieth centuries at the intersection of racialization and radical politics, with a particular focus on representations of the Bolshevik Revolution in US print cultures. A member of the editorial board of *Radical Teacher*, his work can be found there as well as in *Nineteenth-Century Literature* and *English Language Notes*.

Rebekah Walker is the Digital Humanities & Social Sciences Librarian at the Rochester Institute of Technology, USA. Her professional and research interests include digital pedagogy, effective technology instruction, and broadening public access and engagement with digital projects. She has a forthcoming chapter in an *ACRL (Association of College & Research Libraries)* publication.

Daniel Worden is Associate Professor of Art at the Rochester Institute of Technology, USA, where he teaches courses about books, comics, film, magazines, newspapers, and other media. His recent works include the book *Neoliberal Nonfictions: The Documentary Aesthetic from Joan Didion to Jay-Z* (2020) and the edited volume *The Comics of R. Crumb: Underground in the Art Museum* (2021).

Index

Abbey, E. A. 150, 151
"Above the fold" 71, 71 n.40
academia 107, 212, 247
Accessible Technology Services 288
Action Comics #1 204, 204 n.1
Adorno, T. W. 172
adult creative expression 102, 109
advertisements (ads) 32, 33
    Bonner 34, 36–9
    and columns 23–4
Afropean: Notes from Black Europe (Pitts) 93
Ain't I a Woman? 74
"Alas, Poor Richard" (Baldwin) 230
Alemán, J. 244, 245, 253
Álvarez, M. 243, 246
"American idiom, the" 177
American Yawp, The 289
Amiable with Big Teeth (McKay) 85
Amsterdam News 10
Anderson, B. 44–5
Anderson, M. 187, 188
Anderson, V. 34
Antheil, G. 189
"anti-slavery time" 131–3, 132 n.43
Anzaldúa, G. 260
Applegate, D. 130
"April 4, 1968" (Goode) 266
Archie's Girls Betty & Veronica 218
Archipenko, A. 193
Association of University Presses 282
Atlantic Monthly (Bishop) 28
Autobiography of Malcolm X, The (Haley) 232–3

"Bajorrelieve" (Demicheli) 181
Baldwin, J. 20, 226–36
Bambara, T. C. 20, 258–60, 274–5
    Black Woman, The 267–74
    Tales and Stories for Black Folks 267–74
Barnes, J. 27

Barnum, P. T. 171, 171 n.13
Barr, A. Jr. 200
Barthes, R. 86
Batman: The TV Stories 208
Battle of Algiers, The (1966) 270–1
Baxandall, R. 63
Bendann, D. 148
Benjamin, W. 15, 231
Berlant, L. 108
Bernstein, R. 117
Best, S. 118, 119, 119 n.21, 120
Bishop, W. H. 28, 30, 31, 36
Black digital humanities 251
Black feminism 259–60
Black movement 81
blackness 94, 141, 156–8, 251
Black print culture 167–72
Blackwell, A. 266–7
Black Woman, The (Bambara) 267–74
Black women 124 n.29, 171, 172, 259, 267, 268, 270–1, 275
Bla!, The (1916) 196–8
Blind Man, The 173
Bonner, R. E. 24, 27, 31–9
book history 76, 79, 279–80, 288
bookishness 279
Book, The (Borsuk) 277–8
Borderlands Archives Cartography (Fernández and Álvarez) 243–4, 246–7
Borsuk, A. 277–8
Boston 14, 24, 25, 27
bound seriality 45
Breaking the Frames: Populism and Prestige in Comics Studies (Singer) 209–10
Brodhead, R. 23, 26
Brother Jonathan (Day) 27, 27 n.19
Brouillette, S. 100, 109
Brown, J. 140–1, 146, 148, 151, 152, 154, 155
Broyard, A. 227

BuJo 97–102, 105, 106, 106 n.43, 108, 109, 112
Bullet Journal 97–103, 105, 106, 108–12
Bunch, C. 63
Burbank, D. 159

Camera Work (Stieglitz) 173, 182, 187
capitalism 2, 47, 86, 91, 95, 100, 101, 104, 139, 140, 142, 156, 157, 159, 164, 165, 225
Carroll, R. 98, 101, 103, 108
cartes de visite 19, 115, 116, 116 n.5, 116 n.7, 119, 120, 123, 124, 130, 134, 136
Cary Graphic Arts Collection 207, 213, 215, 216, 222, 224
Cavarrero, A. 168
Certified Guaranty Company (CGC) 208
Child Slavery before and after Emancipation (Duane) 116 n.8
Chude-Sokei, L. 171
City Amplified 290
City College 258, 268–70, 272–4
City University of New York (CUNY) 283–4, 288–90
Civil War 19, 115–17, 136, 143, 146, 147, 157
Clark, J. 271
class 34
   conflict 140, 141, 146, 159
   exploitation 52
   politics 111
   race and 49, 156
   relations 47, 50
classic 84
   contemporary 83, 91
   instant 19, 83, 84, 87–92
   unknown 87
classroom
   archival turn in 247–52
   Bambara 268, 269, 272, 274
   centrality of 20
   hybrid 288–91
   transformative 250
Cleveland Gazette, The (Wright) 169, 170 n.10
Cobb, J. N. 116–17, 124
Coleman, G. O. 199

"Color Scheme" 89, 92
Comic Book Marketplace (Cooper) 215
Comic Books Incorporated (Kidman) 219
comics 203, 223
   Detective Comics #230 207–8, 210–13
   digital tools 219–23
   "General Standards" 210
   genres 218
   history 216–19
   print culture 204–10
   synchronic collection 214–16
Comics Code 10, 210, 211, 212 n.22
Comics Code Authority 210, 216, 220 n.42, 221
Conrad, R. 263–4
Contact (Williams and McAlmon) 177
Cooper, S. 207, 214–16, 223
coping economy 99–100, 104
Coronado, R. 244–5
Corona Folding Typewriter 54–5
Courier Post, The 266
Courlander, H. 234–5
Covid-19 pandemic 17, 94, 97, 287
Crane, H. 188
creative economy 100, 109
critical fabulation (Hartman) 235

Daily Graphic 147, 152–3, 159, 163
Davis, S. 173, 195–200
Day, B. 27
DC Comics 206, 208, 209 n.15, 217, 219
Debates in the Digital Humanities (Gallon) 251
Debates in the Digital Humanities (Gold) 285
Delmont, M. 281
Demicheli, D. 180, 181
democracy 240, 241, 252–5
Demuth, C. 199
Denning, M. 25, 26, 28, 34, 36
Detective Comics #230 206–13, 216, 219
digital detox systems 98, 101–4, 108
Digital Ethnic Futures Consortium 253
digital humanities 4, 217, 241–53, 281, 285, 287
"Digital Humanities Manifesto 2.0" (Schnapp and Presner) 250
digital monograph 285–6

digital publishing 20, 277–80, 282, 285, 287, 291
Dirda, M. 82
Dissent 99–100
Distaff 71
distance learning 97, 287
Dow, B. J. 71
Drucker, J. 277–8
Duane, A. M. 116 n.8
Du Bois, W. E. B. 89, 152
Duchamp, M. 173, 186

eBooks 277–8
Edison, T. 168
education 4, 252, 257, 290
　higher 4, 223, 242, 252, 257, 275
　racism 268
　realm of 290
　SEEK program 269
Eliot, G. 289
Ellison, R. 168
emancipation 12, 130, 133
Eng, B. C. 76
ePub 282, 285
"Escenas Camperas" (Rodríguez) 181
"Esthetics of the Machine, The" (Léger) 191
ethnicity 52, 157 n.67
Evans, S. 63
Everett, E. 33, 34
"Everybody's Protest Novel" (Baldwin) 226–8
"Exposición de 'La Casa del arte" 180, 181
"Exposición Pesce Castro" 180, 181

family paper 23, 24, 33–6, 38
Farr, C. K. 75
Feaster, P. 167–8
Federici, S. 164–5
Female Liberation 68 n.20, 69
feminism 63–5, 72, 74–9, 272
Feminist Literacies (Flannery) 74
feminist praxis 78, 242, 274–6
Fernández, S. 243, 246
Fern, F. 33
Ferriss, H. 193
Fire!! (1926) 88, 88 n.20, 89
Flannery, K. T. 74

Flux (Stephen) 109
Flynn, R. 262
Forma: Revista de artes plásticas (1926–8) 174–8, 200
Forty Inns on the Lincoln Highway (Davis) 198–200
Foster, F. S. 120
Fox, C. 243
Frank Leslie's Illustrated Weekly (1877) 146, 147, 151–4, 156, 162–4
Franklin, C. 257, 258
Freeman, J. 70
free spaces 66
"Frenzy, and What Came of It, The" (Abbey) 150, 151
Fuentes, M. 76

Gaceta del Pueblo (People's Gazette) 254
Gallon, K. 251
gender
　identity 160–1
　inequities 71
　oppression 64
　performance 159–65
　race and 66
　racialization 141
gender-bending 82, 88
general strike (1877) 140–5, 148
　periodicals 145–52
　rioting and gender performance 159–65
　striking and racial performance 152–9
　violence 139, 141, 142, 144, 147, 153, 158, 162, 163
ghetto 262, 264, 266
Giardina, C. 77
Gilley, J. 272
Gleaner, The (McKay) 92
Glintenkamp, H. J. 173, 195, 197, 198
global capitalism 86, 95
Going the Rounds 287
Gold, M. K. 285
Goldstein, B. 91
Gompers, S. 159–60
Gonzalez, A. 120
Goode, M. 266
Gordon, L. 63
Graham, D. 94

Grand Comics Database 212
Graphic, The 147, 153
Great Speckled Bird 73
Greeley, H. 32 n.50, 33, 36, 38

Haley, A. 232–5
Hall, S. 157 n.67
Hamilton, B. 73
Happiness Project (Rubin) 98
Harker, J. 75
Harlem Renaissance 81, 84, 85, 87–90, 95, 170, 258 n.5, 259
Harper's Weekly 133–4, 141, 146, 147, 149–52, 156
Hartford Courant 32
Hartman, S. 115, 118, 136, 235
Hayden, C. 77
Heap, J. 187–92, 188 n.56, 194–5, 200, 201
Heffernan, L. 249–50
Hemingway, E. 91
Henderson, D. 265
Henkin, D. M. 31
Henri, R. 195
Herald Tribune 10
Hernton, C. 265
hero block 284
Heyward, D. 91
Hicks, G. 55
Himes, C. 228–30
historiography 65, 74–9, 132 n.43
Hitchcock, P. 45
hoax 130–1, 134
Hoffman, M. 263, 267
Hogan, K. 75
Holmes, L. 271
Home to Harlem (McKay) 88, 89
Hovey, C. 46, 49–51, 54, 62
Howard, V. 264
"How Audiobooks Are Getting Me through COVID-19" (Sackton) 94–5
Hughes, L. 5–12, 20, 88, 90, 262, 273
humanistic inquiry 241, 247, 252–5
Hunter, R. 195
Hurston, Z. N. 85, 88, 259, 270
hybrid publishing 20, 278–91
    book history 279–80
    classroom texts 288–9
    iterative versioning 286–7
    Manifold 283–4
    models of 280–3
    monograph 285–6
    OER 287
    student and community 289–90

"Indignities Imposed" (Wright) 169–70
industrialization 14, 26 n.10, 28, 35
International Theatre Exposition (Heap) 187–92
intersectionality 19, 49, 78, 78 n.70, 79, 108, 174, 206, 252, 253
intertextuality 87, 94
In Vaudeville (Demuth) 199
iterative scholarship 286–7

James Baldwin Papers 226, 236
Jentz, J. B. 158 n.71
Jordan, J. 20, 258–60, 274–6
    Soulscript 260–7, 273–4
    Voice of the Children, The 260–7

Kanellos, N. 244
Kelleter, F. 45
Kelley, R. D. G. 268
Kessler-Harris, A. 164
Kheshti, R. 172
Kidman, S. 219
Kiesler, F. 188–90
King, M. 77
Kirschenbaum, M. G. 279–80
Kitchen Table: Women of Color Press (Smith and Lorde) 259–60
Kohl, H. 261

Lab Book, The 286
labor
    and capital 51
    exploitation 105
    relations 52
    Rockefeller towards 56, 62
    struggles 19
"Labor Question" (Parsons) 139
La Doctrina de Martí (Martí's Doctrine) 247
L.A. Free Press 73
La Pluma (Zum Felde) 173, 174, 179–82, 200

La Revista Ilustrada de Nueva York (New York Illustrated Magazine) 247, 254
Latham, S. 44
Latino Nineteenth Century, The (Alemán) 244–5
Latinx 52, 239, 239 n.1, 241–9
Lause, M. 156
LaValle, V. 15–16
Lazo, R. 244
Léger, F. 191, 193
legitimation 131, 212 n.23
Lehman, D. W. 42, 43
Le Monde Illustré 163
Levay, M. 44
Lew Williams, B. 158
Liberation News Service (LNS) 70
Life of Albert R. Parsons (Parsons) 139
L'Illustration Journal Universel 163
Linebaugh, P. 157
Lippmann, H. 192, 193
literary history 2, 87, 241–7, 249, 253
Little Review (Heap) 173, 174, 187–95
Liu, A. 250–1
Livingston College 272
Locke, A. 88
Locke, J. L. 289
López, M. 250
Lorde, A. 259–60, 265
Lorimer, G. H. 47
Losh, E. 278, 291
Lovecraft Country (2020) 16–17
Lovecraft, H. P. 12, 14–18, 20
lower-class 28, 31, 34
Lozowick, L. 189, 193

McAlmon, R. 177
McMillian, J. 69
Machine-Age Exposition (Heap) 187–95
McKay, C. 19, 81–96
"Mad Hatter of Gotham City, The" 208–9
magazines 187–201
   in the Americas 174–9
   and exhibition 195
   humorous 8
   literary 23, 24, 40
   man and 48
   mixed function 46
   Negro 8
Mailer, N. 227
Major, C. 260
male domination 66, 72, 74, 75, 103, 271
Mandrágora (1938–41) 173, 174, 182–7, 195, 201
Manifold 278, 282–90
Marcus, S. 119, 119 n.21
Mariátegui, J. C. 179
Marshall, D. 232
Marsh, L. 99–100
Martí, J. 239–41, 248, 254
Marvel Comics 209 n.15, 213
Masses (1911–17) 56, 62, 195–8
Maxson, E. 106
Maxwell, W. J. 83
"means" 67, 68
Mellon, A. W. 285
Meltzer, M. 265
Merchant's Ledger 32
Merish, L. 26
Metagaming: Playing, Competing, Spectating, Cheating, Trading, Making, and Breaking Videogames 286
Metropolitan Magazine (Reed) 18–19, 43, 46–50, 52–62
middle-class 12, 108, 123–5, 153, 161–3, 176, 180
Mill on the Floss, The (Eliot) 289
mindfulness 98–102, 108, 109
miscegenation 130–2
Mitchell, M. N. 117
"mob" 149, 151, 154
Modernist Review, The 93
"modes" 67, 68
Molloy, S. 270
Moody, K. 140, 144, 145, 156
Moraga, C. 260
Morgan, R. 77
Morrison, T. 87, 259, 270
"Motherhood" (Clark) 271
Mott, F. L. 26 n.10, 32
Museum of Modern Art (1929) 199, 200

Nadasen, P. 76 n.58
Native Son (Wright) 226

Negro and the Nation, The 289–90
New Black Poetry, The (Major) 260
New Digital Worlds: Postcolonial Digital Humanities (Risam) 246–7
Newman, E. 95
New Negro movement 88–90, 93
New Negro, The (Locke) 88
newspapers 145–6
　Black 168, 169
　Negro 8
　and story papers 24, 29, 30, 39–40
　success of 25
New York 82
New York City 8, 10, 15, 24, 27, 27 n.23, 28, 31, 32, 68, 73, 88, 139, 154, 240, 241, 249, 253–5, 261, 262
New York Daily Times 39
New York Daily Tribune 36–8
New York Evening Mail 196–7
New York Herald (1849) 29
New York Ledger, The (Bonner) 18, 24, 31–9
New York Times 84
Ngai, S. 101
"Niggerati Manor" 89
Nigger Heaven (Van Vechten) 89, 170
None Like Us: Blackness, Belonging, Aesthetic Life (Best) 118
Norton Anthology of English Literature, The 257
nostalgia 9, 108, 205, 206, 206 n.11

Occupy Wall Street 111–12
Odell, J. 100, 101, 103, 104
Ohmann, R. 2 n.1, 46
Open Educational Resources (OER) 287, 288

Panda Planner 97–8, 100, 105, 112
paratext 208, 208 n.12
Parsons, L. E. 139–40, 142, 144, 145, 159
Partisan Review, The 177, 227
Pat Sumi 76
Paz, P. R. 178
Penguin Classics 81, 84–8, 90 n.30, 92–5
"Pennsylvania.-The Railroad Riot at Pittsburgh-The Philadelphia Militia Firing on the Mob" 162, 164

periodicals 145–52
　English and French 163
　feminist 63, 64, 70, 72, 74, 76
　flexibility of 173
　Hughes 8
　industrialization of 26 n.10
　literary 24–5
　production 25, 70
　seriality and 44
　Slotkin and 161
　staplebound 204
Phonographies: Grooves in Sonic Afro-Modernity (Weheliye) 172
phonography 167–9, 171–2
Photo-Journal Guide to Comic Books 215
Pictorial World, The 149
Picture Freedom: Remaking Black Visuality in the Early Nineteenth Century (Cobb) 116–17
Picturing Mexican America (López) 250
Pinkerton, A. 152, 160–2
Pitts, J. 93
Platt, S. N. 188, 195
PMLA 253
Porgy (Heyward) 91
Portrait of America (Rivera and Wolfe) 178
"Portrait of the Hipster, A" (Broyard) 227
Posner, M. 251
Presner, T. 250
print culture 1, 5, 242, 243, 279
　artifacts 1, 10
　Black 167–72
　Borsuk and 278–9
　cosmics and 204–10
　feminist 65, 73–6, 79, 258
　Hughes to 7–10
　and readers 6
　of story papers 23
　studies 1, 2, 4–18, 20, 120, 203, 241, 258
printscape 67, 67 n.15, 68
print-socialism 46
Problem with Work, The: Feminism, Marxism, Antiwork Politics and Postwork Imaginaries (Weeks) 106
productivism 106
"Prop List" 10

"Puerto Ricans" (Hughes) 7–8
Pullman Strike of 1894 144
Purdy, J. 111
Purser, R. 100

Quality of Hurt, The (Himes) 229

race 8, 132, 171
　and class 49
　and gender 19, 66, 140
Racial Innocence: Performing American Childhood from Slavery to Civil Rights (Bernstein) 117
radical writer 41–3
Radio Corporation of America (RCA) 204
"Railroad Riot Extra" 153, 154
Raising Freedom's Child: Black Children and Visions of the Future after Slavery (Mitchell) 117
Ramparts 72
Ramsay, S. 281
Randall, D. 259
Rawhide Kid 213
Readex Hispanic American Newspapers, 1808–1980 database 248, 249
Reclaiming Conversation: The power of talk in a digital age (Turkle) 103–4
Redeeming Productivity 106, 107
redemption 125, 130–3
Rediker, M. 157
Reed, J. 18–19, 41–62
　"Approach to War, The" 56
　Mexican Revolution 43, 44, 48–58, 62
Revista Chicana-Riqueña (Kanellos) 244
Revista de Avance (1927–30) 173, 176, 183, 187
Revolutionary Blueprint, A 276
Rideout, W. 41
Risam, R. 246–7, 251, 253
Rivera, D. 177, 178
Rockefeller, J. D. 51, 56–8, 60, 62
Rockwell, G. 281
Rodríguez, G. 180, 181
Roediger, D. 159
Roggenkamp, K. 30
Romance in Marseille 19, 81–95
　and disability 92–4

Roosevelt, T. 47, 57
Roots: An American Saga (Haley) 232
Rosenberg, H. 177
Ryan, L. 93

Sabner Buurma, R. 249–50
"Salon de 'La Giralda" 180, 181
Scalar 280–1
Schilling, G. S. 145
Schnapp, J. 250
Schneirov, R. 158 n.71
Schomburg, A. 89
Schudson, M. 26 n.10
Scope 262
Search for Education, Elevation, and Knowledge (SEEK) program 268–71
second wave feminism 63–5
sensationalism 28–34, 36, 40, 146
serials and seriality 15, 26, 30, 31, 34, 43–6, 69
"Sex and Caste" (Hayden and King) 77–9
sexism 66, 71, 75, 259, 267
Sheehan, E. M. 45
Silver Age superhero comics 10, 206, 206 n.11, 208, 210, 211, 216
Simple Stakes a Claim (Hughes) 7, 9
Simple stories (Hughes) 5–12
Simply Heavenly (Hughes) 6, 10–13
Singer, M. 209
Siqueiros, D. A. 177
Sisterhood Is Powerful (Morgan) 77
skeuomorphic design 277, 283
Slotkin, R. 161
Smith, B. 259–60
Smith, Z. 208 n.13
social relation 24, 26, 52, 62
Soulscript (Jordan) 260–7, 273–4
sound writing 167
Southern Exposure 275
Sparks, G. 196
Spawn 19, 173, 174, 195–201
Srnicek, N. 100
Starosielski, N. 281
"State of the Press-1976" 79
States-Item 71

Stephen Neil Cooper Synchronic Comic Book Collection 207, 214–16, 223
Stephen, R. 109, 110, 112
Stieglitz, A. 173
story paper 23–4, 26 n.13
　across the city 30–1
　Bonner and 31–9
　as family paper 34–6
　Merish and 26–7
　New York Ledger, The 31–9
　origins of 24–7
　readers 28
　sensationalism of 29–30
Stowe, H. B. 226
Stowell, D. O. 159
Strange Adventures #67 (1956) 214
Strange Adventures #230 (1971) 214
"Strategist, The" 95
"The Street" (Lovecraft) 14, 14 n.33, 15, 17, 18
Student Nonviolent Coordinating Committee (SNCC) 77
Sun, The 29
"Surfacing" 281
S/Z (Barthes) 86

Tales and Stories for Black Folks (Bambara) 267–74
Teaching Archive, The: A New History for Literary Study (Sabner Buurma and Heffernan) 249
technology 3, 19, 25, 67, 68, 101, 103, 104, 112, 167–72
Tell Me How Long the Train's Been Gone (Baldwin) 232, 234
Ten Days That Shook the World (Reed) 42, 43
Theory of the Gimmick, The (Ngai) 101
Third World Women's Alliance 78
This Bridge Called My Back (Anzaldúa and Moraga) 260
Tompkins, K. W. 253
Travis, T. 259, 259 n.12
Traylor, E. 271
Triple Jeopardy 78
Turkle, S. 103–4

unbound seriality 45
Uncle Tom's Cabin (Stowe) 117, 226
Underground Press Syndicate (UPS) 70, 72
Undersea Network, The (Starosielski) 281
University of Minnesota Press 283, 285, 286
University of Washington Libraries and Press 288, 289

Valley Women's Center 68 n.19
Van Vechten, C. 89, 170
Vida-Americana 177–8
Videla de Rivero, G. 179
Viral Texts 287
Voice of the Children, The (Jordan) 260–7
Voice of the Women's Liberation Movement, The (Chicago) 63
voice-writing 167

Wark, M. 100
Warren, K. 257
Waters, D. 285
Webb, M. S. 72
Weekly Louisianan 168
Weeks, K. 106, 108
Weheliye, A. 168, 172
Wells, H. G. 85
Wernimont, J. 278, 291
WeWork 105–6
Wexler, L. 129
What Were Comics? project 212, 212 n.25, 216, 217
Whigham, H. J. 46–7, 56
"White Negro, The" (Mailer) 227
Whitney Museum of American Art (1931) 199, 200
Williams, M. G. 6
Williams, W. C. 177
Willington Enterprise, The 29
Wilson, K. 192, 192 n.78, 194
Wise, S. 77
Women in Print Movement 64, 73, 259
"Women Leading a Mob in Baltimore" 161–2
Wong, E. L. 145
Worden, D. 219

working-class 28, 93, 142, 145, 149–51, 154, 156, 157, 159, 162, 165, 258, 272
"Work of Art in the Age of Mechanical Reproduction, The" (Benjamin) 231
World Not to Come, A: A History of Latino Writing and Print Culture (Coronado) 245

Wright, B. 289
Wright, R. 89, 226–31
Wright, W. C. 169–70

Young, M. 82, 92

Zum Felde, A. 179–82

www.ingramcontent.com/pod-product-compliance
Lightning Source LLC
Chambersburg PA
CBHW070750020526
44115CB00032B/1604